SOLIDARITY BLUES

SOLIDARITY BLUES

Race, Culture, and the American Left

RICHARD ITON

The University
of North
Carolina
Press

Chapel Hill
and London

© 2000 The University of North Carolina Press
All rights reserved

Designed by April Leidig-Higgins
Set in Minion by Tseng Information Systems, Inc.
Manufactured in the United States of America

The paper in this book meets the guidelines for
permanence and durability of the Committee on
Production Guidelines for Book Longevity of the
Council on Library Resources.

Library of Congress Cataloging-in-Publication Data
Iton, Richard. Solidarity blues: race, culture, and the
American left / Richard Iton.
p. cm.   Includes bibliographical references and index.
ISBN 0-8078-2536-0 (cloth: alk. paper) —
ISBN 0-8078-4847-6 (pbk.: alk. paper)
1. United States — Race relations — Political aspects.
2. Racism — Political aspects — United States —
History — 20th century. 3. Radicalism — United
States — History — 20th century. 4. Right and left
(Political science) — History — 20th century.
5. Socialism — United States — History — 20th century.
6. United States — Politics and government — 20th
century. I. Title.
E185.61 I86 2000   320.51′3′0973 — dc21   99-053085

04 03 02 01 00   5 4 3 2 1

FOR CARMEN, JUSTIN, AND ANGELA

CONTENTS

TABLES

ACKNOWLEDGMENTS

I started writing the first draft of this manuscript toward the end of the second term of Ronald Reagan's presidency. As I type these words, Bill Clinton is nearing the end of his own tenure. A number of people have helped me make it from then to now, from there to here.

The dissertation on which this book is based benefited from the advice and support offered by Germaine Hoston, Milton Cummings Jr., Richard Katz, Ronald Walters, and Matthew Crenson while I was a graduate student at the Johns Hopkins University. Harold Waller played a comparable role during my various stays at McGill University (as an undergraduate, graduate student, and instructor) and has been a major source of assistance throughout my academic career. Similarly, Mike Grossman has been a reliable and enthusiastic adviser, besides being a close family friend. Howard University's Joseph McCormick was willing to make time for a graduate student from one of those "other" universities (the fourth chapter in this book grew out of one of those conversations), a gesture I appreciate to this day.

There is a full crew of friends and associates who have helped me maintain my sanity, providing me with strategic support, feedback, and encouragement, if only by making fun of my rate of progress with this labor of love over the last decade or so. Sibyl Anderson, Marvin Ashford, Dave Austin ("Do I make the cut?"), Cameron Bailey, Kim Bailey, Maxine Bailey, Joan Bramwell, Joe Brewster, Jan Campbell, Lloyd Charlton (S/14), Craig Christopher, Perryne Constance, Warren Crichlow, Gary Dennie, Pat Dillon, Heather Dryden, Emile Frazier, Kevin George, Kevin Gilbert, Julian Gordon, Ernest Guiste, Mike Hamilton, Rick Harris, Wayne Harris, Kingsley Henry, Patrick Bernard Hill, Dwayne Hopkinson, Deborah Jordan, the "Karens," Helen Lee, Judy Mapp, Randy McDowall, Dave Messam, Ron Nash, Ron Nazon, Jacqueline Nichol-Hamilton ("Are you still working on that thing?"), Janett Nichol, Sharon Othello, the Pearson family, Ron Peters, Noi Quao, Michelle Ray, Dean Robinson, Dierdre Royster, Martin Ruck, Gary St. Fleur, Kerri Sakamoto, the Saunders family, Michèle Stephenson, Dalours Thornhill, Clement Virgo, Rinaldo Walcott, Ignatius Watson, Shirleen Weekes, Ruth White, Monica Williams, Dulcina Wind, Adrian Worrell, Akhaji

Zakiya, the Each One Teach One posse, and my fellow orderlies in the operating room at the Montreal Children's Hospital (from whom I learned much of what I know about union solidarity, as well as how to curse in many languages): thank you very much. To the following, thanks for teaching me: Anusha Aruliah, Anne Marie Barnes, Joyce Bernasek, Hitesh Chopra, Dean Daley, Claude Davis, Sheryl Davis, Bindu Dhaliwal, Ruth Goba, Marcus Green, Anne Marie Green, Juliet Harriot, Anton James, Karen Jensen, Maurice Knight, Ladislav Kucis, Paul Kutasi, Dane McInnis, Melanie Marshall, Faizal Mirza, Lata Naraswamy, Colin Ojah-Maharaj, Krysta Pandolfi, Lennox Phillips, Monique Pinnock, Matthew Pitter, Chris Ramsaroop, Tracy Rotstein, Patrice Rouse, Ted Salgado, Allan Schultz, Shabana Shaikh, Kenrick Sylvestre, Alexander Vaccari, Nicole Virgin, Leonard Wandili, Courtenay Warren, and Lesley Wilde.

I thank my colleagues in the Department of Political Science at the University of Toronto for advice and support. Ronnie Beiner, Dickson Eyoh (my fellow executive officer in the local branch of the Sepia Club), Gunther Gad, Paul Kingston, Irene Langran, Bob Matthews, Peter Russell, Ian Spears, Graham White, and Melissa Williams have helped me make my way through the maze that is academic life. Similarly, I have appreciated the assistance I have received from the administrative staff at the St. George and Erindale campuses of the university: Rose Antonio, Mary-Alice Bailey ("Roxton Crescent's in the house"), Carolynn Branton, Margaret Hepburn, Elizabeth Jagdeo, Hyla Levy, Ram Mohabir, Slavka Murray, Rita O'Brien, Marian Reed, and Mary Wellman. In the "words cannot express" category, I owe a lot to four individuals. Rob Vipond has been a major source of advice and is responsible in many ways for my being at the University of Toronto. He provided useful feedback on aspects of the manuscript and helped me keep my research goals in clear sight. He is also an extremely decent person. Cecil Houston consistently provided crucial life support for a fading ego, yet at the same time was very good at mocking my attempts at self-pity. As much as I struggle to get up early enough for our regular Saturday lunches, the opportunity to see Toronto, and indeed the world, through his eyes has always been well worth the effort. Jennifer Nedelsky volunteered to be my mentor and read the manuscript from beginning to end. Joe Carens also read this manuscript (and convinced me to revive a separate article I had abandoned during a time of great frustration). The comments I received from Jennifer and Joe, as well as the conversations we had about the claims in this book, forced me to reconsider questions I thought I had already answered and have resulted in a much stronger argument. As important, the personal support I have received from Jennifer and Joe has been immeasurable. Both have helped me maintain forward momentum, even during the more unpleasant periods, and for their friendship, I feel blessed.

Lewis Bateman has supported this project since I first submitted a proposal. His willingness to explain the workings of the "industry" and his calm responses to my various questions helped me keep my cool throughout this process (and I am considering purchasing some bow ties). Along with Pamela Upton, Kathleen Ketterman, Alison Waldenberg, and the other folks at the University of North Carolina Press, he has made this an altogether pleasant, indeed exciting, experience. In this context, I also thank the two readers who provided comments on this manuscript. Their comments were appreciated and have made this book very much better than it would have been otherwise. The final product reads much more smoothly because of the patience and copyediting skills of Nancy Raynor.

My foundation is my family. Accordingly, I offer my thanks and love to my mother and father. Along with my grandmothers, aunts, uncles, cousins, in-laws, and extended family, they have provided a model of community that I carry with me to this day. Although younger than I, my two brothers, along with my parents, are my greatest inspiration. Tony offered much-appreciated financial support when I was a graduate student surviving on two boxes of macaroni and cheese a day (support that was, of course, promptly spent on music). Brian was my roommate when much of the first draft of the book was written, and a number of my arguments here can be traced back to our discussions (often at three o'clock in the morning). Indeed, he was the first "civilian" to read a complete version of this text. Accordingly, this book is dedicated to their children, my nieces and nephew.

To borrow from Bill Withers, thank you all for letting me lean on you.

Last, what follows is very much a "tale of two cities," and in that spirit I have to recognize Montreal and Baltimore for the complicated claims they have made on my soul throughout my lifetime.

Peace and love.

SOLIDARITY BLUES

CHAPTER ONE

Gateway Blues

In the United States of North America, every independent movement of the
workers was paralyzed so long as slavery disfigured a part of the Republic.
Labour cannot emancipate itself in the white skin when in the black it is
branded. — Karl Marx, *Capital*

I think America is growing more and more complicated, and it seems to me that
our conversation is not keeping up with that complexity. This . . . dialogue began
[with the suggestion] . . . that the unfinished business of America is black and
white, but it strikes me that . . . what we really need to do is understand how
complex this country is, with Samoan rap groups and Filipinos and Pakistani
cab drivers, and the racial relationships now in America are so complex and
so rich that it seems to me that we don't have a language even to keep up with
that complexity. — Richard Rodriguez, in "A Dialogue on Race with President
Clinton"

Why is there no "real" American left? How has the United States
managed to avoid the degree of class-based social conflict characteristic of the
politics of most Western societies? Although various arguments have been offered
to explain American exceptionalism and the failure of socialism to establish a
foothold in the United States as it has elsewhere in the West, my discussion will
focus on the significance of one factor — race — and its role in the unmaking of
the American left. I will argue that the particular demographic circumstances that
have existed throughout American history, along with the way in which these circumstances have been interpreted and processed and, in particular, racialized,
have contributed significantly to the unique pattern of social relations one finds
in the United States.

To understand the relationship between race and American exceptionalism
properly requires reexamination of the concepts and approaches that are commonly used to explain the absence of the American left. Unfortunately, investigations into the exceptionalism phenomenon have often employed methodolo-

gies and conceptual strategies that have guaranteed a misunderstanding of the real reasons why there is no American left. Indeed, procedural choices and disciplinary limitations have encouraged some analysts to underrate the significance of the issue itself.

For instance, the historian Sean Wilentz suggests that the exceptionalism debate has resulted from a basic misreading of American labor history and an overstatement of the pace and significance of events in European labor history. Consequently, he argues, "there is a history of class consciousness in the United States comparable to that of working-class movements in Britain and on the Continent."[1] Indeed, Wilentz concludes that the exceptionalism issue is a "colossal non-problem" and that the predominance of the exceptionalism perspective has warped the analyses of American social historians.[2] Similarly, the historian George M. Fredrickson suggests, "The notion that the United States has exhibited radical peculiarities that have made its experience categorically different from that of other modern or modernizing countries has encouraged an oversimplified and often idealized view of the American past."[3] Whether accepting or rejecting Wilentz's and Fredrickson's arguments about the significance of the issue, many American labor and social historians have approached the question in these same terms: the degree of working-class consciousness, and the relative strength of leftist parties and labor union solidarity.[4]

Yet limiting the study of the American left and the exceptionalism issue to the examination of attitudes, events, and movements without considering results and achievements has arguably resulted in a less accurate and nuanced understanding of the significance and derivation of the peculiar nature of the American political culture. Very few analysts approach the study of the left in a comprehensive manner. A "search for" the American left — or any left — should work from the understanding that a left is a means to the creation of a certain kind of society and a certain set of public goods. Beyond the lack of a leftist political party and a "radicalized" working class, the most striking feature of the American political culture is its inability to produce and maintain some basic public goods: comprehensive health care, sufficient housing provisions, effective worker organization and protection, and consistent police protection. To this list one could add gun control legislation, quality elementary and secondary education, public transportation, and inclusive voter registration procedures. In other words, the search for "the American left" might not be, as Wilentz suggests, a "colossal non-problem" but an attempt to understand how and why the American political culture has failed to manifest the collective will to produce a set of public goods.[5]

At another level, any search for the missing American left must make the effort to study the phenomenon in the wider (political) cultural context. Perhaps because American leftists have often been perceived to function as extracultural aliens within the context of their society, able to look into but unable to lock onto the popular imagination as an organic expression of the culture's collective psyche, historians and political scientists have tended to approach the historical development of the left outside the context of American society. In significant contrast, in the other Western societies leftist movements have arisen as organic grassroots expressions of their respective political cultures.[6] The study of the American left, then, needs to proceed beyond the cataloguing of words and sentiments to some understanding of the movement's function—specifically, to create and maintain the provision of a certain set of public goods. These studies must also entail investigation of the social roots of leftist movements, as well as identification of the basic cultural sensibilities and conditions that lead to the development or nondevelopment of a leftist movement. Culture needs to be addressed in the study of the left as a potential source or medium of leftist sentiment and also as a text that can be read in order to expose a society's underlying structure.

Overall, a reorganization of the manner in which the "missing" American left is examined will do much to change the nature of the conclusions that are drawn concerning the causes and sources of its weakness. In other words, a thorough and comprehensive analysis of the history of the American left—including considerations of public policy and popular culture, as well as class consciousness, labor movements, and leftist parties—will clarify that its marginalization has been, to a significant degree, a function of the popular fascination with race.

This preoccupation with race has affected the prospects of American leftist movements in various ways. At the most basic level, the strength of the popular attachment to racial categories has reduced the appeal of class-based movements. Leftist organizations, consequently, have been marginalized because their efforts to mobilize members of the working classes conflicted with the more deeply rooted and developed racial identifications of these constituencies to such an extent that even those leftist campaigns which did not seek to challenge racial norms were still perceived as threats to the racial status quo (e.g., the American Federation of Labor [AFL] before the civil rights era). Thus challenges to the economic status quo have been interpreted, legitimately I might add, as potential or implicit challenges to prevailing racial understandings. In this context those movements of the left which questioned social conventions regarding race explicitly were even less appealing to crucial working-class constituencies (e.g., the American Communist Party after 1928).

The left's ability to organize effectively has also been restricted because of conflicts within and between different organizations over whether antiracist and anti-nativist principles should be adopted and promoted. The energies consumed by debates between nativist and racist elements and those actors advocating inclusive mobilization strategies reduced the left's capacity to launch coordinated campaigns (e.g., the battles that took place within the AFL and the labor movement as a whole). The expression of nativist and racist sentiments by leftists also, of course, alienated immigrant and black workers from leftist causes, an alienation that employers and the left's opponents could exploit for their own purposes to weaken unions and other leftist organizations. This distrust and mutual hostility also resulted in separate labor and political organizations, as those groups excluded from the mainstream left established their own institutions to pursue their own agendas.

Last, with regard to the general ways in which racial dynamics have affected leftist outcomes, leftist organizations (and indeed many analysts of the left) have underestimated the importance of the issues of race and ethnicity and their effects on the left's chances. Even those leftists who were not explicitly racist failed to appreciate the ramifications of leaving the racial status quo unchallenged. For example, until the civil rights movement, the main arena in which racial forces trumped class coalitions was the American South. The South represented—and to a lesser degree continues to represent—the major geographic base of American conservatism. But the left characteristically avoided engaging southerners as aggressively as it did constituencies elsewhere to such a degree that it guaranteed its marginalization at the national level. This is not to argue that if leftist organizations had been more active in the South that the outcomes would have been much different, all things remaining equal. Such a claim would require imagining American leftists being able to rise above the circumstances—the racialized society—that produced them in the first place, as well as a different American South—a different America—somehow more open to these appeals.[7] Rather, the failure of leftists to understand that their absence in the South meant they would have limited influence nationally (e.g., as evidenced in the classic American socialist formulation that racial issues and the South itself could be dealt with "after the revolution") is a reflection of the pervasive influence of race in American life and the common misunderstanding of the stakes involved. The extent to which race has been *naturalized,* to the point that its importance and broader implications are often overlooked, has been reflected in the strategies and priorities adopted by American leftists throughout the nation's history and arguably, to a significant degree, in the work of the analysts—historians, sociologists, and political scientists—who have considered the exceptionalism phenomenon.

Approaches to the Gateway

In their classic text *Voting*, Bernard Berelson, Paul Lazarsfeld, and William Mc-Phee describe the "gateway" as "an entrypoint . . . through which an endless succession of social proposals have passed, are passing, and will pass."[8] For the purposes of this discussion, the gateway can be understood in both this narrow sense and in a broader sense as the barrier, as that collection of restraining influences, dividing the accepted, "normal," and feasible in American politics from the understandings and sensibilities that are common in other (political) cultures.

The relationship under examination in this discussion, then, is that between the individualized interpretation of industrialization (in other words, the combination of a certain conception of how the individual should interact with the collective, and the development of a certain package of technological innovations and possibilities, such as the printing press, the steam engine, the microphone, the automobile) and the nature of the society's response to this challenge. Theoretically, the responses could range from a complete rejection of the individualist interpretation of social possibilities to a partial acceptance and to an enthusiastic endorsement of the ideals and institutions of this new perspective. Overall, then, here I attempt to understand how the forces of individualism and collectivism interact in different contexts.

The emergence of labor movements and socialist parties, the forces that can be characterized as the *conventional left,* is a sign that at least some significant elements within the larger society are willing to oppose the arguments and actions of the individualists. At another level, instead of solely discussing the conventional left, as many analysts have already done, one can focus on the creation, provision, or maintenance of a particular set or type of public goods (i.e., comprehensive and redistributive). Such an elaboration would render the emergence of a conventional left as a related but not essential aspect of the society's resistance. One could argue that a conventional leftist movement is not necessarily the only means by which certain public goods can be produced or maintained, nor is it the only sign of a society's resistance to individualist ideals. From a historical perspective, one might suggest that the conventional left, while the most visible and dominant indicator of resistance at the end of the nineteenth century, is no longer the most likely or even effective means by which resistance can be expressed and operationalized. At the beginning of the twenty-first century, perhaps contemporary efforts to establish and maintain public goods are best mobilized by and situated in other agents and media (e.g., collective economic enterprises, popular culture, and other social movements). These goods could be achieved with-

out the emergence of a conventional left, possibly as a result of some basic social consensus. In this sense, the conventional left can be seen as an intermediate
public good, as a means to the achievement of certain legislation and the preservation of a certain way of life, but not necessarily the only means toward achieving these goals. Certainly the leftist agenda with regard to preferred public goods
and priorities has changed as new conditions, technologies, and possibilities have
arisen and as new information has become available. One should expect, then,
that unions and, to a lesser extent, parties, as the mainsprings of leftist activity
and the main measures of leftist achievement, might not be as crucial today as
they were perceived to be a century or even two decades ago. Consequently, in
the discussion of the conventional left in Chapters 2 and 3, I focus on the period
between the Civil War and the Second World War, while devoting some attention
to subsequent developments; in Chapters 4 and 5, analyzing the New Deal and
public policy, I emphasize developments from the 1930s to the present.

Beyond the emergence of the conventional left and the provision of a certain
kind of public goods, the extent of resistance to the ideals of the individualist perspective can be observed in the way a society makes and remakes its culture, in
the way it reproduces itself. The degree to which the individualist argument has
been accepted should be evident in the extent to which the aggregate culture has
been atomized and fragmented and in the degree to which the common, although
often idealized, understandings that previously gave structure and meaning to
the society have been gutted or abandoned. It is the cultural arena from which
many crucial issues and debates have arisen over the course of the last half century
and from which many of the significant social movements have drawn sustenance.

The left, then, can be understood as having three aspects: the conventional
conception, labor movements and socialist parties; the availability of a certain
set or type of public goods; and the prevalence of a certain sensibility or set of
cultural values (this third realm will be the focus of Chapter 6). These aspects of
the left are also interactive. Conventional leftist organizations—labor unions and
parties—characteristically lobby for public goods such as health care, unemployment insurance, pensions, and access to the franchise, and to the extent that the
conventional left is weak, a key contributor to campaigns for a comprehensive
public policy apparatus is lacking. Similarly, popular culture's ability to produce
and promote collective sensibilities aids the conventional left in its membership
drives and efforts to mobilize support for public policy changes. Comprehensive
public goods that enhance collective sensibilities and attachments break down
the barriers that might weaken the potential support base for unions and social
democratic parties, and they engender the humanistic understanding that might
overcome social differences.

Table 1.1. Unionization Rates (%) in Selected Countries, 1901–1961

	Australia	Canada	United Kingdom	United States
1901	6.1	—	12.42	—
1911	27.9	—	17.72	10.0
1921	51.6	16.0	34.27	17.8
1931	47.0	15.3	21.96	11.8
1941	49.9	18.0	33.7	23.0
1951	—	28.4	40.47	31.3
1961	—	31.6	39.9	27.9

Sources: See Walter Galenson, *Comparative Labor Movements* (New York: Prentice-Hall, 1952), p. 205; *Commonwealth Labour Reports, 1891–1941: Historical Statistics of Canada,* 2d ed. (Ottawa: Statistics Canada, 1983), pp. E175–77; A. G. Hines, "Trade Unions and Wage Inflation in the U.K., 1893–1961," *Review of Economic Studies* 31 (1964): 250–51; and *Bureau of Labor Statistics* (Washington, D.C.: Department of Labor, 1963).
Notes: The statistics for the United States for 1911 are actually from 1910. Similarly, the 1921 figure is from 1920. Reliable historical statistics for union density are not available for most countries (including France, Germany, and Italy).

Defining and Explaining American Exceptionalism

Given this dynamic, where the emergence and promotion of the individualized interpretation of industrialization provokes a society to respond at a number of related levels, what factor or factors can explain the American case and American exceptionalism? In every Western society except the United States, there are relatively viable leftist parties and significant labor movements. Furthermore, in these states certain public goods are taken for granted, such as comprehensive health care, inclusive voter registration procedures, affordable higher education, and a certain standard of public safety. Finally, there persists a meaningful collective sensibility.

This pattern has not been repeated in the United States. Besides the absence of a leftist party espousing socialist or social democratic principles, in terms of labor organization, the United States features the lowest rate of union density among its Western counterparts, except for France, where union membership is not linked to benefits and labor's influence has never been a function of unionization rates (see Tables 1.1 and 1.2).[9] While it can be plausibly argued that the absence of a strong conventional left might not imply the absence of a resilient collectivist spirit (e.g., France) and although it would be inadvisable to base assertions of exceptionalism solely on the weakness of the American left and its labor movement, given that the conventional left is on the defensive throughout most of the industrialized world, a marked difference exists between the public

Table 1.2. Unionization Rates (%) in Selected Countries, 1970–1995

Country	1970	1980	1985	1995
Australia	50	49	40.6	28.6
Austria	60	54	51.7	36.6
Belgium	46	57	42	38.1
Canada	31	35	31.2	31
Denmark	60	77	67.4	68.2
Finland	51	70	61.4	59.7
France	22	19	11.6	6.1
Germany	—	—	30.7	29.6
GDR	—	—	41.1	34.1
GFR	33	37	29.5	24.5
Ireland	52	57	41	36
Italy	36	49	32.9	30.6
Japan	35	31	22.6	18.6
Luxembourg	47	52	48	39.5
Netherlands	37	35	23.3	21.8
Norway	51	57	50.7	51.7
Sweden	—	—	79.3	77.2
Switzerland	31	31	25.4	20
United Kingdom	45	51	36	26.2
United States	30	23	15	12.7

Sources: Jelle Visser, "Trends in Union Membership," in Organization for Economic Cooperation and Development, *Employment Outlook, 1991* (Paris: OECD, 1991), pp. 97–134, and International Labour Organization, *World Labour Report: Industrial Relations, Democracy and Social Stability* (Geneva: International Labour Office, 1997), pp. 237–38.

Notes: The figures in the third column (1985) are all from that year except those for Germany and the GDR (1991) and for Luxembourg (1987). The figures in the fourth column (1995) are all from that year except those for Canada, Ireland, the GDR, and the GFR (1993) and for Denmark, Italy, Sweden, and Switzerland (1994).

goods available to American citizens and those available to citizens of other Western states. Social and regulatory policies are not easily operationalized empirically for the purposes of comparative analysis; nevertheless, the United States has generally been slower than its European counterparts to provide a range of public goods such as worker's compensation, unemployment insurance, and social security (see Table 1.3). The United States is also the only Western industrialized nation that has neither a comprehensive health care program nor a state-sponsored national voter registration system. "For every major domestic program," suggests Richard Rose, the "American government makes less effort than the average OECD [Organization for Economic Cooperation and Development]

Table 1.3. Dates of First Statutory Programs

	Occu-pational Hazards	Invalidism, Old Age, and Survivors	Sickness or Maternity	Unemploy-ment	Family Allowance
Canada	1918	1927	1957	1940	1944
Denmark	1898	1891	1892	1907	1952
France	1898	1905	1928	1905	1932
Germany	1884	1889	1883	1927	1954
Greece	1914	1922	1926	1945	1958
Italy	1898	1923	1910	1919	1936
Netherlands	1901	1913	1913	1916	1939
Sweden	1901	1913	1910	1934	1947
United Kingdom	1897	1908	1911	1911	1945
United States	1908	1935	1965	1935	—

Source: U.S. Department of Health and Human Services, *Social Security Programs throughout the World,* Research Report no. 58 (Washington, D.C.: Office of Research and Statistics, 1981).
Notes: All the Canadian provinces had occupational hazards legislation by 1918 except Prince Edward Island (1931). It should be noted that the dates refer to the first general national programs. Consequently, the United States is considered to have initiated health benefits in 1965 (Medicaid and Medicare) even though these programs covered only the poor and the aged.

nation."[10] Overall, the absence of a significant conventional left has been reflected in the nature of the development of American public policy.[11]

Thus the question is, why has the United States been slower and more reluctant to provide these public goods than its Western counterparts? The oldest explanations for American exceptionalism are those derived from the Turner thesis—the notion that the frontier experience affected American society uniquely by shaping basic societal values and by making possible a significant degree of (conflict-depressing) social mobility.[12] An associated suggestion is implicit in David Potter's *People of Plenty:* the notion that Americans have been particularly blessed in material gifts.[13] These types of explanations face certain problems, though, for as Eric Foner states, they "raise as many questions as they answer. First they rest upon assumptions about the standard of living of American workers that are rarely subjected to empirical verification. Have the wage levels and rates of social mobility of American workers always been significantly higher than in Western Europe?"[14] Furthermore, as Foner notes, mobility and increasing material wealth can be interpreted as both destabilizing and stabilizing factors, as was evidenced in the artisan radicalism of the early nineteenth century.[15] Often greater prosperity and possibilities lead to greater expectations and demands. And greater aggregate wealth has not prevented the persistence of poverty in the United States,

Table 1.4. Children, Elderly, and All Persons
(%) Living in Poverty, by Country, 1979–1982

Country	Children	Elderly	All Persons
Canada	10	5	7
West Germany	8	15	8
Great Britain	11	37	12
Norway	8	19	9
Sweden	5	2	6
Switzerland	5	6	6
United States	17	16	13

Sources: John Palmer, Timothy Smeeding, and Barbara Torrey, eds., *The Vulnerable* (Washington, D.C.: Urban Institute, 1988), adapted from tables 5.2, 5.6, and 5.8; and Arnold Heidenheimer, Hugh Heclo, and Carolyn Teich Adams, *Comparative Public Policy: The Politics of Social Choice in Europe and America,* 3d ed. (New York: St. Martin's, 1990), p. 253.
Notes: Poverty is defined in terms of the official poverty line in the United States converted to other currencies using OECD purchasing power parities and adjusted for family size.

nor has it led to the provision of certain basic social benefits (see Tables 1.4, 1.5, and 1.6).[16]

One could suggest that the timing and impact of wars have crucially influenced leftist development in the United States. Certainly various wars, especially the two world wars, have had significant effects on the fortunes of the American left, but similar effects were experienced throughout the West.[17] Indeed, the disruption of European leftist development caused by the two world wars was arguably greater, especially if one factors in the antileftist influence of the American Marshall Plan. A similar argument would suggest that the division of the American left over tactics (reform versus revolution) and allegiances led to its downfall. This argument, made by such analysts as Milton Cantor in *The Divided Left* and David Shannon in *The Decline of American Communism,* fails adequately to recognize that this division occurred throughout the West, again, possibly to a greater extent in Europe.[18] A third variant of this approach can be seen in *The Corporate Ideal in the Liberal State,* in which James Weinstein suggests that effective labor repression (e.g., the Palmer raids after World War I and the attacks on the left that took place during the McCarthy era), combined with a cunning, co-optive state apparatus, prevented the development of an American left.[19] Once again, this process was not unique to the United States (note, for example, the impact of Otto von Bismarck in early Prussia), and as an answer it only begs the question, Why was this degree of repression possible?

Explanations have been offered on the basis of formal political considerations

Table 1.5. Effectiveness of Transfer Programs in Selected Countries

Country	Families Living in Poverty before Government Transfers (%)	Families Living in Poverty after Government Transfers (%)	Reduction in Poverty due to Government Programs (%)
Canada	24.9	12.5	50
France	36.4	7.9	78
Germany	31.0	6.8	78
Sweden	36.5	5.6	85
United Kingdom	30.0	8.2	73
United States	27.1	17.0	37

Source: Deborah Mitchell, *Income Transfers in Ten Welfare States* (Aldershot: Avebury, 1993), p. 47.

Table 1.6. Portion of Population (%) Living in Poverty after Government Transfers, mid-1980s

Age Group	United States (Whites Only)	Average for Nine Other Nations *
All	9.1	4.8
Children (under 18)	13.2	5.5
Adults (18–64)	7.4	5.2
Elderly (65 and over)	8.0	1.8

Source: Derek Bok, *The State of the Nation: Government and the Quest for a Better Society* (Cambridge: Harvard University Press, 1996), p. 345 (based on unpublished data provided by Timothy Smeeding's Luxembourg Income Study).
* Canada, France, the United Kingdom, Sweden, Norway, Germany, Belgium, Finland, and Denmark

such as the resilience of the two-party system and the manner in which changing political styles resulted in a declining rate of popular participation in the political process, but neither argument explains convincingly why such developments were possible or significant. For instance, Michael McGerr argues that "the decline of popular politics did have at least one tangible consequence of enduring importance. As voter turnout fell in the twentieth century, significant challenges to conventional politics diminished."[20] What McGerr does not explain is why, given the growing depopularization of American politics, the public did not become even more disposed to support and develop unconventional political parties and movements.[21] Furthermore, such explanations tend to overlook the nature of partisan conflict in the American South (not treated by McGerr), which has often involved a series of one-party systems (or no-party systems in some cases, according to V. O. Key) rather than a uniformly competitive two-party system.[22]

Perhaps the most interesting arguments are those which suggest that a certain philosophical tradition shaped or prevented the development of a leftist presence in the American political culture. There are two general philosophical schools. The first approach, argued by Louis Hartz, is the notion that a certain irrational Lockean liberalism has characterized the political discourse and development of the American political culture. Hartz contends that American political culture has been characteristically "Protestant and individualist" and that "by the time of the Revolution a tradition of popular assembly had evolved which made Locke quite a common matter of fact."[23] Given this apparent common disposition toward individualism and the preservation of property rights at all costs, Hartz further argued that "collectivism is the great secret that American history [has hidden] . . . from its economically energetic citizens."[24] In contrast, the republican thesis, as J. G. A. Pocock states, questions "the image of a monolithically Lockean eighteenth century" and suggests that a "civic humanist" interpretation of the common good, an emphasis on the concept and responsibilities of the citizen, and an aversion to social and governmental corruption have also defined the American political culture.[25]

Drawing on the work of such philosophical historians as Pocock and Gordon Wood, Wilentz outlines the working-class variant of the republican vision as "a process of ideological confrontation, negotiation, and redefinition, a fitful process that changed the meanings of old terms as much as it revived them, and that only gradually pitted employers against employees."[26] From Wilentz's perspective, one can argue that the predominant republican ethos permitted and encouraged radical critiques of the emerging industrial order because it contained a certain sense of an inviolable common good.[27] Consequently, he posits, "both entrepreneurs and radicals judged the emerging social order with concepts they shared, and in so doing transformed these concepts into different, and opposing, class visions."[28]

As many have noted, the liberal and republican interpretations are not completely incompatible. James Kloppenberg suggests that one can conceive of the two perspectives as flip side expressions of essentially the same value orientation: "Republicans and . . . liberals were all struggling to achieve autonomy as economic individuals and the right to equal participation as citizens."[29] Similarly, Jeffrey C. Isaac questions the validity of the republican-liberal distinction, arguing that "this account of liberalism, and of republicanism, is flawed. It underestimates both the individualist features of republicanism, particularly in regard to private property, and the communal features of liberalism, particularly with regard to the centrality of the state."[30]

What is intriguing about the philosophical explanations is how little they directly explain about the nature of American political culture and the elements and events that are underplayed by both the republican and liberal schools. In practice, the liberal-republican debate has been a difference over a minute range of substantive issues inside a potentially broad rhetorical and political spectrum. Rhetoric aside, the basic orientation of the two perspectives regarding such significant issues as gender and race relations and the role of the state in the economy have been quite similar historically. As Aileen Kraditor points out, the conflict-consensus dichotomy (Wilentz versus Hartz) is, to some extent, false: "The conflict-consensus framework for looking at the American past can be made meaningful only if the contents of the conflicts and the contents of the consensual ideas and values are included as a necessary part of the framework. To do that is to shift the focus from the ahistorical fact of conflict or the fact of consensus, to the historically-conditioned contents of the conflicts or the shared values and opinions that constituted the consensus. But to do so is to discover at once that the opposition between 'conflict' and 'consensus' is spurious."[31]

The liberal and republican schools have failed to explain how their respective philosophical ideals were transmitted to all the people (including immigrants) who made up the real American working class and the role racial politics has played in the development of the American polity (Hartz probably being the greatest offender in this regard) or, in Alexander Saxton's words, the ways in which "racial identification [has] cut at right angles to class consciousness."[32] As Rogers Smith has argued, it might be more useful to recognize that the "varying civic conceptions" that have informed American life have mixed "liberal, republican, and [inegalitarian] ascriptive elements."[33] Overall, the republican and liberal approaches have failed to account for some of the dynamism evident in the unfolding of American history as well as the fact that American political culture has been defined by a unique combination of demographic circumstances and cultural perspectives through time. In other words, the American experience has been fundamentally heterogeneous.

Making Race

In what sense can one argue that the United States is particularly heterogeneous, and what does it mean to suggest that race explains the weakness of the left? Just as establishing and maintaining a leftist presence is an ongoing process, a dynamic undertaking that can assume different forms at different times (e.g., influence among the ranks of workingmen in the late nineteenth century versus the ability to curry favor with women, service workers, youth, and diverse commu-

Table 1.7. Demographic Variation in Selected Countries

Austria
Ethnic composition: German (99.4%); Croatian (0.3%); Slovene (0.2%); Other (0.1%)
Religious composition: Roman Catholic (85%); Protestant (9%); Other (6%)

Belgium
Ethnic composition: Flemish (55%); Walloon (33%); Other (12%)
Religious composition: Roman Catholic (75%); Other/mainly Protestant (25%)
Linguistic composition: Flemish (56%); French (32%); Bilingual (11%); German (1%)

Canada
Ethnic composition: British origin (40%); French origin (27%); other European (20%);
    indigenous Indian and Eskimo (1.5%); Other (11.5%)
Religious composition: Roman Catholic (46%); United Church (16%); Anglican (10%);
    Other (28%)

Denmark
Religious composition: Evangelical Lutheran (97%); Roman Catholic and other
    Protestant (2%); Other (1%)

Finland
Ethnic composition: Finnish (94%); Swedish, Lapp, Gypsy, Tatar, and Other (6%)
Religious composition: Evangelical Lutheran (97%); Greek Orthodox (1.2%);
    Other (1.8%)

France
Religious composition: Roman Catholic (90%); Protestant (2%); Jewish (1%); Moslem
    (1%); Other (6%)

Greece
Ethnic composition: Greek (98.5%); Other (1.5%)
Religious composition: Greek Orthodox (98%); Moslem (1.3%); Other (0.7%)

Italy
Religious composition: Roman Catholic (99%); Other (1%)

Netherlands
Ethnic composition: Dutch (99%); Other (1%)
Religious composition: Roman Catholic (40%); Protestant/Dutch Reformed (40%);
    Other (20%)

Norway
Religious composition: Evangelical Lutheran (94%); other Protestant and Roman
    Catholic (4%); Other (2%)

Sweden
Ethnic composition: Swedish (91%); Finnish (3%); Lapps and others (6%)
Religious composition: Evangelical Lutheran (93.5%); Roman Catholic (1%);
    Other (5.5%)

Table 1.7. (*continued*)

Switzerland

Ethnic composition: German (65%); French (18%); Italian (10%); Romansh (1%); Other (6%)

Religious composition: Roman Catholic (49%); Protestant (48%); Jewish (0.3%); Other (2.7%)

United Kingdom

Ethnic composition: English (81.5%); Scottish (9.6%); Irish (2.4%); Welsh (1.9%); Ulster (1.8%); Other (2.8%)

Religious composition: Anglican (47.73%); Roman Catholic (9.37%); Presbyterian (3.54%); Methodist (1.34%); Jewish (0.8%); Other (37.22%)

United States

Ethnic composition: White (80.3%); Black (12.1%); Asian or Pacific Islander (2.9%); American Indian, Eskimo, or Aleut (0.8%); Other (3.9%)

Religious composition: Protestant (61%); Roman Catholic (25%); Jewish (2%); Other (5%); None (7%)

West Germany

Religious composition: Protestant (42%); Roman Catholic (35%); Other (23%)

Source: World Quality of Life Indicators, 2d ed. (Denver: ABC-CLIO, 1991).

nities at home and abroad required presently), race is not a given or a static construction. As Barbara Jeanne Fields notes, "If race lives on today, it [is] . . . because we continue to create and re-create it in our social life."[34] Thus even though "data" may suggest that the United States is relatively heterogeneous (see Tables 1.7 and 1.8), such numbers are not rooted in any empirical reality (that can be measured by a linear index as suggested by the latter table) but simply reflect those aspects or signifiers of difference which have been seized on and reified by the analysts (and usually the societies) in question and which are currently perceived to be socially significant.

While these statistics are intriguing on a superficial level and forgetting for the moment that they are based on some problematic assumptions, they need to be put in a broader historical context to understand their limited significance. There are three ways to qualify heterogeneity and scale its probable effects. First, the nature of the heterogeneity can affect its impact on society. The degree of difference between the Flemish, Walloon, and German populations of Belgium is much smaller, for instance, than that between Canadians of Italian and Japanese descent or between British citizens of Welsh and East Indian extraction. A second factor that can affect the impact of heterogeneity on a nation's politics is

Table 1.8. Homogeneity Indicators for Selected Countries

Country	Homogeneity (%)
Germany	97
Italy	96
Norway	96
Denmark	95
Sweden	92
Netherlands	90
Austria	87
Finland	84
France	74
United Kingdom	68
Australia	68
New Zealand	63
Switzerland	50
United States	50
Belgium	45
Canada	25

Source: Charles Lewis Taylor and Michael C. Hudson, *World Handbook of Political and Social Indicators* (New Haven: Yale University Press, 1983).

the distribution of that heterogeneity. If the distribution of the differing populations corresponds to geographic boundaries, then the option exists of diffusing tension by varying the scale of political activity, for instance, by decentralizing decision-making powers. This possibility is enhanced in states in which there is a federal structure, such as Germany, Belgium, Switzerland, and Canada. In these states and in the unitary United Kingdom, the distribution of difference has corresponded roughly to regional boundaries. A third factor that can affect the impact of demographic heterogeneity is the manner in which the different groups "come together." The impact of non-European immigration on the public policy histories of large recipient countries such as the United Kingdom, Canada, and France and on smaller recipient countries such as Germany, Italy, Belgium, and Sweden has, thus far, been negligible because these states had already established the foundations of their public goods systems by the time newer citizens arrived after World War II. While non-European immigration has affected the electoral fortunes of the conventional left as anti-Semitism did in the interwar period — with the French National Front being the best example — the basic policy orientations of these societies have not yet changed.[35] In contrast, immigration to the United States and Canada has had a more profound impact on their respective

Table 1.9. Immigration to the United States, 1820–1989

Period	Number (thousands)	Rate
1820–30	152	1.2
1831–40	599	3.9
1841–50	1,713	8.4
1851–60	2,598	9.3
1861–70	2,315	6.4
1871–80	2,812	6.2
1881–90	5,247	9.2
1891–1900	3,688	5.3
1901–10	8,795	10.4
1911–20	5,736	5.7
1921–30	4,107	3.5
1931–40	528	0.4
1941–50	1,035	0.7
1951–60	2,515	1.5
1961–70	3,322	1.7
1971–80	4,493	2.1
1980–89	5,802	2.7

Source: Statistical Abstract of the United States, 1991 (Washington, D.C.: Bureau of the Census, 1991), Table 5, p. 9.
Notes: The numbers are in thousands. The rate is annual rate per thousand. The rate is computed by dividing the sum of annual immigration totals by the sum of annual population totals for the same number of years.

histories (see Tables 1.9 and 1.10). In both countries the rate of immigration (primarily from Europe and, to a lesser extent, Asia) reached relatively high levels in the mid–nineteenth century and again in the decades before and after the beginning of the twentieth century. These new immigrants forced both societies to reexamine their conceptions of citizenship and tested the elasticity of the prevailing definitions of whiteness and nonwhiteness.

Moreover, although the United States has drawn its population from very different sources, as has Canada, the troubled relationship between American citizens of European and African extraction has no counterpart in the Western world (see Table 1.11). At another level, the distribution of difference in the United States has not corresponded to regional boundaries sufficiently to enable Americans to limit conflict by varying the scale of political activity. States' rights rhetoric has played a role in the development of the American polity, yet the federal structure has not provided an adequate means of responding to diversity. While Canada is by most measures as, if not more, heterogeneous than the United

Table 1.10. Immigration to Canada, 1851–1981

Period	Number (thousands)	Rate
1851–61	352	10.9
1862–71	260	7.1
1872–81	350	8.1
1882–91	680	14.1
1892–1901	250	4.7
1902–11	1,550	21.5
1912–21	1,400	15.9
1922–31	1,200	11.6
1932–41	149	1.3
1942–51	548	3.9
1952–61	1,543	8.5
1962–71	1,429	6.62
1972–81	1,429	5.87

Source: Adapted from *Canada Year Book, 1990* (Ottawa: Statistics Canada, 1990), Table 2.3, p. 2–20.
Notes: The numbers are in thousands. The rates were computed by dividing the immigration totals for the ten-year period by the total Canadian population at the end of the period. The rate reflects the percentage of Canadians who immigrated to the country in the preceding ten years.

States, and conceptions of citizenship in both nations have been formed, to some degree, in opposition to and as a result of the exclusion and exploitation of native populations, Canada's federal structure has functioned as a means of reducing the tensions these demographic conditions can create, particularly with regard to the anglophone-francophone divide.[36] Last, the fact that the majority of African Americans arrived in the United States as slaves has had no little impact on the role heterogeneity has played in the making of the American republic.[37] The historical circumstances under which American national identity has evolved have rendered its demographic heterogeneity particularly significant. As a consequence, despite the heterogeneity one finds in such countries as Belgium and the United Kingdom, these societies have not been marked by the degree of ethnic or racial polarization that one finds in the United States.

It is important, though, to recognize that immigration figures and census data, while useful at a superficial level, assume what needs to be explained and do not reflect what are perhaps the more relevant dynamics: the manner in which difference is calibrated and processed historically or, with regard to the American case in particular, how and why race continues to be a powerful force. In *The Concept of Race,* Ashley Montagu describes the process by which race came to be—that is, the construction of the rudimentary means of classifying humankind, devel-

Table 1.11 American Population, by Race, 1790–1990

	White (%)	Black (%)	Other (%)	American Indian (%)	Asian/ Pacific Islander (%)
1790	80.72	19.28	—	—	—
1800	81.12	18.88	—	—	—
1810	80.96	19.04	—	—	—
1820	81.61	18.39	—	—	—
1830	81.9	18.1	—	—	—
1840	83.16	16.84	—	—	—
1850	84.3	15.7	—	—	—
1860	85.62	14.13	0.25	—	—
1870	87.11	12.66	0.23	—	—
1880	86.53	13.13	0.34	—	—
1890	87.53	11.9	0.57	—	—
1900	87.91	11.62	0.46	—	—
1910	88.86	10.68	0.44	—	—
1920	89.69	9.9	0.4	—	—
1930	89.82	9.7	0.48	—	—
1940	89.79	9.77	0.44	—	—
1950	89.54	9.98	0.48	—	—
1960	88.6	10.5	0.9	—	—
1970	87.6	11.1	1.3	—	—
1980	85.9	11.8	—	0.64	1.66
1990	80.3	12.1	3.9	0.8	2.9

Sources: Adapted from Statistical Abstract of the United States, 1960 (Washington, D.C.: Bureau of the Census, 1960), Table 15, p. 21, and Statistical Abstract of the United States, 1991 (Washington, D.C.: Bureau of the Census, 1991), Tables 11 and 19, pp. 12 and 17.
Notes: The category "Other" was created for the 1860 census, broken down into American Indian and Asian/Pacific Islander in 1980, and re-created for the 1990 census. In 1990, 9% of the population was classified as Hispanic. Hispanics can be found in any of the racial categories.

oped in the eighteenth century by two Enlightenment thinkers, Carl Von Linne and Georges Buffon.[38] Suggests Montagu, "First the races were assumed to exist. Second, they were recognized. Third, they were described, and fourth, they were systematically classified." Continuing, he argues that "if anything could have been more arbitrary it would be difficult to name it."[39]

As the result of a protracted (and ongoing) debate over the utility of the term "race," it has become increasingly accepted in the fields of anthropology and genetics that identifiable, regular, and distinct racial groupings and differences do not exist and that "variation is continuous, not discontinuous . . . [as] populations . . . are always found to grade gradually into or incline toward others." Consequently, the concept of race is deemed problematic because, as Montagu concludes, "(1) it is artificial; (2) it does not agree with the facts; (3) it leads to confusion and the perpetuation of error, and finally . . . for all of these reasons it is meaningless, or rather more accurately such meaning as it possesses is false."[40]

While empirically races do not "really" exist, the obsession with the implications of racial differences has affected the political activities of all Americans, in some manner, regardless of their background. As these categories have been imbued with significance, the behavior and perceptions of Americans have been affected so as to give even greater life to an essentially artificial realm.[41] Consequently, much of the demographic variation that makes Canada a heterogeneous society is contained within the category of "white" in the United States. Similarly, it has been noted that Caribbean Hispanics, upon arriving in the United States, "tend to divide more sharply along black-and-white lines in their residential patterns, primarily because [of] U.S. attitudes about race."[42] The prevalence of racialism has resulted in the preservation of the Hispanic and Asian classifications, even though the categories include a wide range of peoples, cultures, and national origins.[43]

Race cannot provide a moral compass for a people attempting to come to terms with a new environment or changing circumstances. Race, as a consequence of its artificial origins, cannot sustain a coherent system of values; it provides few useful clues as to what is up or down, good or bad, desirable or undesirable. The popular acceptance of race as a significant realm of human existence has left many Americans without a means of making sense of their surroundings.[44] If some sense of a collective identity is necessary to sustain the development of a left, the popular American attachment to an artificial conception of identity—race—undoubtedly has hampered the aggregate's ability to respond consistently and comprehensively to the challenges posed by the experience of modernization.

It is in this context that the increased attention to the growing numbers of Hispanic and Asian Americans is interesting. Predictions that Hispanics will outnumber blacks as the leading minority group by the end of the first decade of the twenty-first century, the growing significance of Asian Americans primarily in the West, and the high rates of intermarriage among all groups (except, it should be noted, blacks) have created the possibility that the bipolar dialectic (i.e., black versus white) that has underpinned American developments for so long might be transcended and perhaps that these changes might encourage Americans to move "beyond race" (see Table 1.12). From a historical perspective, though, the United States has always had a diverse population and has been at the crossroads many times before (e.g., the immigration of "others" such as the Irish,

Table 1.12. Population by Group in New York City, Chicago, and Los Angeles, 1990

Group	New York City	Chicago	Los Angeles
Whites	43.4	38.2	37.5
Latinos	23.7	19.2	39.3
Asians	7.0	3.7	9.8
Blacks	28.8	39.0	13.9

Sources: U.S. Bureau of the Census, 1990; Raphael J. Sonenshein, "The Prospects for Multiracial Coalitions: Lessons from America's Three Largest Cities," in *Racial Politics in American Cities,* 2d ed., ed. Rufus P. Browning, Dale Rogers Marshall, and David H. Tabb (New York: Longman Publishers, 1997), p. 267.

Germans, and Chinese in the mid–nineteenth century, and eastern and southern Europeans in the late nineteenth and early twentieth centuries), and it has chosen every time simply to redefine whiteness (for example, to include the Irish and Germans) and/or blackness (to include Chinese immigrants on their arrival in the late 1840s) so as to maintain the basic dichotomy.[45] Accordingly, Ronald Walters has suggested that Asians and Hispanics might "end up being honorary whites."[46] Similarly, Michael Lind has contended that "what seems to be emerging . . . is a new dichotomy between blacks and nonblacks. Increasingly, whites, Asians and Hispanics are creating a broad community from which black Americans may be excluded."[47] Americans, as they have been at a number of similar junctures throughout their history, are presently faced with demographic circumstances that challenge the binary racial codes that have organized and given shape to their social interactions for so long. It will be interesting to see if these new opportunities produce new outcomes and, to borrow from Richard Rodriguez, a new "language," or if the prevailing racial categories are simply reupholstered.[48]

To return to the issue of the nature of the relationship between race and the left, Americans have faced a unique set of demographic challenges in comparison with citizens of most industrialized nations. These challenges have, thus far, more often presented obstacles than opportunities to leftist movements, dependent as they are on the mobilization of collectivist sentiments. Conceptions of whiteness and blackness have proved to be not only rather elastic but also resilient over the course of American history. Despite the many fluctuations in the texture and temper of American ethnic discourses, the outcomes have been remarkably consistent. Thus, although the meaning and substance of leftism have certainly changed over the last 150 years (roughly going back to the beginning of the industrial era) and although Americans have had numerous chances to remake themselves free of the hindrances of whiteness, blackness, and "otherness" in general, at every opportunity the choice has been to remake race in some potent form at the cost of community.

To date the vast majority of analysts of American exceptionalism have either questioned the validity of the perspective (e.g., Wilentz and Fredrickson) or have sought to explain it by other means: ideology (Hartz, Lipset); the frontier (Turner); material abundance (Potter); institutional factors (McGerr); and divided labor movements and divided lefts (Weinstein, Shannon, and Cantor). Few analysts have argued that American exceptionalism—the lack of a leftist party and a strong labor movement, a range of public goods and policies, and a resilient, solidaristic public culture—whether celebrated or cursed, is, to some significant degree, a function of American demographic heterogeneity, or simply race.[49]

The Set List

The next two chapters will focus on the conventional American left. In Chapter 2 I examine the effects of demographic heterogeneity on the evolution of the American labor movement, paying particular attention to the National Labor Union, the Knights of Labor, the American Federation of Labor, the International Workers of the World, and the Congress of Industrial Organizations. Although labor unions are in retreat in most of the countries in the industrialized world, American unions have always been weaker than their counterparts elsewhere. This chapter will identify the ways in which racially influenced decisions affected the choices made by labor movements and prevented workers from attempting to form the coalitions that might have improved their circumstances. In Chapter 3 I discuss the effect of these same factors on leftist parties, beginning with the preleftist Populist Party and moving through considerations of the Socialist Labor Party, the Socialist Party, and the Communist Party of the United States of America.

The fourth chapter will provide an analysis of the impact of race on New Deal politics and challenge the conventional wisdom that the New Deal—as a means of bringing about substantive change in favor of the working and middle classes—was undone by the disruptive effects of the civil rights movement and the extension of fuller citizenship rights to African Americans in the 1950s and 1960s. In Chapter 5 I examine American public policy choices from a comparative perspective, as well as the role racial considerations have played in shaping these choices (with an extended consideration of voter registration procedures and health care). The sixth chapter will extend the analysis to the realm of culture. I consider how the promotion and acceptance of the concept of race have affected the making of American culture and working-class consciousness or, in the words of David Roediger, "the role of race in defining how white workers look not only at Blacks but at themselves; the pervasiveness of race; [and] the complex mixture of hate, sadness and longing in the racist thought of white workers."[50] This section will also include a consideration of the left's efforts, primarily in the 1930s and 1940s, to establish itself on the "cultural front," to borrow from Michael Denning.[51] In the last chapter I restate the main arguments of the book and briefly consider some of the competing explanations of the exceptionalism phenomenon.

CHAPTER TWO

Race, Ethnicity, and the Cooperative Commonwealth

"But it ain't decent to scab," said Jake.

"Decent mah black moon!" shouted Zeddy. "I'll scab through hell to make mah living. Scab job or open shop or union am all the same jobs to me. White mens don't want niggers in them unions, nohow. Ain't you a good carpenter? And ain't I a good blacksmith? But kain we get a look-in on our trade heah in this white man's city? Ain't white mens done scabbed niggers outa all the jobs they useter hold down heah in this city? Waiter, bootblack, and barber shop? . . . I got to live and I'll scab through hell to live." —Claude McKay, *Home to Harlem*

Labor unions are one of the foundations of the left. In their characteristic struggle over the organization of the means of production, unions are perhaps the primary conventional means by which the collective asserts itself in the economic realm. The move to unionize also symbolizes the development of an identity, an effort to define a collective presence, prior to and usually in conflict with the alternative corporate notions of cultural and national identity. The struggle of unions in the West and elsewhere has been to reconcile the cross-pressures of national identity and one's place in the economic sphere, especially as modernization has created a tension between the two (in other words, the emphasis on interstate competition characteristic of the modernization process has tended to weaken working-class movements within individual countries).

The development and maintenance of a collective identity as demanded by the movement to organize labor depend on a clear delineation of the differences between the interests of capital and those of labor. In societies in which social conflict has developed primarily in the realm of production, an "us-and-them" vision of some sort has been necessary to sustain the unionization effort. In the West, to the degree that it has been agreed that "the other" is capital, labor has been successful. To the degree that the primary other has been a different entity, labor has failed to achieve its goals.

American labor has functioned in an environment in which "the other," more often than not, has not been capital. The development of a collective sensibility has been hampered by the attitudes and fears created by the country's demographic diversity. More to the point, throughout American history racialism and racism—the aggregate decisions to remake and to view as significant racial distinctions—have played a significant role in retarding the union movement. The interplay of racial factors with the unsettling effects of industrialization has created a unique series of cross-pressures for American workers. This has been especially so given the strong but varied attachments most Americans have to their national identity, to their claim to citizenship. Consequently, there has been a reluctance to adopt roles or develop identities that might challenge that citizenship.

Following a brief discussion of the republican roots of American unions, I will focus on the experiences of the major labor movements—the National Labor Union (NLU), the Knights of Labor, the American Federation of Labor (AFL), the International Workers of the World (IWW), and the Congress of Industrial Organizations (CIO)—and their attempts to mobilize workers in the context of a racialized and diverse society. The emphasis will be on the period between the Civil War and the civil rights movement a century later and the ways in which nativist and racist sentiments affected and were reflected in leftist outcomes in the United States. Specifically, the impact of race on labor's influence can be observed in three areas: (1) the popular identification of organized labor with racial progressivism (an association that was accurate at times and ironic at others); (2) the energies consumed by internecine battles within the labor movement between nativist and racist (anti-Asian, antiblack) constituencies and those advocating a more inclusive labor movement; and (3) the decisions made by nativists, racists, and their opponents to forgo challenging the racial status quo and organizing immigrant workers, in the belief that a successful labor movement could be sustained without the participation of these groups, and that these issues and constituencies could be dealt with at some later point after labor had achieved its main objectives. This willingness to exclude or to delay including immigrant and black workers alienated those constituencies from the labor movement as a whole, made it easier for employers to play different groups against one another, and was a reflection of the extent to which nativism and racism were embedded in the collective soul. Given the difficult nature of the battles all labor movements face to mobilize and sustain support for public agendas favorable to the working classes, the popular acceptance of whiteness and race as natural and meaningful categories made the American labor movement's efforts only that much more complicated and, ultimately, from a comparative perspective, less successful.

Versions of Us and Them

American unionism developed tentatively out of a variant of the republican ethos, the sense that all were citizens and equal in rights—that unchecked capitalism and its efforts to make wage labor a commodity (and consequently to degrade wage laborers) would violate the social order. This development was tentative because the move toward labor organization signaled a frustration with the failure of society to reform itself and a recognition that the idealized collective no longer existed, that changes in the commercial realm had brought about a serious Weberesque disjunction between the political, social, and economic spheres. To unionize was to accept that the Garden of Eden was no more and realize that one's citizenship was being devalued as the control over one's own labor was alienated. Labor organization, then, would be an implicit acknowledgment that it was no longer a matter of maintaining the Jeffersonian ideal but instead the less dignified struggle to survive when economic changes inevitably influenced the political. This ambivalence about assuming a (lower) class designation, especially given the extent to which popular notions of class identity have been racialized, and an attachment to a form of the republican vision have marked mainstream American labor to this day.

The first responses to the processes that constitute industrialization and modernization, then, were phrased in terms of republican values. For instance, the authors of the 1834 Declaration of Rights of the General Trades' Union of Boston argued that "labor, being the legitimate and only real source of wealth, and the laboring classes the majority and real strength of every country, their interest and happiness ought to be the principal care of Government." The same publication noted that instead of labor receiving its "just due . . . we already behold the wealthy fast verging into aristocracy, the laboring classes into a state of comparative dependence," and the loss to "the working class [of] that standing in the community to which their usefulness entitles them."[1] As to the relevance and significance of these protestations, David Brody notes that "for many years, the Fourth of July was a workers' holiday"; he adds that although "we lack nineteenth-century opinion polls, we have much else that suggests the resonance of labor's republicanism in the larger society."[2]

The resistance to the developing marketplace's commodification of labor lasted as an issue well into the Jacksonian era. But with the rapid mechanization of American industry and the segmenting effects of Irish and German immigrant labor, the argument that the United States could somehow become "the Palestine of redeemed labor" soon fell by the wayside. Between 1850 and the start of the Civil War, the country's foreign-born population increased from roughly 2.25

to in excess of 4 million individuals, of whom 1.5 million were of Irish extraction and 1.25 million were German, refugees from the potato famine and the 1848 revolutions, respectively.[3] The arrival of these new immigrants set off a wave of ethnic conflicts and violence in Jacksonian America. Anti-Irish violence occurred in Philadelphia, anti-Catholic assaults in Massachusetts, and anti-German incidents in Ohio, Indiana, and elsewhere. While the German immigrants were more likely to be skilled artisans and move to communities with already settled Germans or to form new communities in the West and Northwest, the Irish often found themselves in locales where they were directly vulnerable to nativist passions, especially as they filled the ranks of the unskilled (in some cases displacing child laborers). Also, the more vertical arrangement of the Irish communities and their perceived "Papism" made them easy targets of the Know-Nothing and nativist movements (and natural enemies of labor). Moreover, aggrieved Irish workers often instigated riots that it has been suggested were a form of strike activity.[4] Nevertheless, at midcentury, American labor had yet to move beyond (or be forced to move beyond) its extended negotiation of status and citizenship rights toward a focus on the realities of the workplace: owner-worker relations, wages, hours, and conditions.

The first significant post–Civil War labor organization, the National Labor Union, formed in Baltimore in 1866 as part of an international movement toward national labor organization, was an attempt to realize the labor republicanist vision. The NLU's labor activities were focused in two areas: the drive to reduce the working day to eight hours and monetary reform.[5] Under the guidance of activist Ira Steward, the eight-hour movement was seen as a means of changing the balance of power between labor and capital and "gradually [introducing] . . . the co-operative commonwealth."[6] The concern with monetary reform, or Greenbackism, was a reflection of republican ideals in that it identified labor's interests with those of "producers," including farmers and small business operators. Greenbackism basically sought to curtail bankers' abilities to profit from loans beyond the labor cost of running a banking operation. The aim was to make capital easily available to workers and small business interests and thereby maintain or increase the independence of these groups.

The middle-class aspirations of the NLU set it apart from the agitations and demands of the emerging trade unions and workingmen's associations. Indeed, as Greenbackism became popular, trade union activity, especially against the backdrop of depression, decreased. As the post–Civil War recession faded, the greenback issue likewise lost steam, and the political ambitions of labor gave way to growth-fed trade unionism and the selective activities of the labor aristocracy: the craftworkers. Furthermore, the industrial cooperatives launched in this period, as part of the Greenbackers' program, had largely failed by the end of the 1860s or degenerated into standard corporate entities. By 1872 the NLU was barely functional as a labor movement, having been deserted by the trade unions, or as a political movement, its platform having become less attractive or having been co-opted by the two mainstream parties (especially the Democrats).

Although it was founded in 1869 by seven journeymen tailors in Philadelphia, the Noble Order of the Knights of Labor, the next significant labor movement, did not become an important organization until the 1880s. This was partly a result of the secretive nature of the organization, a characteristic that was maintained until the end of the 1870s. Absorbing former members of the NLU and other workers who were members of unaffiliated locals, the Knights sought to combine all laborers, skilled and unskilled, in a struggle against wage slavery. Suggested the group's founder, Uriah S. Stephens, in 1871: "Living by and on the labor of others is dishonest, and should be branded as such. Labor and capital should treat each other as equals. . . . Knighthood must base its claims for labor upon higher grounds than participation in the profits and emoluments and a lessening of the hours of toil and fatigues of labor. These are only physical effects, and objects of a grosser nature, and although *imperative,* are but stepping-stones to a higher cause, a nobler nature. The real and ultimate reasons must be based upon the more exalted and divine nature of man,—his high and noble capabilities for good. Excess of labor and small pay stunts, and blunts, and degrades those god-like faculties, until the image of God, in which he is created and intended by his great Creator to exhibit, are scarcely discernible, and ignorance boldly asserts that it does not exist."[7]

Under the leadership of Terence V. Powderly, the Knights sought to pursue their goals while forsaking formal political activism. The General Assembly of 1884 decided that "politics must be subordinated to industry" and that the Knights were "in no way bound by the political expression of its individual members."[8] Following in the republican-reformist tradition, the Knights favored negotiation and reconciliation and urged that "every possible effort . . . be made to avoid strikes."[9] The reasons for this disinclination were phrased in classically tentative labor republican terms: "When an employer knows that to reduce wages without first consulting with the organizations represented in his establishment may cause him such a lengthened period of inaction as not only to destroy his profit, but diminish the value of his plant, he will hesitate before action. So, too, the employees will hesitate to enforce their demands for an advance of wages, when they have a sufficient knowledge of the condition of the markets, as well as of the individual enterprise, and know that a strike at such a time would jeopardize their own interests. The Knights of Labor, while attempting peaceful settlement of the inevitable difficulties under the wage-system, use every effort to inculcate the principles of co-operation, and give encouragement to co-operative enterprises."[10]

Like the NLU, the Knights espoused the campaigns for shorter hours and higher wages as a means of elevating all workers and reducing unemployment, and the organization saw cooperative enterprises as a long-term goal. In common with its predecessors, the Protestant corporatism of the Knights of Labor (K of L) also attracted more members as the country slid into recession in the early 1880s. Despite its inclinations to the contrary, it was organizing for strikes and boycotts that swelled the K of L's membership rolls. From its initial seven members in 1869, the organization grew to 20,151 members in 1879, roughly 42,000 in 1882, 51,914 by 1883, over 100,000 two years later, and reportedly 700,000 members by 1886.[11] The Haymarket bombing incident of May 3, 1886, in Chicago, although not officially sponsored by the Knights, tarred the group's image. Along with employer blacklisting attempts, the deployment of union spies, the work of Pinkerton "thugs," a generally violent antilabor campaign, and a series of unsuccessful strikes, the Haymarket incident contributed to the decline of the Knights. As for the effects of strike activity in a context of general labor disorganization, Selig Perlman notes, "The strikes of the Knights of Labor were failures in the large majority of cases . . . [as] the Order operated mainly among the unorganised and the unskilled . . . [and because] the form of organisation of the Knights, well adapted as it was to strikes on a large scale and to extensive boycotts, displayed an inherent weakness when it came to a strike of the members of a single trade against their employers."[12]

By the late 1880s, the original reformist mission of the seven clothesmakers had been pushed aside by the general turbulence of the period. Wrote Powderly in 1893 of the Knights: "Teacher of important and much-needed reforms, she has been obliged to practice differently from her teachings. Advocating arbitration and conciliation as first steps in labor disputes she had been forced to take upon her shoulders the responsibilities of the aggressor first and, when hope of arbitrating and conciliation failed, to beg of the opposing side to do what we should have applied for in the first instance. Advising against strikes, we have been in the midst of them. Urging important reforms we have been forced to yield our time and attention to petty disputes until we were placed in a position where we have frequently been misunderstood by the employee as well as the employer. While not a political party we have been forced into the attitude of taking political action."[13] By 1887, such conflicted efforts and the constantly changing nature and context of American labor reduced the Knights' membership to slightly over half a million. Just six years later that number would be further diminished to less than eighty thousand members.[14]

Pure and Simple: Making a Special Interest

Another factor that contributed to the decline of the Order of the Knights of Labor was the growing trade union movement. At the peak of the Knights' influence in the mid-1880s, there were still roughly a quarter of a million workers organized within the craft unions outside of the organization's sphere.[15] As these were the most skilled and better-paid members of the working class, the Knights sought to compete with the trade unions for their members, setting off a series of conflicts between Powderly and Samuel Gompers of the American Federation of Labor (AFL).

The AFL had grown out of the Federation of Organized Trades and Labor Unions, which had been established in 1881.[16] In contrast to the Order of the Knights and the NLU that had preceded them, the craft unions of the late nineteenth century did not explicitly espouse republican theories, nor did they pursue formal political agendas as doggedly as the NLU had consciously and the Knights had inevitably. Adolph Strasser, president of the International Cigar Makers Union (an AFL affiliate), in an often-quoted piece of testimony before Congress in 1885, stated: "We have no ultimate ends. We are going from day to day. We fight only for immediate objects—objects that can be realized in a few years."[17] His comrade Gompers echoed: "I am perfectly satisfied to fight the battles of today, of those here, and those that come tomorrow, so their conditions may be improved, and they may be presented to them. . . . Every step that the workers make or take, every vantage point gained, is a solution in itself."[18] The craftworkers' opposition to "theorists" and claim that they were "all practical men" signified a basic rejection of the inclusive and socially ambitious programs of the Knights and their predecessors. As Perlman notes, trade union organization in the early days of the federation and its counterparts "was practically restricted to skilled workmen, who organized to wrest from employers still better conditions. . . . The movement was essentially opportunistic and displayed no particular class feeling and no revolutionary tendencies."[19] An offshoot of this practical sensibility was that unskilled workers were left to their own devices, as the new labor aristocracy took care of its own business free of the "nobility of [all] labor" theses of the Order of the Knights of Labor, which had logically required the recruitment, representation, and mobilization of the emerging working class as a whole. As one analyst commented: "The skilled craftsman was supreme. . . .

Organization of the unskilled was considered ill-advised."[20] Indeed, because of the succeeding waves of immigrant laborers, the broad, inclusive efforts of the Knights were seriously hampered — and the logic of the trade unions supported — by the tensions created between immigrant groups and "native" labor and the overlapping conflict of interests between skilled and unskilled labor.[21] "Nativism defended craft-based unionism from a more comprehensive unionism," suggests Gwendolyn Mink, "because industrial workers tended to be new immigrants." Continuing, she notes that "the craft structure of trade unionism thus 'fitted' with the ideology of nativism, because both formalized antagonisms against the class beneath."[22]

While the AFL rejected explicit theorizing and labor philosophy in this period, the activities of the trades unionists in this period were guided by Marxist and socialist principles, ideas that reached American shores with the arrival of German and British workers. Gompers himself was born in London in 1850 of Dutch-Jewish parentage and emigrated with his family at the age of thirteen to New York, where he apprenticed and worked in the cigarmaking industry. His early aversion to the rough American corporatism of the labor republicans was probably a function of his roots and his experience of a society (England) that had already gone beyond tentative Jeffersonian notions toward a full-blown recognition and negotiation of class factors and differences. His vision of the craft unions' role in America clearly centered on some notion of established class differences. "Class conscious?" he asked. "As a matter of fact there is no organization of labor in the entire world that is so class conscious as are the trade unions."[23]

In a sense, the pragmatism of the AFL in this period was based on an accurate assessment of the conditions of American labor and the futility of political cooperation with the interests of capital. As Brody argues, "All of this was grounded on this rock-bottom Marxist maxim: Economic organization and control over economic power were the fulcrum which made possible influence and power in all other fields."[24] Going further, Brody suggests that perhaps the republican vision was unworkable: "Here, then, was a central paradox of American labor history: To embrace the republican values of the larger society was to have a labor movement that would not work. And to have a movement that would work required some degree of disengagement from those American values. It was Gompers's genius to see what had to be done, and he can scarcely be faulted for the choice he made."[25]

In the long run, though, the disengagement of Gompers and the AFL from American values and from any romantic conceptions of the natural rights of American citizens would prove to be flexible. By the turn of the century the socialist and Marxist principles would be explicitly expunged, and as I will discuss later, the Americanist inclinations of the federation would become more obvious partly because of the emergence of a second paradox that would prove to be as troubling for the American labor movement: the possibility that engaging significant constituencies within the working class might necessitate embracing nativism and racism, while recognizing that choosing to leave these sentiments unchallenged might weaken the labor movement as a whole and circumscribe its ultimate achievements.

Pacific Meditation: Race and Labor in the West

Although the increasing heterogeneity of American society created a problem for the organizers of labor, it was a problem that for most seemed "manageable." The dominant attitude was that, with time, various ethnic groups (again primarily German and Irish) would be assimilated, "civilized," and absorbed into the republic. When significant Chinese immigration to the United States started in the late 1840s (see Table 2.1), it was similarly suggested in some quarters that the incorporation of these new citizens would be manageable and of benefit to the wider community. Noted the *Daily Alta California*: "Scarcely a ship arrives that does not bring an increase to this worthy integer of our population. . . . [T]he China boys will yet vote at the same polls, study at the same schools and bow at the same altar as our own countrymen." [26]

The migration of thousands of Chinese individuals into California and the western states in the mid–nineteenth century, though, would provide "native" labor with a stiffer test of its tolerance and a measure of its dedication to particular goals. Almost from the beginning and at the most basic level arose crude reactions that played on fantasies of racial supremacy. One visitor to California in the 1850s posited that "no inferior race of men can exist in these United States without becoming subordinate to the will of the Anglo-Americans. . . . It is so with the Negroes in the South; it is so with the Irish in the North; it is so with the Indians in New England; and it will be so with the Chinese in California." [27] Another individual suggested that the Chinese were enough "to make people wonder that nature and custom should so combine to manufacture so much individual ugliness." [28] Representatives of the Knights of Labor were no more eloquent in their discussions of Asian labor. In their coauthored article Knights associates W. W. Stone and a member of Congress from California simply state that "China is the reservoir of the cheap labor of the world. . . . [S]he has wrought no wonders and performed no service to humanity." [29] As to the effects of Asians upon white labor they suggested "that conflicts should occur between the white miner

Table 2.1. Asian American Population in California, 1860–1890

Year	Total Population of California	Total Asian Population	Percentage Asian Population
1860	380,000	34,933	9.2
1870	560,000	49,310	8.8
1880	865,000	75,218	8.7
1890	1,213,000	73,619	6.1

Source: Lucie Cheng and Edna Bonacich, eds., *Labor Immigration under Capitalism* (Berkeley: University of California Press, 1984), p. 65.

and the Chinese was but natural; for the miner, coming from the centres of civilization, had become somewhat brutalized."[30]

One source of the antipathy among the California Knights was the perception that the Chinese were more loyal to leaders within their ethnic group than they were to the cause of labor, that the group was vertically rather than horizontally structured and oriented: "From his cradle, the Chinese serf is disciplined in the doctrine of nonentity. He was born under a government having a spiritual and a temporal head; and he is, therefore, mangled body and soul. His temporal government is of the patriarchal type, and the sins of one of a family are visited upon the heads of the remainder. It does not require much knowledge of human nature to arrive at the inevitable conclusion that an element trained in such a school cannot possibly sympathize with our plan of co-operation."[31] Consequently, it was perceived that the Chinese individual could not "become either an American citizen or a Christian."[32]

At the local level, anti-Asian sentiment, or anticoolieism, was seen by some as a means of mobilizing and organizing workers. Alexander Saxton argues that "the non-Chinese workingmen of California and their leaders [discovered] . . . in the anti-Chinese crusade a powerful organizing tool."[33] Furthermore, he suggests that the more skilled workers used the issue as a means of manipulating the laboring class overall, including the unskilled and nonunionized, to support the goals of craftworkers: "The Chinese, and the factor of anti-Orientalism which their presence occasioned, furthered the dominance of the skilled trades by enabling those trades to control and direct the energies of the entire white labor force." This result, Saxton contends, came about as a consequence of progressive politicians allying with, supporting, and encouraging unionized skilled labor on the basis of a campaign that relied heavily on anticoolie appeals to all workers. It is in this manner, he notes, that San Francisco became a union town.[34]

There were numerous indications that a "pragmatic" approach to the issue guided the actions of both non-Asian labor and capital. Frank Roney, a leader of the Workingmen's Party in the late 1870s, explained: "I . . . took as active a part as I could . . . to make the party as robust and as progressive as the times and circumstances permitted. It was essentially an anti-Chinese party as was indicated by the motto, 'The Chinese must go.' However, I never warmed to that feature of the agitation. I realized that the cry was superficial, but agreed to sail under the flag so emblazoned in order that I might in time have other and real subjects considered by the people, which I deemed to be of far greater importance to their permanent well-being."[35] For capital, Chinese labor performed two functions: it was cheap, reliable, and plentiful; and it restrained non-Asian labor activism. Without Chinese labor, wrote the president of the Central Pacific Railroad Leland Stanford in 1865, "it would be impossible to complete the western portion of this great national highway within the time required."[36] "A large part of our forces are Chinese," noted E. B. Crocker, future state supreme court judge and brother of one of Stanford's partners, "and they prove nearly equal to white men, in the amount of labor they perform, and are far more reliable. No danger of strikes among them. . . . We want to get a body [of them] . . . and keep them steadily at work until the road [the railroad] is built clear across the continent."[37] Indeed, as they rarely had families to support, Chinese workers often worked for wages far below those of non-Asians. This satisfaction with Asian labor, though, lasted only as long as it was perceived to be efficient. As the Chinese began to set up their own trades and hire their countrymen, the employers who had profited from the deployment of Chinese labor began to support exclusion as vigorously as the workers (Leland Stanford is a good example of this change of heart). This displeasure was further increased by the Chinese willingness to use strikes to gain reduced hours, wage increases, and parity with whites.[38] In some cases the Chinese workers proved to be more aggressive than their white counterparts. In *China Men,* Maxine Hong Kingston records her grandfather Ah Goong as noting, in relation to a brief strike for higher wages against the Central Pacific Railroad, that the workers "would have won forty-five dollars [instead of thirty-five dollars a month] if the thousand demon [white] workers had joined the strike. Demons would have listened to demons. [We, the Chinese workers] . . . went back to work quietly. No use singing and shouting over a compromise."[39]

The ramifications of the anticoolie campaigns in California are instructive. At the local level, the issues of specific interest to labor were swept aside in the rush to promote anti-Asian activity. As anticoolie clubs and the newly formed Asiatic Exclusion League consumed the attention of non-Asian Californians, other issues were crowded out. Indeed, the Workingmen's Party of California, anti-Asian as it was, lost its constituency when its major plank was coopted by the Democratic Party (which used the issue as an acceptable—racist but not specifically antiblack—means of rehabilitation after the Civil War) and then by the Republicans. The latter, naturally, were more resistant to anticoolie appeals, given their economic interests and the party's identification with the antiracist sentiments underlying the Reconstruction effort, but changed course as Asian labor became more expensive and unnecessary given the completion of the railroads, the exhaustion of the mines, and the unending waves of "assimilable" labor coming from the East.

The anti-Asian issue played strongly into the basic ambivalence that has characteristically marked this country's workers and brought together the two paradoxes that troubled American labor: the ambiguous virtues of its hesitant republicanism, and the ramifications of its endorsement of the broader society's racism. Anticoolie agitation provided a means of identifying with (white) America and a certain way of life—a corporate and racialized republican sensibility of sorts. At the same time, the decision to support the exclusion of Asian labor only contributed to the marginalization of labor's economic interests. As Saxton suggests, "In each case [of racial confrontation] . . . white workingmen have played a crucial, yet ambivalent, role. They have been both exploited and exploiters. On the one hand, thrown into competition with non-whites as enslaved or 'cheap' labor, they suffered economically; on the other hand, being white, they benefitted by that very exploitation which was compelling the non-whites to work for low wages or for nothing. Ideologically they were drawn in opposite directions. Racial identification cut at right angles to class consciousness."[40]

At the state level, the California state legislature passed a law in 1880, supported by organized labor, that would prohibit any "Chinese or Mongolian" from involvement as "officer, director, manager, member, stockholder, clerk, agent, servant, attorney, employee, assignee, or contractor to any corporation now existing or hereafter formed under the law of this state."[41] Although this law was subsequently struck down by the courts at the national level, further steps were taken to restrict Chinese participation in American life. The Chinese Restriction Act of 1882 was signed by President Chester Arthur and followed twenty years later by the Chinese Exclusion Act, which was in effect until December 1943.[42] Anti-Asian agitation, riots, burnings, and murders, in California primarily but also in Oregon, Nevada, Arizona, Washington, Wyoming, and Idaho, brought about legislation that severely limited the entrance of Asians (the Japanese and Koreans were later targeted) to the country. At the same time, the issue played a role in deciding the fates of the two mainstream parties and the fate of labor's legislative interests at the national level. As has been the case throughout its history, California was perceived as a crucial state for the Democrats and Republicans. Accordingly, the presidential and congressional campaigns of both parties in the 1870s attempted to identify themselves with the anti-Chinese cause, with the result that the issue became a national concern. For the Democratic coalition, the legitimacy granted to anti-Chinese rhetoric contributed to the rehabilitation of anti-black sentiment and empowered the party's southern conservative wing. After the closely contested election of 1876, the prolabor Jacksonian constituencies were left with nothing more than promises to restrict Chinese immigration, while the core demands of white labor (wages, hours, conditions) were to be neglected by the now dominant southern conservative faction within the party. On the Republican side, the abolitionist impulse that had supported Reconstruction in the South after the Civil War was undermined by the national party's willingness to establish itself as a guarantor of white supremacy in California and the western states. Republican victor Rutherford B. Hayes's subsequent removal of federal troops from the South (as part of the bargain struck in the Compromise of 1877), signaling the abandonment of black civil rights for the next nine decades, can be traced to some extent to the popularity of anticoolie sentiments in the West.[43] On both sides, the more progressive concerns were marginalized, and the economically conservative factions were strengthened.

"The First Time Ever I Saw Your Face": Race and the Labor Republican

The interaction of Africans and Europeans in this country has rarely been a peaceful affair. While the common interests of labor might be expected to draw diverse elements together at least for the purposes of addressing the issues of the distribution of the benefits and the organization of social production, this kind of cooperation has rarely been evident. In the antebellum South, black and white workers established a pattern that was to recur in various forms. Besides working in agriculture, slaves were also used in a range of trades such as tanning, metalworks, and construction. Some were bought by skilled craftsworkers, and others were introduced to the trades while indentured as apprentices. As a consequence, it was natural that owners would use black slaves employed in the nonagricultural sector to threaten the interests of white workers. Slaves were used on occasion to defeat strikes, on the realization that their presence would restrain any aggressive demands on the part of white workers.[44] That slave labor would pose a threat to white workers in the South is not surprising simply given the number of blacks that were in servitude relative to the region's total population. On the eve of the Civil War there were roughly 4,000,000 slaves to 5,250,000 slave-less white farmers, laborers, and tradesmen; about 350,000 slaveholding families representing about 1,750,000 people; and 260,000 free blacks in the South.[45]

Clearly, emancipation did little to free southern blacks in any meaningful sense, and if one overlooks Reconstruction a certain continuity of condition is evident. As one white southerner noted, referring to the prospects of the liberated African's labor, "We controlled his labor in the *past* . . . and *will* control it in the future."[46] While there is some truth to this assertion, the irony is that white labor was to operate under similar conditions and constraints.[47]

Even though the vast majority of blacks were slaves in the South before the Civil War, the attitude of northern white labor toward the relatively small number of blacks on their side of the Mason-Dixon line (240,000 in 1860) was not particularly accepting.[48] As Sean Wilentz writes in *Chants Democratic*, "Outright racism, a fact of lower-class life even in good times, intensified as white craft workers and laborers poured into New York to find blacks well entrenched in some key sectors of the unskilled work force, especially along the waterfront."[49] Wilentz also notes that the racially inspired riots of 1834 in New York were led not by "Southerners and the dregs of society" but by crowds that "consisted largely of small master artisans, tradesmen, and journeymen — including at least one union member."[50] Indeed, it was only after a minstrel performance featuring the stock character Zip Coon that the rioters were satiated and calmed down.

A similar dynamic inspired the New York City draft riots twenty-nine years later during the Civil War itself. In response to the Republican-sponsored Conscription Act of 1863, which allowed citizens to exempt themselves from military service by paying three hundred dollars, working-class whites (predominantly German, Irish, "native," and Democratic) ransacked the homes of antislavery advocates and attacked and killed blacks throughout Manhattan. The conflict was at heart an issue of class — wealthier Republicans could afford to pay the exemption fee, whereas working-class Democrats would have to risk their lives in war — nevertheless, its resolution involved an orgy of destruction and murder (at least 105 dead) in which blacks were the primary target (one black individual, Jeremiah Robinson, tried unsuccessfully to escape the mob and make his way to Brooklyn wearing his wife's clothing, but he was found out, beaten, and thrown to his death in the East River). There were also attacks on Chinese residents in the city and numerous incidents of sexual mutilation (e.g., dragging victims through the streets by their genitals).[51] Although the sincerity of the Republican Party's support for abolition remains a subject of debate, Jacksonian Democrats (North and South) were quite consistent in their restricted labor republicanism before, during, and after the Civil War: blacks and Asians were not — and could not be — properly considered as citizens.

Following the passage of the Emancipation Proclamation Act in 1863 and the formal introduction of free black labor into American society, the unions pursued various responses. On one extreme was the option of active exclusion: the institution of color bars to block blacks' access to the trades whenever possible. Another alternative was to admit blacks but organize them in segregated or auxiliary locals. Theoretically, segregated locals would provide black labor with (separate but) equal representation, although the natural tendency of the white locals was to collect the dues of their darker counterparts while neglecting to respond to their concerns or to allow them to vote for or send delegates to conventions. The members of auxiliary locals were not generally given any representation or access to the decision-making process, although they did contribute dues to the union. Black workers in both segregated and auxiliary locals were commonly restricted to the lower-paying jobs with different seniority rankings and promotion opportunities. A third path was to pursue integrated labor organization. Last, there was the effort to encourage blacks to return to Africa via the various colonization plans popular throughout the nineteenth century. For black workers the efforts of white unionists to restrict their labor often justified and indeed necessitated strikebreaking. Where white unions refused to organize nonwhite workers, blacks often formed their own unions independent of any national affiliation or urged the leaders of the national unions to include black labor to protect their own interests. And some blacks did return to Africa (primarily Liberia) as part of a movement that in various forms lasted well into the twentieth century.[52]

As for official policy, the National Labor Union tried to include in its movement all laborers, regardless of ethnicity. At its 1866 convention it was agreed that "the interests of the labor cause demand that all working men be included . . . without regard to race or nationality; and the interests of the working men of America especially required that formation of trades' unions, eight hour leagues, and other organizations should be encouraged among the colored race, and that they be invited to cooperate with us in the general labor undertaking." [53] Indeed, the NLU's 1869 convention was the first national meeting of white laborers to support the organization of blacks and to include black delegates. Nevertheless, despite its official policy, the NLU was not entirely successful in achieving its goal of a united labor movement. The first splinter occurred as a result of the California delegation's demands that anticoolie planks be adopted by the national organization.[54] A second problem was that official policy could not guarantee the cooperation of the rank-and-file membership and the affiliated unions.[55] As a result, black laborers were reluctant to become involved in the movement given their exclusion from the better trades and white labor's support of that exclusion. For instance, in 1869 Frederick Douglass's son Lewis was denied membership in the

International Typographical Union (ITU), which forced him to abandon his post at the Government Printing Office in Washington, D.C. After Douglass, the predominant civil rights leader of the period, observed that his son's only "crime was his color," the ITU's paper, *Printers' Circular,* stated, "Surely no one who has the welfare of the craft at heart will seriously contend that the union of thousands of white printers should be destroyed for the purpose of granting a barren honor of membership to a few Negroes."[56] Beyond white labor's visible lack of interest in the circumstances of their black counterparts, NLU leader William Sylvis, while recognizing the need to organize blacks, was opposed to the Reconstruction effort in the South, integration, and any changes that might increase social interaction between the races.[57] Another problem that complicated the NLU's relationship with black labor was the political orientation of the former, especially its anti–big business, anti-Republican orientation. Whether pursuing independent or Democratic goals, the NLU's ambitions conflicted with the strong Republican attachments of most blacks in this period (a reality frankly acknowledged by the black unionists in attendance at the organization's 1869 convention).[58]

The record of the Knights of Labor was ultimately the same as that of the NLU, its predecessor. At the level of national leadership the Knights clearly saw the organization of all workers, regardless of background, as a priority. Whereas the NLU's political ambitions and orientation led it into conflict with black goals, the Knights often challenged racist attitudes at the shop-floor level, north and south of the Mason-Dixon line. As Philip Foner and Ronald Lewis describe, seeking "working class solidarity, the Knights of Labor began a definite campaign to enlist black members," going so far as to challenge "southern racial etiquette regarding the segregation of black delegates [at the 1886 convention in Richmond, Virginia]." The efforts of the national leadership, nevertheless, brought mixed results. As Foner and Lewis suggest, the leadership itself was ambivalent about the wisdom of alienating white labor in the South and in the North.[59] Also, like the NLU's leadership, the Knights perceived that the national organization could do little, given white southern resistance. Consequently, some of the locals continued to exclude or segregate black workers from the movement's mainstream. One consequence of the failure to include black workers and assist black locals in many parts of the South was that in times requiring labor solidarity—for example, during strikes—the union movement was easily derailed as employers played one racial group off against the other.

Despite these developments, the efforts of the Knights were appreciated in some quarters of the black community. The journalist and future civil rights pioneer Ida B. Wells described a Memphis meeting of the Knights in glowing terms in the January 15, 1887, edition of the *New York Freeman:* "I was fortunate enough to attend a meeting of the Knights of Labor. . . . I noticed that everyone who came was welcomed and every woman from black to white was seated with courtesy usually extended to white ladies alone in this town. It was the first assembly of this sort in this town where color was not the criterion to recognition as ladies and gentlemen. Seeing this I could listen to their enunciation of the principles of truth and accept them with a better grace."[60] And indeed the Knights of Labor did manage to organize a significant number of blacks into its locals as a result of its willingness, on occasion, to challenge racial norms in the South. But the organization's message and intentions were not entirely consistent, which elicited a mixed reaction from blacks. In response to a Knights proposal that blacks be returned to Africa came this reply in the Philadelphia-based black paper, the *Christian Recorder*, in March 1894: "The Knights of Labor propose to 'deport the negro to central Africa' probably to relieve labor competition. . . . Why not deport the American capitalist? Importation of laborers under contract is illegal, because it practically imports foreign labor prices. Wholesale deportation of nearly eight millions of colored people would affect the labor market considerably. The Knights hope to induce the government to pay for the deportation. That is a thrifty consideration, even if it is not knightly Americanism. Who came to this country first, the negro or the Knight?"[61]

Generally, it appears that blacks in this period recognized the importance of unions as a means of protecting themselves from a new form of exploitation. As Frederick Douglass observed in 1883, "Experience demonstrates that there may be a slavery of wages only a little less galling and crushing . . . than chattel slavery, and that this slavery of wages must go down with the other."[62] It also appears that significant sectors of the group held no romantic notions that their new employers would be the best protectors of their interests, as blacks were often more inclined to organize and demand higher wages and better conditions.

While black laborers may have been willing to pursue their interests aggressively, the attitude of many unions in this period was that letting in the "new" workers was not desirable at a time that August Meier and Elliot Rudwick argue "marked the high point of Negro interest in the labor movement."[63] Organized labor's reluctance to register black workers and its willingness to restrict black entry into many of the trades frustrated the ambitions of some, as one witness to the 1883 Senate Committee on Relations between Capital and Labor testified: "With regard to our race, generally, I can say that it is making some advancement in many respects, and would make more if the trades were open to our young men. The entrances to the different trades seem, however, to be closed against them to a very great extent. There seems to be a disposition on the part of some laborers in some localities to shut our people out. . . . [T]here are very few trades outside of the barber's occupation of which our young men have a chance to acquire a knowledge. . . . There are some labor organizations here which, while they have no definite rules forbidding colored men to enter, yet do practically exclude them. Of course, all this is very discouraging, not only to the young people, but to parents."[64] The result of black perceptions that the better trades were restricted to whites was antiunionism. For the writers of the black publication the *Washington Bee,* for instance, the proper course for black workers was clear. Independent organization was encouraged: "Now the question which occurs to us is, cannot something be done which will unite all colored labor into one strong fraternity with the view to establishing an importance and a power which will either force the white Unions to open wide their doors, or enable sub-fraternities to stand independently of the white striker?" As a backup, strikebreaking was advocated as well: "Would it not be wiser to stand aloof and attract attention and sympathy by filling up the breaks which . . . strikes occasion, rather than manifest undue sympathy for a movement which in practice operates against the interests of colored labor? The time has come when the colored laborer must look to himself for protection."[65] Naturally, black antiunionism and strikebreaking only increased the antipathy of white workers, leading to the reinforcement of color bars and less black interest in unions.

Overall, despite the efforts of both the NLU and the Knights to address the issue of race, white and black labor continued to work at cross-purposes. While the lucrative trades and skilled posts restricted the entry of black workers, both North and South, the result was that blacks provided a ready pool of strikebreakers, thereby contributing to the weakness of the movement as a whole.

The Pure and Simple Revisited

"Every incoming coolie means . . . so much more vice and immorality injected into our social life," lamented Samuel Gompers in reference to Chinese immigration.[66] In 1905 the AFL's chief warned the unassimilable, "The caucasians . . . are not going to let their standard of living be destroyed by negroes, Chinamen, Japs, or any others."[67] And in particular, for black ears only, he suggested that "if the colored man continued to lend himself to the work of tearing down what the white man has built up, a race hatred far worse than any other ever known will result. Caucasian civilization will serve notice that its uplifting process is not to be interfered with in any way."[68] Gompers's statements were consistent with his actions as a leader of the Cigar Makers International Union (CMIU) in the 1870s, when he instituted a white label policy so that cigars made by white union members could be distinguished from those made by Chinese workers (who were refused membership in the CMIU), and with his attempts to encourage employers in the industry to dismiss their nonwhite employees.[69] These views were also symbolic of the AFL's willingness to perpetuate organized labor's resistance to the participation of nonwhite workers. Indeed, after the failure of the Knights' producer ethic to galvanize labor, the emerging craft unions, such as the AFL, made even less effort to organize nonwhites as equals.

These views, offered in the first decade of this century, actually represented an evolution of sorts, at least in terms of official AFL policy. During the federation's first decade an effort had been made, at least rhetorically, to encourage the inclusion of all workers, regardless of "race or creed." Although Gompers himself never advocated the elimination of the social barriers that separated whites and blacks and reportedly "took great delight in telling stories . . . that helped to perpetuate the stereotype [of] . . . darkies, as superstitious, dull, ignorant, happy go lucky, improvident, lazy, and immoral," he recognized that black labor left unorganized could pose a threat to the bargaining ability of the AFL locals.[70] In response to the argument that blacks, like the Chinese, were "cheap" labor, Gompers suggested that "this is all the greater reason why the advantages of organization should be extended to the colored man, in order that he may no longer be so utilized to antagonize our interests."[71] Furthermore, he maintained that to protect against black labor being used "against any effort made by us for our economic and social advancement . . . the Negro workers must be organized . . . or we shall unquestioningly face their undying enmity."[72] In support of Gompers's warnings, Will Winn, an AFL organizer working in Georgia, wrote in the February 1898 edition of the *American Federationist* that "outside a few of the more skilled and organized trades, if a body of workmen generate sufficient temerity to ask for less hours or an advance in wages, the Goliath in command has only to utter the magical word 'negroes,' to drive them back into the ruts in fear and trembling for their positions. . . . Unfortunately, there are but few unions in the South which have the negro as an active competitor that can truly lay claim to stability."[73] To resolve this problem, Winn suggested, "Colonization [the emigration of American blacks to the African continent] would be a practical and mutually agreeable solution of the negro labor problem."[74]

While AFL organizers recognized the costs of excluding black labor, they also had to reckon with the various reasons their rank and file offered for resisting integrated unionization and the opening up of the craft unions (aside from naked racism). One secretary for a New York local noted that blacks could not be involved in some jobs because of the potential "problems": "In regards to Negroes in our line, it is impractical as we go up in office buildings and factories and repair much equipment. In many cases tenants would claim it repulsive. As for instance in the department store, have a Negro repairing a light back of a counter with four or five pretty white girls, — what the results would be! Figure it out!"[75] A Floridian AFL secretary suggested that black members did not sufficiently support union programs: "When the time comes to demand his rights and stand by his oath and obligation he has all kinds of excuses — his house rent is due, his furniture bill is due, his family is suffering, his meal barrel is empty — and so on."[76]

Though recognizing the costs of racial exclusion and color bars, the AFL and the craft unions generally accepted segregation in some cases and exclusion in others. The International Association of Machinists, a union with a color bar, was admitted to the AFL in 1895, one year in which Gompers was not president, after having been denied membership previously. By the turn of the century, Gompers had moved from a pragmatic policy of working to open the unions and shops to all to an acceptance of member unions that segregated and excluded with the hope that perhaps these unions might be persuaded to change their practices. Accordingly, when W. E. B. Du Bois contacted Gompers regarding the conditions of black workers and sent him a copy of his 1902 publication *The Negro Artisan,* the AFL's president replied, "I have more important work to attend to than [to] correct copy for your paper."[77]

Again, separate or segregated locals and unions were perceived as an effective means of including blacks and thereby reducing the strikebreaking risk. Although it usually meant that blacks received lower-paying jobs, little representation for their dues, and few opportunities for upward mobility, for white organizers "separate but equal" was a workable slogan if not reality. "We found . . . below the Mason and Dixie Line," observed Frank Duffy, general secretary of the United Brotherhood of Carpenters and Joiners in 1912 (and later an AFL vice-president), "that when we organized white and colored carpenters into a union, it did not last long. We then decided to organize them into separate local unions. That has been more satisfactory all around."[78] A painters' union offered these five reasons for separate locals: "1 — Arguments between white and colored workers in the meetings often became personal and ended with trouble. 2 — After the Negro enters a mixed union he usually wants the distinction of being the only Negro in there and will not encourage others to join. 3 — It is hard collecting dues from Negro workers. 4 — Negroes 'naturally' get second choice when men are being sent for a job. 5 — Negroes violate union rules more frequently than whites."[79]

Although segregation and exclusion became acceptable practices for the AFL, its affiliates, and their counterparts, only a small number of blacks were actual or potential craft union members, as most worked in low or unskilled jobs of the sort the craft unions had no desire to organize — at least not at this point. Sterling Spero and Abram Harris offer figures suggesting that, as late as 1920, only 16.6

percent of black workers were in the skilled trades, 15.5 percent were semiskilled, and 67.9 percent were laborers. The comparable figures for whites were 32.4 percent, 19.1 percent, and 48.5 percent.[80] As long as the AFL, as the predominant labor movement, continued to maintain a craft orientation, black workers and many white workers would be peripheral to the body's concerns. Significantly, black craftsmen seem to have enjoyed greater opportunity in the South than in the North in this period. "Despite . . . handicaps," writes Ray Marshall, "Negro craftsmen apparently fared better in the South than in the North after Emancipation. In the North, where unions were stronger and there were fewer colored craftsmen, resistance to Negroes was so strong that Negro leaders advised colored workers to return to the South where the skilled crafts were still open to them."[81] Like the NLU and the Knights of Labor, the AFL had little more than moral suasion as a means of controlling its affiliates once they had joined, yet after 1900 the organization began accepting more and more unions that had constitutions restricting or excluding blacks and allowing already-affiliated locals and trades to rewrite their constitutions so as to limit, exclude, or expel black members. Commenting on the role of unions in the reconciliation of the forces of race and class in this period, Marshall asserts that "unions did not create the pattern of occupational segregation in these years, but they were among the institutions used by whites to restrict colored workers to certain kinds of jobs or to remove them from jobs they had formerly held."[82] Notably, at the same time that the AFL was moving toward accepting exclusive unions, theoretically in the hope that perhaps they could be reformed at a later point, it was also dropping its identification with socialist and Marxist rhetoric and principles.

The Gospel according to Booker T.

Faced with the exclusionist and segregationist policies of the unions, black workers often found themselves forced to scab and break strikes. The result was that employers naturally exploited the opportunity to use blacks when it suited their union-busting goals and let them go when cheaper workers were available (newer immigrants) or when unions organized across racial lines and their own prejudice led them to favor white workers. Like the Chinese in the West, black workers were locked into an effective no-win situation as far as their participation in the mainstream economy was concerned.

These circumstances created a dilemma for blacks and black leadership. In the early euphoria of the Reconstruction period and through the 1880s, the attitude of the community's leadership was mostly prounion, with such leaders as Frederick Douglass often using the same republican themes and arguments as the labor movement to urge blacks to participate. It was in this spirit that T. Thomas Fortune, a New York–based newspaper editor (with the *New York Freeman* and *New York Age*) and journalist wrote, "The revolution is upon us . . . and since we are largely of the laboring population, it is very natural that we should take sides with the labor forces in their fight for a juster distribution of the results of labor. . . . [T]he hour is approaching when the labor classes of our country . . . will recognize that they have a *common cause,* a *common humanity* and a *common enemy;* and that, therefore, if they would triumph over wrong . . . they must be united!"[83] When faced with the increasing unwillingness of the unions to permit blacks to participate, this "radical" prounion stance became an equally radical pro-strikebreaking orientation born of deep frustration. In 1907 he wrote, "The determination of trade unions arbitrarily to dominate capital" constituted "robbery of customers and employers."[84] He went on to caution black workers about the unions' "offensive socialistic . . . demands" and their "revolutionary purposes" and became the ghostwriter for one of the most controversial figures in African American history—Booker T. Washington.[85]

Booker Taliaferro Washington, born into slavery just before the Civil War to a white father and slave mother and a subsequent graduate of the Hampton Institute, emerged by the last decade of the nineteenth century as the most powerful and influential leader in black America. Much of his power lay in his ability to attract white philanthropic support and government recognition for his efforts to encourage blacks to pursue thrift and economy, develop Christian character, and not challenge the increasingly widespread acceptance of Jim Crow and the Black Codes. Washington is controversial because the nature of his ultimate agenda was never clear. For some he stands as the archetype of accommodation, an individual who sold out the best interests of "his race" in return for personal glory and power. "This man, whatever good he may do," William Monroe Trotter, a contemporary, argued, "has injured, and is injuring, the race more than he can aid it by his school [a reference to the Tuskegee Institute, which Washington founded to train blacks in the trades]."[86] The historian John Bracey characterizes Washington as the leader of a cadre that "blamed Negroes themselves for their subordinate position in American society and for white prejudice against them . . . [and] flattered southern whites and northern philanthropists [while advising] . . . acceptance of segregation and disenfranchisement."[87] For others, his "pragmatism" was a cunning effort to draw resources from outside the community to develop institutions, such as Tuskegee, that would educate and produce black leaders, craftsmen, and professionals by any means necessary. "This was the typical Washington attitude," argues the historian Harold Cruse on behalf of the second school of thought, "a bourgeois attitude, practical and pragmatic, based on the expediencies of the situation. Washington sought to train and develop a new class. He had a longer-range view than most of his contemporaries, and for his plans he wanted racial peace at any cost." [88] "Can anyone be serious," Cruse asks, "if he thinks that Booker T. Washington could have preached . . . militant separatism . . . in the deep Alabama South?" [89]

On the one hand, Washington's self-help message has resonated throughout African American history; his program led to the establishment of a range of black institutions that might not otherwise have been attempted. On the other, it is hard to believe that Washington's apparent acceptance of the violence that was being showered on blacks (for example, in his famous 1895 Atlanta Exposition speech sanctioning the separate-but-equal doctrine before the *Plessy v. Ferguson* decision) did not play a role in encouraging that violence. If Washington stands as an early symbol of nationalist or nonintegrationist achievement, his message is still a mixed one, especially given his clear endorsement of individualized capitalism, his promotion of the cultural values of the modernist mainstream, his narrow Americanism, and his nativism. [90] "Remember that you are in debt to the black man," suggested Washington to white businessmen, "for furnishing you with labor that is almost a stranger to strikes, lock-outs and labor wars; labor that is law-abiding, peaceful, teachable; labor that is one with you in language, sympathy, religion and patriotism; labor that has never been tempted to follow the red flag of anarchy but always the safe flag of his country and the spotless banner of the cross." [91] Washington's implicit endorsement of nativist sentiments is even clearer in the following passage from his Atlanta Exposition address: "To those of the white race who look to the incoming of those of foreign birth and strange tongue and habits for the prosperity of the South, were I permitted I would [state] . . . [cast down your bucket where you are] among the eight millions of Negroes whose habits you know." [92] As one of his ghostwriters, Robert Park, observed with regard to a trip he had taken with Washington through Europe, "He was an American and thought everything in America surpassed anything in Europe. He just wanted to get the dirt on them [the Europeans] that was all, to discover for himself that the man farthest down in Europe had nothing on the man farthest down in the U.S." [93]

Washington and his allies attempted to organize black America in a manner that resembled the perceived verticalism of the Chinese and Irish communities (and indeed most of the immigrant communities in America, including the Anglo-Saxon). [94] Initially, Washington warned the craft unions that exclusion had its drawbacks. Recognizing that the crafts would practice exclusion and segregation in pursuit of short-term goals, he cautioned: "Race prejudice is a two-edged sword . . . it is not to the advantage of organized labor to produce among the

Negroes a prejudice and fear of union labor such as to create in this country a race of strikebreakers."[95] But while he was cautioning the unions about the consequences of their actions, his main message was being delivered to white employers such as his friends and supporters Andrew Carnegie and John D. Rockefeller. In the June 1913 edition of the *Atlantic Monthly*, Washington assured white capitalists that black labor knew where its loyalties were due: "The average Negro who comes to town does not understand the necessity or advantage of a labor organization which stands between him and his employer and aims apparently to make a monopoly of the opportunity for labor. . . . [He is] more accustomed to work for persons than for wages. When he gets a job, therefore, he is inclined to consider the source from which it comes."[96]

Overall, in the period that saw the rise of the craft unions and particularly the American Federation of Labor, the continued and indeed increasing willingness of white labor to exclude or segregate black labor (having successfully done so to Chinese workers in the West) was met by a willingness to break strikes and adopt antiunion orientations on the part of black workers and leaders alike. Yet, although the late nineteenth and early twentieth centuries were marked by increased racial polarization in the trade union movement, there were instances when the interests of labor prevailed against the pressures of racial difference and misunderstanding. On November 8, 1892, an alliance of forty-nine unions affiliated with the AFL, including teamsters, scalers, and packers, struck for four days against the New Orleans Board of Trade in support of the Triple Alliance. Targeting the racial heterogeneity of the alliance, the Board of Trade made offers to the packers and scalers but declared that it would not enter into any agreement with "niggers"—the teamsters—who were disproportionately black. The *New Orleans Times-Democrat* urged white workers to avoid the efforts of black workers to subjugate them and, along with other publications, published fabricated stories about black attacks on whites. Leaflets were distributed to white workers describing black attempts to take over the city. Last, the governor of Louisiana, Murphy J. Foster, called out the militia to force the twenty-five thousand workers (two to three thousand of whom were packers, scalers, and teamsters) back to work. By that point, however, the unions had agreed to arbitration, and a biracial union committee won most of its demands—a closed shop, wage increases, and shorter hours—except for the request for a preferential union shop.

Another, more significant success in this period was the AFL-affiliated United Mine Workers union (UMW) founded in 1890. The UMW should not have succeeded or fared as well as it did. First, mining in this period was essentially an unskilled craft. There was little variation between the different jobs within the industry, little training required, and therefore few institutional means of regulating apprenticeship and establishing a closed shop. Second, especially in the 1890s, mine work involved an extremely heterogeneous labor force and was therefore prone to strikebreaking. Black strikebreakers were frequently imported to disrupt union plans in the 1870s and 1880s, and in the South in particular, convicts were used in the mines, which further destabilized any potential union organizing efforts. For these reasons, along with such "normal" factors as racial antipathy, black leadership being antiunion, owner manipulation, blacklisting, and state-sponsored violence, organizing mine workers posed a daunting challenge.

Yet because the workers "regardless of race . . . did similar work under the same harsh conditions," fewer means existed to combine racial difference with occupational rank; therefore, a sense that "all were in the same boat" could develop.[97] Although "with all of these differences . . . it [was] . . . an easy matter for employers and foremen to play race, religion, and faction one against the other," as one UMW official noted in 1901, efforts were made to have the union leadership reflect the workers in terms of ethnic and racial background. As Richard L. Davis, a black organizer, explained in 1892, despite the presence of "Polanders, Hungarians, Bohemians, Slavs, etc.," secretaries were chosen "from each nationality," and among the officers elected were "one Hungarian, one Negro, one Polander, one Slav and one white," indicating "that these people mean business and have started about it in the right way."[98] The leadership itself argued that "as far as we are concerned as miners, the colored men are with us in the mines. They work side by side with us. They are members of our organization; [and] can receive as much consideration from the officials of the organization as any other members, no matter what color."[99] Yet very little separates the rhetoric of UMW officials and that of other labor organizations; like their counterparts, the UMW leadership, at least the white leadership, shared the common grievances about "Negroes." One union official "personally believed that the Negro 'standard of morality'" was "not as high as that of white people."[100] Thus the UMW was not immune to the problems faced by other labor organizations, especially in the South, where most of the black 10 to 15 percent of the UMW's four hundred thousand members lived. Nonetheless, the union did manage to establish a significant precedent that laid the foundation for further industrial unionization in the 1930s.[101]

Up on Cripple Creek

The western counterpart of the UMW was the Western Federation of Miners (WFM) founded in 1893 in Montana. As would happen thirty years later in Canada, the WFM and its regional counterparts were to provide the stimulus for the first significant socialist movement in the United States (the Socialist Party) and a radical alternative to the pure and simple unionism of the AFL (in the form of the Industrial Workers of the World, or IWW).

By the last decade of the nineteenth century, the frontier, the mythical and symbolic horizon that inspired Frederick Jackson Turner's work, had virtually disappeared. With the closing of the frontier, Perlman argued, "American labor [had become] . . . permanently shut up in the wage system." [102] Whether or not the frontier had acted as a safety valve, as an outlet to reduce the tension between labor and capital, by the turn of the century its influence had been reduced. As a result, western labor relations (outside of California, which featured a greater degree of heterogeneity) began to resemble those of the East in the sense that direct combat, conflict, or negotiation could not be as easily avoided. Suggests Melvin Dubofsky, "The industrial cities of the mining West represented in microcosm the emerging conditions of life in urbanized, industrial America rather than the simpler social arrangements of the passing frontier." [103] But there was at least one significant difference, Dubofsky contends: "In the West the very rapidity of economic growth brought greater unrest, conflict, violence, and radicalism." [104]

Besides the pace of industrialization, a second difference separated the western labor experience—especially in the mines—from the conditions in the East: the relative homogeneity of the workforce. While the Northeast naturally received and absorbed a significant percentage of each wave of immigrants (except perhaps the Chinese and, of course, the Africans), the workforce in the West remained markedly homogeneous throughout this period, despite the efforts of employers there. As one worker who had lived in both the eastern and western regions remembered, "There was more 'etiquette' on the job than I had observed back east. . . . In the bunkhouse or jungle or job there was this considerateness that was rare back east. Individuality and solidarity or sense of community flourished here together, and with a radical social philosophy. . . . [They] demanded more respect for themselves and accorded more respect to each other than I found back east." [105] As a consequence of the greater ethnic homogeneity evident in the West, small businesspeople and farmers were more likely to support the campaigns of labor unions.

Out of the Western Federation of Miners came the Western Labor Union, the American Labor Union, and then, in 1905, the IWW or, as they were known to many, the "Wobblies." Drawing on the radical inclinations of the miners and lumberjacks who dominated the Western Labor Union, and energized by the relative ethnic unity of western labor, the IWW represented a unique radical vision combining a socialist critique with republican ideals. In the preface of *The Proceedings of the Founding Convention of the IWW,* both Karl Marx—"The emancipation of the working class must be the class-conscious work of the working class" — and Ben Franklin — "Property is the creature of society, and society is entitled to the last farthing whenever society needs it" — are cited.[106]

In a period when the AFL was allying itself with such individuals as Marcus Hanna and Andrew Carnegie of the National Civic Federation and the reformist politics of the Progressive movement, the IWW renounced all ties with capital and rejected Gomperist accommodationism: "The working class and the employing class have nothing in common. There can be no peace so long as hunger and want are found among millions of working people and the few, who make up the employing class, have all the good things in life. Between these two classes a struggle must go on until all the toilers come together on the political, as well as on the industrial field, and take and hold that which they produce by their labor through an economic organization of the working class without affiliation with any political party."[107] Of the many differences in orientation between the AFL and the IWW, two are of particular significance. First, the IWW argued that craft unionism served only the interests of the "aristocrats of labor." Consequently, the IWW organized its unions by industry rather than by trade. Second, the IWW rejected the AFL's discrimination "against workingmen because of their race and poverty."[108] While the AFL was willing to allow locals with color bars to join and lent its support to efforts to restrict immigration, the IWW sought to organize all workers regardless of race or nationality (although the regions in which the IWW was the most successful tended to be "racially" homogeneous).

The IWW's first convention brought together several strands of the socialist and labor movements. Those attending included syndicalist (or, as he preferred to call himself, "industrialist") William "Big Bill" Haywood, the former miner, Socialist Party member, and WFM member; Eugene Debs, who played a major role in Socialist Party politics; and Daniel DeLeon, of the more orthodox Socialist Labor Party. The IWW functioned as a vehicle for the aspirations of these socialists, who were frustrated with the AFL's avoidance of political activity.

The Wobblies enjoyed a brief surge of popularity in the second decade of this century, especially as a result of the IWW's frequently violent confrontations with mine owners in the West (e.g., in Cripple Creek, Colorado) and its successful strikes in the textile industry in the East. In such efforts as the 1912 strike in Lawrence, Massachusetts, the IWW organized a largely immigrant labor force that had previously been neglected by the AFL's craft union in the field, the United Textile Workers. While its membership in this period never seriously challenged that of the craft unions, the IWW's organization of industrial unions across ethnic lines represented a continuation of the policies of the UMW and, to a similar extent, laid the foundation for the later successes of the Congress of Industrial Organizations. By 1915 IWW membership had decreased to a mere fifteen thousand, but the labor historian Henry Pelling suggests that the numbers are misleading because "the importance of the I.W.W. was much more symbolic than actual." [109] While infighting and factionalism did not help matters, the most immediate cause of the Wobblies' decline was probably the violence, state and employer-sponsored, aimed at the union and its organizers.[110] As Dubofsky argues, "so feared were the Wobblies that probably no group of labor agitators before or since has as suddenly or as disastrously experienced the full wrath of state and national authorities." [111] And as will be discussed in the next chapter, the tensions and issues generated by the possibility of world war were a major factor in determining the fate of not only the IWW but the Debs-era Socialist Party as well.

The Crafts in an Era of Industry and Immigration

The same circumstances that brought about the IWW also had an effect on the development of AFL policy. Socialism as an ideology had influenced Gompers and his confreres in the early years of the federation, leading to an emphasis on observable economic gains rather than the citizenship claims made by republicans, but Gompers's socialism had never led him to identify long-term social objectives or to advocate independent political action on the part of labor. This disinclination contributed to tensions within the AFL and Gompers's loss of the presidency in 1894 to John McBride of the UMW, who garnered support from AFL socialists opposed to Gompers's orientation.[112] Gompers returned to the presidency in 1895 naturally even less disposed to socialist politics and especially socialist "politicians." By 1903, the AFL's leader had clearly moved from his early labor socialism to a rejection of the ideology and its proponents: "I want to tell you Socialists that I have studied your philosophy; read your works upon economics, and not the meanest of them; studied your standard works, both in English and in German — have not only read, but studied them. . . . And I want to say that I am not only at variance with your doctrines, but with your philosophy. Economically, you are unsound; socially, you are wrong; industrially you are an impossibility." [113] Though rejecting socialist politics, Gompers did attempt to secure legislation favorable to (craft) labor from Washington with little success as the labor-insensitive Republicans maintained political power until the 1912 Progressive split and Democrat Woodrow Wilson's victory.[114]

Reflecting the mildly corporatist and republican instincts of the prevailing Progressive era, Gompers also participated in the National Civic Federation (NCF), a tripartite (business, labor, and government) organization that sought a reconciliation of labor and capital.[115] The group included among its members Marcus Hanna, Andrew Carnegie, Grover Cleveland, William H. Taft, Gompers, and

UMW official John Mitchell (until he was forced by his union to leave). In Hanna's words the NCF sought to "Americanize the labor movement" and counteract the "radicals" on the left (i.e., the Socialists and IWW) and the right (e.g., the National Association of Manufacturers [NAM], which was pursuing legislation to guarantee the open shop). The AFL's reorientation led to its favorable reception during the war period and especially contributed to the willingness of the government to terrorize "good" labor's enemies, such as the IWW, given Gompers's implicit sanctioning of anti-Wobbly policies and his prowar stance.

While Gompers and the AFL were rejecting direct political action and independent labor politics, elsewhere different processes were occurring. The French union movement was experimenting with syndicalism, and in Germany, Austria, Sweden, and Belgium the trade unions were forming links with socialist parties. In England the trade union movement, specifically the Trade Union Congress (TUC), was organizing the Labour Party, a development the leaders of the AFL were fully aware of given that the TUC and the federation sent delegates and reports to each other's conventions. "It is probable that no phase of the British Trades Union movement has been watched with keener interest by American trade unionists than its political program," reported AFL delegate Frank K. Foster after observing the TUC's 1906 convention in Liverpool, the year the Labour Party was being launched.[116] The federation decided, though, not to follow a similar path because of the different political structures in existence in the two countries, the risk of alienating the AFL's allies in the mainstream parties (should the venture fail), and "a greater homogeneity in their [the TUC's] membership, a greater uniformity of race and creed and outlook than in our many sided and much diversified membership."[117] Gompers believed that the AFL was already an effective representative of labor's interests, and as he would argue later, "The organization of a political labor party would simply mean the dividing of the activities and allegiance of the men and women of labor between two bodies, such as would often come in conflict."[118]

Politics aside, the AFL was also affected by the growing pressure to organize workers industrially—the skilled *and* the unskilled—as opposed to its craft orientation. Indeed, the AFL's largest constituent affiliated union was the UMW, an industrial union, and it had to create loopholes in its governing principles to defend the UMW against attacks from those in favor of strict craft union formation. Despite the charge that the craft orientation would necessitate dual unionism, the AFL began to move toward a compromise. In 1907, the federation established a Building Trades Department to reconcile the interests of the different unions and workers associated with the construction industry. The next year, a similar department was formed in the metal trades, with other fields following suit thereafter, including railways and mining. The success of the NAM's open shop campaigns—to prevent unions from establishing closed shops and thereby reduce strikebreaking—also contributed to the AFL's tentative response to the problems of nonindustrial labor organization.[119]

The interplay between nativist and latent republicanist sentiments contributed to the divisive impact of southern and eastern European immigration. Between 1901 and 1915, 11.5 million immigrants arrived on America's shores, of which 3 million were Italian and 1.5 million were eastern European Jews. This new immigration had a predictable fragmenting effect on the labor movement as each group had difficulty identifying its interests with the others. Again, there were some exceptions; for example, the garment trade workers were to overcome ethnic heterogeneity, especially in New York with the formation of the International Ladies' Garment Workers' Union (ILGWU). And the IWW under Haywood's leadership managed to organize immigrant workers in the Northeast's textile industry. By contrast, the AFL and its leadership grew increasingly resistant to immigrants, not to mention the organization of immigrant labor, viewing excess labor as an effective depressant of wages and a threat to the status of skilled labor.

World War I and the consequent disruption of the flow of immigrants into the United States provided some solace for the new nativists in the labor movement (one must call them "new," for many were themselves immigrants, including Gompers). Seeking a more permanent solution, the federation lent its name to three attempts to restrict immigration: the effort in 1917 to impose literacy tests for prospective immigrants; the Immigration Act of 1921, which linked immigration in any one year to no more than 3 percent of the total of that national group already in the country by 1910; and the even more restrictive Immigration Act of 1924. In what was perceived by some as a victory for labor, the AFL and its nativist allies managed to close off one frontier and prevent the further devaluation of labor through overavailability.

Despite the success of the campaign to block Chinese immigration to the United States (capped by the passage of the Chinese Exclusion Act in 1902), the AFL continued to concern itself with the issue. At its 1920 convention, the following resolution was offered (and adopted): "RESOLVED that we ask of Congress as follows: . . . absolute exclusion of Japanese, with other Asiatics, as immigrants; . . . confirmation and legalization of the principle that Asiatics shall be forever barred from American citizenship . . . [and] amendment . . . of the Federal Constitution, providing that no child born in the United States of Asiatic or Oriental parents shall be eligible to American citizenship unless both parents are eligible to such citizenship."[120] At the next year's convention, agricultural interests (in this case the National Agricultural and Industrial Development Committee) were criticized for lobbying for the admission of Chinese immigrants with the assertion that history had already "proven that the competition of orientals with whites was the greatest evil with which a country can be afflicted."[121]

Throughout these campaigns, at the same time as the AFL promoted a conceivably legitimate concern about the effects of an open immigration policy on labor organization, a racial calculus was also evident. Beyond worries about Chinese, Japanese, and Korean immigration, members lodged protests against potential Filipino and Mexican immigration into the United States, whereas Canadian immigrants, for example, were not perceived to be a problem (although the permeability of the Canadian border—as a possible entry point for non-Canadians—was).[122] As one subcommittee spokesman suggested at the AFL's 1927 convention, "Quota restrictions should [not] be enacted against Canadians . . . whose standards of living are in harmony with those which prevail in the United States."[123] In contrast, "immigrants from certain nationalities did not readily adjust to American customs and standards of living."[124] Not surprisingly, the effect of the combined campaigns of nativists inside and outside the labor movement was to exclude certain nationalities (e.g., Asians), restrict some (e.g., southern and eastern Europeans), and welcome others to the fold.

The Canadian labor movement was as disposed as its American counterpart to exclude nonwhites from its circles. One of the first Canadian unions, the Workingmen's Protective Association (WPA), was organized in 1878 in response to the immigration of Chinese workers to the West Coast, particularly British Columbia. The WPA saw itself as aiding the "mutual protection of the working class against the great influx of Chinese," a goal that would justify using "all legitimate means for the suppression of their immigration." While the association had other ambitions—that members "would assist each other in the obtaining of employment" and seek "means for the amelioration of the condition of the working class . . . in general"—anti-Asian sentiment was the catalyst for the union's formation, a concern that would later extend to include Japanese and Indian immigrants.[125] Subsequent responses to Asian workers in the coal-mining, fishing, lumber, and railroad industries would include anti-Asian riots in Vancouver in 1907, the imposition of a head tax on Chinese immigrants, and the establishment of the Asiatic Exclusion League in 1921 as a result of a campaign spearheaded by the Vancouver Trades and Labour Council. Suggests Gillian Creese, "In the short term, anti-Asian agitation strengthened Euro-Canadian labour organizations [in British Columbia] by providing a successful mobilizing focus, but in the long term it weakened the strength of labour as a whole" by producing a fragmented working-class consciousness and a segmented labor movement.[126] At the national level, the Trades and Labour Congress of Canada (TLC) was espousing similar principles. At its 1920 convention, delegates proposed that the federal government be "petition[ed] to have all Mexicans deported and to bar them from re-entering the Dominion of Canada, on the ground that they are undesirable citizens and interfering with white labour."[127] At the same meeting, the suggestion arose to implement "a system of admission [which] would always provide that the numbers of Orientals in Canada did not exceed one for each thousand of the population."[128] An issue concerning matters quite familiar to audiences in the southern United States was raised at the next year's meeting, as the TLC concluded, "Whereas, the employment of white girls by Asiatics is not conducive to the best interests of Canadian citizenship; therefore be it resolved that legislation be passed prohibiting the employment of white girls by Orientals or white girls and Orientals being employed in the same establishments."[129] Finally, as with the AFL, resistance to immigration within the TLC proved to be flexible in certain cases: "Organized labour in Canada has no desire . . . to prevent the British worker from endeavouring to improve his position by emigrating to Canada to secure any position that may be really vacant. . . . [I]t is advisable that [money] . . . should be advanced to them from a Government fund . . . ensuring the immigrants freedom to work for such employers as they themselves decide."[130] This occurred at a time when it could be safely assumed that emigrating British workers would be white and when British workers themselves were expressing concern about Chinese immigration to South Africa and the threat such a development posed to the interests of the "Englishmen" there.[131] It is not surprising, then, that in this environment the restrictive Chinese Immigration Act was passed by the Canadian parliament in 1923. Thus attempts by white American workers to protect their racial and, in their view, class interests by restricting the immigration of others were consistent with the broader ethnic nationalism of the era, although such efforts would have greater long-term implications for labor and leftist movements in the United States than they would elsewhere.

Coloring the Brotherhood

The effective restriction of European workers in the postwar period at least temporarily addressed the problem of the oversupply of labor in the industrial regions of the Northeast and Midwest. No longer would new waves of European or Asian workers disrupt the efforts of native (i.e., earlier immigrant) labor to control its circumstances and concentrate on its relations with capital. Unfortunately for those who hoped that assimilation would solve the problems of heterogeneity and strikebreaking in due time, a new migrant labor force — blacks moving from the South—began to play a more direct and significant role in the growth of American industry. These new workers, it had long been agreed, could never be assimilated.[132]

Facing the ever imaginative and violent attempts by white supremacists to maintain a form of control through terror in the South and lured by the provocative appeals of northern industrialists seeking a cheap source of labor to further destabilize the unionization movement, blacks began pouring into the industrial centers of the North and Midwest. In 1910, 12 percent of the black population resided outside the South, whereas twenty years later, more than a quarter of all blacks had moved north, pushed by the changing economic circumstances in the agricultural South.[133] At the AFL's 1916 convention, one delegate suggested that the "emigration of Southern negroes to Northern labor centers . . . has occasioned anxiety on the part of the organized labor movement," and a resolution was adopted urging that blacks "in the Southern States . . . be instructed and educated along the lines of the trade-union movement" to "eliminate this menace to the workers in the Northern states."[134] In the spring of 1917 another labor leader argued that the influx had "reached the point where drastic action must be taken . . . to get rid of a certain portion of those who are already here."[135] Nineteen seventeen saw a race riot occur in East St. Louis, and two years later, Chicago erupted with a conflagration of its own. Both disturbances were related to labor tensions and the strikebreaking function of black labor.[136]

As in the past, strikebreaking was not a role natural to blacks but a result of their persistent exclusion from craft unions and skilled occupations. This role was encouraged by cooperative leaders such as Booker T. Washington and his disciples and those employers who perceived that this "race of strikebreakers" would solve any labor problems they might face. Regardless, as the sociologist E. Franklin Frazier observed, the postwar period presented black workers with greater possibilities than before: "In the North the black worker was confined to domestic and personal service, and his appearance in industry from time to time was generally in the role of a strikebreaker. It was not until the First World War that the black worker secured a footing in the industries of the North."[137]

Besides Washington's followers and counterparts in the developing northern black communities, there were efforts by some black leaders to rally black workers to the union cause, but always with misgivings. As Roy Wilkins of the National Association for the Advancement of Colored People (NAACP) lamented, "It is not easy for an Association [he was then assistant secretary] which knows so intimately the raw deals that have been given Negro labor by the AF of L to get out and shout from the housetops to Negro workers urging them to affiliate. At the same time we realize that affiliation would be best for all concerned provided one did not have just as great a battle after getting in the union as one had on the outside." [138] At the organization's 38th convention in St. Paul, Minnesota, in 1918, a report from the executive secretary of the National Urban League, Eugene Jones, was presented to the delegates. Speaking on behalf of a larger committee of civil rights leaders, Jones warned, "The unpleasant incidents in connection with efforts of colored men to get recognition in trades controlled by the American Federation of Labor have been aired. . . . [As a consequence] a general attitude of suspicion has been developed towards union labor on the part of colored working people." [139] Throughout this period, there were consistent efforts to encourage the federation to push affiliated unions to drop their color bars and hire more black organizers.[140] By the mid-1920s, resolutions were also being introduced urging labor to take a public stand on such issues as lynching, Jim Crow, and disenfranchisement "so that Organized Labor [would] become the champion of the Negro's social demands." [141]

Working from the inside of the labor movement, A. Philip Randolph and Chandler Owen struggled to get the AFL to force its affiliates to cease excluding black workers. Coming from a decidedly leftist angle, in 1919 Randolph and Owen formed the National Association for the Promotion of Labor Unionism among Negroes and Socialism to promote "the spirit of class interest between black and white workers [and to] . . . put Negroes in unions for which they are potentially eligible." Disturbed by this double monstrosity, AFL vice-president Frank Duffy commented: "I find it [the Owen/Randolph association] is backed up and supported by the radical socialistic trades of New York, and you can, therefore, realize that I am not in favor of it whatever. We can organize the Negroes along trade union lines, but positively not along party political lines [i.e., in cooperation with the Socialist Party]." This was the same Frank Duffy who, as general secretary of the United Brotherhood of Carpenters and Joiners, had suggested that segregated labor unions were "more satisfactory all around." [142] While Duffy was offering platitudes to the concerns raised by Owen and Randolph, in 1921 the AFL-affiliated Brotherhood of Railway Carmen made segregation and, more important, black misrepresentation an official addition to its constitution. "On railroads where the employment of colored persons has become a permanent institution," the new constitution stated, "they shall be admitted to membership in separate lodges. Where these separate lodges of Negroes are organized they shall be under the jurisdiction of the nearest white local, and shall be represented in any meeting or convention where delegates may be seated, by white men." [143]

Calling the AFL "the most wicked machine for the propagation of race prejudice in the country," Randolph organized the Brotherhood of Sleeping Car Porters (BSCP) in 1925.[144] Although the BSCP would not receive AFL accreditation as an international union until August 1935 (eight years after its first application), the union and its leader were to play a significant role in changing the status of black labor and in determining the evolution of African American politics.[145]

Working for Mister Ford

The Progressive Era attitude of rational negotiation and compromise led to a significant increase in the AFL's membership as well as in the ranks of organized labor on the whole. In 1898 there were five hundred thousand workers organized in trade unions; this number had increased to 1 million by 1901 and had quadrupled to over 2 million by 1904, of which roughly three-quarters were affiliated with the AFL.[146] By 1916, AFL membership totaled over 2 million and by January 1920 had reached an early peak of over 4 million members (see Table 2.2). The number of workers in all unions at this point was over 5 million.[147] The wartime spirit of cooperation that had led to the formation of the American Alliance for Labor and Democracy, Gompers's appointment to committee posts and chairmanships in the Wilson administration, and the retreat of antiunion forces (such as the NAM) did not last long into the postwar period.

The Red scare and antisocialist tenor of the late Progressive Era spilled over into a general antilabor campaign, especially after the Bolshevik victory in Russia. The urge to "Americanize" labor was manifested in an effort to restore the open shop and uphold "the right of any wage earner to refrain from choosing any organization or [to] deal directly with his employer if he chooses."[148] The antilabor atmosphere of the early 1920s was reinforced by a number of factors. Rather than delivering a "new freedom" for the American worker, Congress worked to dismantle the few achievements brought about by wartime cooperation. Blacklisting and significant wage cuts deepened the effects of a depression on unionized labor. Such corruption investigations as the Lockwood Committee in New York and the Daley Committee in Chicago led to a dismantling of many of the building trades associations, strikebreaking, and the reopening of previously closed workshops. Supreme Court decisions such as *Bailey v. Drexel Furniture Co.*, *Adkins v. Children's Hospital,* and *Knickerbocker Ice v. Stewart* represented setbacks for labor on the issues of child labor, minimum wage legislation, and accident compensation, respectively, at a time when the courts were still under the influence of Lochnerist (probusiness, antiregulation) ideals.[149] The early 1920s also saw the antitrust Clayton Act interpreted from an antiunion perspective. New technologies (particularly in mining) led to deskilling and more capital-intensive industry. "Welfare capitalism," the application of new scientific management principles to labor-capital relations, contributed to the problems facing organized labor in

Table 2.2. Membership Totals, American Federation of Labor, 1897–1920

Year	Number
1897	264,825
1898	278,016
1899	349,422
1900	548,321
1901	787,537
1902	1,024,399
1903	1,465,800
1904	1,676,200
1905	1,494,300
1906	1,454,200
1907	1,538,970
1908	1,586,970
1909	1,482,872
1910	1,562,112
1911	1,761,835
1912	1,770,145
1913	1,996,004
1914	2,020,671
1915	1,946,347
1916	2,072,702
1917	2,371,434
1918	2,726,478
1919	3,260,068
1920	4,078,740

Source: See American Federation of Labor, *Report of Proceedings,* 74th convention (Washington, D.C.: American Federation of Labor, 1955), p. 28.

this period and tended to increase the divisions between skilled and unskilled workers by coopting the former and lowering the status of the latter.[150] The emphasis on hierarchy reinforced the reluctance of skilled workers to identify themselves with other workers and the working class overall. Though AFL president Gompers promised that "the workers will prevent these industrial barons from riding horseback over the masses!," he himself passed away in 1924, leaving an unmotivated and uninspired William Green to take his place.[151] By the onset of the Great Depression, the AFL and its trade union counterparts had been decimated. From a high of 450,000, the UMW's membership was reduced to 150,000 in 1930. The AFL itself fell from its postwar high of over 4 million members in 1920 to just under 3 million in 1924 and slightly more than 2 million in 1933 (see Table 2.3).[152]

Table 2.3. Membership Totals, American Federation of Labor, 1920–1933

Year	Number
1920	4,078,740
1921	3,906,528
1922	3,195,635
1923	2,926,468
1924	2,865,979
1925	2,877,297
1926	2,803,966
1927	2,812,526
1928	2,896,063
1929	2,933,545
1930	2,961,096
1931	2,889,550
1932	2,532,261
1933	2,126,796

Source: See American Federation of Labor, Report of Proceedings, 74th convention (Washington, D.C.: American Federation of Labor, 1955), p. 28.

Membership in all unions declined in a comparable manner: about 5.1 million in 1920, 3.6 million in 1924, 3.4 million in 1930, and 2.5 million in 1933.[153]

One response to the depression was government's growing inclination to get involved in economic and social issues. Franklin Roosevelt's New Deal and, in particular, section 7A of the 1933 National Industrial Recovery Act, sought to shore up the negotiating and hence the purchasing powers of the working class. The act stipulated "1) that employees shall have the right to organize and bargain collectively through representatives of their own choosing, and shall be free from the interference, restraint or coercion of employers of labor, or their agents, in the designation of such representatives. . . . 2) that no employee and no one seeking employment shall be required as a condition of employment to join any company union or to refrain from joining, organizing, or assisting a labor organization of his own choosing."[154]

What would seem to be a clear piece of prounion legislation actually provoked intense anxiety among black unionists and their representatives. Given the history of the unions, especially craft unions, and their interaction with black labor, the perception was that legislation strengthening the unions would quite possibly lead to further problems for black workers and prospective black workers. These perceptions were not groundless. Besides the unions that officially barred blacks from joining, others excluded unofficially or included small numbers of blacks to create the appearance of openness. In one case, a local of the racially exclusive Brotherhood of Electrical Workers, organizing new shops in Long Island City, New York, in the early 1930s, demanded of the different managements that the blacks already employed—to whom the union had refused membership—be replaced by white unionists. Their demands were met. There are further instances in which AFL-affiliated unions struck solely to force employers to dismiss black employees. As a result of one such action, black workers were prevented from working on the construction of a black hospital being built in a black neighborhood, and in another case they were prohibited from doing any repair work at any of the area's black schools (both took place in St. Louis). As occurred with the Brotherhood of Railway Carmen, the AFL's unions were not reluctant to use labor solidarity as a means of excluding black participation in the mainstream workforce.[155] The AFL itself, while its leadership consistently reiterated the importance of organizing blacks, seemed reluctant to do much to change the behavior of its affiliates. "The AFL has done everything it possibly can to show recognition to the Negro workers," stated federation vice-president Frank Duffy at the organization's 1934 convention, when from seven to twenty of just over one hundred affiliated unions were then explicitly excluding blacks from their ranks.[156] At the next year's gathering, federation president William Green suggested that "education" as opposed to expulsion would solve the problem of discrimination, and another vice-president, John Frey, warned that further efforts on the part of the AFL might "create prejudice instead of breaking it down."[157] In other words, there were grounds for blacks to be wary of legislation (such as the National Industrial Recovery Act) which might empower unions that were already limiting black opportunities in the labor market.[158]

Consequently, black leadership found itself in the position of opposing seemingly labor-friendly legislation.[159] Jesse O. Thomas, an Urban League field secretary, suggested that "while Section 7A has greatly increased the security of labor in general, insofar as the different labor organizations thus benefitted deny and exclude Negroes from their membership by constitutions or rituals, the position of Negro labor has been made less favorable." Roy Wilkins of the NAACP warned that section 7A would support the efforts of exclusionist locals "to organize a union for all the workers, and to either agree with the employers to push Negroes out of the industry or, having effected an agreement with the employer, to proceed to make the union lily-white." The NAACP's cofounder W. E. B. Du Bois simply wrote that the AFL was "not a labor movement" but "a monopoly of skilled laborers, who join[ed] the capitalists in exploiting the masses of labor, whenever and wherever" they could. At the shop-floor level, one black steelworker in Cleveland posed the problem as essentially a battle between black workers and the unions, resolving "that if labor organizations were to get a footing the colored would lose out. There are [a] few jobs that the colored hold which they [white union workers] would like to get; that is one reason why we have to fight against the labor organization."[160]

As it turned out, section 7A, by itself, was not perceived to be strong enough a measure to improve labor unions' negotiating powers, for some interpreted the legislation's provisions as sanctioning company unions as well as independent labor unions. Also, although the Recovery Act had a psychological impact—in that it signified the Roosevelt administration's support for labor—it was declared unconstitutional on Lochnerist grounds in 1935. Confusion on this issue and a willingness on the part of some to make section 7A effective led New York senator Robert F. Wagner to propose the establishment of a government agency to regulate industrial relations. The 1935 Wagner Act, among other things, made certain antiunion practices illegal, gave workers the right to vote for their own representatives, and created the National Labor Relations Board (NLRB) to ensure that the act's guidelines were followed.

The Wagner Act again led to a face-off between labor representatives, primarily the AFL, and black leadership in the form of the NAACP and the Urban League. Representatives of the two civil rights organizations urged Wagner to include an antidiscrimination amendment, which the AFL opposed, in the bill so as to "safeguard the rights of the Negro," in the words of Howard University dean Kelly Miller. Wilkins contended that given the widespread denial of union membership to blacks, "if the closed shop is legalized by this act Negro workers will be absolutely shut out of employment." A further objection was that the provision forcing employers to rehire striking employees after a settlement would close off the one dependable avenue blacks had traditionally used to secure jobs: strikebreaking. As the NAACP suggested in an office memorandum, "practically every important entry that the Negro has made into industries previously closed to him has been through his activity as a strikebreaker." The irony that an apparently progressive organization such as the NAACP was fighting labor could not have been lost on many.[161] That the AFL and its allies triumphed is not surprising—labor had much greater pull in the halls of Congress than did civil rights organizations. Or, as one commentator suggested, government was far more open to the overlapping objectives of "the industrialists and the A.F.L., both of whom are hostile to Negro labor, the former because they want to keep Negroes as a reserve of cheap labor, and the latter because they want to eliminate Negro competitive labor."[162]

In the wake of these developments, the craft versus industrial issue reemerged, and appeals were made to the AFL to reconsider its policies. Supporters of industrial organization argued that the predominance of the craft approach had resulted in a comparatively unorganized labor force. They argued that whereas only 12 percent of the American workforce was organized in the late 1920s, 35 percent of all workers were organized in Sweden, Germany, and the United Kingdom, over 40 percent were organized in Austria, and more than 50 percent in Australia.[163] By 1937, the conflict over the issue had led to the expulsion of the proponents of industrial unionism from the federation and the formation of the Congress of Industrial Organizations.[164]

Supported and funded to a significant extent by UMW president John L. Lewis, the CIO was more egalitarian in its racial policies and more aggressive in its political aspirations than the AFL (indeed Lewis had been the most reliable supporter of Randolph and the BSCP while he was involved in the AFL).[165] Besides seeking higher minimum wages, social security, and unemployment insurance legislation, the new organization approached the issue of black labor directly, establishing links with the National Urban League, black churches, and such newspapers as the *Pittsburgh Courier* and the *Chicago Defender*. The response was immediate. The African American singer, actor, and civil rights activist Paul Robeson stated that "it would be unpardonable for Negro workers to fail to join the CIO," given his belief that blacks could not "be a part of American Democracy except through labor unions."[166] Similarly, the NAACP's publication *Crisis* urged black workers to join the new union: "[Negro workers] have everything to gain and nothing to lose by affiliation with the CIO and if they fight now, side by side with their fellow workers, when the time comes to divide up the benefits they can demand their share."[167] In the NAACP's *Annual Report* of 1940, a clear contrast was drawn between the reluctance of the AFL and its affiliates to eliminate racial discrimination and the evidence that the CIO "was not satisfied merely with a declaration against racial discrimination in its constitution" but was willing to put into place "a practical program" to eliminate discrimination, "whether [it] be covert or in the open."[168] In addition to providing black support for the CIO, the alliance of labor and civil rights organizations also led to a significant growth in the membership of the NAACP. As Gerald Horne notes, "The NAACP's startling rise in membership during the war years was inseparable from their [the NAACP's] ties with the Congress; . . . correspondingly, the Black advance [social gains] during those same years was inseparable from their advance in CIO unions."[169] Of course, the wartime demands for a larger workforce offered both blacks and women newly expanded opportunities in industry, a set of circumstances that favored the CIO–NAACP–Urban League combination.[170] Walter White, NAACP president, was to suggest that the Truman victory in 1948 was a consequence of the new civil rights–labor alliance: "The results would have been impossible for the Negro without labor, or for labor without the Negro vote. It was the job done by organized labor which narrowed the margin between the two major political parties to the point where the Negro vote could be decisive."[171] The growth in the number of black union members in the 1930s and 1940s was astronomical. In 1930 there were forty-five thousand blacks in the AFL, six hundred thousand black union members ten years later, and over 1.25 million by the peak of the Second World War.[172]

A classic example of the CIO's success in this period is the organization of the United Auto Workers (UAW). Henry Ford, chief of the Ford Motor Company, had been the first car manufacturer to employ black laborers on his assembly lines partly because he believed it would make unionization efforts more difficult.[173] By making strategic contributions to the local black churches and YMCAS, he had managed to set up an arrangement whereby ministers and other community leaders functioned as effective labor recruiters for Ford's antiunion, pro-Republican vision.[174] When the UAW-CIO began attempting to organize autoworkers, it encountered resistance from ministers (prompting one black journalist to ask in the title of a 1938 *Christian Century* article, "Who Owns the Black Church?"). Beyond the churches, local chapters of the NAACP were reluctant to support the UAW's efforts and were in some cases outwardly hostile on account of their ties to Ford.[175] Nevertheless, the NAACP's president, Walter White, participated in the picket lines during the 1941 strike on Ford plants, arguing that the benefits of a united and organized workforce outweighed the patronage of one industrialist.[176] Paul Robeson also visited a number of churches and Ford assembly plants and sang at a crucial rally in support of the CIO's efforts. Although many blacks were initially resistant to the unions' appeals and chose instead to follow the suggestions of their Sunday politicians, eventually enough workers walked out to force Ford to recognize the union and grant certain concessions. Similar developments occurred in the rubber, meatpacking, and steel industries. As the relatively aggressive antiracism of the CIO won over black workers and potential strikebreakers, powerful industry-wide unions were created in the main manufacturing sectors in the North.

Goin' Down South

The organizational successes of the CIO and its stated willingness to organize blacks on an equal basis naturally led the AFL to reexamine its own policies. But not only the CIO's record made the AFL question its laissez-faire attitude toward its affiliates' policies. A. Philip Randolph continued to press the AFL on its orientation from within the organization. Throughout the 1930s he tried, with limited success, to generate AFL support for a range of issues of interest to blacks, includ-

ing antilynching legislation, poll taxes, racially exclusive primaries, the Scottsboro Boys affair, Jim Crow, the Italian invasion of Ethiopia, and, with American
participation in the Second World War, discrimination in the armed forces and
war industries. At the 1941 convention he suggested, "The trade unions to a great
extent have taken over uncritically, without examination, the capitalistic, imperi-
alistic idea of the inferiority of the darker races and they have brought the notion
into the trade union movement."[177] While also criticizing the federation for segregating the seating arrangements at its own conventions, Randolph said that AFL
intransigence in general made it hard for him to encourage blacks to support the
union and noted that the AFL's reputation had weakened it in its competition
with the CIO to organize autoworkers: "Last summer during the election of the
Ford workers, President [William] Green wired me while I was in Jacksonville,
Florida, to come to Detroit for the purpose of working with the Ford men in the
interest of the American Federation of Labor. That is to say, the American Federation of Labor wanted to win the election. I was unable to go there, I didn't get
the telegram in time, but even if I had it is doubtful that my presence in Detroit
would have been very effective in winning support for the American Federation
of Labor, because the Negro workers in the Ford factory were taking the position,
why should they join the American Federation of Labor when the Federation ad-
mits that it cannot do anything to remove discriminations practiced by some of
its Internationals [affiliates]."[178] Green responded by noting, among other things,
that a "line ought to be clearly drawn between the official attitude of the American Federation of Labor itself and the action of some International or National
Unions." Federation vice-president John Frey rejected Randolph's allegations (in
the context of a heated debate about the latter's comments), stating, "If there is
any institution in these United States to whom the colored race owes more than
to any other, it is this American Federation of Labor." Frey also made reference to
what he felt were unfair efforts on Randolph's part to manipulate the convention
and contended that "the delegate [Randolph] . . . has an advantage over every
other delegate who is present. He is the only one who has had the full advantages
of an education in Harvard University. He studied logic, he studied philosophy,
he studied ethics, he studied the humanities and human nature as well."[179] Randolph, despite Frey's suggestions to the contrary, had not attended Harvard, nor
did he have a college degree, despite his oratorical skills.

On the whole, the federation maintained that there was little it could do, that
change did not occur overnight, and that attitudes could not be legislated. While
affiliated unions such as the Brotherhood of Railway Clerks still limited membership to "any white person, male or female, of good moral character," as an AFL
representative Frank Fenton explained, "People cannot be weaned away from the

formative experience of half a century merely by confronting them with a cold, precise order enjoining not only a change of economic arrangement, but by implication also habits of mind." Another argument offered by the AFL's leadership was based on the supposition that separate locals, to some degree, reflected the wishes of black members: "The separate local is rapidly disappearing but it is still found in the South. They were often necessary when local, state laws and community tradition made even the hiring of a hall for a mixed meeting impossible. Curiously enough where they still exist it is more often the Negro members who desire separate locals. Negro workers in the South sometimes feel that if they are a minority in numbers in a union they will not have the best opportunity to participate and control their affairs."[180] There were a few cases where black unionists did prefer separate locals — the musicians union is a case in point — but separate locals as conceived and practiced were hardly created to protect the interests or wishes of blacks. The CIO was not completely desegregated either. Some CIO unions allowed color bars to stand where the choice was perceived to be between unionization with discrimination or no unionization.[181]

By 1946 at least the rhetoric of the AFL had begun to match that of the CIO. In that year George Meany, the secretary-treasurer of the federation urged: "Let there be no pussyfooting on the race issue. The American Federation of Labor is determined to bring into the fold of real free trade unionism all American workers of the South — white and black, Gentile and Jew, Protestant and Catholic."[182] Having reached organizational bottlenecks in the northern industries, the logical frontier for the competition for membership between the CIO and AFL was the largely unorganized South. While the traditional patterns of racial interaction were evident throughout the country, the tensions and implications were more obvious in the South.

A perception that stigmatized unions in the South, especially after the New Deal and the Wagner Act, was that unions were one more arm of the interventionist northern state seeking to upset and destabilize southern tradition. In response to a threatened march on Washington by Randolph in 1941, Franklin Roosevelt established the Fair Employment Practices Committee (FEPC).[183] Seeking to examine employment discrimination on the railroads, in plumbing, in electrical work, within the teamsters organization, and among other transportation workers, the FEPC encountered great resistance and noncooperation from unions north and south. The AFL itself worried that a permanent FEPC might, in the words of President Green, "embarrass some of our labor organizations," and it therefore sought to have some say in the formation of any such body.[184] His fears proved groundless, though, as a block of southern senators secured passage of the 1944 Russell Amendment, which blocked the president from funding any independent agency without congressional approval, thereby guaranteeing the fate of any proposed institutionalized investigation into discrimination in hiring practices. Although the FEPC's achievements were limited, along with the NLRB it signified to southerners that organized labor, despite its observable reluctance to challenge the racial status quo, perhaps represented another means by which northerners might disturb the southern calm. While the FEPC was unable to change practices in the South, state-sponsored investigations (most prominently New York's 1945 Commission against Discrimination) encouraged some unions to drop or amend their racially exclusive membership clauses. As a result of the legislation passed in New York to bar unions that practiced discrimination as a matter of policy, the Brotherhood of Railway Clerks dropped its whites-only clause in 1947, as did the International Association of Machinists the following year. Other internationals, including the Brotherhood of Railway Carmen, left the exclusions in their constitutions but dropped the color bars for their New York locals.[185]

Also hampering the union movement in the South was the contention that unions, especially such industrial organizations as the CIO, were communist-directed or -inspired and that these communists sought to force integration on unwilling communities. This fear had some basis in fact. The post–World War I decline of the socialist movement within the ranks of labor had given way to a significant communist presence by the Second World War. As I will discuss in greater depth in Chapter 3, the communist movement and the Communist Party attracted many blacks and particularly black workers to their cause. Individuals such as Richard Wright (briefly) and W. E. B. Du Bois (eventually) became members of the Party. Communists had supported the 1925 formation of the American Negro Labor Committee (ANLC) to try to win blacks over to the side of labor, as well as the National Negro Congress (NNC), organized in Chicago eleven years later. The CIO itself clearly featured a large Communist Party membership. In the context of the early cold war, Red-baiting and the fear of communist infiltration were effective barriers to labor advancement in some circles. The AFL itself used Red-baiting tactics to try to persuade blacks to affiliate with the federation and not the CIO; indeed, that an organization had been "repudiated as Communist-controlled" by the AFL was cited by congressional committees during the Red scare as a means of identifying "communist fronts."[186] Stated an AFL pamphlet of the late 1940s: "Out of 36 [CIO] International Unions, 21 are dominated by leaders who follow the Communist Party line. It is a well known fact that Moscow has given orders to its American Fifth Columnists to give special attention to spreading unrest and dissension among American Negroes. If you fall for this you are Dictator Joe Stalin's prize suckers."[187] Similarly, the relatively egalitarian approach of the United Packinghouse Workers of America (UPWA) in the South drew charges, to some extent legitimate, that the union's nonracialism was a reflection and consequence of, or cover for, its communism and its desire to subvert local ways and understandings. Indeed, as will become clearer in later chapters, segregation and anticommunism, racism and rightism, have been frequent partners in American history. Even though the AFL had been antisocialist for nearly half a century and despite the CIO's 1950 expulsion of its communist constituency, the perception that Moscow was behind the new drive to organize southern labor aroused the suspicions of many.

Both factors—racism and anticommunism—figure in the results of the 1936 formation of the CIO-affiliated Steel Workers Organizing Committee (SWOC). While the FEPC was cast as the "Devil's Workshop" and an organization that aimed to "force negroes and whites to work together, [and] intermingle with each other," anticommunism functioned as a means of protesting racial interaction. One result was the removal of black Communist organizer Hosea Hudson from the SWOC in 1947. As to whether Hudson's expulsion was race related, Robert Norrell suggests that "the alternative explanations were in fact compatible; most white Alabamians found the idea of blacks' exercising power so disturbing that they took comfort from believing that it originated with an alien force, Communism." Indeed, the SWOC had had to survive an attempt by John Altman, a local AFL organizer, to black and Red-bait William Mitch, the UMW official overseeing formation of the steelworkers union: Altman called Mitch a Communist and warned that "organized Labor will not tolerate social equality between the whites and blacks as advocated by the Communists." [188]

These barriers aside, the CIO's success at organizing the SWOC was definitely a mixed blessing for black workers. Because of the antagonisms perpetuated and institutionalized in the formation of the union, it represented a further strange chapter in labor's compromised challenge to capital's remaking of society. At the turn of the century, the workers in Birmingham's·industries had been roughly three-quarters black, mostly unskilled, and one-quarter white. By 1930, blacks were roughly half the industrial workforce and still largely unskilled. The few blacks who worked in semiskilled or skilled posts for such companies as U.S. Steel were placed by employers to prevent the possibility of shop-floor solidarity. The decrease in black employment in this period was a result of technological developments, which reduced the need for unskilled labor, and hiring favoritism, which in tight times resulted in white workers displacing black workers (in both the North and the South), even in the ranks of unskilled labor.

The successful union organization effort of the mid-1930s did little to improve the conditions of black workers. The SWOC's locals established seniority rules and arrangements with company owners that reserved the good jobs for whites by implementing dual and segregated lines of promotion. Typically, black workers were relegated to promotional tracks that led to low-status jobs, whereas whites could use seniority to move up the occupational ladder or bump black workers with more seniority down. Thus new white employees might be trained by black helpers who had been employed at a company for years but were unable to take the jobs themselves because of the seniority rules. Into the 1950s, as Norrell notes, steel plant managers "played on the insecurities of white workers to encourage opposition to change," warning that the creation of a single seniority system would mean that "these niggers are going to get your jobs." The NLRB assured white unionists that they had nothing to fear from its presence, for it was "not trying the race issue." Even the SWOC's parent body, the CIO, felt compelled to go along to get along. Sensitivity of the CIO to southern criticism led it to publicize its role in the dismissal of black foremen at the ore mines in the 1930s, and when questioned about the contradiction between its national policy and its local practices, the editor of the Alabama CIO newspaper offered the same rationale that labor leaders had given for decades. "The men won't work under negroes," he explained, "and when the union leadership and the men fall out, that's when management steps in and cracks us both. Don't forget that down here no one can afford to be called a nigger lover."[189]

This pattern of separate promotion lines and black displacement continued throughout the first twenty years of the steelworkers union in Birmingham. Combined with the effects of technological innovation, black employment levels continued to decrease. Whereas blacks had constituted 47 percent of all steelworkers in the Birmingham region in 1930 (a number that represented a decrease from the turn of the century), this figure was 41 percent ten years later, 37 percent in 1950, and 32 percent by 1960. In sheer numbers this represented a drop from 12,243 workers in 1930 to 10,666 in 1960 and to 9,512 in 1970. At the same time, white workers not only increased their relative percentage from 53 percent to 68 percent between 1930 and 1960 but also, in a period of industry decline, increased their numbers from 13,896 in 1930 to 22,592 in 1960 and to 19,827 in 1970. Similar numbers and patterns developed in the ranks of the coal and ore miners and in the overall picture, as the percentage of industrial workers who where black dropped from 54 percent in 1930 to 33 percent by 1960 — a level that was maintained in 1970 even though the workforce was smaller.[190] By the early 1960s, black workers, encouraged by the civil rights movement and John F. Kennedy's Executive Order 10925 attacking discrimination in companies holding federal contracts, began to challenge the practices that had restricted them for decades, using the courts when necessary. By the time these cases were settled in the early seventies, Birmingham's steel factories were in the midst of a serious decline.

In both the North and the South, the unfolding of the civil rights movement led to tensions, to say the least, within labor ranks. Nineteen fifty-seven saw the establishment of the United Southern Employees Association (USEA) in North Carolina, an organization that subsequently spread to Virginia, Alabama, Florida, Georgia, and South Carolina. Along with an anti-integrationist orientation, the USEA offered a welfare program and cheap hospital and pension benefits. But the main impetus for the union's formation was resistance to changes being proposed by civil rights activists and the federal government. As put in one pamphlet, "The great majority of USEA members are ex-AFL-CIO union members who have quit the AFL-CIO because of [its] race-baiting tactics. . . . We believe that southerners should organize and control their unions just as we elect our own congressmen from the South to represent us in Congress. We don't need northern rabble rousers to represent us in labor." In response to those who warned that southern resistance to integration might chase away business, a 1959 USEA leaflet entitled "Sterilize the Mongrelizers" stated that "the USEA says to hell with any industry or company that will move South only if we Southerners accept the Communists' scheme of integration." There emerged other, similar movements offering like critiques, such as the Southern Aircraft Workers, the Southern Federation of Labor, the Southern Crafts, Inc., and the Southern States Conference of Union People. The latter argued that the AFL-CIO was "under the control of labor leaders who are aiding and abetting the mixing of the White and Negro races in our public schools and elsewhere, and . . . have contributed many thousands of dollars to the NAACP, an organization dedicated to the elimination of our Southern principle of segregation. . . . Walter Reuther [UAW president and an AFL-CIO official] is a member of the Board of Directors of the NAACP, an organization that is Communist influenced and dedicated to destroying our Southern civilization."[191] The confluence of support for segregation and the labor movement, given the history, is not surprising. The future presidential candidate and defender of segregation George Wallace was establishing his prolabor credentials in Alabama in this same period.

New Shoes for a Different Dance?

At the national level, the December 1955 merger of the AFL and CIO had led to the fear that the latter's egalitarianism (already perceived to be on the wane) would give way to the former's "pragmatism." In the NAACP publication *Crisis* it was stated that the merger "naturally poses the question of the status of the Negro union member in the merged organization. What is the AFL-CIO now going to do about its racially exclusive unions? Unless this problem is attacked head-on it is going to be around to plague organized labor for many a year to come."[192] In its new constitution the AFL-CIO did include commitments to "constitutionally recognize the right of all workers, without regard to race, creed, color or national origin to share in the full benefits of trade union organization in the merged federation . . . [and] to bring about, at the earliest date, the effective implementation of this principle of non-discrimination."[193] Nevertheless, two unions that excluded blacks were admitted shortly after the merger (the Brotherhood of Locomotive Firemen and Engineers in 1956 and the Brotherhood of Railway Trainmen the following year), with every member (except one) of the AFL-CIO's executive council voting in favor (including Walter Reuther). Six years after the merger, the NAACP was still expressing concern about "the failure of the AFL-CIO . . . to take decisive action against the continued existence of segregated locals in the affiliated unions and among the federal locals" and calling for the NLRB to use its powers to force organized labor to lift its remaining color bars.[194]

Continuing to work from the inside, in 1959 A. Philip Randolph (the one member of the federation's executive council who had voted against the admission of the two unions mentioned above) convened, with NAACP support, the Negro-American Labor Council (NALC), an organization to protect and advance the interests of blacks within the labor movement, a body he suggested would be comparable in function with the Jewish Labor Committee.[195] The NALC, Randolph stated, "reject[s] black nationalism as a doctrine and practice of racial separatism, [while] it recognizes the fact that history has placed upon the Negro and the Negro alone, the basic responsibility to complete the uncompleted Civil War through keeping the fires of freedom burning in the civil rights revolution."[196] Closer to the shop-floor level, the Trade Union Leadership Conference (TULC) was formed in 1957 "to interpret the Negro community to the labor movement and the labor movement to the Negro community."[197] Based in Detroit, the TULC was composed largely of black autoworkers seeking to address issues concerning relations between blacks and labor. The union's leaders argued that those blacks who feared that black organization within the union movement would provoke dissent were "hopelessly out of step with the times and totally incapable of making an honest appraisal of the situation as it exists. [They] are suggesting that the Negro should continue to be tractable and content with his lot because the 'other folks' in their 'good wisdom and charity' will see that he is provided for. This is the old 'plantation philosophy.' "[198] Although there were signs of increasing black dissatisfaction with integrationism and the performance of the traditional unions, at the 1962 UAW convention Martin Luther King Jr. argued that "there are more ties of kinship between labor and the Negro people than tradition. . . . [L]abor needs a wage-hour bill. . . . Negroes need the same measures, even more desperately. . . . Labor needs housing legislation. . . . Negroes need housing legislation also. Labor needs an adequate old-age medical bill and so do Negroes. . . . What labor needs, Negroes need; and simple logic therefore puts us side by side in the struggle for all elements in a decent standard of living." [199]

By the middle 1960s, the reception of King's arguments and the civil rights program had changed dramatically. At least perceptually, the background had been reshaped. George Meany, AFL-CIO president, drew attention to a new dividing line while testifying in front of a House Judiciary Committee in 1963 (incidentally, the same year the Brotherhood of Locomotive Fireman dropped its color bar, the last federation affiliate to do so). Preferential hiring, he argued, would be problematic and "would merely replace one kind of discrimination with another." [200] While organized labor—most prominently the UAW's Walter Reuther—did play a role in bringing about the passage of the 1964 Civil Rights Act, the federal agency created to prevent discrimination in the workplace, the Equal Employment Opportunity Commission (EEOC), would prove to be the source of much irritation for organized labor's leadership. Title VII of the act authorized the government to challenge the discriminatory practices of unions with regard to apprenticeship programs and the degree to which promotion practices were racialized, with black, Hispanic, and Asian workers often restricted to jobs that offered few opportunities for advancement. Organized labor, especially the craft unions (e.g., the construction-related unions), perceived the activism of the executive and judicial branches as an illegitimate assault on their right to determine their own policies—specifically, the seniority rights of skilled workers. [201] The Supreme Court's 1979 decision that the affirmative action programs instituted by the Kaiser Aluminum plant in Gramercy, Louisiana, did not contradict the 1964 Civil Rights Act signified a further development in the tortuous relationship between black and white labor. The *Weber* decision signaled a conditional acceptance of management plans to address "racial imbalances" and, in the tone and nature of the majority opinion and dissent and in the editorial responses that followed, provided a sign of things to come. [202] The issue of affirmative action only reinforced the pattern of black-labor relations, perhaps most visibly in the conflicts surrounding the appropriate remedy for the persistent exclusion of African Americans from the construction trades. At the AFL-CIO's 1971 convention, Vernon Jordan, then head of the National Urban League, asked the federation "to intensify the pressures upon [its] backward brothers [in the construction trades] and raise them to the moral and pragmatic standards the rest of the labor movement fol-

lows."[203] When that same year the Nixon administration announced its Philadelphia Plan, which sought to establish goals and timetables for minority hiring
in the construction industry, George Meany suggested that the proposals "divert[ed] attention from the real, solid task of training and qualifying minority
workers" and were "put forth on the basis of very poor information."[204]

Because of the choices and compromises made throughout American labor history, the few significant sources of union growth since the AFL-CIO merger have
been in nontraditional areas. The 1960s and 1970s saw much attention given by
black activists and leadership outside the union movement to the organization
of hospital workers, who themselves were largely black, Puerto Rican, and Filipino. One of the more publicized labor movements of the late 1960s and early
1970s was the United Farm Workers union led by Cesar Chavez in the agricultural sector. Mexican labor became a significant factor in the West, particularly
after the changes in immigration policy in the 1920s restricted European entry to
the United States after World War I. Primarily involved in agriculture, Mexican
Americans were also employed in railroad construction in the Southwest and in
the steel mills, automobile assembly lines, and packinghouses of the North (e.g.,
Bethlehem, Pennsylvania, Flint, Michigan, and Chicago). It would be in agriculture, however, through the use of strikes (*la huelga*) and consumer boycotts in
support of *la causa,* that the presence of Mexican (and Filipino) labor would be
most prominent and where Chavez and his supporters would launch successful,
yet highly untraditional, union-organizing campaigns.[205] Similar, though less successful, efforts were made to organize Hispanic and Asian workers in the garment
industry on the East Coast (primarily in New York City) and West Coast. In both
regions nonwhite workers pushed the International Ladies' Garment Workers'
Union to become more proactive in targeting unorganized and overwhelmingly
female workers and hiring organizers who would be able to speak to these potential (often quite willing) union members. Although a few unions, such as the
CIO-affiliated National Maritime Union and the International Longshoremen's
and Warehousemen's Union (ILWU) in the case of Chinese Americans, had been
relatively progressive in their attitudes toward Asian and Hispanic workers, for
the most part the major unions, craft and industrial alike, either discriminated
against these groups or did not see any reason to organize workers in the secondary labor market of the service sector or in the agricultural sector.[206] This disinclination began to dissipate only because of the increasing diversity brought about
by the 1965 Immigration Act (which made it much easier for nonwhites to migrate
to the United States) and the desperation triggered by organized labor's steadily
decreasing numbers in the 1970s and 1980s.[207]

The experiences of nonwhite workers in the less prestigious and secure ranks of the service sector are also related to one of the fastest-growing segments of the labor force: women. In the garment industry, for example, most of the employees were and are women who remain, as Dubofsky suggests, "locked in the [pink-collar ghetto] typically earn[ing] only 59 percent as much as male workers."[208] In reference to the significance of these circumstances and developments, Herbert Hill argues that "unless organized labor transforms itself into a social movement with broad goals and a new concept of union membership that goes beyond dues-payers in a collective bargaining unit, it will continue its current decline. And if it is transformed, the character of a new dynamic labor movement will be expressed most significantly in its active and special concern for the problems of racial minorities and women at the work place and in the community."[209]

In Context

Ultimately, one must ask, so what? The "words and movements" discussed above might differ in kind from those commonly invoked by mainstream labor historians, but in the end, disconnected from a comparative analysis of labor's achievements and failures, they prove little. Taken out of context, the history of the relationship between white and nonwhite labor, while interesting and often depressing, is hardly remarkable in that the conflicts within the house of labor are no different from those found in every other area of American history. Perhaps this is the point. To analyze American labor is to recognize that it has been riddled with the same tensions and problems that have marked the wider society. As Mancur Olson correctly notes, in a contest in which a broad-based interest such as labor is difficult to organize, any force that further hampers that process is naturally going to give capital and its proponents an upper hand in defining the context, pace, and nature of social development and the terms of the aggregate cultural debate.[210]

For some, organized labor has become a synonym for organized crime, as the circumstances and whereabouts of former Teamsters' president Jimmy Hoffa have functioned as an effective symbol of labor's standing and as fodder for late-night talk show monologues.[211] Logically, as some perceive labor unions through this prism, others have sought to separate "labor" as symbol from "the mainstream," thus playing straight to the hesitant republicanism that has prevented labor from confidently pursuing and expressing its interests. In the *Washington Post,* David S. Broder has described early 1990s attempts by the Democratic Leadership Council (DLC)—a conservative bloc within the Democratic Party—to redirect the party and orient its platform toward "the center." What did this necessitate? A draft

Table 2.4. Union Members (%) Voting for Democratic
Presidential Candidates, 1956–1988

Year	Union Vote
1956	53
1960	64
1964	83
1968	56
1972	43
1976	64
1980	55
1984	57
1988	59

Source: See John Thomas Delaney and Marick F. Masters, "Unions and Political Action," in *The State of the Unions,* ed. George Strauss, Daniel G. Gallagher, and Jack Fiorito (Madison: Industrial Relations Research Association, 1990), p. 332.

resolution argued that the party had to counteract the notions that it put "special interests before the interests of ordinary people" and that it was promoting the "New Deal policies of the past."[212] "Organized labor," Broder notes "has been suspicious from the outset of the DLC and its long list of business lobbyist sponsors . . . [and] has discouraged union officials from attending."[213]

While union leaders have become distrustful of the intentions of centrist and "right-wing" Democrats, significant numbers of union members are voting Republican (see Table 2.4).[214] Notes one analyst, "In many cases, the union agenda [has] . . . not been in step with most of its leadership. . . . Many members long ago decided that they are part of the middle class and not the working class. Many vote Republican. The unions have not been able to respond to this change."[215] Indeed, this Democratic-Republican bifurcation is only the latest stage in labor's conflicted search for identity, constrained by its contradictory goals of wanting the ability to shape society but not wanting to be excluded from the ranks of whiteness and from the mainstream that currently defines social relations to labor's relative disadvantage. Organized labor, currently, as always, finds itself struggling to define itself, for itself. George Meany, former AFL-CIO chief, stated with pride that "labor, to some extent, has become middle class" and that "when you become a person who has a home and has property . . . to some extent you become conservative. And, I would say, to that extent, labor has become conservative. I don't think there is any question of that."[216] A labor movement that identifies itself as conservative and middle-class is not an organization or force that is likely to question the status quo or naturally be able to muster the support to challenge or redefine existing conditions and understanding. Again, one must ask, so what?

Symbols and questions of identity aside, does labor have the means to convey its views, represent its interests, and achieve its goals? On the legislative side, the Wagner Act still stands as the high point of prolabor legislation. Since the New Deal era, the most significant pieces of legislation have acted to "balance" the Wagner Act. The 1947 Taft-Hartley Act gave states the right to circumvent federal legislation and undermine the closed shop with "right to work" bills. Twelve years later, the Landrum-Griffin Act further tightened Taft-Hartley while also targeting Communist participation in the labor movement. Since then, there has been no new legislation that would significantly support union organization and legitimacy (indeed, the major development in American labor relations in the last two decades was probably Ronald Reagan's firing of the striking members of the Professional Air Traffic Controllers Organization [PATCO] in 1981).[217]

If sheer numbers are an important predictor of relative negotiating strength—and they clearly are—then organized labor has lost out on this front as well (see Table 2.5). One might argue that this decline is a reflection of the growth of the service sector (with the increasing numbers of women workers) and the disappearance of jobs in the traditional manufacturing sector. This observation is certainly valid and goes a long way toward explaining the circumstances of labor throughout this century. In fact, the two curves—marking the decline in manufacturing jobs and the decline in union membership—are almost identical.[218] The mitigating factor against the significance of the technology argument is that similar developments have taken place throughout the West to similar effect, yet the levels of unionization in other countries (with one partial exception) are markedly higher (see Table 2.6). The increased competition between nations and the interpenetration of international markets, combined with the decline in the traditional manufacturing sector and the corresponding developments among the young, women, the highly skilled, and increasing numbers of those working under fundamentally insecure conditions, have made union organization more difficult and compelled trade unions to adapt to rapidly changing circumstances throughout the industrialized world. As the 1997 *World Labour Report* suggests, it is "generally agreed that the trade union movement has fallen on hard times . . . [and that] workers' organizations are experiencing serious difficulties almost everywhere and are losing members."[219]

Nevertheless, despite a serious decline in its industrial sector and the Thatcher-

Table 2.5. Unionization Rates in Canada and the United States, 1955–1994
(as a percentage of nonagricultural workers)

Year	United States	Canada
1955	33.4	33.7
1960	28.6	32.3
1965	30.1	29.7
1970	29.6	33.6
1975	28.9	36.9
1978	25.1	39.0
1981	22.6	37.4
1983	20.1	40.0
1986	17.8	37.7
1988	16.8	37.5
1994	15.5	37.5

Sources: Canadian Department of Labour, *Labour Organizations in Canada* (Ottawa: Information Canada, 1995); U.S. Department of Labor, *Bureau of Labor Statistics* (Washington, D.C.: Department of Labor, 1989); and *New York Times,* December 17, 1995, sec. 1, p. 26.

ite assault on labor, British unionization rates have remained above 25 percent since the Second World War. Density rates are near or above 30 percent in Australia, Germany, Austria, and Italy; around 40 percent or more in Belgium and Luxembourg; above 50 percent in Norway and Finland; and above 60 percent in Denmark and Sweden.[220] The one partial exception to this pattern is France, where unionization rates have always been low and obviously do not reflect the political clout of French labor.[221] Currently, Canada also has a substantially more unionized labor force, despite the effects of linguistic and ethnic conflict and the fact that many of Canada's unions were formed as extensions of American unions (see Table 2.5). One factor that explains the increase in the unionization rate in Canada is the growth in union activity in the predominantly francophone province of Quebec since the Quiet Revolution of the 1960s. But this, of course, is not inconsistent with the argument that heterogeneity can make leftist organization more difficult: southern labor presented to American unions a like reservoir of potential members constrained by roughly similar factors and dispositions.[222] Some have argued that the difference between Canada and the United States is that Canadian legislation has been more labor friendly—for instance, David Brody notes that "the rights of workers to organize and bargain collectively are much more effectively protected under Canadian law"[223]—but such an argument only begs the question, Why has Canadian legislation been more favorable?[224]

Table 2.6. Service/Industrial Sector Ratios, Selected
OECD Countries, 1963, 1973, and 1983

Country	1963	1973	1983	Change, 1963–83
Canada	1.71	2.05	2.71	1.00
Denmark	1.02	2.05	2.26	1.24
France	1.02	1.25	1.72	0.70
Germany	0.84	0.95	1.25	0.41
Italy	0.94	1.08	1.43	0.49
Japan	1.33	1.33	1.61	0.28
Netherlands	1.24	1.58	2.41	1.17
Sweden	1.12	1.52	2.16	1.04
Switzerland	0.81	1.09	1.47	0.66
United Kingdom	1.06	1.29	1.90	0.84
United States	1.65	1.89	2.45	0.80

Source: Organization for Economic Cooperation and Development, *Labor Force Statistics, 1963–1983*
(Paris: OECD, 1985), pp. 36–39.

That organized labor has become middle-class, that it is perceived negatively, and that it is rejected as a special interest by mainstream actors are not problems in and of themselves as long as labor is still able to express its interests, realize its ambitions, and, basically, make society in the manner that it wishes. Image and superficial politics aside, labor's job is to insure that its constituency can control the circumstances of its existence. Organized labor in the United States has largely either been afraid to do so or, because of internal and external compromises, been unable to do so. Labor in the United States has not realized any visions beyond the narrow and contradictory objectives established by Adolph Strasser and Samuel Gompers at the end of Reconstruction.[225] "Labor gives off now an almost animal sense of weakness," writes Thomas Geoghegan in *Which Side Are You On?*, his account of his personal experiences as a labor lawyer.[226] And with employers and labor consultants perfecting the science of breaking unions with impunity, it is hard to disagree with Geoghegan's description. The Reagan-era overhauling of the NLRB and the impact of Taft-Hartley have given employers great incentive to force strikes to break unions and fire union organizers knowing full well that it will be a long time, if ever, before any regulatory body responds; knowing full well that any penalties will probably be less than the savings accrued from an unorganized workforce; and knowing full well that labor, organized or otherwise, does not have any real political clout.[227]

It still remains to be proven that demographic heterogeneity has anything to do with these circumstances. Although further discussions of the "So what?" question and the political ramifications of the argument are still to follow, at this point I can make some proposals. Throughout this discussion I have argued that a left can be defined or studied from three perspectives: as a conventional movement (unions and parties), as a means to a set of public goods (possibly including the conventional left itself), and as a sensibility. The establishment or maintenance of any of these three presences requires some sense of a collective, an identity that confidently claims the pronoun "we," a notion that a group exists. American labor, organized or otherwise, has functioned in a world of multiple others in which the "we" claim has been, at the very least, difficult to make. And when organized labor has achieved solidarity, it has established links of racial rather than labor solidarity. It is no coincidence that the most radical movement to emerge in American labor history—and also the one to attract the most violent reception—was the IWW, whose roots lay in a relatively homogeneous sector of American society. Similarly, it is no coincidence that the South has consistently provided a haven for capital, with its working class torn apart by superficial differences reconstructed as a racial divide. "There will never be an effective labor movement in the South so long as the negro workers are not accepted by the unions upon a basis of equality," observed A. Philip Randolph at the AFL's 1936 convention. Tying racial exclusion in the South to the overall fate of the labor movement, he further suggested that "the American labor movement will never be effective so long as there is not an effective labor movement in the south." [228]

At the most mechanical level, the variation of demographic groups within the American working class at different times created the possibility of endemic strikebreaking and continual destabilization. Although this often became a source (and a reflection as well) of black-white conflict, it was also a problem among all the different ethnic groups (although it was commonly "decided" that "yellow" and "black" workers were particularly unassimilable). At the most mechanical level, then, ethnic and racial variation weakened unions and labor solidarity. A lack of solidarity meant the elevation of an apolitical, aristocratic craft movement which failed to make political links when other labor movements in other contexts were doing so and which defined its interests in opposition to Asians, Hispanics, blacks, unskilled workers, and women as often as it challenged capital. Although leftist political movements have increasingly drawn their leadership and membership from nonworkers, the working class has still been, typically, the crucial instigator of the challenge to capital's attempts to remake the aggregate culture. But the American working class has been too divided and preoccupied by ethnic and racial considerations to perform that function, with the result that others—the proponents of individualistic concepts—have been given free reign to remake society.

Last, the creation and propagation of race and racial categories made union-ization itself a mixed blessing, especially for blacks and for nonwhites in general. North, South, and West, unions were used either to exploit or to exclude non-white workers for generations from the skilled and desirable crafts. Ironically, interracial organization often led to worse circumstances for nonwhite workers. Consequently, the otherwise absurd spectacle of the NAACP and other black progressives lobbying against the Wagner Act and its provisions makes sad sense.

Chapters 5 and 6 will develop this argument in terms of the public goods and sensibility conceptions of the left. In the next two chapters I will clarify the effects of demographic heterogeneity on leftist formation at the conventional level as the focus moves from the union movement to an analysis of the implications for the traditional left of the politics of race and of the New Deal.

CHAPTER THREE

Southern Politics and the Unmaking of the American Left

Hold that engine, let sweet mama get on board, cause my home ain't here, it's a long way down the road; . . . Come back, choo-choo, mama's gonna find a berth, goin' to Dixieland, it's the grandest place on earth; . . . Dixie Flyer, come on and let your drivers roll, wouldn't stay up North to save nobody's doggone soul; . . . Here's my ticket, take it, please, conductorman, goin' to my mammy way down in Dixieland. — Bessie Smith, "Dixie Flyer Blues"

The South may not be the nation's number one political problem . . . but politics is the South's number one problem. — V. O. Key Jr., *Southern Politics in State and Nation*

Although the left has institutionalized itself to some significant degree in every Western state except the United States, its emergence was not painless, and its future is neither secure nor guaranteed. Indeed, given the nature of the expectations and fears characteristic of the post–World War I era, one might argue that a major story of the twentieth century was the failure of the left in the West, especially after the late-century jolt that was Thatcherism. Certainly, the conventional left (parties and unions) is currently on the defensive, attempting to safeguard its public policy achievements as it phrases its objectives in increasingly centrist terms (e.g., Great Britain's "New" Labour; the French, Swedish, and German socialist parties; and the former Italian Communist Party).

These developments are not entirely surprising given that sustaining leftist movements involves a difficult and delicate balancing act. The traditional left/ Marxist project has historically been an economically oriented affair, focused on using the modern state as a means of transforming and transcending class differences. Beyond contesting the attractiveness of the market's appeals to individual consumers, it is now clear that the left must be as concerned with cultural issues (e.g., religious and moral attachments, different ethnic experiences) as it has been with the bread-and-butter issues associated with life in the material realm. The events of the last seventy years have provided sufficient evidence that the attempt to mobilize peoples to address their economic alienation while ignoring or even encouraging their cultural alienation (as it can be argued many orthodox Marxists have) is ultimately bound to produce tension and a dissipation of support.

This problem was evident in Europe between the world wars, when the left found itself under attack from constituencies that felt alienated by the acultural aspects of Marxism (and liberalism for that matter), a disaffection that was often energized by anti-Semitism. It was in this context that leftist ideals were easily absorbed and coopted by movements of the so-called right, especially as many early-twentieth-century Marxist movements had struck Faustian deals with the state and nationalist ideologies. Accordingly, Italy's left gave birth to Benito Mussolini and the Fascist Party; the founder of the British Union of Fascists, Oswald Mosley, was a former Labourite, and France's Georges Sorel, with his characteristic attachments to the nation as primary subject and to violence as a necessary means to change, made the leap from orthodox Marxism to voluntarism and anti-Semitism. In a similar manner, German-born Roberto Michels, Belgian Hendrik DeMan, and France's Marcel Deat moved from the socialist camp toward the right. It was also against this backdrop that Adolf Hitler nationalized socialism in Germany.

Although clear distinctions existed between the left and the "far right" in this era, particularly regarding the significance of cultural traditions, their economic orientations were similar. An emphasis on the nation (*volk*) provided a foundation for most of the various leftist movements after the First World War and the different corporatist experiments (which, at their extreme, include Mussolini's Italy, France's Vichy administration, and Hitler's Germany). These movements were not supporters of unrestricted property rights, and along with their counterparts on the conventional left, they sought to resist the institutionalization of free-market capitalism and liberal individualism. In Canada during the same period, the uncertainties unleashed by the depression produced the corporatist (and occasionally anti-Semitic) Social Credit Party and the socialist Cooperative Commonwealth Federation (CCF), the predecessor of the contemporary New Democratic Party. Both movements emerged in opposition to liberalism and the free market and were suffused with Christian ideals. While potential leftist constituencies were splitting in the Canadian West — where both Social Credit and the CCF were rooted — the overall strength of the national left was reduced by the inability of Protestant anglophone socialists to make their movements attractive to francophone voters in the largely Catholic province of Quebec. The weakness of the left in Canada was also connected to the CCF's clear preference for a strong federal government, whereas Quebecers had traditionally been wary of a strong central state (Quebec itself presents an interesting example of the ongoing nationalization of potentially socialist support and the conflation of class and nationalist interests).

Overall, the conventional left has been hampered in its competition with individualism and the free market by the tendency of its natural constituencies to divide over the significance and treatment of cultural issues (and the perception that there is a necessary conflict between cultural tradition and modernity), as well as the problems involved in making a singular political community out of diverse ethnic groups. Over the last three decades, this last issue has become serious in Europe and Canada, as concern over (non-European) immigration has again depressed support for the left and energized parties such as the National Front in France (where the anti-immigration issue was first put into play by the Communist Party), Belgium's Vlaams Blok, Austria's Freedom Party, the German Republican Party, the Italian Social Movement, and, to some extent, Canada's Reform Party. Thus the left, clearly weakened and on the defensive, faces the twenty-first century aware that it cannot phrase its goals in purely materialistic terms. Nevertheless, in Western Europe and in Canada, it can point to certain achievements in the area of public policy, and at the least, the conventional left may not be thriving, but it still survives.

A relatively significant conventional left once existed in the United States, one dedicated to the restructuring of American economic life similar to that undertaken by the socialists and social democrats in other societies in the industrializing West. In common with its Western counterparts, American socialism faced some problems: an insensitivity on the issue of gender relations, and a theoretical blindness to the consequences of large-scale, nation-state–based activism. In other words, the conventional socialist vision featured internal contradictions that reduced the possibility of its ever achieving its goals. As "revolution" became a rhetorical absurdity, there emerged throughout the West a post-Bernsteinian vision of capitalist economies managed and tempered by socialist governments and ideals, complete with its contradictions, limitations, Keynesianisms, and all. In the United States, however, this pattern has not been repeated, for the social-democratic movements common in other Western states have failed to establish a foothold.

The weakness of leftist organizations in the United States can be understood, to a large extent, as a reflection and result of the nation's ongoing decisions to prioritize racial and ethnic identities and difference. Racial conflicts and factors have affected or been reflected in leftist outcomes in the United States in three ways.

First has been the consistent division of leftist activists over the issue of whether organizations should be interracial, segregated, or separate but coordinated. This concern divided the AFL and the CIO in the 1937 to 1955 period and has marked American leftist organization throughout its history. The second means by which the race issue has prevented the left from remaking society in a collectivist mold is through the popular rejection of those movements which have pursued inter-racial alliances (and the related tendency to associate interracialism with "communism"). In this manner the IWW, UMW, and CIO were labeled as being radical by employers and organizational competitors for pursuing a relatively nonracist mode of unionization. Beyond divisive tensions within the left, extramural pressures and attacks have held back movements that have sought to organize across the races. This stigmatization has extended, at times, to all leftist movements re-gardless of their orientation on racial issues (i.e., leftism itself has been seen as an implicit threat to the racial status quo and accordingly rejected). Third, for some leftists the race issue has just been a problem to be solved at some future date or a matter of numbers—of accepting or neglecting 10 percent of the population (e.g., the AFL's belief that trying to force its affiliates to drop their color bars would lead to an overall weakening rather than strengthening of the union movement). While nonwhite peoples constitute a numerical minority within the context of the United States, they have been distributed in such a way that their numbers have had a crucial impact on American politics. Given the various psychocul-tural understandings and misunderstandings that have governed the relationship among races in the United States, the symbolic role of nonwhites—especially African Americans—in American politics also should not be underestimated. Furthermore, nonwhites have been concentrated in those socioeconomic classes which one would naturally expect to support leftist activity. Finally, the South has often played a key role in weakening leftist efforts. Consequently, the decisions by labor unions and other related institutions to dismiss the importance of challeng-ing the racial mores that underpin southern conservative power have had signifi-cant implications. This is not to suggest that the outcomes would have been any different if, somehow, American leftists had paid more attention to the issue of race. They did not, and that choice reflected the extent to which leftists did not consider the ramifications of not challenging the racial status quo and the degree to which race and the South, as presences in American life, had become natural-ized and unremarkable commonplaces.

These three factors—the division of the left on race, the popular pressures to reproduce or reinforce society's racial codes, and the tendency of the left to over-look racial and cultural factors—help explain the weakness of the conventional left in the United States. In Chapter 2 I discussed these factors in the context of the development of the American labor movement; in this chapter I focus on the political parties that have been identified with the left in the United States—the Populists, the Socialists, and the Communists—and their attempts to reconcile the issues of race and class.

Sectionalism and the Roots of Southern Politics

The primary dividing line in American politics for much of the nation's history has been that which separates the North and the South. While it is common to speak of the resilience of the two-party system in American politics, the reality has more resembled a series of regional one-party systems (e.g., the Democratic Solid South) with the main axis running from east to west. From the Compromise of 1877 that marked the end of Reconstruction to the civil rights era, there was very little true competition between the Democrats and the Republicans.[1]

This sectionalism was based on the disparity between those states and regions dependent on slave labor and those dependent on free labor and was directly related to the distribution of Africans in America.[2] One of the first movements to experience the difficulties associated with sectionalism was the American or Know-Nothing Party. Nativism and its publications (such as the various *Native American* newspapers) drew support in both the North and the South, especially in those cities and states where immigrant populations were relatively high, such as New York, Cincinnati, Philadelphia, and St. Louis and Kentucky, Virginia, Louisiana, Maryland, and Texas.[3] The nativists saw these new immigrants, primarily Irish and German, as paupers, criminals, and radicals, threatening to overload or overturn the already-established American way. Although nativist sentiment and violence had been a constant presence since the beginning of the century, the Know-Nothing Party was not formed until 1854 (incidentally the same year the Republican Party was established). Given the timing of its emergence and the general rush toward fragmentation that had been fed by Andrew Jackson's unique combination of personality and pork-barrel politics, it is not altogether surprising that the Know-Nothing Party was fractured by the same tensions that were soon to rupture the Union itself. At a time when sectional issues were predominant, few voters in the North or the South felt they could afford to support a party that was not committed in terms of its regional affiliations. Of course, the narrowness of the Know-Nothing platform—essentially the reduction or elimination of immigration—also restricted its potential popularity.[4]

The Civil War, its establishment of the Republican Party as the dominant national party, and Reconstruction and Redemption in the South led to a slightly adjusted status quo in American national politics. The 1877 compromise gave

Rutherford B. Hayes and the Republicans the electoral college votes necessary to maintain the presidency and left the fate of Africans in the South to be decided by local custom. As mentioned in the previous chapter, the deal is also significant in that it effectively marginalized labor and its interests. As the Republican coalition abandoned blacks, the remade Democratic Party was dominated by southern conservatives who had little interest in the concerns of the party's northern and western working-class constituencies. After the end of Reconstruction, then, the country was left with what was to become the foundation of "Southern Politics." In the North, the Republicans were firmly established as the representatives of industry, whereas most labor and immigrant interests and votes remained within the Democratic camp. In the South, the Republican Party was gradually reduced to the party of southern blacks after the "scalawags" (poor southern whites), "carpetbaggers" (transplanted northern whites), and those whites seeking elected office were gradually drawn away. As the party lost its voting constituency with the institutionalization of Jim Crow, it became an alienated body that focused on the election of national officers at the party's conventions.[5]

Following the end of Reconstruction and the rehabilitation of the Democratic Party, partisan competition virtually disappeared in the South. Given its distribution of land and power, one would have expected the South to produce politicians and movements that questioned the economic status quo. V. O. Key Jr. argued in *Southern Politics* that "the South ought, by all the rules of political behaviour, to be radical. A poor, agrarian area, pressed down by the colonial policies of the financial and industrial North and Northeast, it offers fertile ground for political agitation." But radical politics rarely took root. Instead, southern politics has characteristically sacrificed class politics to racial politics. While there have always been grounds for class conflict, these tensions have never managed to overcome the impact of race and the politics of black and white. As Key noted, "In its grand outlines the politics of the South revolves around the position of the Negro. It is at times interpreted as a politics of cotton, as a politics of free trade, as a politics of agrarian poverty, or as a politics of planter and plutocrat. Although such interpretations have a superficial validity, in the last analysis the major peculiarities of southern politics go back to the Negro. Whatever phase of the southern political process one seeks to understand, sooner or later the trail of inquiry leads to the Negro."[6]

The mechanics of the process by which southern politics shaped national politics until the civil rights era was rather simple. The South was usually divided into two camps, one populated by whites, usually small or tenant farmers and their descendants (the hill counties), and a second populated by blacks, wealthier whites, and their descendants (the delta). Under "normal" circumstances the voting power of each individual would be roughly equal, but after Reconstruction and certainly by the turn of the century, the elimination of the black vote through violence, trickery, and various legal manipulations gave those whites in "black-belt" counties disproportionate influence. The elite manipulation of electoral boundaries further increased the disproportionate voting influence of the whites in the black-belt counties. Simple and effective appeals to white solidarity and supremacy helped prevent remaining poorer whites from pursuing their class interests.[7] In other words, once black voters were removed from the electorate, a small number of relatively wealthy and increasingly business-oriented whites could control state politics. The actions of this class across the South could then present a united front—in the shape of the Solid South—to the nation and hold up any legislation or proposals that might threaten the interests of the southern upper class, especially because southern incumbents were rarely challenged and seniority, pre-Watergate, meant guaranteed access to the exercise of power in Congress.[8] This arrangement (which I discuss in more detail in Chapter 4) lasted well into the 1960s.

National movements seeking to challenge this political status quo have either been solidly rejected in the South, have seen their programs compromised to comply with southern mores, or have accepted truncation (i.e., written off the South), mistakenly believing that national politics could be significantly reoriented without challenging southern cultural relations and understandings. But the key to the Solid South was the relative willingness of economically disadvantaged whites to trade economic and political gains for racial solidarity. Thus non–status quo politics have had to be attractive enough to challenge the racial attachments of these individuals. The story of the first significant post–Civil War movement to test those ties is ultimately one of failure.

Some People's Parties

After Reconstruction, pressure on whites to preserve southern unity resulted in the gradual elimination of all but the Democratic Party. As one individual moving from the Republicans to the Democrats in this period explained, "No white man can live in the South in the future and act with any other than the Democratic party unless he is willing and prepared to live a life of social isolation and remain in political oblivion." Many whites did not have the luxury of philosophizing about the reasons for their actions, which were a response to the threat of violence on top of "social isolation and . . . political oblivion."[9]

Throughout the early years of Reconstruction and until the 1890s, a series of movements sought to shake the prevailing political alignments in the South with little or no success. Among these, the Granger movement, the Greenbackers, and the National Labor Union all failed to make any significant impact on the status quo. The first movement to have some success was the National Farmers' Alliance and Industrial Union (or Southern Farmers' Alliance), founded in Texas in 1877. There were actually two separate Farmers' Alliances: the larger and more aggressive Southern Alliance and, north of the Ohio River, the more moderate Northern Farmers' Alliance. The Farmers' Alliance reportedly had 3 million members at one point, but it is more significant as a precursor of the People's Party, or Populists.[10] Although the southern wing was more radical in its pursuit of banking, monetary, and railroad reform, it rejected attempts by its northern counterpart to draw it into third-party politics because it was content with the Democrats and believed it could achieve its goals inside the larger party without challenging white supremacy. Accordingly, the Southern Alliance refused to organize and involve blacks directly, although blacks and whites alike were faced with the same fiscal constraints and economic circumstances and even though blacks represented roughly half the individuals involved in agriculture in the South. Alliance members actually went so far as to harass and threaten Knights of Labor organizers looking to include black farmers in their movement. Eventually, the Colored Farmers' National Alliance and Cooperative Union was formed in December 1886. Like the Southern Alliance, the Colored Alliance had its roots in Texas and was overseen by a white missionary and former Confederate soldier named R. M. Humphrey. While some of the state Colored Alliances had white leaders (e.g., Texas, Alabama, and Kentucky), in other states the head organizers were blacks (e.g., Georgia, Mississippi, and Louisiana). By 1891 Humphrey was claiming 1.2 million members, a number thought to be grossly overinflated.[11] The numbers involved are nonetheless remarkable, because the Colored Alliance had to withstand the threats of violence by Democratic forces, on the one hand, and the arguments of black Republicans, on the other, who contended that the Farmers' Alliance was too risky a venture to consider dividing black energies. Consequently, black participation in the alliance had to be covert, resulting in a dearth of records of its activities and ambitions.

Overall, few white members saw the contradiction between the Southern Alliance's goals and its continued refusal to question seriously American racial etiquette. Ironically, in a Farmer's Alliance publication it was solemnly stated that "the materialism of to-day does all the time seggregate [sic] human lives. . . . The tendency of the competitive system is to antagonize and disassociate men." [12] These same conflicts and contradictions were to mark the Populist movement.

The year 1892 represented the high tide of independent Populist politics. Standing on the shoulders of the Farmers' Alliance movements, the People's Party, which had been officially launched the year before in Cincinnati, drew support away from the Democrats in the South and the Republicans in the North. The voting returns that year resulted in Populist administrations in Kansas, North Dakota, and Colorado and elected at least eight members to the House of Representatives. The leader of the party's ticket, former Greenbacker James B. Weaver, attracted over a million voters, making the Populists the first third party since the Civil War to gain electoral college votes.[13]

The rise of the Populists certainly did not signify the emergence of traditional Marxist politics in the American context. Populist philosophy was never as rigorous or as pointed in its analysis of the development of American capitalism. Nevertheless, some similarities exist between the two critiques in that they both emphasized the alienating effects of industrialization, as well as the tendency of modern capitalism to concentrate power in the hands of the few. On the whole, no one could mistake the attack by the People's Party on the banking, railroad, and monetary systems as Marxist in the European sense or even in the American sense, but Populism—like its Canadian counterpart that was to lay the foundation for the Cooperative Commonwealth Federation and subsequently the New Democratic Party—did represent a preleftist formation of sorts. The party's 1892 platform called for free silver at a ratio of sixteen to one, a graduated income tax, government ownership of the railroads, the direct election of the Senate, and an end to banks of issue.[14] As one North Carolinian Populist contended, "Both the cannibal and the grinding employer are living on human flesh, the ignorant one devouring it outright and the intelligent one wearing it out for his benefit."[15] The Populists also adopted women's suffrage as an issue, and Barton C. Shaw suggests that "Populism seems to have softened some men's ideas about women. If a man's wife worked in the fields alongside her husband, it was difficult to argue that she was too delicate for politics."[16] This greater sensitivity could also be politically risky given the common linkages between gender, race, and class. One southern paper described "the sight of a woman travelling around the country making political speeches . . . [as] simply disgusting" and warned that "southern manhood revolts at the idea of degrading womanhood to the level of politics."[17]

On the issue of race, Populist attitudes predictably varied according to region. While the northern and border state Populists were generally in favor of including blacks—there were fewer blacks in their states—black political participation was an explosive subject in the states with larger black constituencies and where the Democratic Party and its supporters equated voting the ticket with maintaining the race. Dismissing the economic issues in the Populist platform, the *Richmond Dispatch* made clear the need for whites to support the Democrats, stating "the present Democratic party in Virginia was formed . . . for self-protection against sectional misrule—and without any reference to economic questions."[18] Similarly, the *Atlanta Constitution* offered this analysis: "The old issue of sectionalism is confronting the South and White Supremacy is more important than all the financial reform in the world."[19] Claiming to speak for southern farmers, the *Raleigh News and Observer* argued that the appeals of the Populists would prove fruitless in the South: "Are the honest, manly White Southern farmers ready to receive their lessons in political science from such sources? Can they acknowledge as their leader a foreign-born fanatic like [William Alfred] Peffer [a Populist senator from Kansas], or any Southern White man who hears his degrading race principles and still associates with him? We answer no. The farmers of the South will not follow such men. The chivalry of Anglo-Saxon manhood, reverence for the virtue of Southern women, and respect for ancestral and race pride, all condemn and repudiate such self-confessed demagogues."[20] The *Greensboro Daily Record* chimed in on August 19, 1892: "The Democratic Party of the South is something more than a mere political organization striving to enforce an administrative policy. It is a white man's party, organized to maintain white supremacy and prevent a repetition of the destructive rule of ignorant negroes and unscrupulous whites. . . . The safety of the South . . . as well as the conservation of free institutions on these shores, depend upon the strength, unity and perpetuity of the Democratic Party."[21] It was not merely with words that Democratic unity and white supremacy were maintained. While the nineteenth-century western frontier is often taken as the epitome of American lawlessness, it surely is rivaled if not surpassed by the unrestrained violence that marked southern politics and life in this period. Violence was used to terrorize blacks and dissuade them from voting, as well as to keep whites within the Democratic Party.[22]

For southern Populists the situation was clear. Anticipating V. O. Key's analysis of the essence of southern politics, in August 1892 Georgian Populist leader Tom Watson editorialized in the *People's Party Paper:* "The argument against the independent political movement in the South may be boiled down into one word— NIGGER! Fatal word! Why, for thirty years before our war, did the North and South hate each other? NIGGER. What brought disunion and war? NIGGER. With what did Abraham Lincoln break the backbone of the Confederacy? NIGGER. What impeded Reconstruction? NIGGER. How did the Republicans rule the South for years after Appomattox? NIGGER. What has kept the South in a cast iron straight jacket? NIGGER. What will be the slogan of our old politicians until Gabriel calls them home? NIGGER. Pious Southern people never dreaded death as much as they do now. They fear that when they knock at the pearly gates of the New Jerusalem St. Peter will peep through the key-hole and say: 'You can't come in.' 'Why?' 'NIGGER!' "[23] The Populists, then, were quite aware that to question the political status quo, to test the power of the white upper class, was to encounter directly the issues of race and white supremacy. Referring to those white southerners who joined the Populist cause, John Hicks suggests that "perhaps only a southerner can realize how keenly these converts . . . must have felt their grievances."[24] Indeed, evidence shows that white southern Populists were, at times, as race obsessed as their fellow countrymen. In a July 4 speech, Tom Watson made it clear that he did not seek to undermine white supremacy: "I yield to no man in my pride of race. I believe the Anglo-Saxon is stronger, in the glorious strength of conception and achievement, than any race of created men. . . . Socially, I want no mixing of the races."[25] In the same speech he went on to question the faith of those whites who believed that blacks could threaten white supremacy: "I despise the Anglo-Saxon who is such an infernal coward as to deny legal rights to any man on account of his color for fear of 'Negro domination.' 'Dominate' what? 'Dominate' how? 'Dominate' who? It takes intellect to dominate; haven't we got it? It takes majorities to dominate; haven't we got them? It takes wealth to dominate; haven't we got it? It takes social, financial, legislative, military, naval, ecclesiastical and educational establishments to dominate; haven't we got them?"[26] Yet in 1896 the Georgian Populist platform did take a stand against lynching at a time when the state was leading the nation in terms of victims of vigilante "justice"; Watson, who saw the party as "offering to white and black a rallying point which is free from the odium of former discords and strifes," in one instance personally offered refuge to a black Populist who had been threatened with lynching.[27]

From the black viewpoint, while the franchise was gradually being taken away by means of fraud, violence, and, starting in Mississippi in 1890, law, the logic of supporting the Populists against the Democrats collided with the lingering appeal of Republicanism and the hope that soon Redemption might be reversed. Blacks in this period had trouble distinguishing white Populists from other whites. They could not easily forget the violent nature of their past interactions with the poorer whites who supported the Populist cause and were not reassured of the party's good intentions given its rejection of federal supervision of the voting process. The testimony of William Oxford, a white Populist, at an 1896 congressional committee hearing helps explain this distrust: "Q. Who whipped Calvin Joiner [a black Democrat]? A. I did. Q. Did you ever whip any Negro before you did Calvin? A. Yes, sir, I have whipped a heap of them. I whipped them before I became a Populist and since too."[28] In some areas, though, the Republicans and Populists coordinated their efforts successfully (North Carolina being the preeminent example). The downside of these alliances was that Democrats could then paint the Populists as threats to local customs and puppets of the northern carpet-baggers.

While the nomination of William Jennings Bryan to head the Democratic ticket in 1896 is often seen as the high tide of Populist influence on national politics, by that point Populism had been reduced to little more than silverism (that is, monetary reform that would involve moving from the gold standard to silver).[29] Fusionism — the movement to bring together the Democratic Party and the Populists — symbolized the deradicalization of the People's Party potential and its pursuit of electability over program. By this time, the South was well on its way to institutionalizing Jim Crow: South Carolina followed Mississippi's example in 1895, Louisiana introduced the grandfather clause three years later, and by 1901, Alabama and North Carolina had contrived legal means of restricting the black vote. Indeed the Populist experiment seems to have had two consequences in the South: it accelerated the drive to find permanent means of excluding blacks from formal politics, and it forced the Democratic Party to become more responsive to disgruntled whites.[30] In somewhat the same manner that prounion legislation was to freeze blacks out of the skilled ranks and benefit white workers, the replacement of the convention system with the "progressive" open primary system was of little benefit to disenfranchised southern blacks, but it did increase the access of lower-class whites to the political system to some extent. Nevertheless, the benefits poorer whites gained were constrained and compromised by their adherence to and continued promotion of white supremacist politics. As Key writes, the primaries did not go a long way toward lessening the objective material and political "cleavage between the planters of the Delta and the rednecks of the hill."[31] During the first decade after the election of 1896, the populist agenda was transformed into a white progressivism and ultimately no progressivism at all. It was the politics of race, as practiced by the likes of future anti–New Dealer Carter Glass in Virginia, that were to represent the Populist legacy in the South despite the primary innovation. Watson came to believe that populism's success in the South depended on the elimination of blacks from the region's political life and lent his support to the negrophobic politics of such individuals as Georgia's Hoke Smith.

Why did Populism fail? In *Revolt of the Rednecks,* Albert Kirwan offers a number of reasons: "mismanagement, lack of enlightened leadership, the comparative conservatism of its program, returning prosperity, and the national split resulting from the nomination of Bryan." But he concludes that "most important was probably the race question."[32] John Hicks argues that the "unexpected and disastrous defeats in Alabama and Georgia and the generally poor showing of populism in the South can be fully understood only by taking into consideration what happened to the negro vote."[33] Given the unwillingness of southern whites to risk "negro domination" by abandoning the Democratic Party—an attachment that prompted one black Texan Populist to remark that "the South loves the Democratic Party more than it does God"—the ability of the People's Party to challenge the national status quo successfully was seriously reduced.[34] As former Populists returned to the Republican Party in the North and the Democratic Party in the South, it was not clear that much had changed.[35]

Further Fragments of the Real McCoy:
The Emergence of American Socialism

For Daniel DeLeon, the Populists were "a middle class movement" that needed to be stripped of its socialist pretensions.[36] While the resident philosopher-king of the Socialist Labor Party (SLP) was supportive of the Populists' promise to nationalize such industries as the railroads, he saw the People's Party as more of an obstacle than an ally or precursor of a legitimate socialist attack on capital. The fusion of the Populists with the Democrats in 1896 and the nomination of the Bryan-Sewall ticket similarly led many northern and western Populists to question the value of the party's politics. For some, especially those coming from a labor background, silverism, the battle cry of the Greenbackers, was a poor substitute for an effective challenge to the status quo or, more accurately, given the economic currents of the period, to the rising tide of monopoly capitalism. Socialism, some hoped, would accomplish that task.

Marxian socialism was first brought over to the United States by German immigrants who sought refuge after the uprisings of 1848. One of these émigrés, Joseph Weydemeyer, maintained correspondence with Karl Marx, and the German American community, in relation to the resident population, was characteristically more inclined to freethinking, radicalism, and socialism.[37] By 1877 the SLP had been established (with Adolph Strasser, who would later cofound the AFL, among its initial members). From its establishment until 1890, the SLP was periodically torn by factionalism between syndicalists and reformists, anarchists and socialists, and consequently remained on the margins of the nascent American left. In 1890 Daniel DeLeon became a party member and, at the end of 1891, at the age of thirty-nine, its leader.

DeLeon was a Jewish native of Curaçao who had been lecturing in politics and international law at Columbia University. An early supporter of the ideas and campaigns of Henry George, he was, according to one author, converted to socialism by the works of the French writer Eugène Sue, especially the novel *Le Juif Errant* (*The Wandering Jew*), a text that cast the Jew as protector and ally of the working masses.[38] L. Glen Seretan's description of DeLeon as "probably the most gifted and original Marxist intellectual to focus his attention on the problems attending revolution in the advanced capitalist civilization of the United States" speaks to both the leader's influence and the limited scope of American Marxist inquiry.[39] Recognized by Lenin and other European socialists as a leading Marxist theoretician, DeLeon arguably had more influence (and relevance) overseas than he did in his adopted home. As the leader of the first generation of "impossibilists" in the American left—those activists who were more oriented toward revolutionary correctness than practical advancement and the achievement of political power—his was a philosophy that made few concessions to American realities and often seemed not to recognize that the United States was not Europe.

DeLeon's attachment to an unadulterated, nonrevisionist, and un-Americanized Marxism led to a certain detachment and unwillingness to engage in a real struggle to question and challenge the nature of American society. While he was usually firmly against racism within the socialist movement (although, on one occasion, he did use the word "nigger" in a printed exchange with the former Populist and future Georgia senator Tom Watson), DeLeon did not find the issue of American race relations to be of any great significance.[40] As a classic Marxist universalist, he felt that race had no standing as an issue next to class. Furthermore, DeLeon did not believe that the American Negro, as a result of the experience of slavery, was properly disposed to be a socialist, arguing that "by reason of his race, which long was identified with serfdom, the rays of the social question [reach] . . . his mind through such broken prisms that they are refracted into all the colors of the rainbow, preventing him from appreciating the white light of the question."[41] Subtle color imagery aside, DeLeon's belief that blacks were "wandering in the wilderness" led him to exclude them from his plans for remaking American society. Consequently, at a time when blacks were being systematically denied the franchise, DeLeon ventured, "It matters not how the voting is done; it matters not whether we have the Australian ballot or the Maltese ballot; it matters not whether we have the secret ballot or the viva voce ballot; aye, if it comes to it, it should not matter whether we have the ballot at all. All such 'improvements'—like the modern 'ballot reforms' and schemes for 'referendums,' 'initiative,' 'election of federal senators by popular vote' and what not—are, in the very nature of things, so many lures to allow the revolutionary heat to radiate into vacancy."[42]

This drive to maintain the "revolutionary heat" also colored DeLeon's views on women's suffrage, which, under the guise of impending cataclysmic imperative, were equally supportive of the status quo. The SLP's leader consistently ridiculed the suffragettes as middle-class and "pathetic" and above all as obstacles in the way of the proletarian project. To those who sought party support for the exami-

nation of women's issues, he replied: "There is nothing easier, nor yet more useless to the movement [than] to perceive differences between Woman and Man . . .
for the same reason that there is nothing easier, nor yet more useless to the Movement than to discover the difference there is between a Negro and a white man, a
carpenter and a teacher, etc. More difficult, withal useful to the Movement, is the
discovery of that which may be identical in all—their proletarian character. This
is a creative discovery."[43] DeLeon's approach to the issues of race and gender was
rather evenhanded compared with his views on the Catholic Church and Jesuits in
particular. While Catholics were always more resistant to Marxism, DeLeon aggravated these tensions by launching an unending volley of attacks on the Catholic clergy. The issue of whether Catholicism was inconsistent with socialism was
argued back and forth between DeLeon and Irish socialist James Connolly, who
strove to include Irish and Italian workers in the movement.[44]

The disinclination to forge an American socialism and to examine seriously the
nation's heterogeneous composition was in part a reflection of the SLP's membership, which was largely made up of recent immigrants from southern and eastern Europe. Indeed, it is suggested that "native" Americans represented less than
a tenth of the party's supporters.[45] What is significant about the Socialist Labor
Party, from the perspective of American socialism, is that it was the breeding
ground for three of the more prominent figures in early-twentieth-century, mainstream American socialism: Morris Hillquit, Victor Berger, and Eugene V. Debs.
Along with William "Big Bill" Haywood of the IWW, these individuals would
symbolize the divergent strains within the American Socialist Party (SP).

The Socialist Party was formed in 1901 as an outgrowth of the Social Democratic Party, which had been formed three years earlier in Chicago and which
itself had been an offshoot from the SLP. The Social Democratic faction was
labeled by its SLP loyalist opponents as the "opportunist" wing of the socialist
movement. Besides the former SLPers and Haywood, the party included Bellamy
Socialists inspired by Edward Bellamy's *Looking Backward,* Christian Socialists
largely from the West and Southwest, former Populists, Single-Taxers (reformists influenced by Henry George), and members of the American Railway Union
(ARU).

Morris Hillquit was the leader and representative of the New York City faction of socialists who had left the SLP in response to what were perceived to
be DeLeon's attempts to institutionalize dual unionism. DeLeon had created the
Socialist Trade and Labor Alliance in 1895 after having failed to infiltrate the
AFL and the Knights of Labor—although, as mentioned in Chapter 2, socialists within those organizations did manage to unseat Samuel Gompers temporarily and Terence Powderly permanently—to provide a labor foundation for his

party, similar to the syndicalist creation of the Confédération Générale du Travail in France. Hillquit, a Russian-born lawyer, believed that all labor organization should take place within one organization, the AFL, though he favored industrial unionism over craft organization. As well as perceiving DeLeon to be a dual unionist and dictatorial to boot, Hillquit believed that the SLP was too doctrinaire and rigid in its approach to making America socialistic. "To DeLeon," Ira Kipnis writes, "Hillquit was nothing but a pettifogging lawyer who sought to use the socialist movement to advance his legal practice."[46] Hillquit, who was to represent the centrists within the Socialist Party, was similarly characterized by Leon Trotsky as "the ideal Socialist leader for successful dentists."[47]

Of an even more reformist inclination than Hillquit was Victor Berger. Educated by private tutors as the scion of a wealthy Austrian family, Berger emigrated to the United States in 1882, at the age of twenty-two, on account of family financial problems. Settling in Milwaukee, he found a large number of Germans promoting the socialist ideas with which he was already familiar, and he established a strong following in Wisconsin among socialistically inclined craftworkers loyal to the AFL. He was a proponent of the "bore-from-within" strategy by which it was hoped that the AFL could be reoriented and dual unionism avoided. As to the orientation of the AFL under the pure and simplists, Berger suggested that the "American labor movement [would] . . . remain reactionary as long as [Gompers had] . . . any influence."[48] Like Hillquit, Berger moved from the SLP to the Social Democratic Party and then to the Socialist Party, in 1901, and his socialism did not differ much from turn-of-the-century progressivism, as he advocated government ownership of public utilities, educational reform, and public baths.[49] Berger endorsed Eduard Bernstein's concept of evolutionary socialism and, perhaps as a consequence of his "moderation" (or "opportunism," as some would have it), was elected to Congress as a Socialist, representing Milwaukee from 1910 until 1927 (except for a few instances when he was unseated because of his antiwar activities).

Probably the most renowned socialist in American history, Eugene Victor Debs was brought into the fold by Berger during the former's incarceration in Woodstock Prison for his role as leader of the American Railway Union during the 1894 Pullman strike.[50] Although much of Debs's significance derives from his Americanization of socialism (or perhaps as accurately from the socialization of his Americanism), he was the son of recently arrived immigrants from the Alsace region of France. His parents reached the United States in 1849, and Debs was born six years later. His first and middle names were drawn from the French writers Eugène Sue (the same author whose works influenced Daniel DeLeon) and Victor Hugo. And like Berger (as well as DeLeon and Hillquit to some extent), Debs was not a product of a working-class family. His grandfather had been a factory owner; his father ran a grocery store in Terre Haute, Indiana, where Debs grew up; and as a child he attended both public and private schools. It is also ironic that Debs, the father symbol of American socialism and labor politics, was barely a worker in the traditional sense himself, having labored on the railroads for four years and left the field before the age of twenty.[51] Indeed, the vast bulk of Debs's working life was spent as an accounting clerk, and his involvement in socialist politics grew out of a voluntary association with the local labor movement.

The future Socialist Party leader emerged from a background marked by middle-class aspirations, a hesitant labor republicanism, and "a profoundly negative assessment of working people."[52] Despite these inclinations, Debs's understanding of the degrading effects of capital on labor led him to move from the Democratic Party (by which he was elected to the Indiana State Assembly) to the Populists (who were on the verge of nominating him for a position on the 1896 ticket until he declined), to utopian socialism, the Social Democratic Party, and finally the Socialist Party. By this point he viewed capitalism as "wrong . . . inherently unjust, inhuman [and] unintelligent" and believed "it could not last."[53] Overall, his changing labor and political orientations may be read as desperate attempts to re-create the idealized social harmony of his Terre Haute childhood (it is, arguably, this yearning and sensibility that would distinguish Debs from such individuals as Gompers).[54]

Developing his conceptions of citizen, society, and manhood, Debs was the most visible representative of American socialism in the first two decades of the twentieth century. Running as the SP's candidate for president, Debs garnered 408,000 votes in 1904; 420,000 four years later; nearly 900,000 in 1912, or 6 percent of the vote; and 919,000 in 1920, representing 3 percent of the popular vote (Allan Benson was the party's candidate in 1916).[55] While Debs's numbers and Berger's victories are significant from the perspective of American socialist history, placed in context they suggest that electoral socialism never made much of an impact in this period. Debs's roughly 900,000 votes in both 1912 and 1920 were less than the 1,041,028 votes that James B. Weaver received as the Populist candidate in 1892 and less than a quarter of the over 4 million votes that Theodore Roosevelt received as the Bull Moose candidate in 1912 and Robert La Follette collected as a Progressive twelve years later.[56] From an international perspective as well, the American Socialist Party was quite weak. By 1914, mainstream socialist parties in Europe were receiving markedly higher percentages of the total vote: Austria, 25.4 percent; Denmark, 29.6 percent; France, 16.8 percent; Germany, 34.8 percent; Finland, 43.1 percent; Italy, 17.6 percent; Sweden, 31.1 percent; Switzerland, 10.1 percent; Norway, 26.3 percent; and the Netherlands, 18.5 percent.[57] Only in the United Kingdom, where the young Labour Party received 6.4 percent of the vote in the last election before 1914, does one find a percentage that resembles the American Socialist Party's high of 6 percent in 1912.[58] Furthermore, as Michael Hanagan notes, "In the twenty years after 1914 most European socialist parties increased their percentage of the popular vote. At least for the years between 1890 and 1950, the contrast between the success of socialist parties in Europe and the failure of socialism in the United States is as well-grounded in historical fact as it is in historical literature."[59]

A number of factors have been offered to explain the relative weakness of the American Socialist Party. Nick Salvatore suggests that socialism was, almost by definition, un-American: "In a society that instinctively termed any critical dissent 'un-American,' American socialists had a problem with image from the beginning."[60] Salvatore links this disposition to the circumstances that prevailed during and after the First World War, arguing that "in a fundamental way neither Debs nor the American socialist movement failed. . . . Failure assumes the possibility of success, but that was never a serious prospect for the Debsian movement. . . . As all Americans would rediscover during World War I, their society was not a tolerant one."[61] Indeed, the Red scare during and after the First World War, especially with the occurrence of the Bolshevik movement, involved a widespread clampdown on the Socialist Party. Debs ran his 1920 campaign from behind bars, as he and many other Socialists were imprisoned under the Espionage Act.[62] Another external factor that limited the Socialists' electoral appeal was the crowding-out effect created by the Progressive movement. While Debs and his confreres and consoeurs were directly questioning the role and effect of capital, reform movements were already underfoot to create a superficially more democratic and, of greater importance, more efficient nation. As noted, while Debs received his greatest vote percentage in 1912, progressive Teddy Roosevelt was gaining far more support for his independent effort (with the end result that Democrat Woodrow Wilson won). Furthermore, the efforts of the National Civic Federation to "Americanize" labor, to grant it recognition under the aegis of corporate leadership, and to reduce the socialist threat contributed to the Socialists' misfortunes.[63] The combination of the First World War, the Red scare, and Progressive reformism led many such socialists as Walter Lippman to leave the party and postwar Socialists, such as Norman Thomas and A. Philip Randolph, to Redbait the left as actively and enthusiastically as the Socialists themselves were targeted during and immediately after the war.

Others have argued that the Socialists were opportunists who contributed to their own downfall by seeking to appease the mainstream, resembling more a progressive reform movement than a body seeking to change fundamentally the relationship between labor and capital. For instance, Kipnis contends that "the Socialist Party had been organized to combat the institutions, practices, and values of monopoly capitalism. Instead, it had been corrupted by them. Like other movements sworn to change the American economy, it had proven too willing to settle for a few favors and promises from the dreaded enemy. Whatever the future of socialism, it no longer lay with the Socialist Party."[64] Beyond the possibility that the Socialists were not sufficiently dedicated to anticapitalist objectives, tensions between the "opportunists" and the "impossibilists" and among the left, right, and center factions of the party, along with the consequent fragmentation of the movement, abetted the decline of American socialism. Suggests James Weinstein, "Since the early 1920s, debates between socialists of different tendencies have increasingly become disputes between parties; before 1920 such differences were generally accepted as normal and desirable aspects of the process of developing a viable mass party."[65]

A third internal factor is related to this factionalism: the question of how the party should involve itself with labor. The Berger and Hillquit wings were already linked with the AFL and, despite reservations, resisted any attempt to create an industrial union that would compete with the federation. Their hopes lay in the potential success of the bore-from-within strategy. For the left wing of the party, represented by Debs and William Haywood, the AFL was little better than the labor face of capital. With Debs's support, Haywood was a major force behind the establishment of the IWW, and the perceived radicalism of the IWW's syndicalist vision created tensions within the party.[66] These tensions increased after Debs began to disassociate himself from the IWW, just three years after its 1905 formation, because of the frequently violent nature of the union's conflicts with management, especially in the American West, and after Haywood was removed from the party's National Executive Committee in 1913. Haywood's departure, some argue, led to a significant loss of membership for the socialists.[67] In any case, whether as a result of the IWW's unpredictability or the compromises made to the AFL, the Socialist Party did have problems developing and maintaining a labor foundation, unlike most of its other Western counterparts, especially in the prewar period. The party had an overabundance of intellectuals and middle-class members but lacked a secure relationship with the working classes.

All these factors help to explain the "failure" of the Socialist Party.[68] Yet they provide only short-term explanations of an essentially minor phenomenon. Despite the "native American" twist Debs and Haywood gave to the movement's philosophy, the Socialist Party never really challenged the fundamental nature and structure of American politics and society. This is not to argue that if the movement had crossed the proverbial threshold it would have succeeded in making America socialist. Rather it is to suggest that the reasons given for the party's demise would be different and probably farther reaching.

One fundamental factor that cannot be cited as an indicator of the party's failure to challenge the status quo is that of gender relations. Despite DeLeon's views, the Socialists, for the most part, followed the path established by the Populists in the nineteenth century. On this point Weinstein argues, "No other political party or organization embodied the social values of the various women's rights organizations as did the Socialist Party; no other group fought as consistently for the full enfranchisement of women. In return, women flocked into the Party, playing an active role in its affairs on many levels of the organization, from the lowest to the highest. In this respect, the Socialist Party is unique among American parties, past and present." [69] To some degree the Socialists' collective attitude on gender relations did not go much further than the moderate pedestalism expressed by Eugene Debs — woman is special, she should be placed above and outside the ugliness of life's realities. But some members clearly moved beyond this position to a more developed understanding of the issues of sexual identity and difference.[70] Debs, for his part, was a consistent advocate of women's suffrage, and editorials in the *American Socialist* promised that socialism would "open up to every woman a full and free opportunity to earn her living and to receive her full earnings" and elevate "sex relations between men and women . . . to a place of purity which [could] . . . scarcely be imagined under the present degrading and impossible conditions." [71]

On the issue of immigration, the Socialists were closer to the mainstream orientation despite the fact that the "native American" working class and its leadership were largely composed of recent immigrants (Berger, Gompers, Hillquit) or second-generation Americans (such as Debs). In 1893 Frederick Engels had made an intriguing comment about the fate of socialism in the United States. "In America," he suggested, "I am strongly inclined to believe that the fatal hour of Capitalism will have struck as soon as a native American Working Class will have replaced a working class composed in its majority by foreign immigrants." [72] Perhaps some Socialists sought to bring that "fatal hour" closer. The issue of restricting immigration was a major question within the party, especially at its 1908 convention. The positions taken on the issue tended to correspond to the alignment of the party's factions, with the left favoring no restrictions and the right favoring exclusion. Haywood, who had relative success organizing immigrant labor in New England and elsewhere with the IWW, was against any Socialist campaign to restrict immigration. Debs, his nearest philosophical ally, resisted restrictions on the basis of principle, although his attitudes changed over time.

Like many of his colleagues (Haywood excepted), Debs took a negative view of

Chinese immigration. On the issue of Italian immigrants, he was, at least on one occasion, even more dismissive: "The Dago . . . works for small pay and lives far more like a savage or a wild beast, than the Chinese."[73] Nevertheless, pragmatism and principle seem to have affected his views. Referring to the problem of immigrant labor during the 1896 Populist campaign, he noted that "in Pennsylvania labor is more completely subjugated than in any other state of the Union, and corporate influences better organized. . . . The miners are largely Italians, Hungarians, and Poles, who have displaced American labor and they do not hesitate to vote according to the orders they receive."[74] This observation and his experiences with strikebreakers during the Pullman strike two years earlier led him to believe that socialism and nativism made awkward bedfellows; as a result he argued that "if Socialism, international, revolutionary Socialism, does not stand staunchly, unflinchingly and uncompromisingly for the working class and for the exploited and oppressed masses of all lands, then it stands for none and its claim is a false pretense and its profession a delusion and a snare."[75] Opposing Haywood and Debs on the issue of immigration, Victor Berger invoked the traditional justifications for the exclusion of "others" and promised, "I will fight for my wife and children; I will fight for my neighbor's wife and children; I will fight for all your wives and children against this immigration."[76]

At the party's 1908 convention, one speaker suggested that Marx's "Workingmen of the World Unite" slogan was outdated and no longer a relevant objective of scientific socialism. Another delegate from Wisconsin, Howard Tuttle, argued against open immigration policies and contended that Marx had not said "workingmen of the world rotate"; another contended that a successful political movement had to be homogeneous.[77] Daniel Young, a delegate from Pennsylvania, proposed, "When we go into the game of capitalism we must play the game in accordance with the rules of capitalism. If we try to inaugurate the great and noble ideas of Socialism in a capitalist community . . . we are going to be ground under the wheels of this capitalist juggernaut. Now, there was a law made before the law of the class struggle, and that was the law of self-preservation."[78] In the words of the report submitted to the convention in favor of exclusion, "To deny the right of workers to protect themselves against injury to their interests, caused by the competition of imported foreign laborers whose standards of living are materially lower than their own, is to set a bourgeois Utopian ideal above the class struggle."[79] After G. W. Woodby, a Californian delegate, remarked that it would be a "curious state of affairs for immigrants or the descendants of immigrants from Europe themselves to get control of affairs in this country, and then say to the Oriental immigrants that they should not come here," Mark Peiser of New York acknowledged, "I am a descendant, or rather the son of a German who emigrated to this country," but then added, "I believe that we, the emigrants that emigrated to this country, of the white race, are today working for a higher standard among the working class, while the yellow races are not doing so."[80] The Canadian delegates at the convention displayed a similar willingness to distinguish between desirable and undesirable newcomers. In their report, on the eighth day of the meetings, the assimilation of "the Italians, the Finns, the Jews, the Irish, and people of almost all nationalities" was remarked upon favorably.[81] Yet in the same report the efforts "on the part of the white race to keep the Japanese from overcoming them" were praised, and it was stated that the "problem there [in Canada was] just the same as here [in the United States], exactly."[82]

The issue of immigration restrictions did trigger responses on both sides. Besides Woodby, who invoked the legacy of Tom Paine — "The world is my country" — to buttress his arguments for an open-door policy, other participants urged the convention to reconsider the recommendations in the report being discussed. "I belong to a different race than nine-tenths of you here," remarked Barney Berlyn of the Illinois delegation. "I am not only a foreigner by birth, but I am a Jew." To some laughter and applause, he continued, "You forget that both Democrats and Republicans are united on Japanese and Oriental exclusion, and you want us to blow the little whistle and say 'Me, too.' I do not think that is the mission of the Socialist party."[83] It was Hillquit who engineered a compromise among principle, pragmatism, and prejudice that offered a little something for each camp: "The Socialist Party of the United States favors all legislative measures tending to prevent the immigration of strike-breakers and contract laborers, and the mass immigration of workers from foreign countries brought about by the employing classes for the purpose of weakening American labor, and of lowering the standard of life of American workers."[84]

The question of race relations drew similar responses from the different wings of the party, with the difference that the issue was not considered to be of great significance. Daniel DeLeon's class-over-race orientation largely carried over into the Socialist Party as well. Haywood had no patience for racialism or racism and helped organize the IWW specifically to include those workers, including blacks, who had been excluded by the color bars and policies of the craft unions. Debs, again, although he was not quite as antiracist as the former miner, shared Haywood's views, for the Pullman strike, the American Railway Union's exclusionist policies, and the effects of black strikebreaking helped convince him that racism could be costly.[85] This practical conclusion, however, did not lead Debs to believe that the races were social equals: the "negro, like the white man, is subject to the laws of physical, mental and moral development. But in his case these laws have been suspended. Socialism simply proposes that the negro shall have full opportunity to develop his mind and soul, and this will in time emancipate the race from animalism, so repulsive to those especially whose fortunes are built on it."[86] Like DeLeon, Debs once offered that "there [was] . . . no 'Negro problem' apart from the general labor problem."[87] Like his socialism, Debs's views on race seem to have changed in response to a reality that required a consistent attack on the bases of capital's foundation. Although he grew up in Indiana, which either refused blacks schools or segregated educational facilities, by the time he had become the Socialist Party's perennial candidate he was demanding that his speaking engagements in the South be open to blacks and that the seating arrangements not be segregated. Suggests Salvatore, "By the 1920s Debs's understanding of American race relations led him to a fundamental critique of white American culture itself. He castigated the double standard that allowed white men to abuse black women with near impunity while black men, merely suspected of such activity, often were lynched without trial."[88]

Many Socialists found themselves on the other side of this issue. In the *International Socialist Review,* William Noyes wrote: "Physically, the negroes are as a race repulsive to us. Their features are the opposite of what we call beautiful. This includes, not their facial features alone, but the shape of their heads and hands and feet, and general slovenliness. The odor, even of the cleanest of them, differs perceptively from ours. In a word, they seem like a caricature and mockery of our ideas of the 'human form divine.' An intimate knowledge of negroes still further enables one to sympathize with the common dislike of them."[89] Ernest Untermann, a party member from Idaho, argued, "This is not only an economic question, but also a race question, and I am not afraid to say so. . . . Everyone familiar with conditions in the southern states knows very well what would be the fate of the Socialist Party if we attempted to organize mixed locals of colored and white people there. Everyone familiar with conditions on the Pacific and in the Rocky Mountain states knows that the same result would follow if we attempted to organize mixed locals of orientals and white. . . . I am determined that my race shall not go the way of the Aztec and the Indian. . . . I am determined that my race shall be supreme in this country and in the world."[90] Berger shared few of Debs's feelings concerning the issue of race: "There can be no doubt that the negroes and mulattoes constitute a lower race—that the Caucasian and indeed the Mongolian have the start of them in civilization by many thousand years—so that negroes will find it difficult ever to overtake them. The many cases of rape which occur whenever negroes are settled in large numbers prove, moreover, that the free contact with the whites has led to the further degeneration of the negroes, as of all other inferior races. The 'negro question' will one day give the Socialists a good deal of headache, and will never be settled by mere well-phrased resolutions."[91]

Lynching was discussed within the party after the International Socialist Bureau inquired in 1903 about the American party's stance on the issue. And party member Caroline Pemberton had questioned the rape argument used to justify lynching in a 1901 article in the *Worker*. The statistics she presented indicated that not more than 25 percent of all the Negroes lynched since 1885 were even accused of such an offense as rape and that many of those accused and brutally murdered were clearly innocent. She concluded that this justification of lynching persisted, despite all evidence proving it to be baseless, because it was part of the apparatus of southern white supremacy to keep the Negro in total subjugation and part also of "the Southern capitalists' inherited antipathy to the existence of a growing class of comparatively independent negroes."[92] But in the Jim Crow era and at a time when nativism and progressivism were giving rebirth to a nation, the party chose instead to answer the bureau's inquiry with the suggestion that the arrival of socialism in America would lead to conditions wherein the "lynchable" element could no longer thrive: "The Socialist Party points out the fact that nothing less than the abolition of the capitalist system and the substitution of the Socialist system can provide conditions under which the hunger maniacs, kleptomaniacs, sexual maniacs and all other offensive and now lynchable human degenerates will cease to be begotten or produced."[93]

On the whole, the Socialist Party, at least in the prewar period when it was at its strongest electorally, remained indifferent to the status of black Americans. Kipnis suggests that "there is no record that the party ever actually opposed discrimination against Negroes from 1901 to 1912. . . . [D]espite their theoretical stand for Negro equality, the Left [wing of the Socialist Party] made virtually no effort to use the party in a struggle for Negro rights."[94] Rather, he argues, the party "shared and furthered the racial and national prejudices of the most conservative American Federation of Labor leaders."[95] Haywood's opposition to these policies was mitigated by his outsider position within the party, especially after 1913, and Debs tended to remain above the interparty debates and arguments, leaving a disproportionate amount of the day-to-day shaping of the party's policies to the Hillquit and Berger wings. As Weinstein notes, the Socialist Party did not begin addressing the issue of black Americans in any depth until the war. This attention, he suggests, "did not represent a change in the Socialist view that the Negro question was part of, and subordinate to, the position of the Negro as worker."[96]

The same Socialist Party that refused to admit a local from Louisiana on account of its racist policies had a song called "The Darkies Kingdom" ("in Sunny Dixie, A state for all de darkies, Uncle Sam will gib to us alone"), mocking the aspirations of southern blacks, in the party songbook, *Songs of Socialism*.[97] While the politics of race circumscribed the Socialist Party in a slightly different manner than it did the Populists, both parties were divided on the issue of race, and both were baited by their opponents in the South as threats to white supremacy. Ideology aside, perhaps the most significant difference between the two parties is that the Populists campaigned heavily in the South and as an agrarian and labor movement had no choice but to confront the ramifications of southern politics directly. The Socialists, by contrast, sought to remake America by means of a northern and western labor strategy when the political foundation of revolutionary capital lay (perhaps ironically) in the South. The Socialists might have "failed" in the short term for the reasons discussed earlier, but their long-term insignificance has to be associated with their unwillingness to question and challenge the prevailing aggregate (political) culture consistently. Again, this is not to suggest that if the SP had been proactive with regard to the issue of race that the outcomes would have been any different. Besides the fact that such an argument would require imagining a Socialist Party that did not exist, it would necessitate a different American South and nation as well. Although the compromises, contradictions, and theoretical lapses of the party with respect to the real nature of American politics and the relative significance of the African American population left it far short of the threshold, they must be understood as a reflection of the prevailing popular attitudes regarding race and class identity.

From Society to Community

As the Socialist Party had emerged out of the left wing of the Populist movement, the Communist Party grew out of the left wing of the SP. In the period between the beginning of war preparations and the postwar Red scare, the Socialist Party had attracted a large immigrant following — Finns, Russians, Poles, Hungarians, and other eastern Europeans — whose membership pushed the party's geographical center from the West and Southwest toward the North and East. These groups organized themselves into separate language federations and essentially maintained unchanged the politics they had practiced in their homeland.[98] As a result of postwar attempts of the right wing of the Socialist Party to keep control, these characteristically left-wing bodies were suspended or resigned from the movement. The ethnically based federations, along with those orthodox Marxists similarly displeased with the rampant reformism within the Socialist Party, along with the labor syndicalists and Wobblies who left the SP after Haywood's removal, formed the base of the Communist movement.[99]

The one event that revealed the left-wing/right-wing tensions marking the socialist movement was the February 1917 Bolshevik Revolution. The toppling of the Russian czar and the establishment of a government ostensibly influenced by Marxist concepts made the revolutionary option, as opposed to the Bernsteinian evolutionary or reformist approach, seem viable once more.[100] When the news of the revolt reached American shores, Eugene Debs declared, "From the crown of my head to the soles of my feet I am a Bolshevik, and proud of it."[101] While the revolution did not provoke Debs to leave the Socialist Party, it did lead journalist John Reed to establish the *New York Communist* while still a member of the SP. By September 1919, his enthusiasm for the Russian experiment had led him and others to form the Communist Labor Party at the same time that the expelled language federations were coalescing as the Communist Party. Both groups together composed roughly ten thousand members, the vast majority of which—around 90 percent—were non-English-speaking.[102] In May 1921, under the orders of the recently established Third International, or Comintern (the Soviet-controlled international association of Communist Parties), the two parties merged and in 1929 officially adopted the title Communist Party of the United States of America (CPUSA).

Like the Socialists and other Communist parties around the world, the American party was prone to factionalism from the beginning.[103] In 1929 the CPUSA expelled a group led by Charles Ruthenberg and Jay Lovestone that promoted an "exceptionalist" view of American society (Lovestone originated the term), thus rejecting their perception that the collapse of American capitalism was not imminent.[104] The Trotskyist-Stalinist split in the socialist motherland was replicated in the American party, which also in 1928 expelled James Cannon, a founding member, for supporting Trotsky's permanent revolution theses. By the end of the 1920s the party had settled into a consistent division between "hard-liners" and "soft-liners," the orthodox and the innovationists.

William Foster was to emerge as the leader of the hard-line or "left-wing" faction. Born in 1881 in Massachusetts and a product of a working-class background, Forster supported the Populist movement and Bryan in 1896 before moving on to the Socialist Party in 1901 and, after being expelled from the SP, to the IWW in 1909. Upon returning from France and observing the syndicalist attempts to take over the mainstream unions, Foster rejected the Wobblies' dual unionism and joined the AFL.[105] Pursuing a renewed bore-from-within strategy, Foster established the Trade Union Educational League (TUEL) in 1920 within the larger federation structure, and when the American Communists received instructions from the Profintern—the labor appendage of the Comintern—that dual unionism should be abandoned in 1928, TUEL was identified as the most appropriate means of infiltrating the AFL.[106] Foster would go on, as a partial result of his labor base, to become a significant party leader and a consistent supporter of orthodox Marxist politics within the party. His *Toward Soviet America* outlined a future including an American Red Guard, the nationalization of banks and transportation, the expropriation of the property of the rich, the centralization of industrial planning, the collectivization of agriculture into state farms, and the moving of the capital to Chicago "or some other great industrial center." [107]

The other major wing of the party was led by Earl Browder. Born in 1891 as the son of a schoolteacher, the Kansas-reared Browder became an accountant and, by 1915, through a correspondence school, a lawyer. Like Foster he joined the Socialist Party (in 1907) and left six years later after Haywood's expulsion. Unlike Foster, rather than joining the IWW, Browder became affiliated with the AFL through the Bookkeepers, Stenographers and Accountants Union and after a two-year prison sentence for opposing the war joined the Communists in 1921. While Foster was the perceived chief of the orthodox wing, Browder led the more moderate wing and was seen as being the Comintern's man within the party on account of his willingness to implement the international body's directives.

Until 1928 the party represented little more than an extension of the left wing of the Socialist Party, except that the new orthodoxy derived its credibility from the Comintern rather than Marx's own writings. Until the eve of the depression, two-thirds of the party was non-English-speaking, and indeed native Americans did not constitute a majority of the party membership until the late thirties.[108] Unlike the prewar Socialist Party, which, despite the efforts of Berger and Hillquit, was a relatively decentralized body featuring a range of views, the Communist Party in this period was always marked by a high degree of centralized authority and a low tolerance for philosophical variation and independence.

The Communist movement in America never managed to attract many members. The CPUSA's popularity peaked with around one hundred thousand members during the Popular Front and Democratic Front eras of the late 1930s. Although the party still claimed over sixty thousand members into the late 1940s, the effects of the cold war, the House Un-American Activities Committee (HUAC) investigations, and the inconsistencies dictated by Comintern policy reduced the party to less than four thousand members by 1957 and to more of a symbolic rather than strategic presence in American politics.[109]

The role of the Comintern in the changing fortunes of the CPUSA is well documented elsewhere.[110] The early conflation of leftism with Marxism by the turn of the century in the United States, with the establishment of the Third International twenty years later, led to the popular association of dissent with Communism and the Soviet Union. This change was a significant factor separating American Communism from socialism and populism. While the ideological content of the respective movements might reveal many shared features, the CPUSA's allegiance to the Third International represented a fundamental alienation of authority and hence domestic credibility. The Comintern's persistent tendency to use foreign Communist Parties as agents of Soviet foreign policy was enough to condemn the movement to the margins of American life. Its flip-flops on the virtues of the Nazis and the war effort between 1939 and 1941, evidence of Soviet anti-Semitism, Khrushchev's revelation of Stalin's crimes, and the invasion of Hungary also alienated large groups of party members (particularly Jewish followers) and potential allies. While the southern labeling of the Populists as foreign-born agitators was convenient demagoguery, the questioning of the motives of the CPUSA was, to some degree, understandable and legitimate.

The CPUSA's downfall can also be attributed to many of the same factors that explain the decline of the Socialist Party. On the external side, like the Socialists, the Communists had to contend with a political culture that resisted any significant questioning of the status quo. Secondly, the Red-baiting and McCarthy inquisitions of the late forties and fifties affected the party's circumstances. The year 1940 saw the passage of the Smith Act and the Voorhis Registration Act, the first making it illegal to advocate the overthrow of the government, and the second requiring the dissolution and the arrest of leaders of any organization with foreign affiliations that the attorney general considered a threat to national security.[111] In 1950 passage of the McCarran Internal Security Act required the publication of the names and officers of "Communist-action" organizations. Moreover, if early-twentieth-century Progressivism drew off support from the Socialists, New Dealist politics performed roughly the same function twenty years later.

Internally, it would be hard to argue that the public confused the right wing of the CPUSA with the reform Democrats under Roosevelt, although the Popular Front policies—which involved an attempt to form alliances with the Socialist Party, then led by Norman Thomas, and the progressive wing of the Democratic Party—did often pander to perceived mainstream biases.[112] Browder, as the Communist Party's chief, endeavored to make the CPUSA "correspond more exactly to the American political tradition."[113] A party publication in this period used Browder's family history to support the contention that the movement was American: "It was in the springtime of 1776 and Thomas Jefferson may well have been driving his one-horse shay . . . with a draft of the Declaration of Independence in his pocket, when a certain boy, just turned twenty-one, stepped into a recruiting station in Dinwiddie County, Virginia. He gave his name as Littleberry Browder and was sworn in as a soldier of the Continental Army of George Washington."[114] Similarly, party branches sought to allay fears people might have about "undemocratic" strains within the movement. The Louisiana branch offered these sentiments in one of its circulars: "May we remind you that this is American-ism Week. The Communist Party of Louisiana declares its steadfast loyalty to our Nation's democratic institutions, pledging ourselves in word and deed to fight any 'ism' of any clique, group or minority from within our country or from abroad that would destroy or undermine our democratic institutions." [115] During the war the party also supported the no-strike pledges offered by the AFL and CIO, the internment of Japanese Americans, and the continued segregation of the armed forces. Browder's argument for the soft-line approach was that "the war against fascism . . . was making the American business community, or at least a part of it, democratic and responsive to the needs of the whole nation." [116] It is unclear if the continuation of Browder's policies in the postwar era would have signifi-cantly changed the party's fortunes. He was removed as party chief in 1945 as a consequence of hints from abroad that his innovations had gone too far.[117]

A second internal factor impeding the CPUSA was the traditional tension be-tween the hard-liners and the soft-liners, the orthodox and adventurists, the im-possibilists and opportunists. Like the SLP and the SP—indeed, all movements— the CPUSA was riven from its start by factionalism, ejections, and resignations over policy and personality. The close adherence to "conservative" and orthodox policies in the postwar, post-Browder period by the party under Foster's leader-ship led many to reject the movement on account of its perceived inflexibility. Foster's rejection of Browder's belief that there were "progressive tendencies" in postwar American capitalism collided with the strident defense of the status quo that prevailed within the mainstream culture.

The cold war atmosphere also led to the expulsion of Communists from the ranks of labor, depriving the party of one of its basic foundations. While the CIO had clearly benefited from its alliance with the Communists in the late 1930s, its efforts to recruit in the South, its competition with the AFL, and its unwilling-ness to be Red-baited into submission led the organization to expel individual communists from its membership. Like its leftist predecessors, the CPUSA never managed to establish a firm labor foundation, and by the time of the 1955 AFL-CIO merger, the party found itself the subject of incessant attacks from such union leaders as George Meany.[118]

Placed within the context of American political history, in terms of pure num-bers and real political viability, the CPUSA has to be ranked as a marginal de-velopment at best. Its strongest political showing was the 1948 Henry Wallace campaign under the Progressive Party banner, but Wallace's supporters were primarily activist New Dealers rather than latent Communists.[119] Probably the party's most significant legacy, at least from the perspective of this discussion, was its involvement with American blacks and the issues and tensions that Communist politics generated in both the African American community and the wider community.

Take the "A" Train

The twentieth-century interaction of the American left and the African American population — "the red and the black" as some have phrased it — was shaped by the different concerns the two brought to the table. While the former was typically more concerned with the economic realm and remained unconcerned and unconscious of the problems resulting from a strict emphasis on the material realm, the latter worked from a different orientation. The story of the left's reception in black America and its response to African Americans was often one of linguistic and conceptual confusion on both sides.

It was a group of black socialists, led by W. E. B. Du Bois, who established the Niagara movement in June 1905 in Niagara Falls, Canada — after they had been refused hotels on the American side of the border — a group that was instrumental in launching the NAACP four years later, along with such white socialists as William English Walling and Mary White Ovington. Du Bois's own attachments to the socialist movement and the Socialist Party were tempered by his concerns about the welfare of blacks and particularly the SP's attitude toward African Americans. Like other blacks of the period, he was dismayed by the SP's refusal to address racial issues substantively and the barely restrained racial antipathy expressed by some elements of the party. While he had little time for simplistic attempts to create a parallel black capitalist class, given the choice between the party's racial shortcomings and its role as an agent of economic reform, Du Bois questioned the value of the latter in light of the former.[120] "If American socialism cannot stand for the American Negro," he wrote, "the American Negro will not stand for American socialism."[121] In 1911, on the issue of excluding Asians, he argued, "The Negro race will not take kindly to Socialism so long as the international Socialist movement puts up bars against any race whether it be yellow or black. If Socialism is to gain the confidence of the Negro and get him to join the Socialist party it will have to begin by changing its attitude toward the yellow races. The ban upon Asiatic labor sanctioned by the international Socialist congress will have to be repealed."[122] In 1912 he left the party to support Democrat Woodrow Wilson's presidential candidacy on account of the latter's professed "wish to see justice done the colored people in every matter."[123] Once elected, though, Wilson repaid Du Bois, William Monroe Trotter, and his other black supporters by segregating Washington, D.C., the federal government, and its various departments.[124] Wilson's failure to deliver on his campaign promises, his implicit promotion of white supremacist policies at Versailles, and the dismembering of the Progressive movement and its ideals during the war led Du Bois, who had urged blacks to support the American military effort, to adopt a new approach to the questions of race and culture.[125] "To be frank," he wrote, "the war has increased my radicalism, and from now on my one ambition will be toward a world improvement for the Negro by whatever means available." [126]

Besides Du Bois, prominent in the socialist movement were A. Philip Randolph and Chandler Owen, who in 1917 established the *Messenger* newspaper as an organ for the promotion of socialism within the African American community and were instrumental in garnering support for the socialist movement in Harlem during the First World War. Morris Hillquit, the New York City SP's candidate for mayor in 1917, received a quarter of his votes from black Manhattan largely as a result of the socialist political club Randolph and Owen had established in the area.[127] In the areas of race, culture, and class, Randolph was an advocate of class solidarity before racial organization, using the latter only when necessary (as in the efforts to force the AFL to recognize the Brotherhood of Sleeping Car Porters and beginning in the late 1930s with the threatened marches on Washington).[128] While Randolph consistently rejected placing race above class, he nevertheless saw a need for blacks to agitate for civil rights and suggested "that history [had] . . . placed upon the Negro and the Negro alone, the basic responsibility to complete the uncompleted Civil War revolution through keeping the fires burning in the civil rights revolution." [129]

One of Randolph's major competitors for black support in this period, Marcus Aurelius Garvey, offered a different combination of priorities. The native Jamaican had come to the United States to meet Booker T. Washington, with whom he had exchanged correspondence. His initial intention had been to meet Washington, become better acquainted with his ideas and methods, and then return to Jamaica and implement those ideas. As fate would have it, Washington died before Garvey could meet him face-to-face. Three years later, however, Garvey decided to relocate permanently in Harlem, where he established new headquarters for his Universal Negro Improvement Association (UNIA) in the summer of 1918.

Conceptually, Garvey elaborated on one of the main themes of the Washington approach — economic uplift. As Washington had urged black economic and industrial development, Garvey called for "mass education along scientific and industrial lines" and industrial development as a means to self-sufficiency. "The reliance of our race," he argued, "upon the progress and achievements of others for a consideration in sympathy, justice and rights is like a dependence upon a broken stick, resting upon which will eventually consign you to the ground." [130]

Garvey's industrialism, like Washington's, was intended to help blacks "catch up" economically and worked on the assumption that equality and respect depended on economic capability. Like Washington, Garvey also advocated strikebreaking as a pragmatic, if not principled, response to white union racism. "It seems strange and a paradox," he wrote, "but the only convenient friend the Negro worker or laborer has, in America, at the present time, is the white capitalist."[131] Although he drew from Washington's self-help legacy, Garvey was not as superficially accommodating in his approach to the American racial situation, nor did he ignore civil rights issues such as antilynching legislation and the persistence of Jim Crow law in the South (but unlike the Tuskegee chief, Garvey was not based in the South). Furthermore, inverting Washington's "fingers-of-the-hand" thesis, Garvey resisted white collaboration: "All we ask is a fair share in the fields of industry and commerce and we can take care of ourselves. There can be no coming together of the races, each has a distinct destiny."[132] Another way in which Garvey departed from the Washington legacy was the explicitly internationalist character of his programs. As well as promoting the back-to-Africa concept that had been popularized by Martin Delaney and others in the nineteenth century, Garvey spoke of blacks around the world as one nation.[133]

Within three years of the establishment of UNIA headquarters in Harlem, Garvey led the largest black organization of its kind in the country. Promoting Garvey's policies and the Black Star Line enterprises (a transport company and related businesses), the UNIA attracted between 750,000 and 1.25 million paid members.[134] Garvey's quick rise to prominence during the early Harlem Renaissance also drew some reaction and criticism from other activists. In response to the postwar Red scare, Randolph and Owen had toned down the overt socialism of the *Messenger,* and seeking to garner black support, they launched an attack on Garveyism while increasingly espousing nationalist ideals in their own editorials. A 1920 article stated that "Socialism [is the] only weapon that can be used to clip the claws of the British lion and the talons of the American eagle in Africa, the British West Indies, Haiti, the Southern States and at the same time reach the monsters' heart," thus appealing to the anti-imperialist sentiments the Garveyists had awakened.[135] For his part, Du Bois used the NAACP's publication *The Crisis* to challenge Garvey's policies: "Marcus Garvey is, without doubt, the most dangerous enemy of the Negro race in America and in the world. He is either a lunatic or a traitor."[136] Garvey returned fire in the UNIA's publication, *Negro World,* expressing doubt over Du Bois's racial qualifications, as well as his intentions: "I had promised not to waste much more of the space of the *Negro World* on the cross-bred Dutch-French-Negro editor of *The Crisis,* the official organ of the National Association for the Advancement of 'Certain' People, because it was like washing powder on blackbirds, but this one-third Dutchman, who assumes the right to dictate to the Negro people what they should do and should not do, has become so brazen and impertinent that it leaves me no other course than to deal with him as he deserves. . . . Du Bois is speculating as to whether Garvey is a lunatic or a traitor. Garvey has no such speculation about Du Bois. He is positive that he is a traitor." [137]

The Black and the Red

While the battle between Garvey and Du Bois dominated Harlem's internal politics during the early 1920s, the interaction among the Garveyists and the emerging Communist movement signaled the problems involved with leftist mobilization in a heterogeneous society.[138] After the 1917 revolution the relevance of communist politics to American blacks became a common topic of debate. Whereas socialism and the SP had failed to make any real inroads into the black community (with the limited exception of Harlem), the realization of a revolution in Europe gave the whole question a new viability, especially at a time when race relations were at a low point (e.g., the riots in East St. Louis and Chicago in 1917 and 1919 respectively). In the context of the postwar attack on dissent and the desperate promotion of the economic and racial status quos, these speculations often verged on the hysterical and absurd. A National Civic Federation report wondered about the "radical" aspirations of some blacks and their devotion to the country: "Undoubtedly there are still many loyal Americans among negroes but the hope at least seems very general among them . . . deeply embedded in their consciousness that sometime in the near future they will by some measure come into the fullest and most complete equality with the whites." [139] And as Ira De A. Reid of the National Urban League wrote at the time, some whites made the easy association between the issues of patriotism, anticommunism, and black support for the racial status quo: "Police Commissioner Turley of Dallas, Tex., declared that Communism would not find a fertile field among the Negroes of Texas. . . . *The Philadelphia Bulletin* claimed that the Negro disposition was too happy a one to join that army of discontented. . . . *The Christian Science Monitor* saw no hope in a movement whose tenets taught class hatred or racial consciousness. . . . *The Saint Louis Times* saw no danger in Russian agitators corrupting the loyalty of 'our Negroes.' " [140] Questioning the logic behind such analyses, an article in the black weekly the *Pittsburgh Courier* in late 1919 suggested that "as long as the Negro submits to lynchings, burnings, and oppressions—and says nothing he is a loyal American citizen. But when he decides that lynchings and burnings shall cease even at the cost of some bloodshed in America, then he is a Bolshevist." [141]

Some white observers quickly and conveniently linked antiracist sentiment with procommunism and anti-Americanism, but black Americans were hesitant to endorse the new ideology as well. A. Philip Randolph, as noted, was a firm anticommunist throughout his lifetime, seeing the Communists as a "definite menace, pestilence and nuisance, as well as a danger to the Negro people."[142] The labor leader consistently attacked communist-affiliated bodies and refused to join organizations that he suspected of being Red fronts (his departure from the CPUSA-affiliated National Negro Congress in the late 1930s is a case in point).[143] In the early years Du Bois was also skeptical of the usefulness of communism for American blacks. He was not convinced, he wrote subsequently, "that the communism of the Russians was the program for America; least of all for a minority group like the Negroes; I saw that the program of the American Communist party was inadequate for our plight."[144]

Given the early disposition of the American Communists toward the issue of race, Du Bois's rejection of the party was consistent with his previous departure from the Socialist Party. The CPUSA's 1919 founding convention had declared that the "Negro problem is a political problem and economic problem. The racial oppression of the Negro is simply the expression of his economic bondage and oppression, each intensifying the other. This complicates the Negro problem, but does not alter its proletarian character."[145] In other words, the Communists intended to follow the same line that the SP and SLP had pursued: the race issue was subordinate to the class issue and thus deserved no special attention.

While the socialist inclinations of Randolph and Du Bois led them to resist the communist program, some individuals in Harlem still rallied to the banner of the new movement. During the riot-torn Red Summer of 1919 and before the founding of the American Communist Party, a group of mostly West Indian blacks and former servicemen formed the African Blood Brotherhood (ABB) in Harlem. Though the ABB's membership never exceeded three thousand, it played a significant role as a philosophical forum for some of Harlem's intellectuals, including founder Cyril Briggs, *Home to Harlem*'s author Claude McKay, Garveyist W. A. Domingo, Otto Huiswood, Richard Moore, Grace Campbell, and Harry Haywood, the sole African-American in a leadership position within the organization.[146] While its program initially sought to achieve the "immediate protection and ultimate liberation of Negroes everywhere," by 1921 the Brotherhood had formally become an extension of the Communist Party, running the Harlem West Side branch.[147] The ABB, in addition to functioning as a halfway house for future CPUSA members, also attempted to influence the direction of the UNIA, trying to get the larger body to endorse the communist program. Huiswood and Briggs, among others, were UNIA members. W. A. Domingo was a close associate of Garvey and a writer for the association's *Negro World.* These efforts to reorient the Garveyist movement set off another round of verbal and tactical sparring as intriguing and significant as the Du Bois-Garvey debates.

While Garvey's affection for ceremony and pomp could not be denied, the philosophical underpinnings of his movement could not be easily dismissed either. His racial appeals to blacks were not the sole basis of his popularity, although his unabashed black nationalism did strike a deep chord in the African American community. His attitude toward the American Communists was based on more than a kneejerk or simplistic anticommunism: he had been a labor organizer throughout the Caribbean before his arrival in the United States and was quite familiar with the different approaches to labor organization.[148] As Tony Martin suggests, "In Garvey . . . the communists were faced with an adversary whose knowledge of the black working class, both from the standpoint of the UNIA and the standpoint of labor unions, was very extensive."[149] While the UNIA's leader did admire Lenin and Trotsky and their achievements in the Soviet Union, he believed that race had to precede class in the effort to liberate black America. "We have sympathy for the Workers Party," he said in August 1924, referring to the party by the name it used for electoral purposes, "but we belong to the Negro party, first, last and all the time. We will support every party that supports us, and we appreciate the attention the Workers Party has given us. . . . But the Communists have a long time ahead of them before they can do anything for themselves in this country. When they get there we will be there for them. But meantime we are for ourselves."[150] At times Garvey's comments concerning the Communists were a bit more antagonistic. At one point he stated that he supported the actions of the Bolsheviks in the Soviet Union but was "against the brand of Communism that is taught in America [for the party] constitutes a group of liars, plotters and artful deceivers who twist a one third truth to a whole big lie" and criticized what he saw as the "selfish and vicious attempts of [the party] . . . to use the Negro's vote and physical numbers . . . to smash . . . a system that is injurious to them as the white under-dogs."[151] In the *Negro World,* Garvey tore into the ABB's very light-skinned Cyril Briggs in a tone similar to that he used with Du Bois: "A White Man in New York by the name of Cyril Briggs has started the 'African Blood Brotherhood' to catch Negroes, no doubt. To make it succeed he claims to be a Negro. . . . [T]ake notice and govern yourselves accordingly."[152] Briggs sued Garvey successfully for libel. The Communists, in return, made their intentions clear in the pages of the party's *Daily Worker:* "We are working with the Universal Negro Improvement Association not because its President, Marcus Garvey, has improved enuf [*sic*] or even changed at all in the last two years to suit our view of what the American Negroes must do to win their freedom. As a matter of fact, the reason for our working with the Universal Negro Improve-ment Association is because we desire to win over the masses, organizationally and ideologically, following this association for the Communist program." [153]

Garvey's success in organizing large numbers of blacks (West Indian immi-grants and African Americans alike), his particular style, and the UNIA's am-bitions brought him a wide range of enemies. [154] In Harlem, the black Commu-nists and socialists resented his influence and criticized his philosophy. From the NAACP's headquarters in downtown Manhattan, Du Bois sought to sink the Black Star Line enterprises and its chief operator. At a higher level, the international scale and nationalist goals of the UNIA generated government interest in Garvey's activities. Indeed, both the British and American governments feared Garvey, particularly the former on account of the UNIA's explicit anticolonialism. The re-sults were the "Marcus Garvey Must Go" campaign in New York led by Du Bois, Randolph, Owen, and others (including some of Garvey's former associates) and a government investigation into the UNIA's activities. The culmination of these activities was Garvey's conviction on fraud charges, his imprisonment, and in 1927 his deportation to Jamaica. [155] In short order, many of the American branches of the UNIA folded. [156]

In the meantime, the Communist Party's attitude toward blacks was evolv-ing. At an early Comintern congress, ABB member Otto Huiswood had argued that blacks constituted a counterrevolutionary force, "a reserve of capitalist re-action," within American society, a view that prevailed initially. [157] Nevertheless at the second congress in 1920, Lenin himself suggested that the principle of self-determination applied to American blacks as well: "Communist parties [should] . . . give direct support to the revolutionary among the dependent nations and those without equal rights (e.g., in Ireland, and among the American Negroes, etc.), and in the colonies. Without this last particularly important condition, the struggle against the oppression of the dependent nations and colonies, and the recognition of their right to secede as separate States, remains a deceitful pre-tense, as it is in the parties of the Second International." [158] Within the party, the tendency to dismiss black nationalism such as Garvey's as petty bourgeois behavior began to give way to an understanding that an effort to challenge, re-make, or overthrow American capitalism might have to include and involve the "black masses" directly. Until the late 1920s, Lenin's application of the principle of self-determination to American blacks drew little attention and resulted in few active attempts to involve the black community, save for the early absorp-tion of the ABB. At the Sixth Comintern Congress in 1928, a dramatic change in policy occurred largely as a result of the testimony of Harry Haywood, another early ABB member. The new official policy was articulated two years later in the

1930 Comintern resolution "On the Negro Question in the United States": "In the interest of the utmost clarity of ideas on this question the Negro question in the United States must be viewed from the standpoint of its peculiarity, namely as the question of an *oppressed nation,* which is in a peculiar and extraordinarily distressing situation of national oppression not only in view of the prominent *racial distinctions* (material differences in the color of skin, etc.), but above all because of considerable social antagonism (remnants of slavery). This introduces into the American Negro question an important, *peculiar* trait which is absent from the national question of other oppressed peoples."[159] In practical terms, this new policy meant that in the North the CPUSA would vigorously pursue equal rights for blacks and in the South apply the black-belt thesis, the support of black self-determination in the form of a proposed black nation extending from Virginia to Texas. This new policy, it was hoped, would prove successful in drawing UNIA members and other black nationalists to the communist cause.

The Communists' intentions were evidenced in their efforts to establish such organizations in the South as the Southern Negro Youth Congress, the National Miners' Union, and the Sharecroppers Union, the last of which was met with violence from southern whites. The organization of rent strikes in black neighborhoods also engendered community sympathy for the party's politics. In 1932 the Workers' Party nominated James W. Ford for vice-president, becoming the first significant American party to have a black on its national ticket. With writer and poet Langston Hughes, the party established the League of Struggle for Negro Rights (LSNR), which in 1936 became the National Negro Congress (NNC). The CPUSA hoped to challenge the NAACP with the establishment of this civil rights–oriented organization. To indicate the sincerity of its new orientation, suspected "white chauvinists" within the party were investigated. In March 1931, in a story that made the front page of the *New York Times,* August Yokinen, a Finn, was expelled for his alleged racism.[160] Perhaps most famously, the party undertook the defense of the nine black youths who were charged with raping two white women in 1931 in the Scottsboro case. The result of these efforts was the perception of the Communists as the new abolitionists and as friends of the black American community (at the same time that the AFL, for instance, was arguing that its own hands were tied in this area). Meanwhile, the CPUSA—and Popular Front activists in general—were also becoming more interested in and involved with the circumstances of Mexican American communities in California. Greater concern with Anglo/Latino differences on the West Coast and the refocusing of nativist energies on Hispanic communities (including Filipinos) that followed the restrictions on Chinese, Japanese, and Korean immigration; the Communist Party's involvement in the struggles of Mexican laborers, for instance, in the campaigns that led to the establishment of the United Cannery, Agricultural, Packing, and Allied Workers of America (UCAPAWA) in 1937; interaction with the civil rights organization, El Congreso del Pueblo de Habla Española; and support for the Chicano youths arrested for murder—and subsequently acquitted—in the Sleepy Lagoon case in 1942: these represented noticeable departures from the tendency of leftist organizations to avoid engaging nonwhite constituencies.

The role of the Communists in making an inclusive, progressive politics in the late 1930s was indeed significant (one exception to this pattern was in the area of gender, a circumstance that I will discuss in Chapter 6). Aside from the activities they directly promoted under the CPUSA banner, party members were active in labor circles in the Congress of Industrial Organizations and the NAACP and had a hand in the marked growth of these organizations in this period. The party itself grew from less than ten thousand members at the onset of the depression to almost ten times that number at the eve of the Second World War, growth that can be attributed largely to the Comintern-directed policies of the Popular and Democratic Fronts.[161]

Yet, in pure numerical perspective, the CPUSA was never a significant threat to the mainstream parties. The 1932 William Foster–James Ford ticket garnered 102,221 votes, while the candidate for the past-its-prime Socialist Party, Norman Thomas, managed to attract the support of 883,990 individuals. Similarly, black membership in the Communist Party was never very high: in 1929 there were fewer than one hundred black members, and two years later, only around a thousand. By 1935, however, 11 percent of the party's roughly twenty-seven thousand members were black, and in the South, blacks composed an even higher percentage of the membership.[162] In this regard, compared with the achievements of previous leftist movements, the CPUSA's efforts constituted a milestone. As Mark Naison writes, "At its high point, in 1938, the Harlem CP had close to a thousand black members and activated many thousands more through its work in trade unions, WPA workers groups, the Workers Alliance, tenant unions, legal defense organizations, and cultural groups. No socialist organization before or since has touched the life of an Afro-American community so profoundly."[163]

Negotiating Race, Culture, and Class

While the numbers involved were relatively small, in terms of the tensions and issues that were generated, the interaction of whites and blacks within the forum provided by American communism is significant. Most communists shared two beliefs: society's benefits should be evenly distributed, and creating the new society would require large-scale activity, a belief shared to some extent by modernists and nationalists of all races.[164] It was in the realms of race and culture that real problems arose within the Communist camp. Given the characteristic (cultural) universalism of the Communists, it is not surprising that cultural issues were commonly approached as racial issues—as procedural obstacles that would be overcome once exposed to "the light." This was the same universalism inspired by the Enlightenment thinkers, the utilitarians, the early Marxists, capitalists, and modernizers alike. Many blacks were drawn to the communist movement for its promise to deliver the most marginal to an egalitarian, color-blind utopia.

The author Richard Wright is perhaps the most prominent example of an American black drawn into communism on the basis of its inclusive appeals. The nihilism that Wright revealed in his early writings about his upbringing and African American life made him a ripe subject for the movement. Communism offered him a new citizenship and a means of escaping the past and status he sought to leave behind. Wright's fundamentally negative orientation toward black America never left him, even after he left the party and the country (for Paris) and moved toward his own peculiar brand of Pan-Africanism.[165] In the article "I Tried to Be a Communist" written for the *Atlantic Monthly* after his departure, he lamented, "I knew in my heart that I should never again make so total a commitment of faith."[166] And although the party's general anti-intellectualism, paternalism, and cold reaction to the success of his *Native Son* eventually pushed him to leave the party, he never abandoned his attachment to the ideals of the Enlightenment. As he wrote in *Presence Africaine:* "My position is a split one. I'm black. I'm a man of the West. These hard facts condition, to some degree, my outlook. . . . The content of my Westerness resides fundamentally, I feel, in my secular outlook upon life. I believe in a separation of Church and State. I believe that the State possesses a value in and for itself. I believe that all ideas have a right to circulate without restriction. I believe that art has its own autonomy, an independence that extends beyond the spheres of political or priestly powers. How can the spirit of the Enlightenment and the Reformation be extended now to all men? How can this boon be made global in effect? That is the task that history now imposes upon us."[167]

It was exactly this combination of universalism and integrationism that created tensions between party members and some blacks. The party's persistent inability in the early 1930s to comprehend black nationalism and nonintegrationism—except as inverted, frustrated integrationism or petty bourgeois posturing (which they sometimes were)—shaped its stance toward the function and nature of African American culture. For the party, integration until assimilation was assumed to be the proper course, one that such members as Wright never fundamentally questioned.

The party's unwillingness, at least until the latter part of the 1930s, to recognize cultural differences and realities for what they were—significant although constructed, mutable and unquantifiable—led to difficulties between the universalists and those—mostly blacks—who saw African American culture from a positive or nonantagonistic perspective. While this resistance would begin to dissipate during the later stages of the Popular Front (developments I will discuss in Chapter 6), descriptions of the clash between the white left's characteristic assimilationism and paternalism and the perspectives of many blacks can be found in Ralph Ellison's novel *Invisible Man* and to lesser degrees in the works of Chester Himes (e.g., *If He Hollers Let Him Go* and *Lonely Crusade*) and Richard Wright (e.g., *The Outsider*).[168] The party's reaction to a move by the National Negro Congress, an organization it had helped establish in 1936, to endorse the activities of the black church and black business reveals the movement's hostility to what it perceived as hindrances to the advancement of the working-class cause: "The Left supporters of the [NNC] Congress maintain that the Negro masses must be reached—for that very reason the endorsement of the Negro church and Negro business is, to say the least, most unfortunate. . . . It will bind the Negro worker more firmly to the most reactionary institutions in his heritage, and tend to cut him off even more completely from his natural allies—the working class."[169] As the Canadian left consistently dismissed the significance of the most powerful institution in French-speaking Quebec before the Quiet Revolution—the Catholic Church—the American Communist Party could not establish a modus vivendi that would enable it to draw on the appeal and influence of African American theology. It was unable to make the type of connections with the black church, black business, and black nationalism that it did with black workers in the unions (especially the CIO) and the civil rights movement. The party wanted the Negro "unbound," alienated from any unnecessary ties. Given the events of the late fifties and sixties and the role the black church played in launching the civil rights movement in the South, this shortcoming proved to be indicative of how divorced the CPUSA's policies were from the African American institutional and cultural mainstream. In contrast, although personally a nonbeliever, A. Philip Randolph made frequent references to the Bible, often held BSCP meetings in churches, and led prayers before meetings because he thought that tapping black religiosity might enhance the success of his attempts to mobilize black workers.[170]

Beyond cultural issues also lay problems arising from the perception that the party was not firmly committed to some basic black interests such as anticolonialism and domestic civil rights, problems that largely derived from the twists and turns demanded by changing Comintern policy. George Padmore, the Trinidadian, Howard University–educated intellectual, left the Communist Party after the signing of the 1935 Franco-Soviet Pact that signaled Soviet acceptance of France's colonial policy. Like Richard Wright, though, Padmore's subsequent move to Pan-Africanism did not involve a total rejection of the communist worldview. As he wrote in his *Pan-Africanism or Communism,* "In our struggle for national freedom, human dignity and social redemption, Pan-Africanism offers an ideological alternative to Communism on the one side and Tribalism on the other. It rejects both white racialism and black chauvinism. It stands for racial coexistence on the basis of absolute equality and respect for human personality."[171] He did, however, criticize international communism for "tactical mistakes and psychological blunders" in its dealings with "the darker peoples," and suggested that blacks were "very much alive to the fact . . . that the [Communists'] . . . interest in them [was] . . . dictated by the ever-changing tactics of Soviet foreign policy rather than by altruistic motives."[172] Along with its antistrike policy and disturbing support of the internment of Japanese Americans, the CPUSA's willingness to go slow on civil rights during the Second World War generated further criticism of the party from some members who saw Browderism and the Democratic Front policies as a clear betrayal of basic movement principles.

Perceived paternalism and differences concerning the merits of assimilationism and universalism were also to mark the relations between black and Jewish Communists. Since Marx, communism had provided a number of Jewish intellectuals a means of transcending their status as "the other" in European culture and politics. The Socialist Labor Party's Daniel DeLeon is just one example of a Jewish intellectual whose involvement with Marxism was related to his religious background. "It is estimated," writes Guenter Lewy in *The Cause That Failed,* "that during the 1930s and 1940s, about half of the Party's membership was composed of Jews, many with an East European socialist background, who were drawn to communism as a way of overcoming their marginality. By attaching themselves to a universalist ideology that promised to abolish the distinction between Jews and Christians, Jews hoped to overcome the very categories that defined them as marginal."[173] From the 1930s until the 1950s the Communist Party functioned as a form of sanctuary for the alienated whose ranks included both black and Jewish intellectuals and workers. While both groups' numbers were depleted as a result of the party's tortuous policy changes — the Nazi-Soviet Pact and evidence of Soviet anti-Semitism did much to encourage Jewish departures — during their involvement blacks and Jews established a complex relationship that has persisted to this day.[174]

Play It (Again), Sam? Red Scare II

The collapse of the Communist Party in the fifteen years following the Second World War was first and foremost a result of the cold war and the domestic attack on the movement and its sympathizers. A widespread search for suspected communists made continued party membership dangerous. Like the backlash after the First World War, the second Red scare targeted labor (and the gains it had made during the war), as well as the political left, with the result that many "progressive" organizations sought to purge themselves of any perceived communist taint.

The CIO undertook a housecleaning of its own, partly to fend off the AFL, as did the NAACP (which revoked the charter of its San Francisco branch during this period). The latter's campaign, led by its chief executives, Roy Wilkins and Walter White, created problems between the civil rights organization and Du Bois, who had rejoined the organization in 1944.[175] Perhaps ironically, given the nature of his battles with Marcus Garvey during the 1920s, Du Bois's increased interest in Pan-Africanism and his tactical acceptance of nonintegrated development had led him to leave the NAACP in 1934.[176] His second tenure proved to be more difficult, for the organization's officials became increasingly anxious about Du Bois's willingness to endorse movements perceived to be communist-affiliated or -sponsored and his refusal to engage in Red-baiting. The CPUSA's decision to name its national youth club network after Du Bois did little to allay their fears. Eventually, by New Year's Eve 1948, Du Bois and the organization agreed to go their separate ways, because Du Bois's dogged internationalism and consistent defense of civil liberties separated him from the organization's increasingly cautious civil rights strategies. These same activities also cost him his passport and traveling privileges for a period. Along with the actor, singer, and activist Paul Robeson, the NAACP's cofounder was a frequent target of the HUAC investigations and a remarkably reliable source of resistance.[177] After Robeson was reported to have stated in the spring of 1949 that "he 'loved' the Soviet people more than those of 'any other nation,'" and to have suggested that African Americans would not fight in a war against the Soviet Union, Du Bois was among the few blacks who expressed his support for the Popular Front advocate (while taking the opportunity to make clear his own pessimism regarding black allegiances): "I agree with Paul Robeson absolutely that Negroes should never willingly fight in an unjust war. I do not share his honest hope that all will not. A certain sheep-like disposition, inevitably born of slavery, will, I am afraid, lead many of them to join America in any enterprise, provided the whites will grant them equal rights to do wrong."[178] But Du Bois's isolation from the civil rights mainstream organizations and the black middle classes in general disturbed him: "The intelligen-tsia . . . [and] the successful business and professional men, were not, for the most part, outspoken in my defense. . . . [A]s a group this class was either silent or actually antagonistic."[179] Indeed, the willingness of the NAACP's Walter White and Roy Wilkins to refute virtually every Soviet attempt to score propaganda points by highlighting examples of American racism (often based on the association's own reports), while reducing the organization's vulnerability to Red-baiting, also undermined their own efforts to mobilize support for progress on the civil rights front in the United States.[180]

Like the first Red scare, the sequel resulted in a series of passport restrictions, prison terms, public vilifications, and ruined lives. In labor, civil rights, govern-ment, academia, and the arts (the Hollywood witch-hunt being the most spec-tacular), a new orthodoxy was imposed and reinforced; questioning and dissent became treasonous acts regardless of the nature of the questions or the disagree-ment.[181] What distinguishes the first Red scare from the second and accounts for the different consequences of the two experiences is the context in which the purges took place.

In the international realm, the first domestic attack on the left had coincided with Versailles, the negotiations leading to the League of Nations, and a general Western willingness to maintain the colonial and imperialist status quo.[182] Within the United States, the Red scare and Red Summer were part of the same process. The former targeted the left and labor seeking to put them "in their place" by using the Bolshevik movement as justification for repression. The race riots of the Red Summer, at street level, resulted from the frustration of some whites with the effects of black participation in the labor market. At another level, they sought to reacquaint returning black soldiers—some of whom were lynched upon their return to the South simply for daring to wear their uniforms—with American reality lest they bring home any foreign ideals (liberty, equality, and fraternity, for instance). Together, with the cooperation of Woodrow Wilson's administration, the Red scare and Red Summer were the legacies of the Progressive movement laid bare of its pretensions by the wartime experience, its class biases, nativism, and racism revealed for all to see. These developments, again, were reinforced, if not made possible, by the similar forces and trends arising in the international context. It was still possible at that point to push the genies back into the bottle.

The second time around, the international context was different, and there was less leeway for the kinds of activities that occurred after the First World War. The legislative attack on the left and on labor—the Smith, Voorhis, and McCarran Acts for the left, and Taft-Hartley for labor—was attempted and by most mea-sures succeeded (the CPUSA's Eugene Dennis, Israel Amter, and Benjamin Davis were among those charged under the Smith Act). The interwar increase in stature of both the Soviet Union and the United States left the two as the preeminent superpowers, face-to-face across a perceived ideological canyon. The antagonism between the two made crushing the American communist movement an easy affair. The more ambitious attack on all diversity in the name of anticommunism quelled or delayed the emergence of most of the significant challenges to the domestic status quo (e.g., second-wave feminism).

The one notable exception to the effort to reestablish the prewar status quo was in the area of race relations. Clearly the Red scare did manage to separate the economic challenge associated with African American aspirations from the more procedural issues such as civil rights, segregation, and discrimination. Furthermore, the Red scare and HUAC investigations often equated racial progressivism and communism, thereby weakening both. Investigations of government employees would involve such questions as, "Do you ever entertain Negroes in your house?," "Did you ever write a letter to the Red Cross about the segregation of blood?," and (perhaps appropriately) "How do you explain the fact that you have an album of Paul Robeson records in your home?"[183] The implication was clear: to question one status quo (the racial) made one a likely candidate to question others (e.g., the anticommunist consensus). These linkages surely slowed down the civil rights movement, and few analysts would have predicted before the *Brown* decision (and even after) the significant change that was to follow the civil rights era.

Nevertheless, four factors brought widespread attention to the struggle of American blacks to get their concerns addressed. First, modern technology in the form of television helped make the United States more of a national community and a uniform society. Edward Murrow's televised challenge to the McCarthy investigations on the Columbia Broadcasting System (CBS) is credited by many for turning the tide against the senator from Wisconsin.[184] Second, worldwide media attention made civil rights a national issue that could no longer be avoided or misrepresented. The media dramatized the situation in a way that had not been possible previously. With greater visibility came greater sensitivity. The United States in the post–World War II era could not afford to have its own citizens accusing it of rights violations. Such claims drew greater scrutiny, from Dumbarton Oaks to the United Nations to the capitals of newly independent countries in Asia and particularly Africa (Du Bois's Pan-African congresses and Garveyism played an important role in forging links between Africa and its diasporic populations). Whereas the Versailles powers could ignore the claims of the colonized at home and abroad, in the cold war context, in which the two blocs were competing for support from the new states, visible, "marketable" instances of

America's race problems were inconvenient. As television made a national community, global developments had made an international audience and had likewise reduced domestic leeway in the area of race relations. Noted Dean Acheson, then acting secretary of state, the United States was being "reminded over and over by some foreign newspapers that [its] treatment of various minorities leaves much to be desired."[185] Third, as I will discuss in the next chapter, the emergence of significant black voting constituencies outside the South increased the pressure on the major parties (and particularly the Democrats) to be more sensitive to civil rights issues. The fourth reason the civil rights movement "succeeded" is that Jim Crow, like slavery one hundred years before, had become economically inefficient. The new economies and politics of scale demanded that certain national standards prevail, that certain local customs be overturned. These four factors — the media, the international context, the black vote in the North, and the demands of the centralizing economy and state — made developments in the area of civil rights the one major exception to the general turning back of the clock that took place in the late 1940s and 1950s.[186]

While the first Red Scare had restored American politics to its normal course, the second purge occurred in a fundamentally different context. While antileftism and racism had always been on good terms, the rearrangement of the status quo in the two decades following the Second World War brought about a unique collapsing of the realms of racial and class politics. It also signaled the effective end of the traditional left in American politics and a further truncation of the acceptable range of debate concerning economic issues and alternatives. A gap had always existed between mainstream politics and the left, but in the post-McCarthy era, serious economic challenges to the status quo would be found only on the extreme margins of society, leaving the Democratic and Republican Parties to represent the effective left and right wings of the American political spectrum (it was in this context that A. Philip Randolph would suggest, "A third party, geared to independent political action, not to support candidates of the old parties, must be organized without delay" and that "the Cooperative Commonwealth Federation in Canada furnishes an excellent model").[187]

The coincidence of the second Red scare and the civil rights movement brought about a sudden change in the axis of American politics. While the McCarthy era resulted in the further marginalization of the conventional left, the movement of racial issues to the forefront of American discourse represented a new, "disruptive" force given the nature of American culture and politics. The overall effect was the displacement of the conventional left by those forces insisting on a mainstream reaction to the issues revolving around race. The old-guard parties and their adherents had managed to straddle or ignore the issue for over a century; the potential effects of the civil rights movement on the alignment of the mainstream parties and the political status quo—again, given the nature of the country's history—could not be anything less than profound.

For its part, the traditional left (including the preleftist Populists) never chose to address the implications of American heterogeneity directly, and it misinterpreted the relevance of the issues of ethnicity and race to the making of a left. Neither the Populists nor the Socialists or the Communists successfully deconstructed the symbols, fears, and understandings that gave southern politics—and, consequently, American capital—its power. In the next chapter I discuss how race shaped the New Deal realignment, as well as the ways in which the post–civil rights era interplay of class and race transformed the mainstream political parties.

CHAPTER FOUR

Beyond the Left I
A New Deal for an Old Social Issue

> A simple explanation holds that Negroes rioted in Watts, the voice of Black Power was heard throughout the land and the white backlash was born; the public became infuriated and sympathy evaporated. This pat explanation founders, however, on the hard fact that the change in mood had preceded Watts and the Black Power slogan. Moreover, the white backlash has always existed underneath and sometimes on the surface of American life. No, the answers are . . . more complex. — Martin Luther King Jr., *Where Do We Go from Here?*

By the end of the 1950s, the Socialist and Communist Parties had ceased to be significant forces in American politics. The effective marginalization of the orthodox parties of the left coincided with the emergence of the civil rights movement, and the latter development forced the mainstream parties — the Democrats and the Republicans — to deal explicitly with the issue of race. The focus of this chapter will be the response since the New Deal era of the Democratic Party, the effective party of the left once the Socialist and Communist Parties were rendered inoperative, to the gradual reintroduction of race (and, not coincidentally, black voters) into mainstream American politics and life.

The New Deal coalition — the Democratic Party alliance of organized labor, lower-income voters, Catholics, Jews, blacks, and southerners assembled under the leadership of Franklin Delano Roosevelt (FDR) during the 1930s — is probably as close to the class and interest group alliances that supported leftist parties and policy innovations in other Western societies as any produced in the United States.[1] The combination of forces and circumstances that came together in the interwar period created the foundation for a virtual revolution — to borrow from Theodore Lowi — in terms of the role that the state could play in regulating the economy and redistributing resources.[2] As a result, major institutional developments such as the National Labor Relations Board and policy achievements such as old-age insurance, Aid to Dependent Children, a minimum wage, and unem-

ployment insurance were made possible. The New Deal alignment and the associated policy equilibrium (the American version of the various European postwar settlements) lasted well into the 1960s until the election of Richard Nixon
and possibly until 1980 and the election of Ronald Reagan as the leader of a
transformed Republican Party.[3] It is only then that the basic social welfare policy
commitments that had been made during Roosevelt's reign came under serious
scrutiny.

On the basis of this "conventional wisdom" interpretation of the history, some
have suggested that the changes which have taken place over the last thirty-odd
years signal a new development in the nature of American partisan competition,
and that the issues which emerged in the 1960s, 1970s, and 1980s were as powerful
as the economic concerns that shaped the New Deal era. Perhaps the first major
example of this perspective was *The Real Majority* by Richard Scammon and Ben
Wattenberg, published in 1970. "Suddenly," suggested the authors, "some time in
the 1960's, 'crime' and 'race' and 'lawlessness' and 'civil rights' became the most
important domestic issues in America."[4] The combination of these issues (and
others, such as the war in Vietnam, student unrest, and second-wave feminism)
constituted what Scammon and Wattenberg termed "the Social Issue." On the
basis of these observations, the authors warned candidates for public office, including the presidency, that the key to victory lay in positioning oneself on the
right side of the Social Issue, especially as the (real) majority of voters were "unyoung, unpoor, and unblack."[5] As concerned Democrats, the pair sought to convince their party's candidates that victory lay in sending out a clear message to
"middle America" that it had not been abandoned for young, poor, and black
folks. Indeed, the book started with a discussion of the significance of the segregationist George Wallace's successes in the North in 1964 and Republican Barry
Goldwater's remarkable support in the usually solid Democratic South in the
same year, the implication being that victory in the future (i.e., in 1972 and thereafter) would necessitate coopting the spirit (if not the actual rhetoric) of these
campaigns.[6]

Clearly, Scammon and Wattenberg were making an argument about strategy
rather than public policy (assuming quite logically that to make policy one must
first win office). Consequently, their argument reflected little concern with the
policy consequences of the choices they were recommending. This has not generally been the case with the subsequent versions of the "race ruptures New Deal
coalition" thesis. Thomas and Mary Edsall took the *Real Majority* thesis (most
voters are unyoung, unpoor, and unblack) one step further by arguing that a
"chain reaction" (their book's title) involving such issues as taxes, demands for

Table 4.1. Shares of Aggregate Household Income (%) Received
by Each Fifth and Top 5 Percent of Households, 1967–1993

Year	Lowest Fifth	Second Fifth	Third Fifth	Fourth Fifth	Highest Fifth	Top 5 Percent
1967	4.0	10.8	17.3	24.2	43.8	17.5
1969	4.1	10.9	17.5	24.5	43.0	16.6
1971	4.1	10.6	17.3	24.5	43.5	16.7
1973	4.2	10.5	17.1	24.6	43.6	16.6
1975	4.3	10.4	17.0	24.7	43.6	16.6
1977	4.2	10.2	16.9	24.7	44.0	16.8
1979	4.1	10.2	16.8	24.7	44.2	16.9
1981	4.1	10.1	16.7	24.8	44.4	16.5
1983	4.0	9.9	16.4	24.6	45.1	17.1
1985	3.9	9.8	16.2	24.4	45.6	17.6
1987	3.8	9.6	16.1	24.3	46.2	18.2
1989	3.8	9.5	15.8	24.0	46.8	18.9
1991	3.8	9.6	15.9	24.2	46.5	18.1
1993	3.6	9.0	15.1	23.5	48.9	21.0

Source: National Urban League, *The State of Black America, 1996* (New York: National Urban League, 1996), p. 16.

rights, and, most important, race had not only weakened the Democratic Party electorally but also brought about the replacement of the bottom-up policies of the New Deal era with the top-down politics of the post–civil rights era. "The collapse of the political left and the ascendance of a hybrid conservative populism dominated by the affluent," brought about in their view "through tax, debt, and budgetary policy, a substantial redistribution of income from the bottom to the top" (see Table 4.1).[7]

The Edsalls' arguments were based largely on the results of a 1985 study of former Democratic Party supporters ("Reagan Democrats") in Macomb County, Michigan, conducted by the pollster and Yale professor Stanley Greenberg. Just north of Detroit, the county was home to a mostly white, working- and middle-class population that had moved from regular support for the Democrats to an identification with Ronald Reagan's version of the GOP because they felt the Democrats had abandoned them. Greenberg would later write that "these were disillusioned, angry voters. . . . Their way of life was genuinely in jeopardy, threatened by profound economic changes beyond their control, yet their leaders, who were supposed to look out for them, were preoccupied with *other groups and other issues."*[8] When pressed to explain their reasons for leaving the party that seemed most likely to defend their economic interests, the respondents were quite clear and specific. As Greenberg noted, "These white defectors . . . expressed a profound distaste for black Americans, a sentiment that pervaded almost everything they thought about government and politics. Blacks constituted the explanation for their vulnerability and for almost everything that had gone wrong in their lives; not being black was what constituted being middle class; not living with blacks was what made a neighborhood a decent place to live."[9] On the basis of these observations, the Edsalls and subsequently Greenberg (in his 1995 publication *Middle Class Dreams*) encouraged the Democratic Party to reposition itself and make an effort to increase its support among these alienated white constituencies. They made these recommendations not only because it was good campaign strategy (the main concern for Scammon and Wattenberg) but also because they believed a Democratic Party with majority support would be able to protect and advance the interests of working- and middle-class Americans in much the same way as Roosevelt's party was able to in the midst of the depression.[10]

Undoubtedly, some degree of realignment did take place in the 1960s and afterward, as the major parties, the New Deal Democrats and the GOP, responded to the emergence of race as an issue with clear partisan implications. But also evident is that the New Deal coalition was never as strong or as progressive as some contemporary analysts might suggest (e.g., the Edsalls and Stanley Greenberg). Indeed, it might be more accurate to suggest that the civil rights movement was only the proverbial straw that broke the camel's back and that the New Deal coalition had been unstable almost from the date of its conception. Like the Populists, Socialists, the labor movement, and to some extent the CPUSA, the New Deal Democratic coalition's unwillingness or inability to deal explicitly with the issues associated with race ultimately affected its longevity, restricting its ability to bring about long-term progressive public policy changes. In other words race did not suddenly appear on the political horizon in the 1960s and disrupt the New Deal coalition; it had been a major factor in shaping the coalition from its beginning and in limiting its potential achievements. Moreover, with regard to the future of similar coalitions, legitimate reasons exist to be skeptical about the likelihood that a political party which seeks to reassure alienated whites who believe that blacks "*constituted the explanation for . . . almost everything that had gone wrong in their lives*" will be capable of bringing about a significant improvement in the quality of life of working- and middle-class Americans.[11]

Realignment and Continuity

The New Deal alliance was a striking development in the context of American political history because it brought class, along with the related issue of how great a role the state should play in the economy, to the fore to a greater degree than had even the 1896 battle between the McKinley Republicans and William Jennings Bryan's Democratic-Populist fusion. Following an era in which both major parties had avoided any important differences over class relations and public policy, Roosevelt's effort to increase the scope of the federal government's powers and domain so as to provide security for and to protect common Americans was significant. But restricting these efforts was the reality that the traditional strength of the Democratic Party (at least after the Civil War) lay in the South—especially the white, conservative ("delta" or black-belt) constituencies that controlled southern politics. The Democratic South was hardly uniform in terms of its conservatism (e.g., Alabama's Hugo Black, and Huey Long's unique populism in Louisiana), but it was not a region likely to sponsor or support federal activism on the economy or other issues that might disturb the racial status quo. Consequently, forces within his own Democratic coalition would resist Roosevelt's efforts to remake government and overcome the political and judicial understandings that had protected states' rights.

Nevertheless, the New Deal majority coalition emerged because the party was able to expand its power base outside the South. Specifically, the 1932, 1934, and 1936 elections saw the party increase its influence among working-class constituencies (partly by converting voters and partly because newly naturalized immigrant constituencies were registering and voting Democratic).[12] While religion continued to be a significant predictor of voting behavior (with Catholic and Jewish voters more likely to be Democrats than Protestants), class interests were reemerging as an important aspect of the partisan calculus. The emphasis on economic issues in the 1930s was not a new development in the context of the history of the Democratic Party, but the effects of the depression led to broader support for federal action on a scale that had never been attempted previously.

Another development was the emergence of significant black voting constituencies for the first time since the end of Reconstruction. The changes in southern agriculture, Jim Crow, and the attempts of northern industrialists (with the aid of black newspapers and word of mouth) to attract southern blacks across the Mason-Dixon line, triggered a major migration from the rural South to the cities of the North (e.g., New York, Boston, Philadelphia, and Baltimore) and Midwest (e.g., Chicago and Detroit). While black voters were still essentially disenfranchised in the South, the internal migration created the possibility of black voting blocks, constituencies that — beginning with the elections of 1934 and 1936 — were moving from their traditional home in the Republican Party and taking the advice of such individuals as Robert L. Vann, publisher of the influential black newspaper the *Pittsburgh Courier,* to "turn Lincoln's picture to the wall" and vote Democratic.[13]

The first significant result of the incorporation of these new voting constituencies into the Democratic Party was the reduction in status of the southern wing. The availability of these new voters encouraged the Democrats to broaden their appeals and, beginning with the nonpresidential election of 1934, to target northern black voters, who were seen as a crucial swing constituency. Perhaps the most important long-term change was the decision at the party's 1936 convention in Philadelphia to abandon the requirement that the party's nominee have the support of two-thirds of the delegates. The new simple majority threshold eliminated the South's effective veto over the party's candidates for the presidency, a victory for the northern and more liberal wing that naturally provoked a southern counterreaction. Perhaps symbolically, at the same convention, the segregationist and economic conservative Ellison D. "Cotton Ed" Smith, the party's senator from South Carolina, left the convention hall upon realizing that a black minister had been chosen to lead the prayers that would open the session, exclaiming, "By God, he's as black as melted midnight! Get out of my way! This mongrel meeting ain't no place for a white man."[14] The southern response to the northern liberal gains would, in the long run, be of a more substantial nature.

Initially, most southern Democrats were supportive of both Roosevelt and the New Deal. Roosevelt maintained a second home in Warm Springs, Georgia, and promoted himself in the 1932 campaign as a "Georgia planter-politician." He was careful to respect the preferences of the party's southern membership and signaled as necessary his intention not to challenge "states' rights." His personal popularity in the South was increased by the willingness of Democrats below the Mason-Dixon line, conservative and populist alike, to interpret the early stages of the New Deal as an attack on northeastern privilege: the banks, trusts, and monopoly capital. To the extent that the New Deal would regulate those forces that were perceived to exploit the South, the reforms were popular with the Democratic Party's traditional constituencies. There were exceptions: Virginia's senator Carter Glass saw the New Deal, from the beginning, as "an utterly dangerous effort . . . to transplant Hitlerism to every corner of the nation."[15]

Southerners were also receptive to the early New Deal efforts because the programs were structured in such a way as to allow states to exclude certain constituencies from the new benefits. Given that southerners held most of the important positions of power in the House and the Senate, the pattern of outcomes was not surprising. Accordingly, the legislators decided that the old-age insurance program included under the 1935 Social Security Act, although administered federally, would not be available to agricultural and domestic workers—precisely those occupations dominated by blacks in the South and Hispanics and Asian Americans in the West (a decision, incidentally, which the NAACP and other civil rights organizations opposed but which organized labor supported). Furthermore, as one contemporary noted, the "clauses relating to supervisory control by the federal government" had to be weakened before southern senators would support the legislation, because they did not wish to create an "entering wedge for federal interference with the handling of the Negro question."[16] Similarly, other welfare programs such as unemployment insurance and Aid to Dependent Children (ADC) would be left to the states to control with the probability that the potential recipients in the South would be underserved (relative to their counterparts in more liberal regions of the country). During the 1935 House hearings regarding ADC, Virginia Democrat Howard W. Smith proposed adding "a provision that would allow the States to differentiate between persons [i.e., blacks and whites]" and subsequently noted, "Of course in the South we have a great many colored people, and they are largely of the laboring class," in an effort to restrict federal involvement in the structuring and implementation of these programs.[17] "From a Negro's point of view," lamented Charles H. Houston of the NAACP, in reference to the aggregate programmatic impact of the social security and ADC proposals, "it looks like a sieve with the holes just big enough for the majority of Negroes to fall through."[18] A similar pattern was observable in the programs designed to address the short-term problems that emerged during the depression. In 1934 the NAACP had protested the exclusion of blacks from the provisions of the National Recovery Act and specifically the codes enforced by the Agricultural Adjustment Administration that failed to include the job categories more often occupied by blacks. Over the course of the next four years, the civil rights organization would highlight (and challenge) the southern resistance to any programs that might free black labor from the substandard conditions and seasonal work associated with life in the cotton fields, and criticize the discriminatory impact of the Tennessee Valley Authority (TVA) operations. The NAACP asserted that the TVA "introduced new patterns of segregation and discrimination hitherto unknown to anyone in the Tennessee Valley and . . . increased segregation beyond the usual sectional pattern."[19] Overall, the effect of the short- and long-term programs associated with the New Deal was to strengthen the racially exclusive factions that controlled southern politics by increasing rather than challenging their patronage powers.

After the marked increase in the size of the Democratic caucus in the House resulting from the 1934 midterm elections and after FDR's landslide victory in 1936, a willingness to carry the revolution further developed among the party's liberal and nonsouthern constituencies. Perceiving that the conservative dispositions of members of the Supreme Court were restricting the federal government's ability to regulate the economy and redistribute resources, on February 5, 1937, the president proposed that Congress pass legislation that would allow him to increase the number of justices sitting on the bench. Although the suggestion was popular in some circles and might have provoked a change of heart among the justices sitting on the court (i.e., conservative justice Owen J. Roberts's pro-Roosevelt vote in the *National Labor Relations Board v. Jones and Laughlin* case), it failed to pass Congress and mobilized a coalition of Republicans and (primarily southern) Democrats that was to spell the effective end of the New Deal experimentation.[20] This latter group, including Virginia's Glass and North Carolina's Josiah Bailey in the Senate, suspected that FDR's proposal was intended to bring about a thorough liberalization of the federal courts on both racial and economic issues. Roosevelt's subsequent (and partially successful) effort to increase the proportion of New Deal supporters in his party's southern delegation in the 1938 midterm elections only strengthened the will of his opponents within the party.[21] Glass warned that the South should start "thinking whether it will continue to cast its 152 electoral votes according to the memories of the Reconstruction era of 1865 and thereafter, or will have spirit and courage enough to face the new Reconstruction era that northern so-called Democrats are menacing us with."[22] His colleague Josiah Bailey found the Democrats' efforts to court "the Negro vote . . . extremely distasteful . . . [and] very alarming" and also feared that Roosevelt and the northern wing were "bringing [the party] . . . down to the lowest depths of degradation."[23]

Yet many blacks were displeased that change was not happening faster and that the Roosevelt administration was hesitant to confront segregation. The most obvious symbol of that reluctance was the administration's refusal to support the antilynching proposals that had been circulating in Congress since the turn of the century. Although the number of lynchings was again beginning to increase in the 1930s, Roosevelt was careful not to appear interested in related legislation (despite the occasional urging and efforts of his wife, Eleanor). The few blacks working in the administration were equally frustrated by their exclusion from the decision-making process and the obvious influence of segregationists on the government. Since Woodrow Wilson's election in 1912, the segregation of black workers from their colleagues had blocked blacks' advancement through the ranks of the civil service. Although Wilson defended his actions by suggesting that "segregation [was] . . . in the interest of the colored people, as [it exempted] . . . them from friction and criticism," the changes implemented by his administration resulted in the exclusion of black employees rather than the protection of their interests.[24] Combined with the civil service's requirement that applicants for employment after 1914 provide photographs, the effect of the Democrats' return to power was to place the government solidly behind the defense and expansion of Jim Crow practices.[25] Although Roosevelt made a number of black appointments to the executive branch (including Mary McLeod Bethune, William H. Hastie, and Robert Weaver), these individuals found themselves severely constrained in terms of what they could actually do, given his decision not to challenge the policies instituted by his Democratic predecessor.

On the one hand, the New Deal was launched in a context where the Democratic Party's new nonsouthern constituencies required and allowed it to be more progressive in its policy objectives, especially in view of the exigencies associated with the depression. On the other, the coalition's attempts to build new infrastructures, regulate the economy, and redistribute resources were restricted by the institutionalized power of its southern wing. Generally, Roosevelt remained popular in the South throughout his tenure, but the scope of his revolution was constrained by his refusal to challenge Jim Crow and his dependence on segregationists in Congress for support (especially if one looks at the New Deal revolution from a comparative perspective).[26] Certainly, given the balance between state and federal powers that existed before 1932 and the few mechanisms in place before the New Deal with which the national government could implement regulatory and redistributive policies, Roosevelt's reinterpretation of American governmental norms was breathtaking. Yet the reluctance to engage Jim Crow policies and challenge the warping effects of race on the expression of class politics (of which the New Deal coalition was an imperfect version) meant that the impact of these changes would be limited. By 1938 the New Deal as a mechanism for policy (re)formation was in retreat, and war appeared imminent. Within ten years most of the programs instituted by Roosevelt had been weakened, suspended, or eliminated, including the Wagner Act, the Civilian Conservation Corps, the National Youth Administration, the Works Progress Administration, and the Farm Security Administration.[27] In terms of redistributive policy, one can argue, from a broader historical and comparative perspective, that the New Deal's long-term achievements — old-age insurance, unemployment insurance, and Aid to Dependent Children — were rather meager, especially considering that similar policy innovations had been accepted by liberals and conservatives alike in most of the European countries two decades earlier (the reforms instituted under Lloyd George between 1906 and 1914 have been credited with reducing the impact of the depression in the United Kingdom).[28]

The effort to reconcile the divergent interests of the different Democratic constituencies was not any easier after the Second World War. During the war, organized labor had agreed to a no-strike policy expecting that through cooperation it would be able to increase its influence. The wisdom of this calculation was called into question by Congress's speedy passage of the Taft-Hartley Act in the summer of 1947 (and its override of President Truman's veto) and the extent to which the anticommunism of the period included organized labor among its targets. In both these instances, the union members in the Democratic Party found themselves at odds with their own party's southern contingent.

As for race, organized labor and the Communist Party were willing to "go slow" on racial issues during the war, but black leaders and civil rights groups were not similarly disposed. At this point black voters in the North were a crucial part of the Democratic coalition and consequently felt empowered to make demands on the party. By threatening to lead a march by African Americans on Washington, A. Philip Randolph had forced Roosevelt to issue an executive order (8802) in June 1941 that prohibited discrimination in hiring in the war industries. Similar pressures encouraged Harry Truman and the Democratic Party to pursue a much more aggressive strategy on civil rights issues, especially in view of the efforts of Paul Robeson and others to persuade blacks to support Henry Wallace's Progressive Party. Thus Truman was the first president to address the NAACP, and in October 1947 the Committee on Civil Rights, which the president had appointed, issued a report calling for federal action to protect the civil rights of minorities. Truman's endorsement of some of the committee's recommendations (including the abolition of poll taxes, an antilynching statute, and the reestablishment of the Fair Employment Practice Commission) and the party's decision to include a similarly progressive civil rights plank in its platform at the 1948 convention (an effort spearheaded by the mayor of Minneapolis, Hubert Humphrey), although supported and welcomed by liberal, pro–civil rights constituencies, only increased the tension between the party's southern and nonsouthern wings.

The reaction in the South to this series of events was predictable. Initially the party's southern supporters promised to withhold support from any candidate (including Truman) who did not uphold "states' rights" and to have the two-thirds rule for selecting the party's nominee reinstituted at the party's convention in Philadelphia in the summer of 1948. Eventually, though, a significant number left and launched the States' Rights (or "Dixiecrat") Party, led by South Carolina's governor Strom Thurmond with his counterpart from Mississippi, Fielding Wright, as the movement's vice-presidential nominee. Thurmond, fearing "police state tactics . . . federal gestapo[s] . . . a totalitarian state and . . . the threat of Communist infiltration," stated his intention to prevent Washington from forcing "negroes into . . . [southerners'] homes, their schools, their churches and their places of recreation and amusement."[29] Wright was confident that Jim Crow would be maintained. As he advised in a radio address targeted at blacks in his home state: "As governor of your state, I must tell you that regardless of any recommendation of President Truman, despite any law passed by Congress, and no matter what is said to you by the many associations claiming to represent you, there will continue to be segregation in Mississippi. If any of you have become so deluded as to want to enter our hotels and cafes, enjoy social equality with the whites, then kindness and true sympathy requires me to advise you to make your home in some state other than Mississippi."[30]

Consequently, Truman faced competition not only from John Dewey and the Republicans in the 1948 election but also from the Dixiecrats in the South and the Progressives led by former Democrat Henry Wallace. Although he won the election in 1948, he was unable to muster support from a largely uncooperative Congress. It was in this context that his own Fair Deal languished and his attempts to create a national health care program failed.

Convergence and Disillusionment: Southern Politics after the Civil Rights Era

The 1948 Dixiecrat revolt was the first stage in the gradual realignment of the two major parties. Although the South remained a relatively reliable base for the Democratic Party throughout the 1950s, it was a period during which the party's leadership posed no threats to the interests of the Dixiecrat constituencies. This changed, of course, with the civil rights movement, which compelled both national parties to respond to the new developments and abandon their characteristic post-Reconstruction straddling of the issue (with the exception of the Truman Democrats mentioned above).

Starting with the *Brown* decision in 1954 and culminating in the 1964 Civil Rights Act and 1965 Voting Rights Act, the civil rights movement created the possibility of a significant realignment. As James Sundquist notes, "Only the restraining influence of sectionalism, which held so many southern conservatives in the Democratic Party, seemed to be keeping the two major parties from realignment as class parties on the European pattern."[31] Logically, one would have expected that, given the apparent force of the integrationist tide, any aggregate realignment would involve a further affirmation and rationalization of the pro–New Deal and anti–New Deal coalitions: the working and middle classes, regardless of ethnic or regional background, would move closer to the Democrats, whereas the upper classes would gravitate toward the GOP. Indeed, this is what some analysts expected at the time. In his 1972 text *Class and Politics in the United States,* Richard Hamilton argued that Republican success in the South, in the long term, would derive from the upper class and upper middle class as it did in the North: "The successes of Republicanism [in the South] appear to be dependent on upper-middle-class conversions, distractive [i.e., racial] appeals and very low electoral participation." Believing that "the real existential concerns of the majority of the Southern population, both black and white [would prevail]," Hamilton thought it "unlikely that . . . distractive appeals could have any long-term success." He went on to suggest that the Democrats would in time become the "permanent majority party" and that "in order for them to lose they would have to make colossal mistakes, mistakes of such a magnitude as to drive their supporters away to the opposition."[32] Hamilton dismissed racial issues as capable of generating much reaction among voters and instead foresaw the creation of a national Democratic majority based on the working and middle classes.

Of course, this did not happen. Rather than nationalizing and rationalizing the New Deal coalition, the effect of the civil rights revolution was to rupture the already fragile alliance. The southern wing of the Democratic Party had been able to maintain itself when northern blacks emerged as a crucial constituency within the coalition; that arrangement was no longer viable once the party's national leadership was forced, by default and by circumstances, to support the challenges to Jim Crow being made by southern blacks. While Lyndon Johnson won the 1964 election by a landslide, the most significant indicator of the future direction of American politics was the level of support given to Republican candidate Barry Goldwater: 87 percent of the vote in Mississippi, 69.5 percent of the vote in Alabama, 57 percent in South Carolina and Louisiana, and 54 percent of the vote in Georgia.[33] Goldwater's opposition to the civil rights movement and the Civil Rights Act of 1964 attracted the same constituency (southern whites of both upper- and lower-class backgrounds) that had supported the States' Rights/Dixiecrat campaign in 1948. It was also Goldwater who enunciated what would become for the next three decades the Republican position on the black vote: "We're not going to get the Negro vote as a bloc in 1964 or 1968, so we ought to go hunting where the ducks are."[34] His opponent, Lyndon Johnson, recognizing the role of race in determining white southern partisan allegiances, suggested in a 1964 speech he gave in New Orleans that all southerners "ever hear at election time is nigra, nigra, nigra"; on another occasion he stated that the Democratic Party's support for civil rights legislation would "[deliver] the South to the Republican Party for a long time to come."[35]

These same constituencies were the primary base of support for the segregationist and former New Dealer George Wallace, who supported increases in Social

Table 4.2. Estimated Voting-Age Blacks (%) Registered in Eleven Southern States

State	1947	1956	1964	1968	1976	1986
Alabama	1.2	11.0	23.0	56.7	58.4	68.9
Arkansas	17.3	36.0	49.3	67.5	94.0	57.9
Florida	15.4	32.0	63.8	62.1	61.1	58.2
Georgia	18.8	27.0	44.0	56.1	74.8	52.8
Louisiana	2.6	31.0	32.0	59.3	63.0	60.6
Mississippi	0.9	5.0	6.7	59.4	60.7	70.8
N. Carolina	15.2	24.0	46.8	55.3	54.8	58.4
S. Carolina	13.0	27.0	38.7	50.8	56.5	52.5
Tennessee	25.8	29.0	69.4	72.8	66.4	65.3
Texas	18.5	37.0	57.7	83.1	65.0	68.0
Virginia	13.2	19.0	45.7	58.4	54.7	56.2
Total South	12.0	19.0	43.1	62.0	63.1	60.8

Source: Harold W. Stanley, *Voter Mobilization and the Politics of Race: The South and Universal Suffrage, 1952–1984* (London: Praeger, 1987), p. 97.
Notes: Percentages are probably higher than the real numbers because out-of-date decennial census data were used to compute the levels of registration.

Security, health care improvements, and stronger collective bargaining rights for organized labor in his 1968 campaign under the banner of the American Independent Party. But in the long term it was the Republican Party that would reap the benefits of the changes in partisan affiliation in the South.[36] Aiding this conversion was the traditional conflation of civil rights claims with concerns about "law and order" and "crime" (i.e., the Social Issue). These understandings and coded references lay at the root of the Republican Party's "southern strategy" and its attempts, beginning with the election of 1972, to establish itself as the party of the white South. These efforts were only assisted by the increasing registration and voting of blacks in the South and their participation in and support of the Democratic Party (see Table 4.2).[37] To borrow from "Cotton Ed" Smith, in the South the Democratic Party would not be the sponsor of too many "mongrel meetings," for the movement of blacks into the party coincided with the exodus of whites.

The issues generated by the second wave of feminism (e.g., the proposed Equal Rights Amendment and abortion as considered in the 1973 *Roe v. Wade* decision) and the movement of Christian evangelicals to the Republican Party after the 1978 decision by the administration of Democrat Jimmy Carter to deny tax-exempt status to segregated Christian academies in the South contributed to the post–civil rights era realignment of southern white voting constituencies.[38] The GOP's 1980 nomination of Ronald Reagan, who was clearly on the "right side" of these social issues, only accelerated the process of conversion in the South. If one examines the eleven states that are typically considered to constitute the South, the change in partisan alignment that has occurred over the last four decades is striking.[39] At the presidential level the white South has been voting Republican consistently since 1964. In terms of the federal legislature, in 1960, 94 percent of the southern representatives in the House were Democrats, and a year later Texas's John Tower became the sole GOP senator from the region.[40] After the midterm elections of 1998, only 43 percent of the southern representatives in the House were from the Democratic Party, and fourteen of the twenty-two members of the South's senatorial delegation were Republicans.[41] Whereas incumbency used to favor and empower southern Democrats, in 1998 the speaker of the House was Newt Gingrich, a Republican from Georgia, and the Senate majority leader was Trent Lott, a Republican from Mississippi.[42] In retrospect, Strom Thurmond's career stands as an accurate reflection of the changes that have taken place in the region: a Democrat in the 1940s (who was perceived to be a liberal in comparison with his peers) who leads the Dixiecrat revolt against the civil rights activism of Harry Truman in 1948, filibusters for a record time of over twenty-four hours against a relatively weak civil rights bill in 1957 as a senator from South Carolina, switches allegiance to the Republican Party after the passage of the 1964 Civil Rights Act, and campaigns (successfully) to be reelected to office in 1996, at the age of ninety-three, to be South Carolina's senator into the twenty-first century.

The South is clearly still in transition, and it is not yet clear whether the region will become as solidly Republican and effectively conservative as it was Democratic and conservative before the New Deal era. Currently, eight of the South's eleven state legislatures are controlled by the Democratic Party, although seven of the region's governors are Republicans.[43] Nevertheless, over the last three decades the trend has been toward greater Republican strength in the South: in Congress and in the state legislatures. Moreover, the Democrats that have prevailed in the South have been mostly white and from moderate to conservative (i.e., the "blue dog" caucus), outnumbering the few liberal (mostly black) representatives.[44]

Identifying the Alien Child

In *The Liberal Tradition in America,* Louis Hartz suggests, "The South . . . has been the part of America closest to Old World Europe. It has been an alien child in a liberal family, tortured and confused, driven to a fantasy life which, instead of disproving the power of Locke in America, portrays more poignantly than anything else the tyranny he held."[45] If anything is clear about twentieth-century American politics, it is that the South was hardly on the margins of American life but that the region most visibly expressed the values and inclinations that dictated the nation's politics. It is not a coincidence that, with the possible exceptions of John F. Kennedy and Harry Truman, every Democratic president in the last century was, in some way, a southerner.[46] At the same time, it is evident that the "race-trumps-class" phenomenon has not been unique to the South. Southern politics have long revealed a willingness to marginalize class issues in the name of white supremacy (however constructed), but politics outside the South have increasingly been characterized by similar conflicts and conflations. The failure of the New Deal coalition to nationalize and rationalize itself after the civil rights movement is related to processes that unfolded throughout the country. Perhaps one of the most telling developments related to the correlation between region and the extent to which politics are racialized are the changes in racial composition of public schools in the different parts of the country. Between 1968 and 1980, racial segregation in American primary and secondary public schools dropped in every part of the country, including the South, except the Northeast, where by every measure it increased significantly.[47]

It is in this context that the Macomb County phenomenon is significant. At the most basic level, these white Reagan Democrats (and Bush Democrats) in Michigan, experiencing unemployment rates as high as 17.6 percent, feeling victimized by blacks, and abandoned by the Democratic Party, are a classic example of the cross-pressured constituencies that have defined and circumscribed American working-class politics.[48] Although the reasoning is not as explicitly racialized as it was in the South before the civil rights era and may be complicated by the emergence of such issues as affirmative action and the effects of the Great Society effort, the basic pattern is familiar: the party of the left is perceived as being overly indulgent of blacks and is therefore rejected by whites (essentially regardless of class). For similar reasons, preleftist and leftist movements such as Populism, Socialism, and the CPUSA were unable to attract sufficient support.

Perhaps more striking is the interpretation given to these developments. Thomas and Mary Edsall argue that a values barrier has developed which separates "Democratic liberals and much of the electorate at large" and which "because of the underclass . . . has taken on a racial cast." They suggest that "this conflict has evolved, in complex ways, from one of the major struggles of the twentieth century: the struggle between so-called traditional values and a competing set of insurgent values." These traditional values include "commitments to the larger community—to the family, to parental responsibility, to country, to the work ethic, to sexual restraint, to self-control, to rules, duty, authority, and a stable social order." The insurgent values, from this perspective, have been "the focus of rights-oriented political ideologies, of the rights revolution, and of the civil rights revolution"—revolutions calling for "freedom from oppression, from confinement, from hierarchy, from authority, from stricture, from repression, from rigid rule-making, and from the status quo."[49] In their description of the values barrier, the Edsalls offer an accurate rendering of the symbolic construc-tions that have proven so effective in contemporary American politics, in terms quite similar to the sentiments of the alienated residents of Macomb County.

Yet the values barrier, as outlined by the Edsalls, is the result of two differ-ent but related processes. The revolutionary force of the last two centuries has been the promotion and popular acceptance of the combination of values clus-tered around individualism and the individual-oriented economic perspective, as promoted by the expansion of the free market. It is an anomic individualism which has eaten away at the foundations of "tradition" and which has shattered the (often idealized) harmonies that formed the basis of earlier conceptions of community. The second story has centered on the significance of race as a factor in American politics. In suggesting that the civil rights movement was one aspect of this drive to enthrone these new insurgent values, the Edsalls implicitly posit that racism and white supremacy are traditional values in the American political culture. Indeed, Jim Crow *is* one of the idealized harmonies whose rupture has brought about the developments of the last three decades, including the new poli-tics of frustration and cynical symbolism as practiced by both Republicans and Democrats.

Consequently, in *Middle Class Dreams* Stanley Greenberg portrays the citizens of Macomb County as victims, as voters betrayed (and "doubly betrayed") by Great Society liberals.[50] Although he does not gloss over the visceral racial an-tipathy that informs their worldviews, Greenberg clearly believes that a reborn Democratic Party must reestablish its credibility with these disaffected voters in a manner that is both disturbing and arguably contradictory. On the one hand, he encourages the belief that these voters are victims and seems unwilling to ques-tion or critique the raw racial sentiments that underlie their calculations. On the other, Greenberg's constant usage of the modifier "middle class" seems to imply that he too believes that "not being black [is] what constitute[s] being middle class." The privileging of "middle-class dreams" arguably has serious implica-tions. When he argues that the Great Society programs "distorted the Democrats' bottom-up vision . . . [and made] it into something constricted and racial," he is romanticizing the New Deal and overlooking the extent to which Roosevelt's revolution was itself constricted and racialized. What is particularly noteworthy in this regard, however, is how his definition of the middle class—"people who work for a living, receive wages or salary but who do not own a business or play an executive role"—effectively eliminates the working class (for example, in Macomb

County, 40 percent of the households were union households). In other words, the cross-pressures of race and class seem to be so strong that constituencies one would objectively classify as working class dare not speak their own name and must for political reasons be called "middle class." The implication is clear and consistent with the hesitant and constricted republicanism of the labor movement in the nineteenth century: working-class whites do not or should not exist, membership in the white republic precludes a (lower) class designation. It is in this context that David Roediger refers to "white workers, who are . . . defined much more by the adjective than by the noun."[51]

The political implications of this post–Great Society Democratic vision have been illustrated by the Democratic Leadership Council (DLC). The DLC emerged in 1985 as a movement within the party representing the traditional southern conservative perspective. The Super Tuesday idea—the grouping together of the southern primaries to improve the viability of a southern conservative Democratic candidate (in a sense, an attempt to re-create the two-thirds rule abandoned by the party in 1936)—was a DLC product.[52] In response to the perceived hold of the left on the party, the DLC has sought, with some success, to pull the Democrats back into the mainstream in accordance with the warnings of Scammon and Wattenberg, the Edsalls, and Greenberg. While the DLC has succeeded in achieving its primary goal of, as one member has stated, delineating "a new middle ground of Democratic thinking on which someone can run for president and be elected," this new thinking has often found its proponents at odds with organized labor and civil rights interests.[53]

It is in this context that Bill Clinton's presidency is understandable. A founding member of the DLC, Clinton sought to establish a policy middle ground that was not quite as revolutionary as that pursued by the GOP, yet to the right of even most moderate Democrats. With the assistance of Stan Greenberg (who was one of his advisers), Clinton invoked the mantra of the middle class (e.g., "middle-class bill of rights," "the forgotten middle class") in an almost paint-by-numbers fashion during the 1992 campaign and made sure to visit Macomb County on three separate occasions.[54] Furthermore, the confrontation with Jesse Jackson (the "Sister Souljah" incident) during the 1992 campaign established Clinton as a Democrat not beholden to black interests symbolically, just as his abandonment of Lani Guinier's nomination to the Justice Department after his election indicated his willingness to avoid any subsequent undue association with civil rights "activists."[55] As for organized labor, the Clinton administration's dismissal of trade union concerns in its negotiation of the North American Free Trade Agreement (NAFTA) and its decision to propose and then abandon a relatively unattractive health care reform bill illustrate the basic "New Democratic" orientation toward labor's interests.[56] The decision to sign the legislation that would "end welfare as we know it," despite organized labor's opposition, only reinforced the impression that an administration obsessed with the "middle class" would be of little use to lower-income constituencies and, ultimately, middle-class constituencies as well.[57]

The developments in the 1990s suggest that there are limits to the extent to which politicians can experiment as long as the coded cultural and racial understandings that define American politics continue to shape popular sensibilities and conceptions of identity. To the right, the failure of the Newt Gingrich–led GOP to realize the full range of objectives contained in the Contract with America indicates that there is a residual, aggregate attachment to certain public welfare programs (e.g., Medicare and Social Security).[58] But the 104th Congress (1995–96) was successful in setting the agenda and reestablishing the leftward limits of the political culture, a culture still seemingly immune to many of the policy norms (e.g., universal health care coverage) that have been accepted in other industrialized societies.

Macomb County Blues

Analysts such as Richard Scammon and Ben Wattenberg, Thomas and Mary Edsall, Jim Sleeper, and Stanley Greenberg have suggested that the move from "warm acceptance" to white backlash was motivated by the pace of the "Negro revolution," by the quick evolution of the nonviolent marcher into the rioting urban warrior.[59] While the imagery is quite provocative, it bears little resemblance to reality. The unfocused anger that reared its head in Watts and especially in the riots after Martin Luther King's murder in 1968 was not new. Even the ritual was not new, as the 1935 uprising in Harlem had established the riot as one means of expression for black Americans.[60] As for the philosophy of nonviolence, this approach derived its legitimacy from the peculiar circumstances pertaining in the South in the late 1950s and early 1960s. To superimpose the urban rioter on the civil rights demonstrator is to confuse contexts, circumstances, and regions and to engage in the most superficial symbolic analysis.[61] Similarly, to suggest that New Deal politics collapsed because of the ramifications of the civil rights revolution is to romanticize the achievements of the New Deal era and to overlook the effects of race on New Deal politics.

More striking are the continuities between pre- and post–civil rights era American politics. While there have been changes in the terms of political debate and partisan alignment and the situation of the various African American geographic and income communities, post–New Deal politics continue to be shaped by the same basic forces that influenced the earlier eras. The substantive policy leeway available to American politicians, whether they are Republicans or Democrats, will continue to be limited and defined by American attitudes toward race as they always have been. A significant American left, comparable to those found in Europe or even Canada, will not be possible given the dominant role played by race.

It might be argued that if leftists — or, in this case, self-identified progressives — were to attempt to deconstruct the gateway, that is, to challenge racial divisions and misunderstandings directly, they would lose support and have to cede the power to make decisions to parties of the right. Indeed, the experiences of the IWW, CIO, the Populists, the CPUSA, and to some extent the Democratic Party support this notion. Consequently, one might understand the efforts of progressives to avoid being marginalized in this way by choosing either not to challenge or even to reinforce these racial codes. It is in this spirit that Thomas Edsall writes, "Recapturing the ability to build a winning alliance requires . . . developing a conscious awareness of precisely what the electorate will support politically [and] what it will not," a statement that captures the essence of the gateway.[62] What needs to be recognized — and it is precisely this understanding that is lacking in the analyses of Edsall and Greenberg — is that such a strategy, besides being morally suspect, is not likely to deliver much in terms of progressive policy achievements. In other words, playing by the existing rules of the game and seeking to reassure "threatened" white working- and middle-class constituencies that the racial status quo will not be challenged has meant accepting relatively limited returns and, as I argue in Chapters 5 and 6, forsaking the public goods typically maintained or achieved through leftist organization.

CHAPTER FIVE

Beyond the Left II
Making the Public Good

The common or collective benefits provided by governments are usually called "public goods." A common, collective, or public good is here defined as any good such that, if any person . . . in a group . . . consumes it, it cannot feasibly be withheld from the others in that group. . . . Students of public finance have, however, neglected the fact that *the achievement of any common goal or the satisfaction of any common interest means that a public or collective good has been provided for that group.* — Mancur Olson, *The Logic of Collective Action*

Is there then, any place for Socialized Medicine? Since all experience shows and history attests to mankind's unquenchable thirst for freedom with justice, it follows that any system which limits freedom and justice, which imposes coercion and restricts voluntary effort towards self-betterment—has no place in the advanced and just society. A system which commits its citizens to mental and fiscal imprisonment, which in its aim to abolish uncertainties unavoidably eliminates opportunity and challenge, and leaves only the boredom of a limited certainty—such a system can only be regarded as reactionary in the historic evolutionary process of man. — Matthew Lynch and Stanley Raphael, *Medicine and the State*

The left, it has been suggested throughout this discussion, can be approached from at least three different perspectives. The conventional approach focuses on parties and labor movements and their attempts to garner popular support. A second approach would extend the discussion beyond unions and parties and examine the conventional left as one possible element within the larger movement to establish or maintain the provision of a range of public goods. In this context, the conventional left would be seen as an intermediate public good, as a means to the achievement of other public goods.[1] From this perspective, I posited, it would be possible to achieve or maintain the provision of these public goods, conceivably without a conventional left, as a result of some basic underlying societal consensus expressed and mobilized through other media and mechanisms (e.g., popular culture, collective economic enterprises, and newer social movements). A third, more abstracted approach to the study of the left would involve examining basic cultural sensibilities and artifacts for evidence of behaviors or mechanisms conducive to the expression and realization of collectivist or group-oriented sentiments. This third perspective would focus on the fundamental forces and understandings that shape developments related to the intermediate and conventional conceptions of the left. In Chapter 6 I will pursue the study of the left from this third perspective.

In Chapter 4 I argued that the New Deal coalition was limited and ultimately fractured by the same racial and ethnic factors that constrained the development of the labor movement and such leftist forces such as the Socialist and Communist Parties. Besides the effect of these tensions on the survival of the conventional left and left/liberal movements, I suggested that to the extent that leftists or progressives underestimated the significance of racial conflicts, their efforts to bring about changes favorable to the working classes would be unproductive. In other words, comprehensive and redistributive public goods cannot be maintained in a society that cannot support an inclusive, public-minded sensibility. The role racial understandings have played in the struggles to establish some of those public goods is the focus of this chapter.

Regardless of ideology, the making of public policy is an often difficult balancing act. For instance, only a fine line sometimes separates policies which respect cultural and regional differences from those which effectively encourage prejudices to develop unchecked. It is this type of issue that underlies the establishment clause of the First Amendment to the Constitution and the Supreme Court's attempts (e.g., *Lemon v. Kurtzman,* 1971) to establish a balance between religious and cultural diversity and the needs of the secular state.[2] Similarly, it can be difficult to distinguish policy innovations which enable people to improve their circumstances from those which ultimately hinder that ability by creating a structured dependency. Welfare policies are probably the best examples of this problem. In other words, it is not clear that the results of state activism have been entirely consistent with the objective of preventing the institutionalization of alienation, a Durkheimian anomie, or economic exploitation.[3]

In terms of the concerns of the left, especially because public goods need not be provided solely by the formal state, we can argue that in making policy, one would have to be concerned with the possible negative ramifications of an activist state, particularly its attempts to aggregate power and establish mechanisms of control. The frequent clash between economic priorities, on the one hand, and scalar and cultural priorities, on the other, is directly related to the issue of power.

The right to make decisions and the search for the system that best reproduces the circumstances under which that right is equitably distributed are issues with which a consistent leftism must be concerned. This search for a consistent set of guiding principles must be founded on the basic principle of respecting the dignity of groups and individuals. Policies that seek to establish uniform conditions or behaviors in a culturally diversified or regionally varied polity increase the likelihood of institutionalizing alienation and in "making power," or attempting to do so, undercut the efforts to reduce the alienating effects of economic exploitation.

For instance, the centralization that tends to accompany universalization practically requires the institutionalization of alienation and, frequently, deceit as popular expectations exceed the policymaking center's ability to deliver.[4] The left must question inclinations to "make things big," to universalize, and to centralize, occasionally to the point of adopting a wary anarchism, because an overloaded center can produce an alienated and frustrated populace (as well as deceitful politics). Whenever possible, decentralization should be a priority if one's intention is to avoid the institutionalization of alienation—the sense of having lost control over one's own circumstances or some aspect(s) of one's being. A sensitivity to difference is also required. Furthermore, to the degree that the energy and development of the aggregate depend on the interaction of its various elements, the attempt to eliminate or repress that variation through universalization is counterproductive. A consistent leftism, then, involves seeking and maintaining a delicate equilibrium. Leftists need to recognize the risks of seeking universalization through large-scale state activism while understanding that broad-based, state-sponsored programs are often the most effective way of preventing exploitation, marginalization, and alienation.

In this sense the dichotomy that is often suggested to exist between individual and group priorities is false. The debate, as it is usually posed, is between two abstracted, polar principles: an anomic individualism that is seemingly based on a conception of the individual existing outside of and prior to society (e.g., some contract theories), and an equally anomic collectivism that is incapable of handling or processing difference to the point of denying any but the most empty and existential identities (e.g., the more simplistic socialisms and nationalisms). This exaggerated contrasting of "freedoms to" and "freedoms from" fails to recognize that individual and collective identities are necessarily intertwined in a dynamic and dialectic fashion. It is as a result of the energies and questions generated by the interactions among different entities that ideological frameworks are developed, conflicts and contradictions recognized and occasionally resolved, and change occurs. A workable leftism has to move beyond these questionable dichotomies toward a deeper understanding of how viable political cultures are made.

Approaching the Welfare State

Some public goods, at least from a long-term perspective, are not necessarily desirable from a leftist perspective. Certain policy developments associated with the minimalist welfare state might represent means of preserving the institutions of the economic right more than the achievement of the goals of the left. For instance, the argument that the New Deal was an attempt to save rather than to transform American capitalism has merit. "In many places growing fear of the Left intensified the interventionist trend," suggests Peter J. Coleman. "Generally speaking, social democrats, not radicals, dominated political life. They sought to reform capitalism, not overturn it. But criticism from the Left produced a siege mentality in both business and politics and led to strategies of co-option as the best way to defend capitalism." Noting Bismarck's program in late-nineteenth-century Germany, Coleman goes on to suggest that "the politics of co-option also animated much of the New Deal. Franklin D. Roosevelt's critics from the Right may have seen him as an enemy to his own class, but it is widely believed that his policies saved American capitalism from its own worst self." [5] In other words, the New Deal programs were, in some respects, poor substitutes for the more comprehensive redistributive programs available elsewhere and provided fewer opportunities for citizens to pursue nonmarket possibilities (decommodification) than has been the case in many other Western states (with Sweden marking the other extreme). Roosevelt went out of his way to downplay the scale of his "revolution" by claiming that his intention was to save rather than undermine capitalism and the market, and that the changes being made were consistent with those made by German conservatives in the late nineteenth century and British Tories in the first two decades of the twentieth century. Aware of the gap that remained between American policy norms and those accepted elsewhere, Roosevelt told a journalist in 1938, incidentally after the New Deal reform process had stalled, "In five years I think we have caught up twenty years. If liberal government continues over another ten years we ought to be contemporary [with our counterparts in Europe] somewhere in the late 1940s." [6]

While the desirability of these minimalist programs can be questioned from a leftist perspective, their availability has been relatively restricted in the United States. Direct cross-national comparisons are complicated by the American federal structure and by the leeway states have in establishing their budgetary priorities and taxation schemes, but the redistributive policy apparatus in favor of the lower-income classes is less developed in the United States than elsewhere in the West (especially after the 1996 rollback of the entitlement status for Aid to Families with Dependent Children, or AFDC).[7] Relative to other industrialized nations, the American ratio of government expenditure to gross domestic product (GDP) has been consistently low. Similarly, U.S. expenditures on social welfare programs as a percentage of total government expenditure and as a percentage of GDP are also relatively low (see Table 5.1).[8]

Not only are social spending levels low and redistributive policy expenditures relatively small in the United States, but the establishment of social programs has also occurred later than in its European counterparts. Germany in 1883; the United Kingdom in 1897; France, Denmark, and Italy in 1898; and the Netherlands and Sweden in 1901 — all instituted programs to deal with occupational hazards before the United States, which first did so in 1908 during the Progressive Era. A similar pattern can be found in the area of unemployment benefits, with only Sweden (1934) coming close to the United States (1935) in the tardiness of its beginning such a program. France initiated a program for the unemployed in 1905, Denmark in 1907, the United Kingdom in 1911, the Netherlands in 1916, Italy in 1919, and Germany in 1927. Likewise, it was not until 1935 and the institution of the Social Security Administration that the United States established a program benefiting its elderly. Germany did so in 1889, Denmark in 1891, France in 1905, the United Kingdom in 1908, the Netherlands and Sweden in 1913, and Italy in 1923.[9] Overall, even in comparison with such other liberal welfare states as Australia and Canada — to use Gøsta Esping-Andersen's terminology — the United States's public policy apparatus is rather underdeveloped and minimalist.[10]

One reason the American welfare state is so unambitious is because of racial factors. Certainly, from Reconstruction until the civil rights era, southern states and their congressional representatives resisted the creation of new federal programs that might challenge the racial status quo. Accordingly, such New Deal programs as Aid to Dependent Children (which later became Aid to Families with Dependent Children) were left to the states to administer.[11] The choice to let the states control these programs with little federal regulatory influence reflected a weaker commitment to "welfare-type" programs, as well as the racial pragmatism of the New Deal legislature and executive. Southern representatives in Congress were also able to have clauses removed that would have required states to establish a single state authority to administer these programs and to provide assistance at a "reasonable subsistence compatible with decency and health." Similarly, southern congresspeople were able to exclude initially from the Social Security and unemployment insurance programs those groups which were most likely to

Table 5.1. Social Welfare Expenditures as a Percentage of Gross Domestic
Product and Total Government Expenditure, 1987 and 1995

Country	Government Expenditure as % of GDP (1987)	Welfare Expenditure as % of Government Expenditure (1987)	Social % of GDP Consumed by Social Welfare Expenditure (1987)	Welfare Expenditure as % of Government Expenditure (1995)
Australia	—	—	—	34.8
Austria	40.3	45.8	18.5	47.5
Belgium	52.9	39.4	21.1	—
Canada	24.2	33.4	8.1	40.8
Denmark	39.8	40.0	15.1	44.9
Finland	31.9	34.0	10.8	43.4
France	45.1	—	—	40.4
Germany	—	—	—	45.9
West Germany	30.1	—	—	—
Greece	50.9	—	—	19.6
Ireland	60.4	25.5	15.4	29.6
Italy	52.0	29.1	15.1	—
Netherlands	57.7	35.7	20.6	40.0
New Zealand	—	—	—	37.8
Norway	40.6	35.1	14.2	38.5
Sweden	42.9	48.5	20.8	54.0
Switzerland	—	49.9	—	49.2
United Kingdom	38.9	28.6	11.1	32.9
United States	23.3	28.4	6.6	32.0

Sources: George Thomas Kurien, *The New Book of World Rankings,* 3d ed. (New York: Facts on File,
1991), pp. 82, 91; *Government Finance Statistics Yearbook, 1991* (Washington, D.C.: International
Monetary Fund, 1991), p. 111; and *Government Finance Statistics Yearbook, 1997* (Washington, D.C.:
International Monetary Fund, 1997).

Notes: Some expenditure statistics are not available. The 1984 figures for government expenditures
on social security, welfare, housing, and community amenities (i.e., a subset of the programs included in the second column in the table above) are West Germany, 21.45% of GDP; France, 20.2%
of GDP; the United Kingdom, 15.1%; Canada, 12.38%; and the United States, 9.71%. The 1995
social welfare expenditures include spending on housing and community amenities, social security, and
welfare. All the figures are from 1995 as indicated except those for Canada (1994), France (1993),
Germany (1991), and Ireland (1994).

be largely black (e.g., agricultural workers and domestic laborers), as well as to structure the Tennessee Valley Authority so as to guarantee that few of its benefits would accrue to black southerners.[12] Given that sharecroppers were rarely paid in cash and consequently were dependent on their employers, the southern resistance to programs that might put real money in the hands of these workers was hardly surprising. Overall, as Jill Quadagno notes, "Race was a key component in battles over New Deal policymaking."[13] Indeed, as part of a process that started with Woodrow Wilson's administration, the expansion of the federal government that occurred during the New Deal era not only failed to challenge Jim Crow practices in the South but also introduced segregation into new regions and realms of American life.

Thus on account of the developments I discussed in Chapter 4, the overall weakness and fragmentation of the American welfare policy state is not surprising. Until the War on Poverty in the 1960s, when blacks might have benefited, programs were minimalist, left to the states, or abandoned. Since that period and the Great Society attempt to address some of the shortcomings of the American welfare state, income maintenance and other public programs have been stigmatized in the (mistaken) belief that the only beneficiaries of government spending are blacks and other nonwhites. A general pattern has emerged over the course of American (public policy) history: significant extensions of rights or services to include blacks and nonwhites have usually thrown the gears of American public policy making into reverse. Accordingly, the 1960s Great Society correction to the racial exclusions of the New Deal result in the (increased) demonization of welfare recipients and the defunding of welfare programs throughout the 1970s and 1980s until a promise to "end welfare as we know it" was acted upon in the 1990s. In this context, the proposal of new spending programs becomes much more difficult and the actual implementation of these programs much less likely.

Besides income maintenance programs, one could contend that certain public goods constitute a leftist minimum: goods for which there is little reason for the state not to get involved and for which there are indeed compelling reasons—efficiency and legitimacy—for public sector investment. These goods involve establishing universal programs but do not represent unnecessary attempts to make power or to institutionalize alienation. They can be approached as components of the immune system that any viable political culture must develop, as those provisions on which a real civilization might depend. Of these goods, I will examine the availability of two—health care and inclusive voter registration procedures—from a comparative perspective to illustrate some of the ramifications of the interplay of class and "race" in the United States.[14] The debate over health care reform indicates how difficult new policy (and spending) ventures can become in a political culture in which state activism is seen through a racialized lens even when there appear to be good reasons to undertake comprehensive reform. The history of the evolution of the franchise illustrates the pattern referred to above: how efforts to extend basic citizenship rights to nonwhites can result in the deterioration of those rights for all.

Individualized Medicine

In this section I examine the American provision of health care benefits from a comparative perspective in order to underline some of the ramifications of the weakness of the conventional left in the United States, a force that has in other societies pushed successfully for comprehensive health care provisions. I then consider the debates that took place in the early 1990s about whether and how the American health care system should be reformed. Finally I look at the role racial factors have played in American health care debates and in limiting the popular willingness to support — to demand — substantive health care reform.

The United States has chosen to place the responsibility for securing sufficient health insurance on the individual and to leave the provision and distribution of medical services to the machinations of the free market. Changes over the last two decades have led to an increased questioning of the wisdom of this choice. The postwar baby boom, the steady increase in life expectancy rates for the general population, and the impact of new illnesses have brought about a greater demand for medical services. For instance, the number of people over the age of sixty-five will more than double, from 30 to 65 million, during the next four decades. One demographer has suggested that the United States is "certainly on the threshold [of] . . . a health care crisis," and a spokesperson for the Alliance for Aging Research has warned that the country is facing "a tremendous national problem" because of the pressures that will be placed on the health care sector.[15] At the same time, with the overall restructuring of the economy — the relative growth of the service sector, the decline of unions and union activism, the deregulation of business, and the streamlining of industry — there has been an increase in the percentage of individuals who are under- and uninsured. It is estimated that roughly 44 million Americans, or one-sixth of the population, including between 10 and 11 million children, are completely uninsured. This number has grown every year since 1987 (when 37 million Americans were without health insurance) and does not include the elderly covered by Medicare or the poor covered by Medicaid. Nor does this figure reflect the fact that very few Americans actually have complete, comprehensive health care insurance.[16]

While many Americans lack adequate medical insurance, the percentage of

Table 5.2. American Health Care Cost Increases as Compared
with Changes in Gross Domestic Product, 1929–1990

Period	Health Care Costs as % of GDP at End of Period	Average Change in GDP per Year for Period	Average Increase in Health Spending per Person per Year for Period
1929–40	4.0	0	1.4
1941–50	4.5	3.1	4.0
1951–60	5.3	1.5	3.6
1961–70	7.3	2.5	6.5
1971–80	9.1	1.7	3.8
1981–90	12.2	1.7	4.4

Source: New York Times, May 16, 1993, p. E3.

the gross domestic product (GDP) absorbed by health care costs has steadily increased (see Table 5.2).[17] The nation's spiraling health care costs have drawn funds away from other basic infrastructural needs such as public works, research and development, and education. Also, American industries have lost a step relative to other countries' industries because of these costs (see Table 5.3). Whereas foreign competitors are free from the responsibility of providing basic health care, American companies must deal with the issue. One negative effect of this responsibility is the bitterness that can develop between employers and employees as they negotiate health care arrangements. For all businesses, health spending increased from 2.2 percent of wages in 1965 to 8.3 percent in 1990. Small business owners have been particularly hard hit because the impact of these increased costs has required them to consider whether they can continue to provide health care coverage to their employees and if they do provide such coverage whether they can afford to hire or keep on individuals who might have particularly expensive health care needs. At the individual level, hospitals have engaged in "patient dumping"—refusing care to the under- or uninsured—and insurance companies have become increasingly unwilling to insure those with certain preexisting health problems (e.g., diabetes, cancer, ulcers, arthritis).[18] Last, deaths from treatable diseases such as asthma, cervical cancer, pneumonia, and heart disease continue to occur because of a lack of preventive care.

As problems in the health care area have affected the overall economy, business, and individuals, the programs instituted by the state are facing uncertain futures as well. Medicaid, created in 1965 during the Johnson administration, cur-

Table 5.3. Share of Gross Domestic Product (%) Spent
on Health Care, Selected OECD Countries, 1960–1991

Country	1960	1970	1980	1990	1991	Ratio, 1960/1991	Increase, 1980–90 (%)
Britain	3.9	4.5	5.8	6.1	6.6	1.70	5.3
Canada	5.5	7.1	7.4	9.0	10.0	1.82	21.6
Italy	3.6	5.2	6.8	7.6	8.3	2.31	11.8
Japan	3.0	4.4	6.4	6.5	6.6	2.20	1.5
Sweden	4.7	7.2	9.5	8.7	8.6	1.83	−8.4
United States	5.3	7.4	9.3	12.4	13.4	2.53	33.3
West Germany	4.8	5.9	8.5	8.1	8.5	1.77	−4.7

Source: Organization for Economic Cooperation and Development, *Labor Force Statistics* (Paris: OECD, 1992), and Theodore R. Marmor, with Mark Goldberg, "American Health Care Reform: Separating Sense from Nonsense," in *Understanding Health Care Reform,* ed. Theodore Marmor et al. (New Haven: Yale University Press, 1994), p. 2.
Note: The 1980–90 percentage increase for Britain has been changed here from 4.7 in the Marmor text.

rently covers 47 percent of the poor under the age of sixty-five and 30 percent of those sixty-five and over. Nevertheless, the program's expenses have risen faster than the federal and state governments have been able to pay, creating a burden on state budgets, especially as the qualifying income levels for Medicaid are set by Congress and not by the states themselves. Whereas Medicaid costs constituted 4 percent of state expenditures in 1970, by 1990 these costs represented 14 percent of state expenditures. In 1988 total Medicaid expenditures were $54.1 billion. These costs rose to $72.5 billion in 1990 and to $115 billion by 1991. Because the established fees for Medicaid procedures are pegged below market rates (74 percent of the actual cost), as are Medicare rates (91 percent of cost), many doctors refuse to treat Medicaid patients.[19] The result is that Medicaid "mills" providing questionable service have emerged. As a study conducted by the Kaiser Family Foundation concluded, "Increasingly it is a program on paper—increasingly it has no delivery system."[20]

The Medicare program has faced a similar set of problems. Up to this point, the Medicare hospital trust fund has been funded by a 2.9 percent payroll tax, but the prediction is that the program's costs will be 3.42 percent of wages by the year 2000. Should no significant change be made in the funding mechanism, the hospital trust fund is expected to go bankrupt by some point in the early twenty-first century. A spokesperson for the government's Social Security Advisory Council has suggested that "it is a very sick future for Medicare unless policy-makers take

Table 5.4. Public/Private Health Care Spending Ratios in Selected Countries

Country	Public Health Exp. as % of GDP (1984)	Total Health Exp. as % of GDP (1984)	Ratio of Public Health Exp. to Total Health Exp. (1960)	Ratio of Public Health Exp. to Total Health Exp. (1987)	% Public Coverage for Hospital Care (1960)	% Public Coverage for Hospital Care (1987)
Australia	6.6	7.8	47.6	84.5	77	100
Canada	6.2	8.4	43.1	74.4	68	100
France	6.5	9.1	57.8	71.2	85	100
Germany	6.4	8.1	67.5	78.2	86	95
Greece	3.6	4.6	57.9	79.3	30	98
Italy	6.1	7.2	83.1	84.1	87	100
Japan	4.8	6.6	60.4	72.1	—	100
Norway	5.6	6.3	77.8	88.8	100	100
Portugal	3.9	5.5	—	71.1	18	100
Sweden	8.6	9.4	72.6	91.4	100	100
United Kingdom	5.3	5.9	85.2	88.9	100	100
United States	4.4	10.7	24.7	41.4	22	40

Source: James Simmie and Roger King, eds., *The State in Action: Public Policy and Politics* (London: Pinter Publishers, 1990), p. 77.

the window of opportunity afforded to them before the baby boom starts to retire in ten short years." The other Medicare fund, which covers doctors' bills and is three-quarters funded by the Treasury and one-quarter by the program's beneficiaries, is also becoming significantly more expensive. Together these two funds, which currently cost about 2 percent of GNP and cover over 33 million individuals (compared with the 26 million covered by Medicaid), have emerged as the fastest growing major programs in the national budget. Between 1980 and 1990 the cost of the hospital program grew at a clip of almost 10 percent a year, whereas expenses for doctors' services rose at a rate of 15 percent per annum.[21]

Overall, then, the American nonsystem has preserved market conditions for the majority of its population, but major problems exist. Health care expenditures have consumed an increasingly larger share of GNP, businesses have been burdened by extra costs, many individuals have been ill-served, and the minimal safety nets instituted for the poor and elderly — Medicaid and Medicare — are themselves in trouble.

In contrast to the American preference for institutionalized individualism and unwillingness to construct a comprehensive health insurance program, other so-

Table 5.5. Portion of Population (%) Covered by Public Health Care System, 1991

Country	Inpatient Care	Ambulatory Care	Pharmaceutical Costs
Canada	100	100	34.0
France	99.0	98.0	98.0
West Germany	92.2	92.2	92.2
Japan	100	100	100
Sweden	100	100	100
United Kingdom	100	100	100
United States	44.0	44.0	12.0

Source: OECD Health System: Facts and Trends, 1960–1991, OECD Health Policy Studies no. 3 (Paris: OECD, 1993), 1:267–69.

cieties, by various means and through a range of different plans, have chosen to socialize the costs and distribution of health care expertise and technology (see Tables 5.4 and 5.5). The first national health insurance program to be instituted was established in Germany in 1883 by the Bismarck administration. The program, guaranteeing free services and sick benefits and involving compulsory insurance, was at first limited to manual workers, for it was Bismarck's intention to coopt the issues and constituency of the left in what Barrington Moore has termed a "revolution from above."[22] Gradually the ranks of the insured were expanded to include transportation and office workers (1903), agricultural and forestry workers (1911), seamen (1927), and most other workers, as well as the unemployed, by the establishment of the Federal Republic. The program, funded two-thirds by employees and one-third by employers and currently covering roughly 95 percent of the population, is largely administered by the *landers* (the states). Those not covered by the program have private health insurance arrangements.[23]

The Belgian health care system is both complex and relatively decentralized as a result of the country's heterogeneity. The current system emerged out of turn-of-the-century legislation that subsidized preexisting sickness funds that by 1920 had been amalgamated into five national unions. In 1945 the state's financial intervention was increased to create an effective system of compulsory insurance that currently covers over 99 percent of the population to varying degrees (the self-employed, for example, are covered only for the more expensive and riskier medical procedures). Like the German system, funding is drawn from general social security payroll taxes paid by workers and employers.[24] Britain's National Health Service (NHS) was established in July 1948 and was, as Rudolph Klein notes, "the first health system in any Western society to offer free medical care to the entire population."[25] The NHS was also the first comprehensive health care system instituted by a state to operate on the principle that health care is a universal right rather than a service tied to contributions. As Klein suggests, "It was a unique example of the collectivist provision of health care in a market society," or as former Labour Party leader Michael Foot has written, the NHS is "the greatest Socialist achievement of the Labour government." [26] The creation of the NHS involved the aggregation of preexisting public and private institutions into a unified administrative and delivery system. Despite the Thatcherite attack on the public sector during the 1980s, the NHS has prevailed because of the common perception that it is an intrinsic aspect of the British political culture or, in Klein's words, a "protected species." [27] Although the NHS was created while the Labour Party was in power, the basic outlines of the proposed institution were developed during the postwar coalition with Winston Churchill's Conservatives. In other words, as in Germany, the perception that the time for national health care had come was shared by the left and the right and was not dependent on the triumph of the conventional left as the ruling party. Although the forms of the systems vary, all Western democracies except the United States have some form of national health care. Some are centralized (e.g., Norway) and others decentralized (e.g., Belgium); some are oriented toward a contribution-for-insurance principle (e.g., Germany and France) and others to the notion that health care is a basic right and collective responsibility (e.g., the United Kingdom). And though the funding systems vary, it has generally been accepted that health care is one good whose distribution should not be left to the dictates of the free market.

The American preference for the free market has not produced a cost-efficient system. Health care costs have risen throughout the industrialized West, but from a comparative perspective, these costs and the rate of their increase in the United States as a percentage of gross domestic product are high. For instance, in 1984, when 10.7 percent of American GDP was consumed by health care costs, the next highest figure in the West was Sweden, with its British-style system, at 9.4 percent. Germany's health care percentage was 8.1 percent; Japan's, 6.6 percent; France's, 9.1 percent; and the United Kingdom's, 5.9 percent. [28] Although the American expenditure on health care has been proportionately greater, the percentage of the population covered, as noted, is relatively low, and the nation's infant mortality, immunization, and life expectancy rates higher, lower, and shorter, respectively, than one might expect (see Tables 5.6 and 5.7). [29]

Perhaps the most appropriate comparisons can be made between the United States and Canada. While health costs were 12.2 percent of GNP in the United States in 1991, the comparable figure for Canada was 9 percent. The per capita cost for health care for the two countries in 1993 was $3,299 in the United States and $1,971 in Canada (see Table 5.8). The number of physicians who treat patients per

Table 5.6. Comparative Life Expectancy and Infant Mortality, 1995

Country	Life Expectancy (in years)	Infant Mortality (deaths per 1,000 births)
Canada	78.3	6.8
England	77.0	7.0
France	78.4	6.5
Germany	76.6	6.3
Japan	79.4	4.3
Sweden	78.4	5.6
United States	76.0	7.9

Source: U.S. Bureau of the Census, *Statistical Abstract of the United States, 1995* (Washington, D.C.: Bureau of the Census), pp. 849–50.

Table 5.7. Children Immunized (%) against Three Major Diseases in the United States, Sweden, the United Kingdom, and Canada, 1990–1994

	United States	Sweden	United Kingdom	Canada
Diphtheria	88	99	91	93
Polio	79	99	93	89
Measles	84	95	92	98

Source: UNICEF, *The State of the World's Children, 1996* (New York: Oxford University Press for UNICEF), p. 85.

one hundred thousand population (1989 figures) are roughly comparable (194 in Canada and 197 in the United States), while the hospital beds per capita (1988) is one for every 148 people in Canada and one for every 188 people in the United States. Again, on two basic measures of performance, life expectancy and infant mortality, the Canadian record is slightly better.[30]

Many cultural and historical similarities exist between the two countries, but their choices in terms of health care policy have been quite different. In contrast to the American nonsystem, Canada has a national health insurance scheme that, like the British system, covers the whole population for doctors' bills and hospital costs, as well as such other items as pharmaceuticals to different degrees in different provinces. Like the Belgian system, the Canadian system is administered not at the federal level but by the provinces. Nevertheless, the different provinces provide essentially the same services. The movement toward comprehensive health insurance was started by the Co-operative Commonwealth Federation in Saskatchewan and adopted in stages (first hospital insurance and then

Table 5.8. Comparative Costs of Health Care, 1993

Country	Health Care Expenditures per Capita ($)	Health Care Costs as Share of GDP (%)
Canada	1,971	10.2
France	1,835	9.8
Japan	1,495	7.3
Sweden	1,266	7.5
United Kingdom	1,213	7.1
United States	3,299	14.1
West Germany	1,814	8.6

Source: U.S. Bureau of the Census, *Statistical Abstract of the United States, 1995* (Washington, D.C.: Bureau of the Census), p. 853.

coverage for doctors' fees) by the different provinces and the central government beginning in the late fifties and culminating in the passage of the Medical Care Act in 1966.

The Politics of American Health Care Reform

One of the most significant differences between the American and Canadian systems is the amount that is spent on administrative costs.[31] In 1987, of each dollar spent on health care in Canada, eleven cents went toward administrative costs; in the United States the figure was twenty-four cents.[32] Accordingly, many of the groups advocating health care reform in the early 1990s, at a time when health care was reemerging as a significant issue on the national agenda, predicted that the implementation of a Canadian-style system would produce significant savings. A 1991 study conducted by Steffie Woolhandler and David Himmelstein, members of Physicians for a National Health Program (PNHP), concluded that the adoption of the administrative principles underlying the Canadian system would bring about savings of $100 billion each year and, according to a report issued by the Economic and Social Research Institute, $241 billion in the first year alone. Even the nonpartisan Government Accounting Office (GAO) suggested in 1991 that reforms of this nature would save $67 billion a year.[33] Yet a 1992 study undertaken by the Republican staff of the congressional Joint Economic Committee estimated that a national health insurance system would increase health costs by $81.5 billion a year.[34]

That the conclusions made in the study produced by the Republican staffers differed to such a great extent from the conclusions made by the pro–health care reform organizations (and the GAO) was (and is) an indication of the partisan alignments on the issue and the nature of the underlying debate over whether the American health care system should be changed. Then Republican House minority leader Robert Michel argued that "assertions that Americans would save money with national health insurance are baseless. . . . It's about time someone broke through the myths of the Canadian health care system."[35] The Bush administration's secretary of health and human services Louis Sullivan similarly contended "the belief that, by itself, putting an insurance card in every pocket will cure all our health-care ills is false prophecy from those preaching easy solutions."[36] The groups that would have been most affected by any Canadianization of the American health care apparatus — for instance, the American Medical Association (AMA) and the Health Insurance Association of America — were also quite vocal in their opposition to "socialization." Although some elements within the AMA had made mild reform proposals over the years in an effort to avoid state intervention and a complete overhaul, the organization warned the public about the effects a Canadian-style system would have on physician-patient relations. Individuals in Canada were (and still are) completely free to go to any doctor they please, yet for the AMA, waiting periods for some surgical procedures and government-established budgets for health care expenditures constituted "rationing," an inevitable outcome of socialized medicine. "We know our own health care system has severe problems," James Todd, deputy executive director of the AMA conceded, "but there is no question that it is the best in the world. People who think that the Canadian approach is a magic solution need to think harder. Americans want choice. I don't believe for a minute that they would settle for that kind of rationed care and limited access."[37]

Of course, the advocates of a Canadian-style health insurance program did not share this perspective. In reference to the high cost of administration and paperwork in the health care system, PNHP national coordinator Woolhandler observed, "We have 1,500 different health insurance programs, each with its own marketing department, claims processing apparatus and coverage regulations. The multiplicity of insurers inflates insurance overhead and inundates doctors and hospitals with the paperwork needed to keep track of every bill for every Band-Aid and aspirin."[38] And in response to the rationing argument, Woolhandler argued, "In the U.S., we are rationing medical care based on ability to pay. This would be a tragedy if there was a shortage of medical resources in this country, but . . . one of three hospital beds is lying empty. . . . It takes a lot of effort to keep sick people out of empty doctors' offices and empty hospital beds. In fact we spend a tremendous amount of administrative time and money to keep needy patients separated from available resources."[39]

Even Canadian physicians, some of whom fought the Medical Care Act vigorously, were struck by the portraits of the Canadian health care system that some were offering in the United States. In an editorial in the *Canadian Medical Association Journal,* it was suggested that exposure to the AMAs stateside campaigns might make Americans wonder "if any of us [Canadians] are still alive, given the pitiful state of health care here."[40] Another Canadian doctor contended, "I don't think you would find too many of my colleagues saying they find the American way more attractive than ours."[41] In response to the suggestion that the American system encourages greater technological innovation, a Canadian health care policy analyst countered, "High-quality care has to be judged on achieving the best results with the least possible intervention. To say [Americans] . . . have better medicine because [they] . . . spend more on high technology or fancy specialties than we do is crass, gross and untrue."[42] And in response to the rationing charge, the executive director of policy development for the Ontario Ministry of Health stated, "As a society, Canada chooses what it can afford to spend on health care. So do . . . [Americans]. The fact that rare Americans have access to distinguished medical services, so that millions have none, seems like rationing to me. I have never understood why Americans stand for it."[43]

Despite definite signs that health care was a powerful mobilizing issue (e.g., the 1991 senatorial elections in Pennsylvania and New Jersey in which reform advocates were victorious), health care interests in the private sector and their strongest supporters in the mainstream parties managed to control the direction of public policy debate. "What you've got here," suggested one congressional aide, "is that the people that have the most to lose [from significant health care reform] are very well organized, very vocal and well-heeled."[44] With more than two hundred political action committees (PACs) and large amounts of funds to draw on, the antireform lobby had established itself as a major player in congressional circles. Of the 535 members of Congress in 1991, 519 had received money from these PACs. Significantly, this money was concentrated in the campaign funds of those members having policymaking ability in the health care area, in the House Ways and Means Committee, in the health subcommittee of the House Energy and Health Committee, in the Senate's Medicare subcommittee and in the Senate's Finance Committee. Whereas PAC contributions rose 90 percent, on average, over the course of the 1980s, antireform PACs increased their contributions 140 percent over the same period.[45] Furthermore, labor's decline, in terms of numbers and influence, reduced the policy-shaping ability of one of the more consistent advocates of reform, and even the American Association of Retired Persons (AARP), one of the potentially strongest interest groups, was compromised on the issue of health care reform because it was earning significant revenue (about one-third of its budget) as an insurance broker for its membership.[46]

Of course, health care reform had been high on the public agenda before. Ironically, for a brief period during the Progressive Era the American Medical Association was actually supportive of a government-organized health care system. Since 1916, though, it has been the most consistent opponent of such efforts. Perhaps even more ironical, when in the middle of the second decade of this century the first serious campaign to institute a health care program emerged, one of the most vocal opponents of any government action was the AFL, at that point still led by Samuel Gompers. Meyer London, a Socialist member of the House of Representatives, elected from New York City's Lower East Side, introduced a resolution that called for the establishment of a national health insurance fund which the AFL dismissed as "an assumption of attitude wholly repugnant to the rights, interests, freedom and welfare of the workers."[47] The craftworkers' unwillingness to support London's bill was undoubtedly partly a reflection of the tensions between some factions of the federation and the Socialist Party. Gompers—who questioned whether it made sense for labor to support legislation that would "open up opportunities for government agents to interfere lawfully with the privacy of the lives of wage earners"—was then also under the influence of his corporate colleagues in the National Civic Federation, who were similarly averse to any government-sponsored health care program.[48] The AFL went so far as to label "impracticable and ill-advised" any suggestion that it might set up a system to provide sick and death benefits for its own members at its 1916 convention (again, at a time when such programs were commonly administered by its counterparts in other countries). Some members of the AFL did want to see a state-sponsored health care system, but the federation would not officially endorse such efforts until 1935 under the leadership of William Green. Given these dynamics, defeating reform efforts was not very difficult, even without the added suggestions that government-run Medicare was a product of "the kaiser" (i.e., Germany) and not appropriate for American citizens.[49]

The issue came up again in the 1930s during the depression and in the context of Franklin Roosevelt's remaking of the federal government. Although it was considered, FDR chose not to include a health care proposal in his 1935 Social Security legislation for fear that it might prevent passage of the programs he considered most important and because he did not perceive any strong popular demand for action. Nevertheless, individuals within the administration were working on the issue (e.g., Harry Hopkins, Arthur Altmeyer, and Isidore Falk), and in his second term a National Health Conference was held to review the status of the nation's health provisions and possibly to make recommendations for reform. The participants (including the AFL's William Green) made a number of suggestions including proposals that the federal government focus on providing improved services to women and children, devote resources to hospital construction, use a model similar to the Social Security plan to extend medical care coverage, and transfer funds to the states to provide health care to the poor.[50] Actual legislation did not result because the proposals coincided with Roosevelt's clashes with Senate Democrats (and Republicans) after his court-packing proposals in 1937 and with his efforts to replace his opponents within his own party in the 1938 midterm elections. Furthermore, despite organized labor's support for reform, the tensions between the AFL and the CIO after their 1937 split consumed most of their energies. Even the limited federal hospital construction plan that Roosevelt proposed died in committee in the House.

While Roosevelt's attention was increasingly focused on foreign policy issues and the revolt from within his own party, Arthur Capper, a Democrat from Kansas, and New York's Robert Wagner introduced different bills in the Senate regarding health care reform, proposals that also were unsuccessful because of the internecine conflict among Democrats and war preparations. The reality that few Americans had access to quality health care (see Table 5.9) and reports that more than 40 percent of the men called up for service in 1941 were unfit provoked widespread concern about America's health in general, and against the backdrop of England's announcement of its intention to set up what would become the National Health Service, there was renewed support for government action.[51] With labor's support and involvement, Senators Wagner and James Murray of Montana (Democrat), together with House member John Dingell (Democrat), introduced proposals for a public sector plan in 1943. Roosevelt recommitted himself to the issue in his State of the Union addresses in 1944 and 1945, and recognizing that the momentum might be moving against them, the AMA launched an extensive campaign against reform (this time targeting the "socialistic" British, as they had the Germans three decades earlier and as they would Canadian arrangements four decades later). Unfortunately for advocates of change, Roosevelt died on February 8, 1945, before he could lend his full support and his skills to the effort.

Furthermore, the elevation of the United States to superpower status after the war reduced the willingness of American policymakers to take any cues from their European counterparts. Suggests Daniel T. Rodgers, "The years between the 1870s and the Second World War . . . [represented] a moment when American politics was peculiarly open to foreign models and imported ideas," a period "when other nations' social politics . . . were *news*" and Americans were able to

Table 5.9. Portion of Population Uninsured (%) in the United States, 1940–1998

Year	Uninsured
1940	90.7
1950	49.3
1960	27.7
1970	13.6
1980	14.8
1990	13.9
1992	14.7
1998	16

Sources: Derek Bok, *The State of the Nation: Government and the Quest for a Better Society* (Cambridge: Harvard University Press, 1996), p. 250, and *New York Times,* August 9, 1998, pp. 1, 18.

access "a world mart of useful and intensely interesting experiments." [52] Although, as noted elsewhere, key decision makers in government and labor circles had always tended to resist adopting European innovations, the disinclination to pay close attention to developments on the other side of the Atlantic only increased with the circumstances and developments brought about by World War II. "After 1945," contends Rodgers, "when the United States found itself suddenly astride a global system of its own, the exceptionalism theme [i.e., the celebration of American differences] returned, full volume," with the perception that the "strangers abroad are not us; their experience is not usable." [53]

Harry Truman continued the push for reform and released a proposal for health care legislation in November that contained many of the recommendations made by the 1938 National Health Conference seven years earlier, including support for federal spending on research and hospitals and to cover mothers and children, a social security tax to insure workers and their dependents, as well as a wage insurance fund for the sick. Nevertheless, lacking FDR's oratorical abilities and confidence, Truman was even less successful in his efforts, although his identification with the issues seems to have been stronger. The Republican victories in the 1946 midterm elections made health care reform unlikely for the short term as the deepening Red scare would make "socialistic" and "communistic" programs rather difficult to sell. The new conditions encouraged one of the more prominent groups promoting reform, the Committee for the Nation's Health (CNH), to pass a resolution ensuring that its members not "supply bulletins or other information . . . to organizations which in the judgement of the officers [of the CNH] are associated with the Communist party or led by members of that party." [54] Accordingly, in this context Ohio Republican Robert Taft could label the most recent reform proposals from his Senate colleagues Wagner and Murray as "the most so-cialistic measure that . . . Congress has ever had before it."[55] Taft's successful sponsorship of labor legislation in 1947 (the Taft-Hartley Act) marked the beginning of the decline of organized labor and indirectly further disabled the campaign for health care reform.[56]

Despite Truman's support for health care in his 1948 presidential campaign and the Democrats' recapturing of Congress that same year, the opportunities to secure passage of reform legislation were lacking. By this point the Red scare was in full swing, and Truman's opponents in the Senate were able to block even the most modest reform proposals. Before the commencement of the Korean War, the Senate's 60-to-32 vote in 1949 against allowing Truman to upgrade the Federal Security Agency to cabinet status (as the Department of Welfare) was widely understood as a strike against health care reform, an issue on which the secretary of welfare was expected to focus. Thirty-seven of the sixty votes came from Republicans, and twenty of the twenty-three Democratic votes against Truman's proposal came from southern Democrats (one of Truman's few southern supporters was Texas's Lyndon Baines Johnson). In characteristic fashion, the AMA responded to Truman's 1949 health care proposals by suggesting that a compulsory health insurance program offered "neither hope nor promise of progress" but was a "discredited system of decadent nations which are now living off the bounty of the American people." Contending that "the voluntary way is the American way," the association concluded that Truman's proposal was "one of the final, irrevocable steps toward state socialism — and every American should be alerted to the danger," and it went so far in 1951 as to call for an investigation of the nation's schools to identify and remove any teachers or books that promoted "the fallacies of collectivism."[57]

Race and the Quest for Comprehensive Health Care Reform

Not surprisingly, from early on racial considerations also played a role in the various health care debates. The unique combination of racial and class factors operating in the South gave power to the senators who were the most reliable opponents of health care reform. Their opposition to reform was only strengthened by Truman's activism on civil rights issues during the 1948 election campaign, his desegregation of the armed forces, and his unsuccessful attempts to restore the Roosevelt-initiated Fair Employment Practices Committee. Similar dynamics delayed the passage of what were to become Medicare and Medicaid for more than a decade until after the Kennedy assassination and the Johnson landslide in 1964.[58]

Table 5.10. Uninsured Nonelderly Residents (%)
in the United States, by Ethnicity, 1979 and 1989

Ethnicity	1979	1989
All United States	14.8	17.5
All Latino	25.7	39
Mexican	27.8	41.6
Puerto Rican	16.5	22.6
Cuban	22.1	22.1
Other Latinos	28.9	44.3
Anglo	12.7	13.8
Black	22.7	24
Asian and other	22.1	21.8

Source: R. Burciaga Valdez, Hal Morgenstern, Richard Brown, Roberta Wyn, Chao Wang, and William Cumberland, "Insuring Latinos against the Costs of Illness," *Journal of the American Medical Association* 269, no. 7 (February 17, 1993): 891.
Note: "Other Latinos" includes Central and South Americans.

Furthermore, given the segregation of public institutions that prevailed legally in the South and elsewhere until the *Brown* decision in 1954, it is not surprising that little support existed for the rationalization of health care provisions (e.g., a number of the federally funded Veteran's Hospitals were segregated or refused admission to black veterans altogether). The AMA itself, the most consistent opponent of health care reform over the course of the last century, refused to allow any black doctors to join until 1949 and accepted state and local chapters that excluded black members until 1968. As labor's color bars often denied blacks the right to work, in many of these states and jurisdictions one had to be a member of the AMA to get a license to practice medicine.[59]

As for contemporary health care debates in the early and mid-1990s, at a symbolic level the ability of the antireform interests and the apparent willingness of the media to downplay the gravity of the problems of the uninsured were related to racial considerations. The immediate perception was that the completely uninsured were disproportionately nonwhite (see Table 5.10). This encouraged the belief that significant health care reform was not necessary but rather another attempt to institute a welfare program.[60] This argument was made in a 1991 editorial in the AMA's own publication, the *Journal of the American Medical Association:* "Access to basic medical care is still not a reality in this country. There are many reasons for this, not the least of which is long-standing, systematic, institutionalized racial discrimination. . . . It is not a coincidence that the United States of America and the Republic of South Africa—the only two developed, industrialized countries that do not have a national health policy ensuring that all citizens have access to basic health care—also are the only two such countries that have within their borders substantial numbers of underserved people who are different ethnically from the controlling group [South Africa has since taken steps to institute such a program]."[61] Reflecting the extent to which racial considerations have shaped the broader health care policymaking environment, Robert Blendon, of the Harvard School of Public Health, has suggested that rationing—reform efforts that would include the uninsured—is "the Willie Horton [referring to the escaped black convict and rapist the Bush campaign team used to great effect in 1988] of national health care."[62]

It is in this context that the failure of health care reform in 1994 was remarkable yet not surprising. The developments following from the emergence of health care as a hot-button issue in 1991 to Bill Clinton's adoption of the issue as a central plank of his 1992 campaign platform seemed to indicate—at the time—that some degree of serious health care reform was inevitable. Indeed, the issue was high on the public agenda, a new president seemed committed to reform, and he had majorities of his own party in both Houses of Congress with which to work. Yet Bill Clinton had campaigned as a "New Democrat" and consequently was restricted in terms of the range of proposals he could make once in office. As Theda Skocpol suggests, "Having stressed anti-government themes on their way to Washington, the Clintonites were not very comfortable featuring explanations of governmental structures or processes in their public messages about Health Security."[63] This discomfort meant that a Canadian-style type of reform proposal could not be advanced because it would be categorized as "socialized medicine" and as yet another "Old Democrat" tax-and-spend policy that would threaten individual rights and the operations of the private sector. Accordingly, the proposals that finally were produced (and sold as "guaranteed private insurance") were an awkward attempt to improve the provision of health care services without challenging any of the powerful actors in the private sector (particularly the hospitals, doctors, and insurance companies) that were the source of some of the basic problems related to cost and coverage.[64] Reflecting their "New Democrat" origins, the plans were drawn up without serious consultation with labor or the more liberal Democratic constituencies in the House and Senate (although clearly these groups would have been happy to support anything ultimately), and the real debate took place between centrist (southern "blue dog") Democrats of Clinton's ilk and the Republicans who were, at heart, opposed to any real reform. Once one factors in the political marginalization of the un- and underinsured, the cooptation of both major parties by antireform PACs, the telling history of health care reform failures over the course of this century, and the basic fear of change and the unknown that hampers any effort to sell public policy, the final result becomes more understandable.[65]

The main factors blocking reform—including the significance of PAC money and the corresponding weakness of organized labor, the predominant role played by southern conservatives in both major parties, and the popular resistance to government activism—can also be understood, to varying degrees, as reflections of the influence of race in American politics and policymaking. Although deliberations about public policy no longer involve explicit references to race as was the case until the 1930s, assumptions rooted in racial understandings have been internalized and incorporated into the processes associated with making health care policy and public policy in general. The president who came in pledging to "end welfare as we know it," given the class and racial connotations associated with that promise, was not likely to have a strong mandate (or the confidence) to undertake comprehensive health care reform or to make health coverage for the uninsured a national priority.

The Clinton campaign's decision to use "middle-class" as a prefix for every policy initiative it proposed also had implications for the shaping and selling of health care reform. The consultants, including Stan Greenberg, who worked on the packaging of the health care proposals urged that the administration's ambition "to serve ordinary people" be highlighted and that the plan be designed in such a way as to reassure crucial constituencies that the reform was "about their lives, *not somebody else.*"[66] The author of one memo took a position that, in light of the Macomb County phenomenon, could not be any clearer in terms of its understanding and endorsement of racial codes: "This is not an argument about 'access' . . . or 'extending coverage' or 'the uninsured.' . . . Since most Americans have insurance, they think of the uninsured as 'them'—this creates an 'us and them' mentality. We should not even talk about '37 million uninsured' because that is not who the proposal is designed to protect."[67] Overall, as Skocpol observes, "Carried over from the 1992 presidential campaign was a concern to reassure the middle class that this was not just another Democratic welfare program."[68] Nevertheless, this careful positioning still allowed the opponents of reform to use such phrases as "socialized medicine" and "another welfare program" that would trigger negative responses based on the historical conflation of racial and class understandings and weaken support for any proposed legislation. The supposed advocates of reform were afraid or perhaps simply unable to speak in clear terms about the health care problems all Americans were facing, regardless of race, and to offer appropriate solutions of the sort that are taken for granted in other industrialized nations, because they did not wish to alienate the crucial constituencies they classified as middle class. In other words, given the signals and code words used by Clinton and the Democrats to win in 1992 (what was a split-field victory), the basic groundwork necessary to develop broad-based support for reform had not been done: New Democrats cannot reinvent themselves mid-term. Clinton's racial calculations and his effort to distance himself from "old" Democrats meant that he would have very little leeway with which to fashion a feasible and effective health care package.[69]

Shaping the Ballot

Similar processes have unfolded with respect to the evolution of the franchise. That a government has been constituted in accordance with the explicit wishes of the electorate represents the fundamental means by which claims to democracy can be legitimated. Although in some cultures voting may be merely a matter of endorsing the status quo and in itself no guarantee of democracy, a political culture in which large numbers, verging on a majority of the members, do not directly participate in the electoral process can barely claim to be a functioning democracy. In comparison with its Western counterparts, American government cannot genuinely claim to represent the explicit wishes of a significant percentage of the populace. This is not to argue that Americans have been directly denied the right to vote. At least in theory, the franchise is available to all free (i.e., not in prison), competent American adults over the age of eighteen. But there is a large gap between theory and practice. In other Western democracies, voter turnout percentages have been markedly higher than in the United States (see Table 5.11). For instance, in the most recent major national elections held as of 1993, the voter turnout percentages were above 80 percent in Belgium, Sweden, and Italy and at or above 70 percent in Germany, the United Kingdom, and Canada. For France, the corresponding figure was 65 percent. In the United States, 55 percent of the electorate turned out to vote in 1992.

Beyond questions about the legitimacy of American democracy and concerns that low turnout might diminish the symbolic function of the electoral process, there are other reasons why low voter participation rates are significant. If the electoral system is meant to function as a check on the actions of government, the nonparticipation of roughly half the electorate could lessen the effectiveness of that balancing and shaping mechanism. More specifically, it has typically been the working and lower-income classes that have constituted the nonvoting population, and as Frances Fox Piven and Richard Cloward note, "The United States is the only democratic nation in which the less well off are substantially underrepresented in the electorate."[70] One can argue that consistent large-scale nonvoting by these classes has affected the aggregate political culture by leaving underrepre-

Table 5.11. Electoral Turnout (%) for Selected Countries
(for most recent election before end of year given)

Country	1963	1968	1973	1978	1983	1988	1993
Belgium	87.2	83.9	84.2	88.3	86.1	86.7	93
Canada	79.7	74.8	74.9	68.9	68.9	75.0	70
France	68.7	80.0	81.3	83.2	70.9	78.5	65
Germany	—	—	—	—	—	—	78
West Germany	87.7	86.8	90.7	87.8	84.4	84.3	—
Italy	92.9	93.0	90.1	90.8	89.0	88.5	89
Sweden	85.9	89.3	90.8	91.8	91.4	83.0	86
United Kingdom	78.7	76.0	72.2	72.9	72.8	75.4	76
United States	65.4	62.3	57.1	55.8	55.1	52.8	55

Sources: Elections since 1945: A Worldwide Reference Compendium (Chicago: St. James, 1989); *The International Almanac of Electoral History,* 3d ed. (Washington, D.C.: Congressional Quarterly, 1991); and Matthew Cossolotto, *The Almanac of European Politics, 1995* (Washington, D.C.: Congressional Quarterly, 1995), p. 19.
Note: The 1993 figures are rounded to the nearest whole number.

sented those groups which might seek to contest the "revolutionary" remaking of the republic.[71] In this vein, Piven and Cloward contend that "the distinctive pattern of American industrial development at least partly stems from the fact that the United States was not a democracy, in the elementary sense of an effective universal suffrage, during the twentieth century."[72] Perhaps wider popular participation would eventually lead to more prolabor legislation, possibly a greater number of parties and greater party responsiveness to voter concerns. Accordingly, one of the major objectives—and achievements—of working-class constituencies in the eighteenth and early nineteenth centuries in Europe was universal manhood suffrage.[73] For example, it is hard to believe that the debate about welfare reform would proceed as it does if not for the fact that the decision makers on both sides of the aisle know that welfare recipients are less likely to vote.

The suggestion that the participation of nonvoters would change political outcomes has certainly been challenged on the basis of studies of nonvoters which indicate that their partisan dispositions are not necessarily very different from those of the individuals who regularly go to the polls. Given the current party system and electoral options, this might be true.[74] Yet the sort of America that would see institutionalizing state support to increase voter turnout as an important priority and public good would be a different society from the one that currently exists. Thus it is reasonable to speculate and to expect that to generate widespread public and legislative support for inclusive voter registration procedures would require a fundamentally different conception of American community. That new community would logically engender a wider range of parties and options and a context in which current nonvoters would support other candidates (from those available now) and in which the aggregate gap between the preferences of current nonvoters and current voters would be broader.

Two kinds of explanations exist for the consistently high level of nonvoting in the United States. One category focuses on the individual voter and her or his personal reasons for choosing not to participate in the electoral process. Some have suggested that it is the contented who tend not to vote and that nonvoters, by not participating, are tacitly endorsing the status quo. According to Seymour Martin Lipset, "It is possible that nonvoting is . . . at least in the Western democracies, a reflection of the stability of the system [and] a response to the decline of major social conflicts."[75] In an article entitled "In Defense of Nonvoting," George Will writes, "The fundamental human right is to good government. The fundamental problem of democracy is to get people to consent to that, not just to swell the flood of ballots. In democracy, legitimacy derives from consent, but nonvoting often is a form of passive consent. It often is an expression not of alienation but contentment, or at least the belief that things will be tolerable no matter who wins."[76] As Piven and Cloward point out, though, it seems strange that lower-income groups would be the most contented.[77] Another school of thought argues that high levels of participation can be interpreted as signs that the "system" is breaking down. In "The Inactive Electorate and Social Revolution," Francis G. Wilson contends that "in a society in which only fifty per cent of the electorate participates it is clear that politics does satisfy in a way the desire of the mass of the individuals in the state. As the percentage of participation rises above, let us say, ninety per cent, it is apparent that the tensions of political struggle are stretching to the breaking point the will toward the constitutional."[78] Going one step further, Lipset suggests that the "evidence confirms [the] . . . thesis that a sudden increase in the size of the voting electorate probably reflects tension and serious governmental malfunctioning and also introduces as voters individuals whose social attitudes are unhealthy from the point of view of the requirements of the democratic system."[79]

Clearly a lack of education, income, status, or interest correlates with nonvoting (see Table 5.12). But this fact does not account for the relatively high levels of nonvoting in American society. Some individuals will choose not to vote, and in most modern democracies those individuals tend to be disproportionately less educated, less well off financially, the very young, and the relatively old. It still remains to be understood why American nonvoting levels are significantly higher than elsewhere.

Table 5.12. Voters (%) Claiming to Have Participated in 1984 American Elections, by Race, Gender, Employment Status, Education, and Region

Subgroup	Percentage
National	59.9
White	61.4
Black	55.8
Hispanic origin	32.6
Male	59.0
Female	60.8
Employed	61.6
Unemployed	44.0
Not in labor force	58.9
0–8 years elementary school	42.9
1–3 years high school	44.4
4 years high school	58.7
1–3 years college	67.5
4 or more years college	79.1
North and West	61.6
South	56.8

Source: Frances Fox Piven and Richard A. Cloward, *Why Americans Don't Vote* (New York: Pantheon, 1988), p. 205.
Note: In 1984, 9.9% more people claimed to have voted than actually did.

A second set of explanations focuses on the structure of the American electoral and political systems and, in particular, the obstacles to the exercise of the franchise. "In the United States," writes Ruy A. Teixeira, "voting is primarily an individual responsibility. The individual must surmount the bureaucratic obstacles necessary to vote . . . [and] must, by and large, mobilize himself or herself to go down to the polls and cast a ballot. The individual, in short, has the burden of voting on his or her shoulders, rather than having that burden collectively shared, as in other countries."[80] Add Piven and Cloward, "American registration procedures are Byzantine compared with those that prevail in other democracies. The major difference is that governments elsewhere assume an affirmative obligation to register citizens."[81] Similarly, Walter Dean Burnham notes that "everywhere else in the West (including neighboring Canada), it was early accepted that it was the state's task to compile and update electoral registers."[82] While the responsibility for registering to vote rests on the individual in the United States, other obstacles also make voting difficult. Partly as a consequence of states' rights agitation, the registration process is complicated by the different sets of regulations that prevail in different states, especially given the high rates of geographic mobility in the United States. In some states, once registered a voter must maintain her or his registration or risk being dropped from the ranks of eligible voters in the regular purges of the polling lists. Furthermore, absentee voting is often not easy, nor are there laws mandating that employers allot time on election days for their employees to go and vote.[83]

Customs concerning electoral participation are different in the other Western democracies. In Canada, for instance, voter registration is carried out essentially by the state. The government, on a commission basis, pays representatives of the two leading parties in each polling district to go out in pairs, once during the day and if necessary a second time during the evening, to register voters. The resulting lists are then posted throughout the voting district so that individuals can check to see that they have been enumerated. An individual who has not been listed at this point can still have her or his name included. The United Kingdom practices a similar procedure.[84]

Interestingly, universal manhood suffrage, or at least universal white manhood suffrage, was achieved in the United States relatively early. A similar extension of the franchise was not realized in France until the Third Republic, in England until the 1880s, and in Italy, Germany, and Russia until the twentieth century.[85] The relatively early "granting" of the franchise to white males in the Jacksonian era made sense given the rhetorical and philosophical roots of the American Revolution (including the republican ethos and its various interpretations), and the associated lack of a cumulative mythology that would enable the formal state to put off recognizing the voting rights of its free citizens.[86]

The highest rates of political participation in the United States occurred in the mid–nineteenth century after the gradual elimination of the property qualifications that had limited popular access to the ballot and an increase in the number of offices available in the growing federal system (see Table 5.13). It was only after the 1877 compromise, which lessened the threat that federal troops would be deployed in the South to enforce the Fifteenth Amendment, that rates began to drop. In the late nineteenth century, southern state legislatures created a series of devices to circumvent the Fifteenth Amendment and the potentially disruptive effects of the Negro vote where fraud, force, and random violence failed to suffice. In 1877, Georgia began enforcing a poll tax. In 1882, South Carolina devised a literacy test that Florida copied seven years later. In 1890, Mississippi instituted a two-dollar poll tax as well as a literacy test. Other variations on this theme included retroactive and cumulative poll taxes, grandfather and fighting grandfather clauses (restricting the vote to those whose grandfathers had voted and to those whose grandfathers had fought for the Confederacy, respectively),

Table 5.13. American Voter Turnout (%), 1840–1924

Year	National	South	Non-South
1840	80	75	81
1844	79	74	80
1848	73	68	74
1852	69	59	72
1856	79	72	81
1860	82	76	83
1864	76	(Civil War)	76
1868	81	71	83
1872	72	67	74
1876	83	75	86
1880	81	65	86
1884	79	64	84
1888	81	64	86
1892	76	59	81
1896	79	57	86
1900	74	43	83
1904	66	29	77
1908	66	31	76
1912	59	28	68
1916	62	32	69
1920	49	22	55
1924	49	19	57

Source: Walter Dean Burnham, "The System of 1896: An Analysis," in *The Evolution of American Electoral Systems,* ed. Paul Kleppner et al. (Westport: Greenwood, 1981), p. 193.

undefined tests requiring that the prospective voter indicate an "understanding" of the Constitution, and equally vague "good-character" tests.[87]

Blacks were the direct target of the disenfranchisement efforts, but many whites who lacked the means, education, and influence demanded by the new laws dropped into the ranks of the nonvoting as well. As C. Vann Woodward notes, that these campaigns would restrict white access to the franchise was camouflaged by the emphasis on the need to uphold white supremacy: "To overcome the opposition and divert the suspicions of the poor and illiterate whites that they as well as the Negro were in danger of losing the franchise — a suspicion that often proved justified — the leaders of the movement resorted to an intensive propaganda of white supremacy, Negrophobia, and race chauvinism. Such a campaign preceded and accompanied disenfranchisement in each state."[88] Even in those cases where the restrictions were vague, some whites chose to avoid the discomfort these new procedures might cause. As a result, voter turnout continued to drop in the South.[89] Added to the virtual elimination of a competitive party system, the sharp reduction in the size of the electorate and the dispositions of the remaining participants in active political life undoubtedly had a significant effect on the shape of southern politics.

The remaking of the electorate was not limited to the South. At the same time that labor and elements of the left were supporting legislation to limit immigration (and the Socialist Labor Party's Daniel DeLeon was dismissing the significance of voting arrangements altogether), the leaders of the Progressive movement were making changes in the registration requirements in the northern states that would make it more difficult for new Americans to vote and influence the prevailing political arrangements. Whereas the white South feared that the black vote would threaten white supremacy, in the North some progressives worried over the unpredictable and occasionally corrupt politics of the often immigrant-supported political machines that were developing throughout the country, as well as the possibility that these new citizens would support socialist politics (e.g., the Socialist Party strongholds in Milwaukee, Wisconsin, and New York City's Lower East Side that sent Socialists to Congress). These developments "convinced elites everywhere that unlimited suffrage fueled disorder."[90] To prevent "the severance of political power from intelligence and property," as *The Nation* phrased the problem, eleven nonsouthern states implemented literacy tests between 1890 and 1926.[91] While these tests succeeded in preventing numbers of immigrants (European, Mexican, and Asian) from voting, the states instituted more effective means as an unintended consequence of the drive for efficiency and "clean government."[92] Maine, Connecticut, and Massachusetts had had voter registration laws before the Progressive Era, but by 1929 all the states had such systems, except Indiana, Texas, and Arkansas (Texas and Arkansas already had other devices to restrict the vote, and eventually all three would also adopt registration systems). As nativist fears, under the guise of progressivism, deepened, these registration procedures became increasingly intricate. Those states which had sponsored and instituted registration procedures gradually implemented systems that would require prospective voters to present themselves at particular offices during specified periods to register to vote. As Piven and Cloward note, "Where once the door-to-door canvass had been used to add electors to the list, now it was used exclusively to eliminate them."[93]

Perhaps ironically, the suffragette movement phrased its appeals for the right to vote in terms that exploited the fears of nativists. Advocating an "expediency strategy," National American Women's Suffrage Association (NAWSA) leader

Carrie Chapman Catt argued, "The government is menaced with great danger. That danger lies in the votes possessed by the males in the slums of the cities and the ignorant foreign vote." As a solution, Catt suggested that the nation "cut off the vote of the slums and give it to women."[94] With the support of pioneer feminist Elizabeth Cady Stanton, the NAWSA convention of 1893 decided to adopt this strategy as a means of winning over southern whites and northern nativists: "Resolved that without expressing any opinion on the proper qualifications for voting, we call attention to the significant facts that in every state there are more women who can read and write than all negro voters, more American women who can read and write than all foreign voters; so that the enfranchisement of such women would settle the vexed question of rule by illiteracy whether of home-grown or foreign-born production."[95] While Susan B. Anthony did not support the expediency strategy explicitly, she did endorse state efforts to restrict the franchise and discouraged black women from participating in NAWSA for fear that southern white women would be alienated.[96]

The advent of literacy tests and cumbersome registration procedures were only two features of an overall change in the style of American politics.[97] The move from pork-barrel politics to the administrative state, the Progressive push to make government "efficient," and the decline of competitive party politics in the post-1896 era — all contributed to the remaking of the American political culture.[98] As in the South, the evolution of the primary system in the name of reform coincided with the depopularization of formal political life in the North, although the drop was not as great as it was in the South. As a result of the combined efforts in the North and the South, less than half the legally eligible voters actually voted in 1920 and 1924.[99] Overall, in the period in which the American working class was crystallizing and at a time when a social democratic party might have been expected to emerge, the theoretical electorate was being surgically reduced as a direct result of its growing heterogeneity. Though it might be tempting to focus on the actions of the elitist Progressives, organized labor and elements of the conventional left contributed to the creation of an atmosphere in which this effort could be undertaken: in the South against blacks, in the Northeast and Midwest against European immigrants, and in California against Asians. The price was an inclusive voter registration system that might encourage the parties and the policy-making system in general to reckon with the claims of the working classes (incidentally, at a time when the reverse process was occurring in Europe and access to the vote was increasing).

The changes in registration procedures that occurred in the late nineteenth and early twentieth centuries cannot be the sole reasons for the current voter turnouts (see Tables 5.14, 5.15, and 5.16).[100] Furthermore, despite the passage of the 1965

Table 5.14. American Voter Turnout (%), 1928–1996

Year	Voter Turnout
1928	56.9
1932	58.4
1936	61.0
1940	62.4
1944	55.9
1948	53.3
1952	63.8
1956	61.6
1960	65.4
1964	63.3
1968	62.3
1972	57.1
1976	55.8
1980	55.1
1984	55.0
1988	52.8
1992	55.2
1996	49

Sources: Walter Dean Burnham, "The System of 1896: An Analysis," in *The Evolution of American Electoral Systems,* ed. Paul Kleppner et al. (Westport: Greenwood, 1981); Thomas Mackie and Richard Rose, *The International Almanac of Electoral History,* 3d ed. (Washington, D.C.: Congressional Quarterly, 1991); *Kessing's Record of World Events, 1992* 38, no. 11 (1992); *New York Times,* November 7, 1996, and November 5, 1998.

Voting Rights Act, which removed many of the restrictions that had depressed black suffrage in the South, white turnout rates continue to be higher than those of blacks (roughly by 5 to 8 percent) and much higher than those of "Hispanics" (less than 30 percent).[101] Beyond the inconvenience of registration there are undoubtedly other reasons for the high degree of nonvoting in the United States.

Suggests Burnham, the "low and declining turnouts [also] reflect a pervasive and deepening crisis of political integration . . . symptoms of [which] . . . include the continuing decay of the political parties and the proliferation of intense single interest lobbies in the political process."[102] It does stand to reason that, after generations of working with a restricted electorate, the parties have become accustomed to employing a certain range of political styles and responding to a certain set of popular demands. Moreover, as contemporary electoral politics have become a function of political action committee money, the willingness and ability of the major parties to respond to the theoretical electorate have lessened.[103] On the other side, as the formal political and policymaking systems have remained

Table 5.15. Reported Registration Rates in the American
South, by Race, 1946–1992 (as % of population)

Year	Whites	Blacks
1946	—	3.1
1960	—	28.7
1964	61	41.9
1968	71	58.7
1972	70	55.8
1976	67	59.9
1980	66	55.1
1984	68	66.9
1988	67	63.7
1992	68	65.0

Source: Derek Bok, *The State of the Nation: Government and the Quest for a Better Society* (Cambridge: Harvard University Press, 1996), p. 176.

removed from the populace, this alienation has become accepted and institutionalized. This "disconnection," to use Penn Kimball's term, has made electoral participation seem even more futile. Also, the decline in influence of unions, one of the more dependable mechanisms of voter registration for the working class, has further reduced the number of voters registering.

One possible source of change in voter turnout patterns might be the National Voter Registration Act (the so-called motor-voter legislation), which went into effect in January 1995 and requires states to make voter registration more accessible (i.e., at motor vehicle administrations and social services outlets). Thus far the impact of the legislation is unclear. Some analysts predicted major increases in voter turnout (one suggested, erroneously, an additional 40 million voters by 1998), whereas others believed that—for a number of reasons, including state resistance—the new legislation would not make much difference. Although Republican governors were generally slow to implement the legislation (some argued unsuccessfully that it was an unfunded mandate) and feared it might increase support for the GOP's opponents, new voters have been most likely to register as independents rather than as Democrats or Republicans. How many individuals are added to the rolls and how many of these actually turn out to vote remains to be seen, especially as voting levels are falling among the less affluent and increasing in wealthier constituencies.[104] Although a number of factors are involved besides registration, the turnout levels for the 1996 and 1998 elections seem to indicate that the 1995 legislation, by itself, will not lead to a significant increase in voter turnout.

Table 5.16. Portion of Population (%) That Reported Voting
in Presidential Elections in the South, by Race, 1964–1992

Year	Whites	Blacks
1964	59.5	44.0
1968	61.9	51.6
1972	57.0	47.8
1976	57.1	45.7
1980	57.4	48.2
1984	58.1	53.2
1988	56.4	48.0
1992	60.8	54.3

Source: Derek Bok, The State of the Nation: Government and the Quest for a Better Society (Cambridge: Harvard University Press, 1996), p. 176.

Formal political activity and elections are hardly the only means by which the left's goals can be realized, but they are two strategies by which the conventional left has managed, in other contexts, to achieve its objectives. That voting has been made relatively difficult in the United States results from the aggregate society's attempts to grapple with its increasing heterogeneity and its unwillingness or inability to overcome the barriers that ethnic and especially racial misunderstanding can create. Regardless of how votes might be cast, a society in which roughly half the electorate does not participate and in which voting is effectively discouraged lacks one mechanism through which it can maintain a basic sense of community.

Externalities

If American exceptionalism meant nothing more than the failure of the conventional left to establish itself, an extended examination of the phenomenon might not be justified. But this is not the case. Regardless of one's ideological orientation, it is clear that a fundamental difference exists between the "absolute value" of the public goods available in the United States and elsewhere in the West ("public goods" understood in both the narrow and broad senses). The relative weakness of American unions and the related absence of comprehensive health care policies and inclusive voter registration procedures are other ramifications of American exceptionalism. And while one may question the desirability of minimalist welfare state provisions (as opposed to comprehensive programs), if avoiding the institutionalization of alienation is a priority, these programs are less developed in the United States as well. Beyond these differences, the spirit that has traditionally informed American policymaking has also affected protection of the environment, regulation of business and banking activities, the extent and nature of gun control regulations, the development of worker safety programs, and the nature of the urban planning and public transportation schemes adopted in the United States. Gender relations and policies have also been racialized.[105]

Certainly, other factors may explain the nature of American public policy, such as regionalism, a general resistance to an activist federal government, the crowding-out effect that defense spending can have on domestic policy, and the influence of the frontier experience, among others. Contemporary debates about American public policy are very rarely phrased in terms of "white people won't . . ." or "because black folks will. . . ." Yet the characteristic interactions of class and race, the absence of a resilient transracial collective sensibility, and an understanding American electoral history lend credence to the suggestion that race plays a role in the unique development of American public policy. Suggests Martin Gilens, on the basis of surveys designed to determine the extent to which welfare policy preferences can be affected by racial perceptions, "racial attitudes are a powerful influence on white Americans' welfare views. Indeed . . . racial considerations are the *single most important factor* shaping whites' views of welfare."[106] Similarly, Gwendolyn Mink observes that "into the 1990s, the racial mythology of welfare cast the welfare mother as Black, pinned the need for reform on her character, and at least implicitly defined Black women as other people's workers rather than their own families' mothers. Racially charged images of lazy, promiscuous, and matriarchal women have dominated welfare discourse for quite some time."[107] In an interesting contrast, Theda Skocpol suggests that "the stigma of policies targeted on the poor cannot be attributed mainly to the presence of the black minority. Until recent decades, blacks were overwhelmingly concentrated in the South, where there were few public social policies of any kind. Antipoverty policies were very stigmatized in the North, where most of the poor were white."[108] Skocpol's argument, of course, rejects the notion that northern understandings of community and citizenship were also affected by racial considerations long before the beginning of significant black migration to the North early in the twentieth century, and the implications of Alexis de Tocqueville's observations, based on his journeys through Jacksonian America, that "the prejudice of race appears to be stronger in the states that have abolished slavery than in those where it still exists; and nowhere is it so intolerant as in those states *where servitude has never been known.*"[109]

The willingness throughout American history of crucial constituencies to interpret their circumstances in terms of race (e.g., the residents of Macomb County,

Michigan) helps explain the contemporary weakness of the social welfare state in the United States. To understand why American cities are deserted after five o'clock in the evening, why Americans are increasingly "bowling alone," and why American public spaces are more often empty spaces, one might want to consider the influence of the constructed reality that is race.

CHAPTER SIX

Memphis Diversities
Race, Class, Identity, and Popular Culture

> Africanism has become . . . both a way of talking about and a way of policing mat-
> ters of class, sexual license, and repression, formations and exercises of power,
> and meditations on ethics and accountability. Through the simple expedient of
> demonizing and reifying the range of color on a palette, African Americanism
> makes it possible to say and not say, to inscribe and erase, to escape and engage,
> to act out and act on, to historicize and render timeless. It provides a way of con-
> templating chaos and civilization, desire and fear, and a mechanism for testing
> the problems and blessings of freedom. — Toni Morrison, *Playing in the Dark*

> Now tell me your philosophy on exactly what an artist should be. — Lauryn Hill,
> "Superstar"

In the previous chapters I have considered the effects of the acceptance of race as a meaningful axis of difference on the circumstances of American
leftist organizations and public policy. Labor unions, leftist parties, and progressive policy objectives have all suffered in the United States as a result of the potent
combination of race and class. The role played by racial understandings with regard to the exceptionalism phenomenon is even clearer in view of the sentiments
and values that have been promoted in the arenas of popular culture.

Popular culture is one means by which people can grapple with the changes associated with modernization. The making and remaking of cultural forms with
which different constituencies can identify and through which they can process
and come to terms with the various aspects of their alienation are relevant to
the left because these public goods allow for the formation of solidaristic conceptions of community, the kinds of understandings that are crucial to successful leftist enterprises and campaigns. In the first part of this chapter I will discuss some of the problems encountered by leftists in their dealings with notions

of "tradition," as well as the challenges solidaristic movements face on the cultural front, in industrializing societies generally and in diverse societies particularly. I then examine the complex and nuanced ways that racialized understandings of citizenship have made maintaining these collective sensibilities even more difficult in the United States. The significance of the minstrel show will be explored in an effort to understand the role race has played in shaping American popular culture, followed by a consideration of the left's influence on American popular culture stemming from the policies and artistic coalitions produced during the Popular Front. Finally, I assess these developments in light of the ironic tensions that have characterized American popular culture in the post-McCarthy era, specifically the willingness to borrow freely from and engage with reconstructed images of blackness and yet reject the possibility of racially inclusive social and political communities.

Making Modern Culture

The battle over how the different technological possibilities, created by mechanization, electrification, and the introduction of systems of mass production and communication over the last two centuries, should be incorporated into the social (re)production process has been a cultural conflict, with culture understood in both the broad and narrow senses.[1] The economic right has attempted to institutionalize the rights associated with an abstracted individualism in the process of adapting these new technologies, consequently challenging the customs that, for others, have given structure and meaning to the collective experience. These others (e.g., the various socialist, cultural preservationist, and fascist movements) have sought, in different ways and to different degrees, to maintain the occasionally idealized harmonies (e.g., understandings of family, community, and virtue) that characterized their societies before the process of industrialization began, perceiving that the promotion of this abstracted individualism would result in a widespread anomie and the institutionalization of alienation.

Throughout the world, this latter reaction has been conflicted. Historically, most European socialist and communist parties have chosen to emphasize the economic effects of industrialization and have consequently been rejected by groups concerned with the cultural implications of this process. The conventional left has often responded to the abstracted individualism of the economic right with an equally abstracted collectivism that has allowed no role for cultural considerations. In its adoption of the universalist outlook of the Enlightenment, the conventional left has ceded much of its potential agenda, accepting many of the values promoted by the forces it has sought to overturn.

A second approach, reflected to varying degrees in George Sorel's syndicalism, Benito Mussolini's fascism, and Adolf Hitler's national socialism, has traditionally emphasized the cultural realm and the importance of the *volksgeist,* to the relative exclusion of economics, thereby undercutting the appeal and long-term feasibility of its programs. Apparently neither movement has considered the potentially alienating effects and implications of the moves toward centralization and "making things big" associated with the process of industrialization. This decision not to resist the institutionalization of this anomic individualism, in all its aspects — economic, cultural, and scalar — has compromised the effectiveness of these efforts to influence the remaking of the republic. Neither the economists nor the culturalists have countered consistently the attempts of the economic right to atomize society; neither has perceived that emphasis on one realm, to the exclusion of others, has done little to challenge the potentially alienating effects of the experience of industrialization. The splitting of the left into universalizing socialists and universalizing culturalists has helped to give the economic right the space to establish its own institutions and the opportunity to universalize its own ideals (e.g., the importance of private property and the notion that labor can be legitimately understood as nothing more than an alienable commodity).

This splitting of the left — or of potentially leftist sentiment — has not prevented European societies from maintaining some collective values. Depending on the resulting class alliances, however, different patterns of state development have emerged. As Gøsta Esping-Andersen has noted, in those states in which cultural institutions such as the church were the focus of the resistance to the free market (e.g., to varying degrees, France, Italy, Germany, and Austria), corporatist welfare state provisions, typically inclusive but not particularly redistributive, have been the result. In those states in which the conventional left has had more access to the state and decision makers and in which cultural actors have had less sway (e.g., Sweden, Denmark), social democratic outcomes (e.g., comprehensive and redistributive programs) have been more likely.[2] Although the emergence of the economic right did contribute to the fragmentation of European society, a fragmentation that had begun long before the Industrial Revolution, these societies have managed to maintain a range of public goods and, as the need has arisen, to create new means of socializing the effects of industrialization. These goods have included labor movements and unions; communist, socialist, and social democratic parties; worker protection legislation; public housing and transportation schemes; health care coverage; affordable higher education; old-age security, and public safety. Moreover, significantly, these societies have maintained culture itself, in the narrow sense, as a public good.

Just as a socialized health care system can provide critical support for a certain way of life, culture, again in the narrow sense, can be approached as an institution, as a means by which the collective maintains itself, and as a medium through which new developments, technologies, and challenges are processed.[3] As with other public goods, a society's particular chosen method of developing or making culture can provide some clues as to the basic nature of the society itself.

There are three fundamental ways in which a society's methods of making culture can affect the extent to which alienation is institutionalized and the relative strengths of the right and left. In the economic realm, a society can develop its cultural institutions in such a way as either to allow individuals to exploit popular attachments to these artifacts or to socialize the material benefits of the cultural (re)production process. Second, the making of a society's culture can either promote a group's traditions or negate them by adopting new notions of how the group should identify and constitute itself. The third issue of scale is relevant in that the process of making culture can be different from the processes associated with the creation or maintenance of other public goods. Whereas many of the other conventional public goods are also susceptible to particularistic challenges (e.g., health care, education, policing), cultural production is especially prone to such challenges.[4] Thus, a society can make culture in such a way as to emphasize regional and ethnic variations, or it can choose to ignore these particularisms and promote a universal and possibly more alienated set of institutions and practices. Naturally, in all three areas — economics, culture, and scale — a society can choose a course that moderates the extremes. Given these choices, the making of culture throughout the West has increasingly tended to be a profit-driven, antitraditional, and large-scale enterprise. With each new technology, from the printing press through the microchip, given the choice between pursuing individualistic and socialistic cultural production and consumption possibilities, the tendency has been to choose the former.

Not coincidentally, the onset of industrialization led to the acceleration of the process of cultural fragmentation. The often romanticized customs that formerly gave meaning to the collective experience have become divorced from their original context to such an extent that they can no longer support a coherent worldview. As church and state, science and religion, and *homme* and *citoyen* have become separate and even opposing entities, and with the overall societal division of labor, the ability of the collective to make sense of and to process new developments and challenges has diminished.[5] The partitioning of mind, body, and soul that has marked cultural development in the West (and elsewhere) has rendered many practices and institutions — for instance, the church, leisure, music and the arts, sex, and education — that formerly constituted aspects of an integrated, multidimensional, and unified worldview into alienated rituals and anachronisms, frequently approached in terms of such unidimensional dichotomies as good and evil, weak and strong, inferior and superior.

The implications of this transition from the traditional to modern "mass culture" have been the subject of the writings of a number of theorists. For instance, the crux of Walter Benjamin's work was that this fragmentation and commodification, the making of what he called "postauratic" society, could be liberating, as mythologies would be demystified and democracy enhanced. His concern that much of the Nazis' appeal derived from Adolf Hitler's manipulation of German tradition and his invocation of an aura led Benjamin to believe that the new "technique[s] of reproduction [would] detach the reproduced object from the domain of tradition," that the application of industrial techniques to the production of culture would challenge the foundations of the Nazi movement and other regimes that used tradition in a similar manner.[6] In this spirit Orson Welles, who was responsible for the 1938 broadcast of "The War of the Worlds" and devoted to producing antifascist popular culture, contended that radio was "a popular, democratic machine for disseminating information and entertainment."[7] In contrast, Benjamin's Frankfurt school colleague Theodor Adorno contended that mass culture "assumes a malicious and miserable tone which barely and momentarily disguises itself as harsh and provocative" but ultimately encourages the perception that "nothing may exist which is not like the world as it is."[8] For Adorno, the commodification of culture and its mass production were not liberating, as earlier art forms and methods of cultural production had the potential to be, but rather symbolized compromises with the status quo.

To some degree, the Benjamin-Adorno debate paralleled the communist-fascist contest that was taking place in Europe in the interwar period. Both Frankfurt school theorists seemingly dismissed the possibility that new technologies could be adapted without rupturing the values that defined the collective. Similarly, the fascists and the communists cast the solution to the problems created by modernization and the actions of the new individualists as being either a matter of resisting exploitation in the economic realm or resisting alienation in the cultural realm. Thus the debate within the Frankfurt school was based on a false dichotomy in that the techniques of producing mass culture could have been used to perpetuate as well as further democratize traditional culture (a process that could include challenging misogynist, homophobic, and racist assumptions as well). These new technologies, then, depending on the motivations under which they were adapted, could have been used to socialize or atomize, to preserve or destroy preexisting cultures. "The way Adorno sets it up there is no way out," suggests Cornel West. Continuing, he contends: "The market itself is a crucial terrain in the struggle for nonmarket values. The opposition that is always already in the market does, in fact, have impact regarding the possibilities of alternative views, of critiques, of sustaining traditions of resistance. The market . . . is a terrain that, in its dominant form, is tilted to status quo. It is tilted to reproducing things as they are. But there are always, within the market itself, oppositional possibilities."[9]

In the economic realm, these new technologies could have been used to increase the leisure time available to all citizens as easily as they were used to heighten and institutionalize the exploitative relationship between employers and employees. Similarly, the advances made in terms of scientific knowledge could have been used to break down the barriers that separate people from one another and to make the attempts to manipulate tradition more difficult. In other words, these procedural developments could have been employed to maintain, reinforce, and restore the interactive quality on which viable and resilient cultures depend. Instead, this knowledge has been used, more often than not, to further alienate individuals from one another and from an understanding of the productive process itself.[10] Last, in terms of scale, these new technologies (e.g., video cameras) could have been used to maintain regional peculiarities as easily as they have been used to eliminate these differences.[11] These new practices, ideas, and techniques need not have been used to "make things big" and uniform; nevertheless, this has been the tendency. Altogether, the bundles of new technology that constituted "industrialization" and "modernization" need not have been used to separate the functions of employer and employee, artist and audience, and to establish cultural centers, hierarchies, and uniformities. While the possibility of adopting these new technologies without a consequent "shattering of aura" existed, the uncoordinated and inconsistent response by the two wings of the left to the efforts of the economic right contributed to the further fragmentation of the various worldviews that had previously bound Western society.

The tensions generated in the making of a society's culture have also been affected by the relative homogeneity or heterogeneity of its population. Since the Second World War many European nations have had to reconsider their conceptions of citizenship and national identity with the arrival of immigrants from other parts of Europe, Africa, Asia, and the Caribbean. Beginning with Great Britain, these societies have had to question whether their already fragmented cultural identities and often superficial corporate national identities were resilient enough to accommodate peoples from other parts of the world. The role of immigrant communities in changing the sound and look of European popular music has been one means by which the continent has been compelled to acknowledge its diversity. Another important realm is sports. The 1998 World Cup forced countries such as the Netherlands, England, and particularly France to reconcile their nativist tendencies with the reality that many of their football heroes were the children of immigrants or immigrants themselves. Accordingly, suggestions made by Jean Marie Le Pen, leader of France's xenophobic National Front, that the country's 1998 World Cup team, led by the children of Algerian, Armenian, West African, and Caribbean immigrants, was not worthy of the nation's support proved to be unpopular with his fellow citizens (especially after France's victory). That immigration has become such a potent issue in most European countries is evidence of the fragility of these various national identities.

As a result of such tensions, the making of culture in Canada, a largely immigrant society, has been a complicated process. There have been government efforts to institutionalize bilingualism across the country—for instance, Pierre Trudeau's 1969 decision to require that government services be available in the two official languages, French and English—and thereby, at least in the realm of language, to create a national culture. Accordingly, parallel French and English divisions exist within the state-owned television and radio network, the Canadian Broadcasting Corporation. At the same time, in contrast to the more corporate or melting-pot conceptions of national identity that have been propagated in other contexts, the Canadian government has offered rhetorical and financial support for multiculturalism, promoting the notion that Canada is a "community of communities." This support has undoubtedly been offered in belated recognition of the fact that immigrants to Canada have tended to retain their native cultural attachments in the New World, yet it symbolizes a marked departure from the programs pursued elsewhere. Certainly both bilingualism and multiculturalism have met resistance. Identification of French Canada with Quebec and English Canada with the rest of the country has led to less of a geographic basis and less national support for bilingualism. Similarly, as the more recent immigrants have come increasingly from non-European societies, "native" Canadians have questioned the merits of the mosaic conception.[12] Although in Canada's political culture (broadly defined) there is a common agreement that certain public goods should be provided, as a consequence of its heterogeneity it would be difficult to identify the shared cultural values (culture narrowly defined) that make Canadians unique, except for those created by cold weather, a collective tolerance of particularisms and regional ways, and, perhaps most important, a profound ambivalence toward the United States of America.

After World War I, there was an effort to create a Canadian cultural identity that led to the launching of a number of periodicals and magazines, increased popular support for Canadian writers and poets, and the paintings of the self-consciously Canadian Group of Seven. These cultural products reflected an essentially Anglo-Saxon determination to promote a Canadian sensibility distinguishable from Great Britain and did not involve, to any great extent, the other immigrant communities. This movement also failed to overcome the linguistic and cultural barriers that were only reinforced by the 1917 decision to institute a draft which would require French-speaking Canadians to serve in the war under the British flag (as would all Canadian troops).[13] As John Herd Thompson and Allen Seager suggest, "the most obvious crack in the foundation of the temple of cultural nationalism was French Canada."[14] Nevertheless, since that period there have been attempts to establish a Canadian culture, perhaps most notably with the 1968 creation of the Canadian Radio-Television Commission (CRTC) and the subsequent launching of the Maple Leaf System, which stipulated that Canadian television and radio programmers feature a certain percentage of Canadian product.[15] These movements have brought different Canadian artists to the forefront, but they have not created a dominant Canadian style or a particular cultural perspective. Some see this as a problem, fearing that the United States is exerting too strong an influence on Canadian culture; others argue that this effective cultural pluralism has been a blessing.

The making of culture in the West has been affected by the same dilemmas that have affected the making of other public goods such as the conventional left, labor unions, health care, and public policy in general. Different actors have pursued their own conceptions of the proper orientation in the economic, cultural, and scalar realms, and in those societies with heterogeneous constituencies, the making of culture has been a more challenging process. The making of culture in the United States has been similarly marked by these tensions as well as by race, an additional factor that has constituted the basis of American exceptionalism.

Defining the Boundaries of the Blackface Republic

A society's culture, way of life, worldview, artifacts, and institutions are reference points that the members of the community can use to make sense of their perceptions and experiences even as their environment is changing. To the extent that these institutions, understandings, and practices cohere and reinforce one another, a society's culture can function as an effective means of mediating change. Conversely, to the extent that these customs and artifacts lose meaning and become contradictory, a society's culture no longer functions as a map or compass by which the collective can interpret its circumstances and define its future options sensibly.

The ability of American society to generate a culture resilient enough to mediate change has been affected by the aggregate rejection of collectivism and group identities. As culture is a function of the interactions of the collective—by definition an individual cannot create or sustain a culture—the popular attachment to individualism has militated against the preservation of any cultural traditions (apart, perhaps, from those embodied in the Constitution). The demonization of collectivism and collective action that has occurred over the course of the re-making of the republic has removed one of the basic foundations of a coherent culture. Furthermore, the proponents of the individualized conception of American society have contributed to its reduction to little more than an abstracted, rhetorical entity.[16]

Similarly, while cultural traditions and "roots" have helped other societies to respond collectively to the modernization challenge, another trait that distinguishes American culture is its disavowal of any such inheritance. In other words, while a culture's survival would seem to depend on the recognition and promotion of tradition, Americanism has thrived on the eradication and repudiation of these customs and ways of life. "American nationality has always been creedal," suggests conservative columnist George Will, and the nation, he further contends, has always "aspired to be a transforming nation, severing roots and dissolving ancient manners and mentalities."[17] Consequently, there has always been the notion that the United States should be free from the "decadence" of Europe and what have been cast as the restrictive traditions of other countries.[18]

The acceptance of individualism as a cultural priority and the institutionalization of an almost nihilistic approach to the cultural practices developed in the societies from which the United States has drawn its citizens are also consequences of the heterogeneous composition of American society. In a heterogeneous society, the making of culture becomes a delicate process if the particular traditions that define different subconstituencies are to be represented and perpetuated. In fact, in a significantly heterogeneous society, a national culture cannot be made without the institutionalization of a certain degree of alienation and possibly deceit, if not outright violence. Nevertheless, just as there has been a push to make states and create political orders, there has been a push to make national cultures. The historical record in Europe and in Canada reflects the occasional inability of heterogeneous societies to reconcile the properties of identity and difference. These countries have also struggled to avoid the temptation to establish universal, normative hierarchies and exaggerated dichotomies.

As in Canada, the development of the American republic has been affected by the heterogeneity of its citizenry. As I noted in Chapter 2, much of the skirmishing that occurred in the early labor movement in the United States was due to tensions among different groups of immigrants, as well as between their "native" offspring and the Chinese, Italians, Scandinavians, and eastern Europeans who began to arrive later in the nineteenth century. The battles fought over such issues as religion and language often resulted in the reinforcement of vertical, ethnic loyalties and the weakening of potential horizontal, class identifications.

These tensions provoked demands that immigrants assimilate into American society as well as nativist movements. It was in this spirit that Theodore Roosevelt criticized German immigrants to the United States for their hyphenated Americanism. "When two flags are hoisted on the same pole, one is always hoisted undermost," argued Roosevelt. "The hyphenated American always hoists the American flag underneath. . . . German-Americans who call themselves such and who have agitated as such . . . are not Americans at all, but Germans in America."[19] Although this particular attack on the German American community was precipitated by the antagonisms associated with preparations for the First World War, it was not an isolated incident. Different forms of Know-Nothingism had emerged since the first significant non-Anglo-Saxon immigrant cohorts began arriving in the United States in the early nineteenth century.

While some of the newer Americans rejected demands that they assimilate, others in their actions effectively encouraged and reinforced the sentiments of the nativists. Argues Guido Dobbert, for example, in reference to the German community in Cincinnati, if the community "died during the [First World] war, its death was of its own making; the war served only to heighten its agony. In this sense, nativism, upon reaching its full strength at war's end, had found only a dead or dying horse to flog."[20]

The notion that immigrants to the United States should assimilate and that a failure to do so would be a sign of backwardness is expressed in the following statement by a journalist writing for the Interchurch World Movement: "The process of assimilation . . . [has] reached an advanced stage, owing to . . . [the] intelligence and progressiveness" of the Czech American population. The writer understood assimilation as "the incorporation of these people into our American population to such a degree that we are no longer able to differentiate between them and other elements . . . on the basis of nationality or race."[21] And to a large degree, this is what happened. Writing nearly sixty years later from the other side of the native-immigrant divide, Joseph Chada suggests: "With its wealth and characteristics [the Czech community] has now all but retreated into history, as have the communities of other immigrant groups. . . . The bustle and noise of its holidays and holyday celebrations or national commemorations have ceased. The air has been cleared of the aroma of spices and herbs intended to garnish the family meal."[22] Noting the effects of American life on the community, Chada proposes that some members of the community "found it difficult to retain their emotional ethnic stance or respect for their cultural heritage," choosing instead to substitute English for Czech in the home, to Americanize their religious practices and institutions, and frequently to marry outside the group.[23] Contends Chada, this "void created by . . . departures from former lifestyles, values, and ideals was eventually replaced by a combination of loyalties and practices derived from the experiences of daily life in the mainstream of economic, industrial, and technological America."[24] Thus, in contrast to the mosaic conception that has been pursued in other immigrant societies such as Canada, the melting pot has been the preferred approach, at least at the superficial level, in the United States. Whereas some societies have been built on the notion that cultural differences need not be eliminated in the pursuit of a national identity, it has been demanded of prospective American citizens that they abandon all "non-American" traits to become accepted members of the republic.[25]

The interplay of these tensions in the making of (white) American culture was evident at the turn of the century. The period between the Populist challenge and the emergence of the Progressives saw a marked revision of American cultural practices. In response to the waves of new immigrants there was a movement by "native" Americans to reinforce the preexisting political order by establishing a cultural order. Thus when the franchise was being restricted and the formal political system restructured, culture itself was being refitted to assimilate the new Americans, as well as to insulate the "native" population. The effort to create a cultural hierarchy, to distinguish highbrow, "refined" culture from lowbrow, primitive culture, was evident in the changes instituted in the presentation and production of the various public arts (e.g., opera, theater, museums, and movie houses) and the efforts to make art itself a profession. As the distinctions between performer and audience were clarified and reinforced by cultural sponsors, arts critics, and performers themselves, the ability of the masses to interact with the artists and with one another was reduced as the attempts to do so were discouraged. For instance, Lawrence Levine suggests that "nothing seems to have troubled the new arbiters of culture more than the nineteenth-century practice of spontaneous expressions of pleasure and disapproval. . . . By the middle of the twentieth century polite applause and occasional well-placed 'bravos' were all that remained." As a result, he contends, "audiences in America had become less interactive, less of a public and more of a group of mute receptors [as] art was becoming a one-way process: the artist communicating and the audience receiving." As individualism was being promoted as a value and contributed to the atomization of the political culture, "the promoters of the new high culture . . . convert[ed] audiences into a collection of people reacting *individually* rather than collectively."[26]

Defenders of the "higher" art forms perceived the increasing heterogeneity of the population as a hindrance to the creation of an aggregate American culture, given the problems involved with creating national cultural forms in an ethnically and regionally varied polity. Accordingly, noted the critic Frederick Nast in 1881, "American music cannot be expected until the present discordant elements are merged into a homogeneous people." [27] While these attempts to create harmonies or, as one music critic defined the objective in 1875, to prevent the institutionalization of an "intellectual and aesthetic communism" could only involve artifice in an increasingly heterogeneous society, the effort was nevertheless made to create a culture that could silence the voices emanating from these multiple communities of others.[28] It is in this sense that the military marches created by John Philip Sousa, one of the first significant European American cultural achievements, mirrored and reinforced larger social changes. Notes Levine, "One of the several factors underlying John Philip Sousa's importance as a cultural figure at the turn of the century was his image as an apostle of order in an unstable universe." [29] Sousa, appropriately, was also one of the main features at the Atlanta States and Cotton Exposition in 1895 at which Booker T. Washington made his classic address signaling acceptance of racial segregation. Michael Rogin suggests that a similar process of assimilation took place with regard to film audiences in the early twentieth century in which industry executives "saw themselves as transforming motion pictures from sites of class and ethnic division to arenas of modern, mass entertainment, from threats to agents of Americanization." Continuing, he argues, "The 1920s motion picture palace, with its narrativized features, live orchestral accompaniment, lavish appurtenances, and mass audiences, silenced and incorporated the participant, immigrant crowds." [30]

As the labor movement and the conventional left struggled and ultimately failed to legitimate their use of collective pronouns, tensions developed in the making of popular culture in late-nineteenth-century and early-twentieth-century America. These tensions undermined the popular ability to interpret and challenge the arguments and actions of the individualist revolutionaries. As the franchise that had been granted to all white men during the Jacksonian era was whittled down over the course of the next nine decades, the ability of Americans to summon shared cultural referents to respond to their changing circumstances was similarly diminished. As Levine suggests, Americans "in the nineteenth century . . . shared a public culture less hierarchically organized [and] less fragmented into relatively rigid adjectival boxes than their descendants were to experience a century later." [31]

That a legitimate and coherent national culture could no longer be sustained need not have been a problem, because an agreement could have been reached to respect the "right to culture" — specifically, a universal agreement to accept particular cultural attachments — to use Otto Bauer's phrase.[32] The cultural differences between Americans could have been processed in a less artificial manner and without creating dubious cultural hierarchies. This approach to making culture, though, has never been given much credence in the United States. Neither nativists or, more important, various immigrant cohorts have supported cultural pluralism (i.e., the mosaic conception).

This effort to make a national culture in a society founded by different, particular peoples is reflected in the kinds of calculations made by television programmers. In seeking not to "offend" the American viewing audience, programmers have typically avoided making reference to specific ethnic groups. It was "an unusual, even risky move," suggested a television critic, for CBS to air *Brooklyn Bridge,* a series about a Jewish family living in Brooklyn in the 1950s, "because the show was so specific to New York and so centered in urban ethnic culture." The show that, in the producer's words, would be "very ethnic . . . [one] where Jewish people are Jewish and Irish people are Catholic," might have, the critic suggested, "alienate[d] some viewers in other parts of the country."[33] Similarly, the comic and actor Jackie Mason complained, after the cancellation of his similarly particularistic ABC series *Chicken Soup,* about the perspective that programs had to be made to "appeal to the whole country."[34] Referring to the possible implications of making culture in a heterogeneous society, one critic suggests: "In a homogeneous society the artist has only to contend with one set of prejudices. . . . Though his instincts, opinions and judgements often add up to bias, to the artist himself they may be the driving forces of his creativity. What really limits and devitalizes art are not the artist's prejudices but his audience's prejudices, of which in a vast heterogeneous society like the United States there is an almost infinite variety. The artist has trouble enough with one censor. When he has twenty, his art becomes a day-to-day accommodation."[35] This need to appeal to the whole country by playing to the lowest common denominator has encouraged members of different ethnic groups to remake themselves to assimilate into the mold prescribed by the nativists (and for film and television it has meant the underrepresentation of African Americans and the virtual absence of Native Americans, Hispanics, and Asian Americans). As a consequence, sensing that "ethnic" names might not play well in middle America, the country singer Loretta Lynn felt comfortable enough while campaigning with George Bush in 1988 to make light of the possibility that a "Doo-kaw-kis," emphasizing the Democratic challenger Michael Dukakis's Greek background, could be elected to the presidency. Similar pressures have encouraged actors and singers, as they have other individuals, to change their names (e.g., Mladen Sekulovich to Karl Malden, Robert Zimmerman to Bob Dylan) — and occasionally their features — to obliterate any particular traits that might prevent their reaching the widest audience possible.

The gap between the rhetoric of the melting pot and the realities that have resulted in the prioritization of certain ethnic identities and the rejection of others is illustrated by the tension between Ronald Reagan's pronouncement that "anyone can come to America, and anyone can be an American," and the statement by a prospective voter during the 1992 New Hampshire Democratic primary regarding presidential hopeful Paul Tsongas: "I just wish he had a name like Smith."[36]

Many of these tensions occurred in the process of making Canada as well. The heterogeneity of Canada's population contributed to the left's inability to mount a sustained resistance to the economic right and its attempts to commodify labor and laborers. And although nativist sentiment never reached the level it did in the United States, there were similar attempts to reduce immigration and hasten the assimilation of foreigners. Accordingly, J. S. Woodsworth, one of the early leaders of the Co-operative Commonwealth Federation (predecessor of the social democratic New Democratic Party), initially was drawn to public life and formal politics by his concerns about the nature of the immigrants entering Canada in the early twentieth century. As in the United States, there was some acceptance among immigrants of the values of Canadian mainstream culture, despite its vagueness. What has differentiated the Canadian experience from the American is that, in the American instance, the legitimacy and significance of these conflicts, as well as the ability and willingness of particular ethnic groups to resist the push toward universalization, the flattening of cultural diversity, and the avoidance of cultural specificity, were undercut by a particularly attractive conception of whiteness. Although anti-Indian (e.g., aboriginal or "First Nations" peoples), anti-Asian (e.g., in British Columbia), and antiblack (e.g., in the Maritimes and southern Ontario) notions of whiteness have emerged throughout Canadian history, these sensibilities have never been as pervasive or systematically codified as they have been in the United States. Making a white people and a white culture in the United States has encouraged the downplaying and dismissal of the particular identities, customs, and practices that defined these immigrants on their arrival. The popular Manichean view of the opposition between white and black in the United States has contributed to the dissolution of the various European cultures and the anomic character of American culture.[37] "Even in an all-white town, race was never absent," recollects David Roediger. "I learned absolutely no lore of my German ancestry and more than a few meaningless snatches of Irish songs, but missed little of racist folklore."[38] Similarly, in *How the Irish Became White*, Noel Ignatiev describes the process by which "the Catholic Irish, an oppressed race in Ireland, became part of an oppressing race in America" and how "in becoming white the Irish ceased to be Green."[39]

This achievement of identity through negation (anti–Old World, antiblack) has had its ironic aspects. While blacks have often functioned as the equivalent of the Antichrist in American life, black styles, language, and culture or, to be more accurate, white views thereof have been used as media through which Americans have confronted their fears and confusions.[40] In other words, they have been used effectively as a substitute culture, as a shared heritage of sorts through which non-black Americans can grapple with their changing circumstances.

The first significant manifestation of this inclination was the minstrel show. Notes Robert C. Toll, as a consequence of the first efforts to remake the republic culturally and economically, Americans "desperately needed amusements that spoke to them in terms they could understand and enjoy, that affirmed their worth and gave them dignity. They needed a substitute for their folk culture— something that could establish a new sense of community and identity for them and their neighbors."[41] This need for an identity that was "anti-European, and . . . [that] white 'common men' could all unite around" provided the minstrels with an opening through which they could insinuate themselves into the emerging popular culture.[42] Accordingly, Mark Twain would observe after the heyday of minstrelsy, "If I could have the nigger show [i.e., the minstrel show] back again in its pristine purity . . . I should have but little further use for opera."[43]

Although blackface performances had been common since the turn of the century, especially in the South and Midwest, it was not until the 1840s that minstrel shows became the predominant form of American entertainment. The first minstrel troupes actually developed in New York City (Christy's Minstrels) and Boston (Ordway's Aeolians), and it was in the North that the genre was particularly popular. Like any effective medium of popular culture, the minstrel shows, with their stock characters such as Zip Coon (city dandy) and Jim Crow (country bumpkin), were a means by which the masses could address and process, or seek to escape, the pressing issues of the day. Populist and antielitist in tone, at the peak of its popularity minstrelsy was closely tied to the spirit of Jacksonian America and to the Democratic Party (nonpartisan minstrel shows would not become conceivable until after the Civil War, given the association of the Republican Party with abolitionism and the anti-Whiggish orientation embedded in the medium).[44] As a consequence, the rituals allowed commentary on issues such as immigration (German, Irish, Chinese, Japanese); the American Indian question; the effects of modern, urban life on the society's moral traditions; and the challenge women presented to male status, as well as the expression of a cloaked and occasionally not-so-subtle homoeroticism (suggests Eric Lott, "White male desire for black men was everywhere to be found in minstrel shows").[45] The shows' spontaneity and immediacy gave Americans an opportunity to "work out their feelings about even the most sensitive and volatile issues."[46] Given the onslaught of new information and the rapidly changing circumstances northerners were facing in this era, the minstrel shows also functioned as a means of escape, as a nostalgic exercise through which American whites could evoke a more rewarding past.[47]

Performances not only explored and celebrated a more certain past but also functioned as a means by which whites could deal with their feelings toward blacks. As a people unsure of their present circumstances, a people whose basic citizenship was being challenged by the rising propertied class, as well as the immigrant "hordes," the degradation of blacks encouraged by such unbounded public communions gave these restless classes some status. If the remaking of the republic involved the creation of a hierarchy, minstrel shows reassured whites that they, at least, were not at the bottom. Minstrelsy, then, was both egalitarian in its criticism of the emerging social order yet desperately racist (and sexist), because it mirrored the frustrations and insecurities of its audience and its performers. As such, it embodied, quite accurately, the compromises made by many white Americans in their attempts to come to terms with their changing environment. By asserting that blacks were fundamentally foolish, inferior beings, minstrelsy also allowed whites throughout the country to square the circle, to reconcile slavery with the ideals expressed in the Constitution and the Bill of Rights. The values expressed in the minstrel shows were the cultural counterparts of those expressed by white labor in its hesitant republicanism, in its fundamentally conflicted search for identity.

The minstrel tradition, the use of blackface, and the assumption of what were perceived to be black mannerisms lasted well into the twentieth century and became means by which formerly excluded groups could make the transition into whiteness. Michael Rogin suggests that "by the turn of the twentieth century Jewish entertainers were the major blackface performers" and that the combination of the new medium of film and "motion picture blackface . . . by joining structural domination to cultural desire . . . moved . . . ethnics into the melting pot by keeping racial groups out."[48] From Al Jolson's starring role in the first talking picture, *The Jazz Singer* (1927), through the beatniks and the hippies, *Amos 'n' Andy,* rock 'n' roll, and, more recently, such acts as New Kids On the Block, Vanilla Ice, a group of "white" youths who actually called themselves the Young Black Teenagers ("black is an attitude"), and Macomb County, Michigan, native Eminem, American popular culture has continued to draw its sustenance from black folkways.[49] Asked one writer in 1845 in the *Knickerbocker Magazine,* "Who are our true rulers? The Negro poets, to be sure. Do they not set the fashion, and give laws to the public taste?"[50] In Norman Mailer's hands, this becomes a desire for the life of "the Negro hipster," his life "in the enormous present . . .

[the] Saturday-night kicks . . . [and the ability to relinquish] the pleasures of the mind for the more obligatory pleasures of the body." And as Jack Kerouac was moved to lament, "the best the 'white world' [had] . . . to offer was not enough ecstasy . . . not enough life, joy, kicks [nor] music" and wish that he could "exchange worlds with the happy, true-minded, ecstatic Negroes of America . . . [and be] anything but . . . [himself], so pale and unhappy, so dim." [51] In Kerouac's longings and Mailer's suggestions clearly lies a certain degree of positive identification with "blackness," but ultimately their views are quite consistent with the complex combination of transgression and containment that Eric Lott contends characterized blackface minstrelsy.[52] In other words, while these creations often involved explicit challenges to social norms and conventions and occasionally featured sympathetic renderings of Negro life, they ultimately were founded in and upheld existing and racist attitudes toward African Americans.

Ballads for Americans: Labor on the Cultural Front

Despite the broad acceptance of blackface artistry and the extent to which the medium's acceptance prevented the development of the solidaristic understandings that might have supported challenges to the economic status quo, leftist-influenced cultural creations and alliances have had an influence on American popular culture. This effect was greatest during the Popular and Democratic Fronts, the high point of leftist influence and the CPUSA's attempts to form alliances with progressive forces such as organized labor (particularly the CIO), the liberal wing of the Democratic Party, and the civil rights movement in the 1930s and 1940s.

Michael Denning has argued convincingly that the left's influence on American popular culture in this period should not be limited to a study of the CPUSA and the involvement of a number of creative artists with the party but should also include those individuals who were not formally involved with the party—or the New Deal Democrats—but through their work and gestures indicated their support for the broad ideals of the "cultural front": the promotion of the goals of organized labor, antifascism, ethnic inclusiveness, and antiracism. Denning also suggests that this movement, largely spearheaded by "fellow travelers" rather than "card-carrying members" of the Communist Party, survived the McCarthy era and the cold war; indeed, the efforts of artists in the 1930s to sustain a "structure of feeling"—Raymond Williams's term—that was supportive of working-class concerns could still be observed into the 1970s and afterward (e.g., in such films as *Norma Rae, Sounder, The Molly Maguires, Serpico, M.A.S.H.,* and *Reds*). Denning's liberation of progressive creative artists from the circumstances of the

Communist Party is important, as is his claim that the study of the left in general, including the cultural arena, needs to move beyond the member/nonmember dialectic. This second argument is significant given that various artists left the party (e.g., Howard Fast, Richard Wright, and Elia Kazan) because of its abrupt policy changes and revelations concerning Stalin's pogroms but still continued to identify themselves with the broader Popular Front movement and produce art consistent with the Front's concerns.[53]

Despite the efforts of the Progressives to institutionalize protections for a narrow conception of whiteness (i.e., literacy tests, reform initiatives that were partly energized by nativist sentiment), the New Deal coalition forged in the 1928 to 1936 period "brought the immigrant to the center of American politics," and the cultural creations of the subsequent decades promoted what Denning terms a "working-class ethnic Americanism."[54] Much of the latter activity was made possible by the support offered to artists in programs sponsored by the Works Progress Administration (WPA), as the depression itself, by creating a sense of crisis, encouraged Americans to recognize the common bonds that united them, a process that was only accelerated by the preparations for and entry into the Second World War. In this context the left was able to ally itself with liberals and progressive institutions and exert a remarkable influence on the substance of American popular culture. The artistic efforts characteristic of this era include John Dos Passos's *U.S.A.* (1938), John Steinbeck's *The Grapes of Wrath* (1939), Charlie Chaplin's work in *Modern Times* (1936) and *The Great Dictator* (1940), Orson Welles's portrait of newspaper baron William Randolph Hearst in *Citizen Kane* (1941), modernist classical composer Aaron Copland's *Lincoln Portrait* (1942) and *Fanfare for the Common Man* (1943), Frank Sinatra's 1945 recording of "The House I Live In," the comedy of Zero Mostel, and the folk recordings of Woody Guthrie. Other artists who supported Popular Front causes include the musicians Benny Goodman and Artie Shaw and the writers who launched their careers in magazines such as *New Masses* and developed their literary skills in activities and productions supported by WPA funds.

These artists and their productions were often closely linked with the labor movement and its activities, particularly the CIO. The attempts to organize industrial unions were supported by the conscious creative efforts of these individuals and through public appearances and speeches. For example, the 1930s campaign to organize farmworkers in California who were primarily Mexican, Filipino, Chinese, and transplanted migrants from southwestern Dust Bowl states such as Oklahoma was supported by Welles, actor Will Geer, and Mexican Americans Rita Hayworth and Anthony Quinn, leading eventually to the formation of the United Cannery, Agricultural, Packing, and Allied Workers of America

(UCAPAWA) in 1937. The dramatization of the circumstances of these workers in Steinbeck's *The Grapes of Wrath* and the recordings of Woody Guthrie (e.g., "Tom Joad" from his *Dust Bowl Ballads* album) helped bring wider attention to labor's issues. A similar coalition, involving actors, writers, and such organizations as El Congreso del Pueblo de Habla Española, would develop in support of the seventeen Mexican Americans arrested for murder in the Sleepy Lagoon case of 1942.[55] Overall, during the late 1930s and early 1940s, West Coast Popular Front causes and creations helped bring together a range of labor activists and the emerging left-liberal Hollywood community at a time when nativist concerns were shifting toward Mexican Americans.[56]

Similar coalitions were attempted, primarily on the East Coast, involving organized labor, left-leaning artists, and African Americans. The Sleepy Lagoon incident, of course, had its counterpart in the Scottsboro Boys case for which significant legal support was provided by black CPUSA members Benjamin Davis and William Patterson. The National Negro Congress, launched in 1936, played a role for blacks vis-à-vis Front activities similar to that played by El Congreso for Hispanics and the American Slav Congress for eastern Europeans. The successful campaign by Ben Davis, a Harvard law school graduate, for the New York City council seat vacated by Adam Clayton Powell Jr. in 1943 also provided Popular Front forces with a useful focal point and a means of mobilizing leftists and civil rights constituencies toward a common, labor-oriented agenda. Davis's campaigns in 1943 and 1945 (when he was reelected) drew support from musicians such as Count Basie, Duke Ellington, Leonard Bernstein, Lena Horne, Teddy Wilson, Hazel Scott, Billie Holiday, Ella Fitzgerald, Coleman Hawkins, folksinger Josh White, and Paul Robeson, one of the candidate's closest friends. Such actors as Rex Ingram, Canada Lee (one of the stars of *Body and Soul* [1947]), Will Geer, and José Ferrer also endorsed Davis, as did the writers Jerome Robbins and Langston Hughes, the boxer Joe Louis, and Powell himself.[57] Other events associated with the movement featured jazz musicians Dizzy Gillespie, Charlie Parker, Sidney Bechet, Benny Carter, Miles Davis, and Fletcher Henderson, as Front-affiliated groups helped launch the acting careers of Sidney Poitier, Ruby Dee, Ossie Davis, and Harry Belafonte.

Reflecting the willingness of Front-affiliated artists to challenge the racial status quo consciously, Orson Welles's Mercury Theatre group presented an all-black production of *MacBeth* and a stage version of Richard Wright's *Native Son,* and Welles developed a film project with Wright and Duke Ellington (which was never completed). Similarly, the Café Society Downtown, a Greenwich Village club managed by white leftists such as Barney Josephson, sponsored events and programs with the intent of bridging the racial divide. It was in 1939 at Café So-

ciety that Billie Holiday first performed what was to become one of her signa-
ture tunes, "Strange Fruit" — "Southern trees bear a strange fruit, blood on the
leaves, blood at the root, black bodies swinging in the Southern breeze, strange
fruit hanging from the poplar trees" — a critique of lynching that was written by
the communist schoolteacher Lewis Allan (aka Abel Meeropol). In this period,
one of the club's main supporters, producer, talent scout, and Front member John
Hammond, would record jazz artists such as Benny Goodman and Count Basie,
arrange racially integrated studio sessions, write for *New Masses,* and coordinate benefits for various Front causes (e.g., the Scottsboro Boys). Duke Ellington's
Jump for Joy, including "I Got It Bad (And That Ain't Good)," and Count Basie's
"It's the Same Old South" ("where the bloodhounds that once chased Liza, chase
a poor CIO organizer"), featuring the vocals of Jimmy Rushing, were also products of this era and the general attempt by artists and activists to challenge the
prevailing racial and economic status quos (separately or together).[58] Perhaps the
high point in terms of the achievements of the cultural face of the Popular Front
was Paul Robeson's triumphant return to the center stage of American life in late
autumn of 1939 after an extended stay in England (where he was personally affected by his encounters with the struggles of organized labor). His performance
of Earl Robinson's "Ballad for Americans" (originally "Ballad for Uncle Sam") on
CBS radio on the evening of November 5 (a performance that was repeated on
New Year's Eve that same year) captured the spirit of the Popular Front in terms
of its effort to engage Americans yet provoke them to reexamine the nation's
basic values and commitments. In light of Mark Naison's argument that "no cultural figure in modern American history, with the possible exception of Woody
Guthrie, so completely identified his life and art with the fate of American labor"
as did Robeson, the significance of his acceptance by a broad spectrum of Americans becomes even greater.[59] The subsequent recording of the song by Robeson
proved to be immensely popular at a time when the country was caught up in a
groundswell of patriotic self-celebration. Other hits in this period included "I'm a
Yank Full of Happiness," "Defend Your Country," and "I'm an American." At the
Democratic Party's convention in 1940, the theme song was Irving Berlin's "God
Bless America," and only because Robeson was unavailable, the GOP's gathering
featured Ray Middleton singing "Ballad for Uncle Sam" (Woody Guthrie wrote
"This Land Is Your Land" in response to this outbreak of patriotism and specifi-
cally in response to the blandishments espoused in Berlin's "God Bless America").

These victories on the cultural front, though, were always qualified. The same
compromises integral to the CPUSA's strategies during the Browder era of the
late 1930s — the efforts to bridge communism and Americanism and the consequent willingness to advocate no-strike policies during the war, to urge a go-slow

approach to civil rights, to support Japanese internment and suspend Japanese American party members—were also reflected in the activities of the Popular Front. Accordingly, Robeson's "Ballad," which references a range of freedom struggles beginning with the Revolutionary War, is ultimately an awkward attempt to reconcile the ideals and the realities embodied in American history. The song "does not attempt to resolve the history of conflict it narrates," suggests Hazel Carby. "On the contrary, it concludes that the struggle to found an equitable nation continues."[60] Similarly, another high point in terms of Popular Front cultural influence, the success of Orson Welles's *Citizen Kane,* reflects the same fundamental ambivalence as evidenced in its treatment of the main character, Charles Foster Kane, as portrayed by Welles himself (and clearly modeled on William Randolph Hearst).[61] While the movie graphically details the protagonist's excesses, self-absorption, and near fascist pretensions, the movie's critique is ultimately undercut by its occasionally sympathetic rendering of Kane's struggles and the romantic depiction of his childhood separation from his mother and boyhood. Although the film was certainly a great artistic and dramatic achievement (indeed it was the twenty-five-year-old Welles's directorial debut), the decision to anchor the story in an "auratic" narrative of American innocence lost was at tension with the broader Popular Front desire to challenge prevailing understandings of class and status (and it represented an incomplete bridging of the Benjamin-Adorno divide). In other words, faced with the real dilemma of how best to engage Americans in order to challenge their assumptions, Popular Front productions often tended to accomplish the former at the expense of the latter. The Popular Front was also relatively silent on some of the major issues that would define American politics (and popular culture) in the postwar era, specifically gender and sexuality. If anything, the cultural productions of the era characteristically revealed a certain anxiety about these realms. This anxiety perhaps reflects the historical linkage of gender issues to concerns regarding race (in other words, the likelihood that a racial "revolution"—e.g., the abolitionist and civil rights movements—would have to precede progress on the gender front); the highly charged debates about lynching, which provided incentives for progressive activists to avoid acknowledging "the sexual mountain," to use Calvin Hernton's term; and, from a broader perspective, the generally antifeminist politics that prevailed, across the political spectrum and throughout the West, in the period between the wars.[62] Betty Friedan's launching of second-wave feminism in the 1960s might then be understood as a response to her experiences as an organizer and journalist with the *Federated Press,* a leftist publication, and as a participant in the Popular Front and its lack of attention to issues of gender.[63]

With regard to race, the story of the Popular Front and its cultural ramifications is complicated. The broader movement certainly encouraged more ethnically inclusive and cross-racial encounters and coalitions than were characteristic of the "outside world." In this spirit, Billie Holiday speaks of Orson Welles, a frequent visitor to Café Society, in glowing terms: "He's a fine cat—probably the finest I ever met. And a talented cat. But more than that, he's fine people." [64] The marriage of Mexican American activist Josephina Fierro de Bright to leftist screenwriter John Bright (coauthor of *The Public Enemy*) is also symbolic of the kinds of bonds that were established in this period across cultural lines. The warmth with which the author Howard Fast describes his dealings with Paul Robeson is yet another example. The strength and durability of some of these linkages is evident in actress Ruby Dee's explanation for her support for Ethel and Julius Rosenberg in the early 1950s: "I was aware of so many instances when Jews had joined in our Struggle for justice, protesting the persecution and the murder of blacks. My deeper self felt an obligation here." [65]

Despite these commitments across lines of ethnicity and race, the cultural left's efforts to combine antiracism and class consciousness did encounter some problems. One major issue (which I discussed in Chapter 3) was the question of agency and specifically the extent to which blacks, Hispanics, and Asians participated in Popular Front productions as creative forces or merely as actors in a story scripted by others. For instance, Denning notes, "Most critics and historians have seen Café Society as a marriage of convenience between radical white entrepreneurs like [Barney] Josephson and [John] Hammond and apolitical black musicians." [66] In this context, Billie Holiday's role in the creation and recording of "Strange Fruit" is often cited as an example of black artists simply taking their cues from others (in this case Josephson, the club's manager, and Lewis Allan, the song's composer), although this interpretation of Holiday's contribution to the overall project has been challenged. [67] "Most of the Negro intellectuals," Claude McKay would write in 1940, "were directly or indirectly hypnotized by the propaganda of the Popular Front." [68] This debate about the relative autonomy and agency of blacks within the movement would, of course, be one of the central concerns of Harold Cruse's controversial 1968 publication *The Crisis of the Negro Intellectual*.

The CPUSA's initial reluctance to consider certain forms of cultural expression as progressive was also a source of conflict. For example, at the beginning of the 1930s the official party position was that useful, black art had to be specifically protest-oriented and that efforts to produce marketable, commercial cultural goods were to be criticized and dismissed as "bourgeois and decadent." [69] Furthermore, a conception of authenticity was advanced that tended to emphasize folk and blues artists (e.g., Josh White) and disregard jazz musicians. This was not purely a black versus white issue. For example, Paul Robeson, although never a party member but certainly a central figure throughout the period in leftist circles, felt that jazz "reflect[ed] Broadway, not the Negro" and that it was not "the honest and sincere folk-song in character [nor] genuine negro music."[70] Over time, the left's attitude toward jazz would soften. The CPUSA, partly as a reflection of its desire to create a broad, inclusive coalition of black organizations during the latter part of the 1930s, "began to speak of the black arts (with the exception of vaudeville and musical comedy with sexually explicit themes) as politically 'progressive,' in and of themselves."[71] Robeson regularly attended jazz shows at the Apollo in Harlem and at Café Society Downtown during the 1940s; formed friendships with musicians, including Dizzy Gillespie; and in 1958 commented, "For my money, modern jazz is one of the most important musical things there is in the world."[72]

Internal conflicts aside, the left's successes on the cultural front, as elsewhere, were obviously affected by the Red scare that occurred after the Second World War. Although Denning is correct in his assertion that the "laboring" of American popular culture which took place in the 1930s and 1940s outlasted the CPUSA and survived McCarthyism to some extent, the influence of Popular Front artists was nevertheless dramatically reduced by the domestic unfolding of the cold war. The atmosphere created by the HUAC investigations had a particularly significant effect on Hollywood and the film industry. While individuals such as Orson Welles and Charlie Chaplin simply went into exile, others, most notably the director and former CPUSA member Elia Kazan, testified and "named names" before Congress.[73] The changing context also elevated the actor Ronald Reagan, who played a major role in this period as president of the actors' union, the Screen Actors Guild, and as a source of information for the Federal Bureau of Investigation (FBI); indeed, the Red scare raised the public profile of the two dominant personalities in Republican politics in the second half of the twentieth century, Reagan and California congressman Richard Nixon. As a result of these developments, many of those associated with the Popular Front found themselves blacklisted: Welles, Leonard Bernstein, Aaron Copland, John Garfield, Will Geer, José Ferrer, Ruth Gordon, Uta Hagen, Dashiell Hammett, Burl Ives, Burgess Meredith, Arthur Miller, Arnold Perl, Earl Robinson, Edward G. Robinson, Pete Seeger, Artie Shaw, Sam Wanamaker, Zero Mostel, the director Martin Ritt, and the screenwriters Arthur Laurents and Howard Fast, among others.[74] Fast's unsuccessful efforts in 1951 to secure a contract for his novel *Spartacus* because of the pressure put on the major presses by J. Edgar Hoover and the FBI is an indication of the impact of McCarthyism on the publishing industry.[75]

Because few blacks had established careers in the film industry and Broadway, in contrast to Hollywood, was less affected by the HUAC investigations and the general panic that ensued because its gatekeepers were more willing to resist the tide, the impact of the Red scare on black actors and creative artists was different.[76] Nevertheless, this resistance did not extend to television and radio, where blacklisting occurred and black artists were beginning to make inroads. Furthermore, one of the focal points of the McCarthy investigations was the actor and singer Paul Robeson, and attempts to isolate the activist forced a number of black artists to make difficult choices as well. Robeson's emergence as one of the central personalities in the McCarthy era—Ossie Davis suggests that he "was America's question mark"—was a reflection of his willingness in the 1940s to identify himself not only with the Popular Front but also with the Soviet Union (an identification so strong in the latter case that he apparently was willing to overlook the anti-Semitic purges taking place in Stalin's Russia).[77] For most of the 1940s, Robeson neglected his artistic career in favor of his political concerns, a decision that certainly cost him financially.

The contrasting popular responses to Robeson's activities are symbolized by the extremely warm reception accorded his performance of "Ballad for Americans" in 1939 and the reaction to his speech in April 1949 in Paris at the Congress of the World Partisans of Peace. Whereas "Ballad" was read as a celebration of the United States and American history, the Paris address, in which he contended that blacks would not "make war on anyone . . . [and would] not make war on the Soviet Union," was interpreted as seditious in the context of the cold war. Although Robeson received support from W. E. B. Du Bois (who, along with Pablo Picasso, had been in attendance at the Paris conference) and the first-wave feminist and civil rights icon Mary Church Terrell, these gestures were lost in the swell of voices attacking Robeson's speech (or at least the version of it that was reported in the American press). Jackie Robinson, who had broken the color line in baseball in 1947 (perhaps ironically just two years after Robeson and others had spoken to a meeting of club owners in support of integrating the sport), was only the most prominent black to speak out against Robeson—he called Robeson's comments "silly"—before the House Un-American Activities Committee.[78] After making an initial statement in response to a request from the State Department affirming the loyalty and "Americanness" of blacks, the NAACP's Walter White wrote an article for *Ebony* magazine entitled "The Strange Case of Paul Robeson" which questioned Robeson's devotion to African Americans, suggested that he might be too wealthy to understand the circumstances of blacks, and implied that he might suffer from paranoia. More predictable criticisms surfaced in articles written by Roy Wilkins for the NAACP's publication *Crisis* and in statements issued by A. Philip Randolph (who, despite his socialist leanings in the 1920s, had become a reliable anti-Communist), Charles H. Houston, Mary

McLeod Bethune, the boxer Sugar Ray Robinson, and Adam Clayton Powell Jr., among others.[79] Many of these statements were the orchestrated result of a meeting convened by A. Philip Randolph, at Roy Wilkins's request, concerning the appropriate response by the civil rights establishment to Robeson's declaration.

Given the publicity accorded Robeson's comments and the suspicion in some quarters that he had been at least partially correct in his assertion that blacks might be hesitant to volunteer to fight for a country that refused them basic civil rights, a number of prominent blacks in the entertainment industry were invited to testify in front of HUAC. Hazel Scott, a singer who had launched her career at Café Society and had become Adam Clayton Powell's second wife in 1945, was encouraged by her husband, by that point Harlem's representative in the House, to appear before the committee. Stating that she was "not ready to hand over America's entertainment industry to Moscow," Scott urged that the "entertainment unions should oust any Communist member." At the same time, she did ask the committee to "protect those Americans who have honestly, wholesomely, and unselfishly tried to protect [the United States] . . . and make the guarantees in . . . [the] Constitution live."[80] Josh White, a friend of Robeson's — indeed, in tears, he told Robeson beforehand that he felt that he had no choice but to testify — appeared before Congress and expressed his disappointment with Robeson's activities and declared his own willingness "to fight Russia or any enemy of America."[81] He subsequently wrote an article for *Negro Digest* under the title "I Was a Sucker for the Communists." When Duke Ellington was facing similar pressures — he was supposed to have signed the Stockholm Peace Petition — he defended himself by stating that "movements of a political nature . . . any kind but orchestral movements — have never been part of my life. . . . The only 'communism' I know of . . . is that of Jesus Christ."[82]

The response of some black artists to the Red scare and the nature of their HUAC testimonies reinforced the notion that the Communist Party was manipulating naïve and innocent blacks and brought the issue of agency back to the surface. Hazel Scott claimed that Café Society's Barney Josephson had required her to perform at a Ben Davis campaign event; Josh White suggested that it was his ignorance regarding politics that had led him into communist circles. As the actor Ossie Davis has recently recollected, "There was Langston Hughes, who had to publicly eat his previous words to square himself with the House Committee; there was Josh White; and there was Canada Lee, who couldn't find a job anywhere and died of a broken heart. Some of these black heroes had to publicly attack Paul Robeson, or at least swear that Paul had duped them."[83] Despite their testimonies, Scott, White, Hughes, and Lee were blacklisted (or remained blacklisted). Such others as Lena Horne and Ruby Dee who did not cooperate were listed in the 1950 publication *Red Channels,* which identified those individuals in the radio and television industries suspected of being communists (or "fellow travelers").[84]

Geography and Context: Making the Bigger Picture

Although the Popular Front era did produce significant victories for the left in the cultural arena, the ease with which the Red scare shattered the progressive cultural alliance that had formed in the 1930s suggests that the movement had only a tenuous grip on the imagination of American mainstream audiences. The achievements of the Popular Front also need to be placed in a broader geographic context. As Denning observes, "As with many American social movements, the strength of the Popular Front was regional and local, rooted in particular cities and industrial towns."[85] The cultural impact of the Popular Front was still more restricted, even if one factors in the disproportionate influence of the cultural industries in New York and Los Angeles on the rest of the country's consumption habits.

Efforts to challenge the racial status quo faced the problem of producing progressive art in a context which demanded that blacks be portrayed stereotypically, if at all. Beyond the issue of creative skill—as Duke Ellington observed, making "a statement of social protest . . . without saying it" requires a "real craftsman"—there was the reality that attempts to challenge the racial status quo were rarely appreciated and were perceived to be unmarketable.[86] "*Jump for Joy* provided quite a few problems," noted Ellington with regard to his own efforts in this area. "There was the first and greatest problem of trying to give an American audience entertainment without compromising the dignity of the Negro people. Needless to say, this is the problem every Negro artist faces. He runs afoul of offensive stereotypes, instilled in the American mind by whole centuries of ridicule and derogation. The American audience has been taught to expect a Negro on the stage to clown and 'Uncle Tom,' that is, to enact the role of a servile, yet lovable, inferior."[87] Although Holiday's "Strange Fruit" represents one of her greatest artistic achievements—Angela Davis suggests "her performance of the song . . . almost singlehandedly changed the politics of American popular culture"—its making also reflected some of the obstacles, socially constructed and self-imposed, facing racially progressive artists at the time.[88] Holiday, herself, was reluctant to perform the song, "thought it was a mistake" and expected that "people would hate it."[89] Indeed, she rarely performed the song in the South— "I didn't want to start anything I couldn't finish"—and her label, Brunswick, declined to release the song because according to the company's executives, "They won't buy [the record] in the South . . . [and] we'll be boycotted . . . [because] it's too inflammatory."[90] For similar reasons, Columbia was anxious about the reaction to the 1940 Josh White release *Chain Gang*.

Although the southern market was relatively small when viewed from a national perspective and certainly from an international perspective, the effect of these fears and calculations was to restrict black artists to unchallenging roles which reinforced the prevailing racial understandings (e.g., Stepin Fetchit and Butterfly McQueen) or which simply rendered them invisible, as was the usual outcome in terms of the film industry. The few films that did feature African Americans in nonstereotypical roles were banned from southern theaters or edited so as to remove the offending scenes. Consequently, Hazel Scott's performance of "The Man I Love" was excised from Warner Brothers's 1945 release *Rhapsody in Blue* to satisfy southern censors, and as Donald Bogle notes, Lena Horne's films "were constructed so that Horne's scenes could be cut when the movies were shown in the South."[91] The most powerful of these gatekeepers was Lloyd T. Binford, the son of a slaveowner and the head of Memphis's Board of Censors from 1928 to 1955. Binford's views were so influential that the film studios used his tastes as an indicator of the likely response throughout the South; a movie that had been recut to satisfy southern preferences was described within industry circles as having been "binfordized." Suggests Robert Gordon, Binford "forbade anything portraying blacks on a social level equal to whites" as well as other films whose politics or aesthetics he found disturbing (e.g., Charlie Chaplin's work).[92] Besides guaranteeing that southern audiences were not likely to see Lena Horne in southern theaters, Binford banned the musical *Annie Get Your Gun* because it had a Negro railroad conductor ("We don't have any Negro conductors in the South. Of course it can't show here. It's social equality in action.") and *Brewster's Millions* because one of its stars, the black actor Eddie "Rochester" Anderson, had "too familiar a way about him, and the picture presents too much racial mixture."[93]

The Popular Front's efforts to promote popular culture that supported the broad goals of the working classes and racial inclusiveness must be assessed, then, against the backdrop of the wider environment in which many of these products were either never seen or edited in such a way that their progressive impulses, which in the case of race relations were usually quite mild, were undermined. Indeed, the most popular films of the first half of the twentieth century either reinforced the racial codes that had been established during the minstrel era—*The Jazz Singer* and *Gone with the Wind*—or sought to revise these understandings in ways that were even more problematic, for instance, D. W. Griffith's celebration of the Ku Klux Klan, *Birth of a Nation*, which, among other things, made the argument that any liberalization on the racial front would put white southern womanhood at risk.

The Office of War Information (OWI), established in the summer of 1942, was one significant arena in which many of these conflicts regarding class, gender, ethnicity, and race were, if not exactly resolved, at least engaged. Given OWI's mandate to provide information that was supportive of American interests abroad and would aid in the mobilization of domestic support, it was inevitable that it would have to reckon with some of the same tensions and conflicts faced by the Popular Front. Indeed, some degree of overlap existed between the two: OWI defined its mission in rather liberal, New Dealist terms, and such Front members as Howard Fast and Archibald MacLeish worked for the government agency. One of the major concerns about war propaganda was the film industry.

Attempts by outside actors and interest groups to influence the content of films were not unprecedented. Although civil rights groups were unable to block the release of Griffith's *Birth of a Nation* in 1915, they were able to prevent its screening in some cities.[94] The 1935 Warner Brothers release *Black Fury,* about the struggles of coal mine workers, was rewritten in response to complaints from the National Coal Association. A copy of the script for a 1938 movie, Metro Goldwyn Mayer's (MGM's) *Idiot's Delight,* based on an antifascist play written by Robert Sherwood (who would later work with OWI), was sent to Benito Mussolini for approval. Indeed, Hollywood studios avoided making explicitly antifascist films until 1939 because they did not want to alienate audiences in Italy and Germany and limit market access. William Randolph Hearst, who made relatively friendly comments regarding Adolf Hitler and Mussolini throughout the 1930s, sought to block the release of Orson Welles's *Citizen Kane* in 1941. Thus efforts by OWI in the early 1940s to encourage Hollywood to reflect certain interests favorably were made in a broader context in which it was perceived that pressure could be effectively exerted on the studios.

Recognizing the impact of the American film industry on the foreign policy front abroad, OWI convinced MGM's Samuel Goldwyn not to reissue *The Real Glory* in 1942 because of the film's focus on the American occupation of the Philippines just over four decades earlier, and not to release *Kim,* a movie whose focus was British imperialist activity in Asia. Similar concerns were brought to bear on MGM's *Dragon Seed* (1942) and its depiction of Chinese life, because of the importance of maintaining positive relations between China and the West in this period. This sensitivity, not surprisingly, did not extend to representations of Japan and the Japanese, especially after Pearl Harbor. As Clayton Koppes and Gregory Black observe, "The cinematic Japanese remained monolithically diabolical."[95]

Domestically, OWI's agenda was complicated by the same pressures that restricted the cultural efforts of the Popular Front. The most significant obstacle was that of race, especially in view of the increased activity on the civil rights front by blacks in the northern states and their access to key decision makers (particularly in the Democratic Party), along with the continued resistance of southern authorities to any challenge to the racial status quo. To the extent that mobilizing blacks to support the war effort was complicated by what the *Pittsburgh Courier* called the Double V campaign—for democracy abroad and civil rights at home—that is, the linkage of African American support for the war to progress on the racial front domestically, OWI had to find a way "to improve Negro morale without incurring too much criticism from whites," as one of its own analysts presented the dilemma.[96] This mission was further complicated by the fear that blacks might begin to identify with the Japanese as fellow colored people.[97]

At the time, the American military was still segregated; Jim Crow was still the norm in the South, the border states, and certainly elsewhere; and OWI's own surveys indicated that there was significant resistance to any change in these arrangements. The OWI interviewers found that 96 percent of whites favored residential segregation, and 76 percent favored Jim Crow policies on buses and streetcars. With regard to the military, nine of ten whites believed that blacks and whites should be trained separately; three-quarters of blacks disagreed.[98] Faced with these conflicting cues, the War Department's Bureau of Public Relations sought to control the images of the war that circulated domestically. After the publication of photos of black servicemen dancing with (white) Englishwomen in the United States provoked an uproar, the military's censors were instructed to block the release of all such images (a policy that was relaxed by General Dwight Eisenhower to allow black GIs to send the photos home after they had been marked "For personal use only—not for publication"). As George Roeder Jr. notes, this concern about images and the racial status quo extended to the kinds of roles in which blacks could be portrayed in military publications, meaning that "material intended for white audiences seldom depicted blacks in aggressive poses."[99] In this context a poster of the boxer Joe Louis holding a rifle was just barely acceptable with respect to prevailing concerns about black male aggression. Ironically perhaps, not only aggression was found to be an undesirable quality in black males, for photographs of wounded African American GIs were also censored, partly because of a perception that the "negro press [tended] to unduly emphasize" the contribution of black units to the war effort.[100] In 1942, OWI launched its initial campaign to shore up black support for the war effort with the publication of a pamphlet written by Chandler Owen, A. Philip Randolph's former ally in the Harlem branch of the Socialist Party in the 1920s, entitled *Negroes and the*

War. Owen's argument that black progress in the United States had been significant and would only be enhanced by black support for the war abroad angered southern whites, who saw the pamphlet as "subversive"; displeased elements of the Republican Party who viewed the release as pro–New Deal propaganda; and failed to engage blacks, who found the vague promises and suggestions offered by Owen to be "palliative, wasteful, and ineffective."[101]

These awkward attempts to manage the images of and responses to the war were accompanied by OWI's concerns about the depiction of blacks in films produced during the war and its conviction that if "the prime determinant of morale within a nation at war is *the identification of the individual with the community,*" Hollywood's tendency to erase blacks from the "community" altogether or to restrict them to roles that granted them no dignity was problematic.[102] Again, activities of the OWI were motivated by a New Deal liberal—and at times leftist—agenda. The war against fascism abroad was seen by many as involving a battle for democracy, including racial desegregation at home, and as noted earlier, many of OWI's staffers were drawn from the institutions of the Popular Front. Because these concerns were shared by the civil rights movement, OWI initiated an informal alliance with the NAACP and other civil rights groups in this period; as A. Philip Randolph put it, before the end of the war "blacks want[ed] to see the stuffing knocked out of white supremacy."[103]

Attempts by OWI to encourage Hollywood studios to produce more "positive" images of blacks first bore what turned out to be rather bitter fruit in the 1942 campaign to modify MGM's *Tennessee Johnson.* Rooted in the same reading of Reconstruction that gave rise to Griffith's *Birth of a Nation,* the original script for the movie portrayed Abraham Lincoln's successor, Andrew Johnson, as a political hero and his opponents among the Radical Republicans, particularly Thaddeus Stevens, as threats to democracy. The loose coalition of OWI and NAACP staffers was mobilized after the CPUSA's newspaper, the *Daily Worker,* published a story about the planned project, drawing attention to its reinforcement of the understandings that underlay Jim Crow. Given its concern about black loyalty and developments that might increase black alienation, OWI's chief of its Bureau of Motion Pictures, Lowell Mellett, after receiving correspondence from the NAACP's Walter White that the movie might do "enormous injury to morale," asked MGM either to change the script or, as a reflection of the shallowness of OWI's commitment, to delay the film's release until after the war. In response, the studio offered the interesting defense, in light of the industry's willingness to satisfy southern censors, fascist dictators, and industrialists, as the need arose, that "a minority in the country . . . [should not] dictate what shall or shall not be on the screen."[104] Eventually, OWI decided to back off from its efforts to "soften" or block *Tennes-*

see Johnson because it believed that the major source of complaint was not the civil rights community with regard to the movie's treatment of race but rather the Communist Party and its desire to have Thaddeus Stevens presented in a positive light. The perception was that the left was involved because it saw Stevens as a hero and defender of the former slaves and future sharecroppers in the fight against southern property owners (that is, paralleling the Bolshevik-led revolt of Russian peasants), an interpretation that led OWI to decide that the Republican was "a hero of the left-wingers rather than of the Negro people." Ultimately, the film was released with its glorification of Andrew Johnson intact (apparently Harry Truman strongly identified with the film's protagonist, played by Lionel Barrymore), and to satisfy complaints in the civil rights camp, the number of blacks featured was significantly reduced (thereby removing the grounds for any complaints about negative portrayals). A protest campaign against the film supported by actors, including Zero Mostel, Vincent Price, Dorothy Gish, Canada Lee, and Ben Hecht, proved to be unsuccessful.

The ability of OWI to monitor Hollywood's releases was limited after the spring of 1943 when a coalition of Republicans and southern Democrats voted to cut the agency's domestic operations budget by more than 90 percent. Nevertheless, some sensitive portrayals of African Americans did emerge during the war years, including Dooley Wilson's role as Humphrey Bogart's piano-playing associate, Sam, in *Casablanca* (1943), and Kenneth Spencer's performance in *Bataan* (1943), which was one of those rare instances where the film world was ahead of the real world in terms of its treatment of blacks: the movie featured an integrated army unit *before* the military was desegregated in the Korean War.

As an institution of the New Deal and, to some extent, the Popular Front, the OWI's limited impact on the film industry and American popular culture as a whole is significant. Despite their efforts and some notable successes, Hollywood proved to be relatively immune to the racial agenda of the liberals and the more broadly progressive ambitions of the leftists.

The King Crosses the Cultural Front

Even though the influence of Popular Front artists would be felt after the collapse of the CPUSA and the left, the post-McCarthy era was characterized by a new "structure of feeling." The combination of the effective elimination of the left and the emergence of the civil rights movement, along with the subsequent entry of racial issues onto the main stages of American life, was accompanied by changes in the cultural realm that would ultimately make the maintenance of solidaristic identities as difficult as ever, but in slightly different ways.

Part of this reorientation can be traced to the renewed southernization of American popular culture that took place in the 1950s. Ira Katznelson and Michael Denning both argue that one of the major factors that weakened the New Deal coalition and the Popular Front's hegemony was the migration of whites and blacks from the southern states to the North and increasingly the West as well.[105] Suggests Denning, "The extroadinary wartime migration of black and white southerners . . . remade the American working class. . . . The second-generation immigrant working class that had built the CIO and the Popular Front was displaced . . . and the shape of working-class politics and culture was changed irrevocably."[106] In this context Denning refers to the emergence of the novelist William Faulkner, notes evidence of a "Popular Front uncertainty about Elvis Presley," and contends that Benny Goodman, Count Basie, and Frank Sinatra were replaced by such artists as Muddy Waters and Hank Williams.[107] As a reflection of these changes, Sinatra would dismiss rock and roll as "phony and false" saying that the new music was "sung, played, and written for the most part by cretinous goons."[108]

This internal migration and the resulting exportation of southern mores to other parts of the country certainly helped reintroduce Americans to issues that had been largely ignored throughout the period of peak influence of the New Deal coalition. The eclipse of the left inside the United States, the striking increase in attention to the civil rights struggle, and the fragmentation of the New Deal political and cultural alliances, however, were largely results of the cold war and the increased influence and reach of the media rather than reflections of the impact of southern emigration. Moreover, the combination of McCarthyism and the civil rights movement also troubled relations among New Deal constituencies. For example, Catholic Democrats responded differently from Jewish Democrats to the Red scare and to the dilemmas posed by the second Reconstruction (i.e., integrated housing campaigns, busing, and affirmative action). As Jonathan Rieder notes, "McCarthyism highlighted the festering ethnic tension within the Democratic party, in which Jewish liberals decried Catholic authoritarianism and Catholics reciprocated with charges of Jewish bolshevism."[109] If one includes the changes that took place at the local and state level, as well as national politics, is is clear that the relationships between different ethnic and religious constituencies evolved in ways even more complex than a simple southern-versus-northern or Catholic-versus-Jewish contrasting suggests (e.g., within the Catholic and Jewish communities, different individuals reacted differently to the challenges presented by the civil rights era). Although the postwar southernization of American politics and popular culture does help explain the collapse of the left and the weakening of the New Deal, many of the constituencies allied in the 1930s and 1940s would prove quite receptive to the messages (and messengers) exported from the South. Furthermore, it is not clear that these communiqués were always more racially polarized or class demobilizing than those produced by Popular Front artists. Indeed, starkly contrasting northern New Deal constituencies before the war as inherently progressive and the resouthernized working classes of the post-McCarthy era as thoroughly regressive does a disservice to the real nature of the transition that took place over the course of the New Deal era, a transition that reflects developments beyond those in the realms of class, race, and ethnicity.

In many ways the new cultural formations that came into being after the McCarthy era were simply an updated version of the blackface republicanism that had been developed in the mid–nineteenth century. The gender and racial anxieties characteristic of classic nineteenth-century minstrelsy, though, were revised after the war in two significant ways. The most important transformation was the beginning of the entry of women into public life and popular culture as creators and consumers. Nineteenth-century political life and its popular cultural manifestations largely excluded women certainly as creators (hence the cross-dressing characteristic of minstrelsy) and, to a lesser degree, as participants and consumers. In contrast to a Popular Front that was ill-prepared to respond to issues of gender (and certainly sexuality) — "only rarely did a Popular Front feminism develop," notes Denning — the new cultural forms that emerged in the 1950s were energized by a nascent feminism and an overt sexuality quite distinct from the often chaste offerings of the 1930s and 1940s.[110] There was also a clear generational aspect to this transition. The postwar boom freed American teenagers of both sexes to establish a cultural economy of their own. The understandable absence of a politics of pleasure in the New Deal era, given the economic circumstances and the war, would not be replicated in post-McCarthy American life: put more accurately, an explicit struggle over these issues would occur in the 1950s and 1960s as opposed to the lack of dialogue around these possibilities in the Popular Front era. Indeed, the beginnings of this dialogue can be traced back to the gendered and generationally bounded response to Frank Sinatra during the Popular Front era, a reaction that established precedents on which such artists as Presley and the Beatles would build.

There would also be a liberalization of cultural mores on the racial front, at least in the period between 1954 and 1968. Over the course of the first half of the twentieth century, literal blackface lost its legitimacy, a change observable in the difference between Al Jolson's engagement of the medium in *The Jazz Singer* in 1927 and Larry Parks's arm's-length reference to Jolson's blackface practices in *Jolson Sings Again* in 1949. As Michael Rogin observes, "1950s minstrelsy could no longer root itself in open blackface display," largely because of the same factors that contributed to the successes of the civil rights movement: southern out-migration and the growth of the media and its impact on cold war–era competition between the Soviets and the Americans.[111] The early rock-and-roll era featured a greater degree of transgression and, in some ways, progressive transgression (as opposed to the mere pursuit of the thrill of breaking taboos). Sam Phillips, Elvis's first producer, would claim with pride to have "knocked shit out of the color line," and he reportedly "sensed in Elvis a kindred spirit, someone who shared with him a secret, almost subversive attraction not just to black music but to black culture, to an inchoate striving, a belief in the equality of man."[112] Similarly, the cultural historian Greil Marcus, writing in 1982, said Elvis "embodies [and] . . . personalizes so much of what is good about [the United States, including] . . . the kind of racial harmony that for Elvis, a white man, means a profound affinity with the most subtle nuances of black culture combined with an equally profound understanding of his own whiteness."[113] The King's visit to the Fairgrounds Memphis amusement park on "colored night" on June 19, 1956, is consistent with this reading of Presley's significance on the racial front.

The rock-and-roll revolution of the mid-1950s involved an unprecedented degree of "race mixing." It would be in 1954 that the Chords, a black vocal group, would cross over into the pop charts with "Sh-boom" at the same time as Bill Haley and the Comets, and subsequently Elvis, Buddy Holly, Chuck Berry, Little Richard, and others, were making an impact on listeners in the pop and black radio communities—developments that bothered gatekeepers in both camps. Thus while Earl Warren's Supreme Court was working toward issuing a unanimous decision—*Brown v. Board of Education*—that de jure segregation would (eventually) have to give way, the dam had already broken on the cultural front. It was in this period that African American Jesse Stone would author Bill Haley and the Comets's "Shake, Rattle and Roll"; Otis Blackwell would compose "Great Balls of Fire" for Jerry Lee Lewis and "All Shook Up" and "Don't Be Cruel" for Elvis; and the songwriting team of Leiber and Stoller would create hits for black artists (the Coasters) and white artists (such as Presley). As Jerry Leiber recollects, "Even though we were white, we didn't play off a white sensibility. We identified with youth and rebellion and making mischief. We thumbed our nose at the adult world. We crawled inside the skins of our characters, we related to the guys in the singing groups, and the result was a cross-cultural phenomenon: a white kid's take on a black kid's take on white society. Color lines were blurred, but the motif was always absurdity."[114] It is in this broader context that Brian Ward refers to the black teenagers who "adored Elvis Presley in the late 1950s and early 1960s" and the "young white women" drawn to black R & B artists.[115]

Of course the strong resistance to any challenges to the associated racial and gender status quos limited the impact of these actions. Some states (such as Louisiana) passed prohibitions on interracial dancing, and as Ward notes, "the campaign against rock and roll became inextricably linked to the rise of organized white resistance to desegregation and black insurgency in the region." [116] Against this background the battle in the late 1950s over a bill to amend the Communications Act of 1934, which would have prevented radio broadcasters from owning record companies or music-publishing firms, devolved into a debate about rock and roll and rhythm and blues, because ASCAP, the music-publishing company closely associated with pre–rock and roll musical forms, feared that its competitor BMI was becoming too powerful because of its dominance in the emerging rock, rhythm and blues, and country markets. The battle between the two publishing companies paralleled the contest between the AFL and the CIO in that BMI was willing to sign artists in the new musical fields that ASCAP, like the AFL, had no interest in. The legislation introduced by the Florida Democrat and segregationist George Smathers in the late summer of 1957 was supported by Massachusetts's John F. Kennedy and Arizona's Barry Goldwater in the Senate. Kennedy and Goldwater saw an attack on rock and roll as a means of making inroads in the South at a time when both were considering the possibility of launching bids for the presidency. When hearings were scheduled for the bill in 1958, Frank Sinatra also voiced his support for the anti-BMI effort, suggesting that as a "singer of songs," he felt something needed to be done to reverse the tide and respond to the popularity of hits such as "Hound Dog," "BeBop-a-Lula," and "All Shook Up." [117] The amendment eventually failed, but not before an attack on Hank Williams and country music provoked a response from Tennessee senator Al Gore, reportedly a capable fiddler himself and one of Nashville's representatives in the Senate (Nashville being the capital of the country music industry).

The late 1950s and 1960s would feature a remarkable degree of interpenetration between the white and black music communities and a complexity, although faithful in many respects to the minstrel roots of American popular culture, in some ways more supportive of broader solidaristic formations than the sober, antifeminist, tentatively integrationist, and geographically limited creations of the Popular Front. If progressive intent is measured in terms of willingness to engage real conflicts, the politics and culture of the post-McCarthy era were possibly more progressive and ambitious than those of the Popular Front, except, perhaps, on the class frontier. Accordingly, Lyndon Baines Johnson's willingness, as a southern transgressor verging on "race traitor," to violate racial *and* class understandings, in the political realm, with his support of the Civil Rights Act, the Voting Rights Act, the Great Society programs, and the War on Poverty, in contrast to the efforts of Franklin Roosevelt, reflects and parallels some of the cultural developments of the period.

Nevertheless, while I do not want to overstate the importance of the cultural politics of the post-McCarthy era from a progressive standpoint, the inability of the American left to survive the era that produced the civil rights movement and second-wave feminism says something about the American left, as well as American society. The exploitation and denigration of blacks characteristic of nineteenth-century minstrel shows were still evident in postwar rock-and-roll culture. The ability of pop artists such as Pat Boone and others to make their careers copying the recordings of such artists as Little Richard (e.g., "Tutti Frutti") speaks to the nature of the racial dynamics of the era, as does the composition of the audience for rock and roll (especially after the mid-1960s, when black and white listening tastes began to resegregate). While Elvis was seen by many as the "king of rock and roll" and a hero to many inside and outside the Confederacy (including the young Bill Clinton), his "white Negroisms," to use Mailer's term, have been read differently by different audiences. In contrast to the favorable interpretations of the Presley phenomenon that have been offered by Greil Marcus and others, there are the economic and racial implications of the often quoted statement by Presley's first producer, Sam Phillips: "If I could find a white man who had the negro sound and the negro feel, I could make a million dollars."[118]

A certain ambivalence existed in the responses of blacks to Presley and rock and roll which reflected the different economic, gender, generational, and political concerns brought to the table by different constituencies. Yet some African American youths responded enthusiastically to the new culture. The future civil rights leader Julian Bond recollects, "Three friends of mine and I sang . . . 'Teddy Bear' . . . and I remember thinking it not all that remarkable that we would sing this Elvis Presley song. So here's these four black young men singing, 'Just wanna be, your teddy bear, put your arms around my neck and lead me anywhere.' And looking back on it now, it seems remarkable to me. . . . We just said, 'this is ok . . . this guy is alright.' I think my peers thought Elvis Presley, at least in that early stage, was ok."[119] Some blacks also read rock and roll's emergence as supportive of the integrationist movement, therefore viewing the form's dependence on black music as something to be publicized and celebrated. Accordingly, such publications as *Jet* magazine would run articles citing Presley's musical roots and mentioning his acknowledgment of this debt. As one publication noted, "Presley makes no secret of his respect for the work of Negroes, nor of their influence on his singing."[120]

On the other hand, there was resentment, particularly on the part of those in the black music industry who felt their work was being exploited and, in the case of radio programmers, that their ownership over the music was being challenged. At a deeper level, as a product of the South, Presley's racial politics, despite his statements and actions, were always suspect in some quarters, a caution justified perhaps by the nature of his reception by white audiences. The widely circulated rumor that Presley had stated that "the only thing that Negroes can do for me is shine my shoes and buy my records," true or not, is a reflection of this distrust.[121] This accounts for the distaste expressed in the rap group Public Enemy's 1989 recording "Fight the Power": "Elvis was a hero to most but he never meant [expletive] to me, you see, straight up racist that sucker was simple and plain, [expletive] him and John Wayne." [122] Given the willingness of prominent rock artists to engage black music traditions and racism (e.g., the Rolling Stones' recordings "Brown Sugar," "Sweet Black Angel," and the infamous combination of misogyny and racism, "Some Girls," which includes the suggestion that "black girls just want to [expletive] all night"), the black uncertainty about Elvis had legitimate roots. Although the cultural forms that emerged in the post-McCarthy era challenged the status quo to a greater degree than did earlier forms of blackface minstrelsy, ultimately the containment aspect of these new ironic, yet still racialized, cultural public goods would remain in place.

By 1968, the progressive potential of the resouthernization of American politics and culture had largely been exhausted. The collapse of interracial cultural alliances after the reestablishment of the racial impasse in the South and elsewhere following Martin Luther King's murder marked a significant turning point in American life, culture, and politics, just as the Memphis riots of 1866 had presaged the end of the first Reconstruction. That 1968 also marked the end of the age of Sidney Poitier (i.e., *Lilies of the Field, A Patch of Blue, To Sir with Love, In the Heat of the Night,* and *Guess Who's Coming to Dinner?*) is an indication of how far the film industry lagged behind the music business in its ability to reflect the changes taking place in American society. The year saw the end of a unique experiment involving a willingness to reassess the gender and cultural assumptions underpinning American life, an experiment that was made possible because of the cold war competition between the United States and the Soviet Union and the consequent sensitivity of American authorities to the concerns of the civil rights movement.[123] It is worth noting that this "near revolution" on the racial front occurred at a point when class politics as defined by the left, labor, and even the New Deal Democrats were effectively marginalized or on the wane.

Elvis Is Dead

That Elvis Presley briefly revived his career in 1968—by slimming down and re-turning to some of the musical traditions, including rhythm and blues ("In the Ghetto" and "Suspicious Minds"), that had originally informed his creations—is just another irony in the context of a political culture mired in absurdity. Along with Frank Sinatra, he would soon offer his support and services to Richard Nixon and the Republican Party. While investigations of popular culture supply data that might be inaccessible or unavailable in more truncated analyses of political life, it is always important to note the disjunction that exists between formal politics and cultural processes in the United States. Popular culture allows, thrives on, and usually demands a degree of nuance that formal political pro-cesses do not always permit.[124] Accordingly, drawing direct, unambiguous mean-ings from popular culture is a risky venture.

Beyond Paul Robeson's "Ballad for Americans" and Orson Welles's *Citizen Kane,* various examples from the last decades of the twentieth century reveal the ease with which cultural messages can be read differently by different audi-ences (regardless of the author's intention), as well as the extent of the right's consciousness regarding the possible uses of popular culture. For instance, dur-ing the 1984 presidential campaign, Ronald Reagan and his staff were attempt-ing to secure endorsements from prominent popular entertainers. As part of this effort, Reagan invited Michael Jackson to the White House to offer public sup-port for his campaign against drunk driving. Subsequent, although ultimately unsuccessful, efforts were made to involve rock and pop artists, including John Mellencamp, Billy Joel, and apparently ZZ Top, in the reelection bid (the latter because their guitarist's parents were friends of Vice-President George Bush). But the GOP was able to attract support from country artists such as Roy Acuff and Lee Greenwood. It was in this context and with the recommendation of colum-nist George Will (who frequently used the sport of baseball as a metaphor to sup-port his conservative visions), that Reagan's staff tried to establish linkages with Bruce Springsteen, who at that point was at the peak of his popularity, having released his *Born in the U.S.A.* album that summer. The decision to reach out to the "Boss" (Springsteen's nickname) was interesting and in some ways a clever calculation. Springsteen's music had roots in the new pleasures and possibilities unearthed by Elvis Presley (e.g., "Born to Run," "Candy's Room," and "Dancing in the Dark"), Bob Dylan, and increasingly the Popular Front aesthetics of one of Dylan's inspirations, Woody Guthrie (e.g., Springsteen's live performances of Guthrie's "This Land Is Your Land," his 1982 album *Nebraska,* and the 1995 release *The Ghost of Tom Joad*). Nevertheless, like most popular artists in the 1980s, the

Boss was not politically engaged publicly, and his work reflected the conflicted impulses of the white ethnic working classes. Although his bands had always included black musicians (e.g., David Sancious, Ernest Carter, and, most prominent, saxophonist Clarence Clemons) and his music drew from rock and R & B traditions, his lyrics remained relatively silent on the issue of race.[125] On one track from *Born in the U.S.A.*, "My Hometown," Springsteen comments on his high school days in the mid-1960s — "fights between the black and white" — and the fact that "troubled times had come to [his] hometown."[126] The title track from the same album makes references to unemployment ("hiring man says 'son if it was up to me'") and the frustrations of Vietnam War veterans ("sent off to a foreign land to go and kill the yellow man"), and against the backdrop of the backlash against affirmative action and the racial resentments that mobilized the Reagan Democrats, it could conceivably be read as support for the conservative populism that brought the GOP to power in 1980.[127] The historian Jim Cullen suggests that Springsteen had little to say on racial matters possibly because he believed "the topic [was] too incendiary . . . [and] many white audiences simply did not want to listen to stories about black people."[128] A similar ambivalence could plausibly be observed with regard to his feelings about the nation as a whole. "Born in the U.S.A." could be interpreted, at least on the surface, as a patriotic celebration of the American spirit. By the mid-1980s Springsteen had left behind the beatnik and Dylanesque aesthetics of his early work in the 1970s and adopted a much more muscular physique quite consistent with the *Rambo* chic popular at the time (i.e., the roles played by GOP supporter Sylvester Stallone in the *Rocky* movies and *Rambo* itself). Given the possibly conservative interpretations that could be made of Springsteen's popularity, then, the Reagan campaign's attempt to appropriate the singer's image made a certain amount of sense. After attempts to reach Springsteen directly failed, at a campaign stop in Hammontown in southern New Jersey on September 19, Reagan told the assembled crowd, "America's future rests in a thousand dreams inside your hearts; it rests in the message of hope in songs so many young Americans admire: New Jersey's own Bruce Springsteen. And helping you make those dreams come true is what this job of mine is all about."[129]

Initially, Springsteen did not respond directly to the widely publicized comments except to wonder to which exact records of his the president had been listening. He would, though, make the following comments at a show, before a performance of "The River," shortly after Reagan's statement:

There's something really dangerous happening to us out there. We're slowly getting split up into two different Americas. Things are gettin' taken away from people that need them and given to people that don't need them, and there's a promise getting broken. In the beginning the idea was that we all live here a little bit like a family, where the strong can help the weak ones, the rich can help the poor ones. I don't think the American dream was that everybody was going to make it or that everybody was going to make a billion dollars, but it was that everybody was going to have an opportunity and the chance to live a life with some decency and some dignity and a chance for some self-respect. So I know you gotta be feelin' the pinch down here where the rivers meet [i.e., Pittsburgh, where the show was taking place].[130]

Following his performance of the song, he added, "That was for Local 1397 [one of the more militant locals affiliated with the United Steelworkers of America], rank and file."[131] Indeed, if Reagan's handlers had really been paying close attention to Springsteen's work, they would have realized that, despite the limitations of his labor republicanism and the potentially conservative, auratic meanings that could be read into his conception of "the beginning" in the quotation above, he was not a likely supporter of the GOP's agenda. After Reagan's first victory in 1980, Springsteen told an audience in Arizona, "I don't know what you thought about what happened last night [in reference to Reagan's victory the night before] but I thought it was pretty terrifying."[132] Although he had not made his political beliefs explicitly understood before the Reagan incident, thereafter Springsteen's convictions were made quite clear: "You see the Reagan reelection ads on TV—you know, 'It's morning in America'—and you say, well, it's not morning in Pittsburgh. It's not morning above 125th Street in New York. . . . And that's why when Reagan mentioned my name in New Jersey . . . I had to disassociate myself from the President's kind words."[133] Speaking to John Hammond, the Popular Front activist, who had discovered and/or initially signed Billie Holiday, Count Basie, Benny Goodman, Aretha Franklin, Bob Dylan, and Springsteen himself, Springsteen noted: "When you start to get real popular, you have to be careful that there isn't a dilution into some very simplistic terms of what you're doing. There are times when you have to get up and say, 'wait a minute, this isn't right. This is it: this is the way I feel.'"[134] More than a decade after the Hammontown speech, Springsteen would observe, "They basically tried to co-opt every image that was American, including me. I wanted to stake my own claim to those images, and put forth my own ideas about them."[135] Besides the support he had given to the anti–nuclear power movement in the late seventies, he would offer financial support and publicity to causes associated with Vietnam War veterans, the homeless, women's groups, civil rights interests (e.g., the battle against Proposition 209 in California), and farmers. Again, if Reagan and George Will had paid any attention to Springsteen's lyrics and their consistently sympathetic rendering of the circumstances of working-class Americans, they would have known that he was not a realistic candidate for an endorsement, despite his noticeable silence on racial and gender issues. Yet the possibility and probably the likelihood exists that Reagan's advisers knew this but gambled that few artists would be willing to resist the public appeals of an extremely popular president, if only for financial reasons. Worth noting is the refusal by the basketball star and Nike shoe spokesperson Michael Jordan to endorse Democratic candidate and African American Harvey Gantt in his 1990 contest with archconservative Jesse Helms in Jordan's home state of North Carolina, because, in his words, "Republicans buy shoes too" (especially when contrasted with the choices Paul Robeson made regarding his career and financial security).[136] Shortly after the Reagan incident, Walter Mondale, the Democratic nominee in 1984, and subsequently New Jersey Democrat Bill Bradley would make equally awkward attempts to attach themselves to the Springsteen juggernaut.[137]

Fried Ice Cream Is a Reality

In 1988, George Bush's campaign featured African American jazz/pop singer Bobby McFerrin's novelty hit "Don't Worry, Be Happy": "Ain't got a place to lay your head, someone came and took your bed, don't worry, be happy; landlord says your rent is late, he may have to litigate, don't worry, be happy; . . . in your life, expect some trouble, when you worry you make it double, don't worry, be happy." Although the Bush campaign seemed to read the song as a straightforward endorsement of the GOP's remaking of American politics and society during the 1980s, it was a remarkable choice because the lyrics are clearly sarcastic in tone and McFerrin, along with the comedian Robin Williams, who was featured prominently in the video for the song, would probably be considered as "fellow travelers" of the contemporary Hollywood left.[138] Another example of the complicated relationship between the understandings that structure American institutional politics and the sentiments that characterize the more informal cultural politics of the nation is the late Lee Atwater, an expert practitioner of racial politics (for instance, his role in the infamous Willie Horton advertisements during the successful 1988 campaign to elect Republican presidential candidate George Bush) *and* avid rhythm and blues fan.[139] The willingness of the blues guitarist Eric Clapton, who has based his career on borrowing from different black musics (e.g., his return to popularity with his version of reggae musician Bob Marley's "I Shot the Sheriff" in 1974), to offer support for the British National Front and its leader Enoch Powell and call for the "repatriation" of nonwhite Britons, also speaks to the incongruity between the realms of popular culture and formal politics.[140] A similar tension has marked the history of Memphis, Tennessee, one of the most crucial sites with regard to the development of American popular culture, especially in terms of music (and film, in view of the influence of longtime city censor Lloyd T. Binford). While B. B. King, Sun Records, Elvis Presley, Aretha Franklin, Stax Records, Otis Redding, Isaac Hayes, Al Green, and Earth, Wind and Fire's Maurice White can all claim roots in Memphis, the frequent cross-racial cultural alliances the city has produced have not been reflected in the history of its politics. The music historian Larry Nager suggests that Memphis has always been a place "where social segregation was the rule but cultural integration was a fact of life."[141]

The popular American attraction to reconstructed images of African American folkways has been historically accompanied by, in the realm of formal politics, a conflicted language of self and community that has rejected identification with blacks and imbued even the claims of those movements seeking to challenge the status quo (i.e., labor unions and leftist parties). Although American popular culture has typically tended to reinforce racial and racist understandings, it has also frequently involved the blurring of categories, some level of engagement with the "black" other or, as is the case in many American towns and cities, literally "crossing the tracks." That engagement has occurred rarely in the arenas of formal political activity, where the conceptions of liberty and community have lacked the sense of racialized (and inevitably sexualized) longing one finds in American popular culture. In this broader context, Bill Clinton's sax playing on Arsenio Hall's talk show in 1992, his obvious ease with African Americans (at least in contrast to the majority of his predecessors), his Elvisisms, and the troubling suggestion by some commentators, black and white, that his experiences in the White House (i.e., the personal scandals) made him the nation's first "black" president, combined with his willingness to pander to white racism, are intriguing but not particularly surprising.[142] Overall, the Clinton phenomenon is hardly inconsistent with the general American propensity to engage otherwise taboo issues and sentiments in blackface. Unfortunately, these transgressive possibilities have always been undercut by the distancing incorporated into the process and the preoccupation with racial lines, and race itself, rather than the real issues on the table (e.g., economic exploitation, gender conflict and insecurities).

Despite the transgressive elements contained in American popular culture, ultimately significant is the historical tendency of these forms to reinforce and uphold racial categories and attitudes and to delegitimize more inclusive conceptions of community. The racialization of American culture, together with the aggregate willingness to "make things big"—the totalizing tendency toward large-scale fantastic enterprises rather than smaller, more subtle portraits and particularistic triumphs — has relegated some ethnic groups to the margins of American popular culture (e.g., the Chinese and Japanese American communities), just as it has effectively consumed and regurgitated the various Native American cultures as a series of convenient stereotypes and symbols (e.g., the noble savage, the stoic victim, the sports team mascot) and the foil for the heroic exploits of white Americans in the western film genre. Similarly, these inclinations have resulted in the institutionalization of a bewildering array of popular attitudes and orientations toward African American cultures ranging from hatred and benign neglect to admiration and imitation. The continued popular attachment to African American cultural forms and the American tradition of dreaming in blackface are symptomatic of a fundamental alienation and an inability to maintain a value system through which one's own circumstances can be understood and confronted.[143]

This unwillingness of many Americans to process difference without creating hierarchies (as Johann Herder and Harold Cruse, among others, have proposed) and the zero-sum calculations made by the defenders of American national culture are an outgrowth of an inclination on the part of some peoples to avoid facing their own alienation by denying the existence of any cultural alternatives. This effort to achieve identity through negation, this "universal drive for recognition" (Hegel) or "will to power" (Nietzsche) is evident in Marx's statement that "I am nothing and I should be everything" and the actions of those who have attacked the validity of other cultures (and occasionally culture itself) while failing to examine the condition of their own.[144] In the United States, this cultural nihilism has become institutionalized. To the degree that the artificial realm of race has been accepted as the fundamental axis of difference, Americans have been particularly incapable of producing a culture (or more accurately cultures) resilient and coherent enough to enable them to maintain the collective sensibilities other peoples have in other national contexts. The result has been a complex array of cultural public goods, some as unidimensional and alienated as the values and conceptions that have been institutionalized in the making of American formal politics (e.g., Griffith's rendition of the minstrel tradition in *Birth of a Nation*), and others more nuanced in terms of their fidelity to the jumbled roots of the American cultural project. If one recognizes culture as a crucial public good in the making and maintenance of a left, as a way of identifying and mobilizing sustainable and progressive communities of interest, and as a means of achieving other public goods, the aggregate response of American people to their heterogeneity and preference for racial constructs and categories has hampered the development of this medium as it has affected the overall making of the left.

CHAPTER SEVEN

Making Love in America

Everyone has a *bottom line*. The choice here is to put "love" on the *bottom line*. Is this a culture that is producing love? This question may seem strange because it has not been on the agenda of serious scholarship for some time. . . . The language that has emerged in . . . America is magnificent in many respects, but it is deficient on the *bottom line* of love-production. . . . We need to use our language carefully, so that we speak to each other's common humanity, and assist in the production, accumulation, and distribution of love in our culture.
—Raymond Gozzi Jr., *New Words and a Changing American Culture*

If you're thinking of being my baby, it doesn't matter if you're black or white.
—Michael Jackson, "Black or White"

Race has had a significant impact on the choices Americans have made throughout the nation's history, and racialized understandings of citizenship and community have been major contributing factors to the popular willingness to reject leftist movements and appeals. That the crucial role played by racial tensions and conflicts has often been overlooked by analysts seeking to understand the weakness of the American left is partially a consequence of the methods that have been used to investigate the exceptionalism phenomenon. Specifically, I have tried to improve on previous efforts in three ways: by developing and applying a comprehensive definition of the left that includes considerations of public policy and popular culture, by approaching the American left from a comparative perspective, and by considering the evolution of the left over an extended period of time (as opposed to focusing on one era).

First, the study of American exceptionalism must extend beyond an emphasis on one realm—for example, philosophy, the conventional left, a particular public policy area—to consider the phenomenon in a thorough fashion.[1] An adequate account cannot end with a discussion of the philosophical influence of one ethnic group, the analysis of a single movement in a particular context, or other isolated phenomena. The left must be approached as one presence among others *and as a functional entity.* One needs to go beyond words and movements to understand the relative provision of other public goods and the relationship among the political, economic, and cultural aspects of the society in question. An analysis limited to one realm is less likely to reveal the impact of the broader social processes and dynamics related to race on American life. It is after considering the histories of labor unions, leftist parties, efforts to institutionalize comprehensive and redistributive public goods, and popular culture that the common role played by race in each of these areas becomes significant — a significance often dismissed or overlooked because racial factors seem to play a relatively minor role in the development of isolated components of the overall phenomenon (e.g., the American Socialist Party, the history of the efforts to establish a national health care program). Similarly, the argument that race matters in the study of American exceptionalism is reinforced when the interactions between the different components are fleshed out: the unions that are already weakened by racial conflicts are missing at the policymaking table when the rules relating to the franchise are being established and health care reform is debated; the same individuals who devote their leisure time to minstrel shows do not respond to the (occasionally sincere) appeals of the leaders of their national unions to accept nonwhite members in their struggle to increase the leisure time available to all (e.g., the eight-hour movement); the absence of viable and quality public institutions such as schools, hospitals, and transportation systems, because of the impact of political traditions rooted in racial understandings, makes it harder for people to cross the racial divide and imagine themselves as citizens sharing a common fate.

Second, I have attempted to contribute to the existing literature by approaching the American left, defined broadly, from a comparative perspective. It is difficult to analyze a society properly in terms of concepts and data generated by that society alone. For example, Theda Skocpol's suggestion that "it is hard to doubt that there would have been a deep and persistent stigmatization of policies targeted on the poor, even if African American slaves had never been brought to this nation, and even if black sharecroppers had not migrated in huge numbers to urban areas from the 1940s onward," begs a comparative analysis because the evidence suggests that social welfare policies are not as stigmatized elsewhere as they are in the United States.[2] The instruments and theories used to interpret American developments need to be tested in other contexts for them to have any comparative validity. An example is the tendency to invoke the terms "left" and "right" in American politics without analyzing the contents of these terms. Consequently, some have argued, for example, that parallels can be drawn between the British Conservative Party, the German Christian Democratic Party, and the American Republican Party (or Britain's New Labour, the German Social Democratic Party, and the American Democratic Party). Rarely is it noted that the platforms of these movements, as well as the political contexts in which they function, are quite distinct. The willingness to use "left" and "right" simply as code words for the forces of change and the forces of reaction makes comparative analysis and understanding difficult if the contents of the demands for change, the contents of the calls for retrenchment, and the underlying status quo are not investigated. Such an examination would reveal that many dimensions exist to these debates and that the specific issue conflicts are different. Simplistic situational characterizations such as liberal and conservative, pro–status quo and anti–status quo, or pro-state and antistate fail to capture the essence and multi-dimensional nature of these different conflicts. Similarly, they encourage a sloppy form of analytic shorthand (e.g., "the Reagan-Thatcher axis" or "the collapse of the left throughout the West") that glosses over the distinct national contexts and political cultural configurations. The conceptual shortcomings of many analyses of the American left and American exceptionalism have been compounded by an unwillingness to undertake an accurate comparative examination of the relationship between the American "right" and the European "rights," the missing American left and the fading European conventional lefts. In this discussion, an effort has been made to develop a resilient and coherent definition of the left that is comprehensive, empirically observable, and applicable to other contexts. The application of such an understanding of the left and leftism would make it clear that, in contrast to the situation in every other Western, industrialized nation, there is no left to speak of in the United States.

Yet a comparative approach also reveals that the dynamics evident in the United States, related to heterogeneity and class, are not unique to the American case and that there might be a need to reexamine some of the terms and labels that have been used to classify political parties. Some analysts still suggest, for instance, that the contemporary emergence of such movements as the French National Front, the Austrian Freedom Party, and the German Republican Party is evidence of "far right" activity, movements separated from the conventional left by the economic right. This tendency to force all ideological expression into one dimension (left to right) has resulted in the argument that, by accommodating the complaints of the various anti-immigrant lobbies, the European party systems are moving to the right even though the issues being raised are not directly economic. To the extent that these movements are concerned with economic issues, they are not calling for economic individualism, the atomization of the collective, or the elimination of collectivist public goods but rather collectivism under the guise of ethnic nationalism and the withholding from others of the benefits of citizenship and of community itself.

It is in this spirit that Catherine Mégret, the National Front mayor of Vitrolles, a suburb outside Marseilles, promised on election, "We will immediately stop all state subsidies to immigrants and give the money to French people, [although] unfortunately, there are some services we have to keep providing to immigrants . . . there won't be a centime beyond those."[3] Naturally the effort to limit the number of immigrants and their access to public goods and the splitting of the conventional left's constituency over these issues have paved the way for the economic right to increase its influence. Nevertheless, economics and culture are two different dimensions of ideology and political life, and there has been no consistent pattern of association between the poles of these different realms. Indeed, it was the Communist Party that first raised the immigration issue in France, just as it was the Italian left that gave birth to Benito Mussolini's Fascists and the ideas of Georges Sorel, Martin Heidegger, and Friedrich Nietzsche that inspired both leftists and the so-called far right. Similarly, while the increase in support for the anti-immigrant and economically conservative Reform Party in Canada is seen as coming solely at the expense of the center-right Progressive Conservatives, the new party has also cut into the voting base of the leftist New Democratic Party (in the province of Ontario to a small extent and to a larger degree in the Western provinces). "A working man pays his bills and all he sees are increasing taxes. And what's it for? It's for the minorities. Why should I support them when they should be supporting themselves?" asks an autoworker and union member in southern Ontario, explaining his decision to switch parties and vote for Reform.[4]

If one approaches ideology as a means of grappling with various forms of the other, as well as the possibility of alienation in several realms (economics, culture, scale, geography, gender, aesthetics), it becomes clear that the study of the left must reflect these potential tensions and nuances. The failure to consider these various dimensions has led to conceptual confusion as to the contents of the "left" and the "right" and the relationship between the different movements that have emerged over the course of the experience of industrialization.[5] Last, a comparative approach reveals that the United States is still unique in the degree to which these dynamics have shaped its politics, indeed to the extent that the conventional left has been completely marginalized.

Finally, I have tried to improve on previous efforts to understand American exceptionalism by extending the analysis beyond a focus on one particular era (e.g., Jacksonian America; the Progressive, New Deal, or post–civil rights eras). In the last twenty-odd years, a number of analyses of the impact of the politics of race have emerged.[6] Unfortunately, most of these analyses, while provocative, have failed to examine the phenomenon from a broader historical perspective. Racial politics are not new in the United States, and their impact has spread far beyond the realm of formal politics. The common tendency to dismiss the significance of race or to suggest that race became an issue only after (or, as some seem to imply, because of) the Watts riot or some other convenient cutoff point is to misunderstand the nature and scale of the phenomenon. The United States's obsession with race certainly precedes the modern ghetto and the affirmative action baby. While it might suit certain agendas to suggest otherwise, the historical record is clear on this point. It would be difficult for one to consider every era in American history thoroughly (and certain eras have been given less attention than others in this analysis). But by considering the evolution of the conventional left from the beginning of the industrialization era in the United States to the end of the McCarthy era, the unfolding of the modern American public policy state from the 1930s to the present, and the subterranean but potent role played by the interactions of race and popular culture throughout the history of the nation's left, I show that the relationship between a weak or missing left and the popular attachment to racialized identities cannot be restricted to or explained solely in terms of the developments of the last four decades (or any isolated period, for that matter). Perhaps more important, it becomes more likely that a convincing explanation of American exceptionalism must involve long-term, as opposed to short-term, dynamics or processes.

Whose Blues and How?

Approaching the United States from a comparative and long-term perspective shows that the exceptionalism claim is justified. The main point is not that the United States has a relatively weak labor movement and lacks a viable leftist party. If that were the extent of the difference between the United States and other industrialized countries, there might not be grounds for further investigation of the phenomenon, especially because the conventional left is not the only means by which a society can respond to the uncertainties of the free market and because the left has been on the retreat, for the most part, in Europe and Canada for the last two decades (although leftist parties are currently in power in France, the United Kingdom, Italy, Sweden, and Germany). Rather, a useful approach to the study of American exceptionalism, broadly defined, has to consider other realms and in particular must consider the public policy orientation of the United States in comparison with its counterparts. The United States has been slower than other countries to institute basic programs (e.g., old-age and unemployment insurance), shown relatively little commitment to the programs it has instituted (e.g., many of its income maintenance programs), or has not yet implemented these programs (with health care being the most glaring example). While

Table 7.1. Homicide Rates per 100,000 Population, Selected Countries, 1996

Country	Homicide Rate
United Kingdom	0.5
Japan	0.6
France	1.1
Canada	2.04
Finland	3.2
United States	7.4

Source: New York Times, July 26, 1998, sec. 4, p. 1.
Note: The figure for Canada is from 1994.

some analysts have noted a basic convergence between the policy preference patterns evident in Europe and North America, such an assertion ignores the consistent difference between American choices and those operationalized even in states such as Canada and the United Kingdom, where means-tested, minimalist programs have often been the norm (in contrast to the preference for comprehensive solutions found in Sweden, for example).[7] Furthermore, the absence of a state-sponsored process for registering voters is not a minor oversight. The struggle for the unrestricted right to vote was one of the major accomplishments of the European working classes in the decades before and after the end of the nineteenth century. It might seem odd to focus on the franchise as an important public good for the left, but only because many Americans are unfamiliar with arrangements elsewhere and take the right to vote for granted. When one considers these absences—a viable conventional left, an effective welfare state, state-sponsored health care, and an inclusive franchise—as well as the other circumstances unique to the United States, such as the shortage of public housing, public transportation, and accessible (urban) public spaces in general, suggestions that a basic convergence is occurring or has occurred are not particularly plausible. In light of the 1996 abandonment of a national commitment to provide income support for poorer Americans, of the most minimal safety net, the notion that the United States has shared a common policy trajectory with other industrialized nations becomes especially unconvincing. Last, incarceration rates are higher in the United States than in any other industrialized society, and despite the United States's unique preference for capital punishment as a deterrent to would-be criminals, American lives are more often at risk (see Table 7.1). Thus grounds exist for investigating the exceptionalism phenomenon and trying to understand why the United States has pursued this unique path.

Broadening the field of inquiry—by defining the left in a more comprehensive manner, incorporating comparative references, and extending the analysis across eras—makes more tenable the suggestions that the United States is exceptional and that racial tensions have significantly weakened class identities. These claims become stronger after one considers other possible interpretations of the history of the American left.

Three important factors have both contributed to the weakness of leftist movements in the United States but also had a significant impact throughout the West (and therefore cannot be cited as explanations of American exceptionalism): the way in which gender relations have affected social organization and (re)production; the effect that participation in the "world system" can have on the individual society; and the philosophical contradictions contained within the perspectives endorsed by many conventional leftists. The manner in which gender relations are manifested has a significant effect on the nature of a society's evolution and its pattern of public good production, especially with the weakening of the dichotomy between public politics and the private realm over the course of the twentieth century. As Sandra Burt suggests, "The meaning of women's issues has changed substantially over time, and today the term embraces social and moral questions, definitions of rights and obligations, as well as the nature and distribution of power in society."[8] The general inability of each sex to accept the "other" on its own terms but rather as an inferior or superior continues to influence strongly societal politics (e.g., the lesser production of certain public goods such as equal pay regulations, parental leave for child care—and generally those benefits which support the development and maintenance of "family values"—and the encouragement of misogynist and homophobic attitudes). While leftist theorists (going back to Marx and Engels) have questioned modern conceptions of gender roles more consistently than their counterparts on the right, and although socialist-influenced or -governed societies have been more responsive to gender-related issues, with a few exceptions (e.g., Sweden and Norway) these changes have represented essentially superficial reforms—largely in response to the demand for women workers in the labor market—rather than fundamental restructurings of the popular treatment of the questions of sexual identity and difference.[9] Furthermore, given the historical identification of the conventional left with the interests of male workers, labor and other related, older social movements have often been resistant to the newer social movements such as second-wave feminism.[10] Nevertheless, on the whole, bearing in mind the problems involved in making comparative, empirical evaluations of these policies, there appears to be some relationship between a society's responsiveness to class issues and its sensitivity to gender issues (see Tables 7.2 and 7.3).

As for the second factor, class relations within states have been dramatically

Table 7.2. Ratio of Women's to Men's Hourly Earnings,
Nonagricultural Workers (%), 1970 and 1990

Country	1970	1990
France	78	80
Japan	51	50
Sweden	80	89
United Kingdom	60	70
United States	62	72
West Germany	69	74

Source: Francine D. Blau and Lawrence M. Khan, *The Gender Earnings Gap: Some International Evidence* (Washington, D.C.: National Bureau of Economic Research, 1992).
Note: The Swedish figure in the second column is from 1989, and the British figure in the second column from 1984.

affected by the relations between states. This understanding is the crux of the imperialist and dependency critiques as developed by Lenin and Cardoso, respectively.[11] In some states the influence of the international context has lessened potential class conflict by enriching the whole society relative to other societies while maintaining or even increasing class differentials (as has happened in most Western "developed democracies"). Televisions, motor cars, VCRs, blue jeans, and indoor facilities are all good reasons to become satisfied or complacent. Instead of increasing class tensions in the last century and a half in the West, we have seen the adoption of middle-class values and lifestyles by larger percentages of the population. Although some of this growth around the middle is more mythical (in other words, in the minds of the satisfied working classes) than real, an identifiable, service-oriented class has emerged.

The tensions that have been internalized historically in the philosophical orientation of the conventional left have also contributed to the ability of the proponents of individualism to establish a foothold in the various Western political cultures. The conventional left's failure to transcend a range of false dichotomies (e.g., individualism versus a certain conception of collectivism, technology versus culture) and its apparent attachment to certain principles in the realm of culture (i.e., an Enlightenment-style "humanism") and to the state as the primary vehicle of policymaking have made it vulnerable to the attacks of the individualists, as well as susceptible to internal division.

Yet these three factors—the influence of gender relations, the relative "satisfaction" of the Western working classes, and the ramifications of some philosophical confusions—are not satisfying explanations for the exceptionalism phenomenon, for they have had an impact on all Western conventional lefts. Perhaps, then, one

Table 7.3. Maternity Leave Provisions in Selected Countries, 1997

Country	Length of Leave	Wages Paid (%)
Australia	1 year	0
Austria	16 weeks	100
Belgium	15 weeks	82 for 30 days, 75 thereafter
Canada	17–18 weeks	55 for 15 weeks
Denmark	18 weeks	100
Finland	105 days	80
France	16–26 weeks	100
Germany	14 weeks	100
Ireland	14 weeks	70
Italy	5 months	80
Japan	14 weeks	60
Luxembourg	16 weeks	100
Netherlands	16 weeks	100
New Zealand	14 weeks	0
Norway	18 weeks	100
Sweden	14 weeks	75 for 360 days, + 90 days at a flat rate
Switzerland	8 weeks	100
United Kingdom	14–18 weeks	90 for 6 weeks, flat rate thereafter
United States	12 weeks	0

Source: International Labour Organization, *Gap in Employment Treatment for Men and Women Still Exists* (Geneva: ILO, 1998), pp. 5–8.

might suggest that the tendency to adopt individualistic solutions for social prob-lems best explains the American case. Arguably, the characteristically American resistance to collective strategies reflects an attachment to the rights and preroga-tives of individuals over and above the claims of any particular communities. But this explanation, as developed by such analysts as Frederick Jackson Turner, Louis Hartz, and Seymour Martin Lipset among others, really only begs the question. Why have American public policy choices been so consistently and thoroughly informed by individualistic choices? Although Hartz's fragment thesis is a fas-cinating effort to place American developments in a comparative perspective, it fails as an explanation for the outcomes I consider here. The resistance to the left and comprehensive public policy options, while often phrased in stridently, indi-vidualistic terms, logically has more likely been a response to the racial conflicts that have shaped American life. When one considers the full range of actors in-volved in the struggle to define community in the United States—workers and labor unions, employers and plantation owners, women and men, politicians in-side and outside the South, and the state and courts—it is a common understanding of race that connects them, not an attachment to Lockean liberalism and individual privilege. Indeed, the resistance to the left in the United States, as in contemporary Europe, has often been rooted in ethnic collectivism and phrased in such terms (e.g., the need to maintain white supremacy), rather than a reflection of the endorsement of individualist claims. The liberal individualism Hartz and others have cited has been the rhetorical residue remaining after the battles among the competing "we" claims promoted by different ethnic and racial communities. In other words, while an examination of the speeches of politicians might reflect a particularly American preference for individual liberties, the unstated realities have often been shaped by the ethnic and racial calculations made by different groups. Against this backdrop, Hartz's argument becomes even less persuasive.

By the same token, arguments that focus on short-term developments or institutional differences such as tensions within one union or party, the personality of one individual, or features peculiar to the American nation-state (e.g., the state-federal arrangements, the electoral college) are not convincing explanations for what is clearly a rather far-reaching phenomenon. Can the failure of the Socialist Party explain the wholesale absence of leftist forces in the United States, especially when socialist parties in other countries also made mistakes or found themselves at times "on the wrong side of history" (e.g., France's Socialist Party)? Was the influence of Samuel Gompers on American developments so strong by itself that it outweighed the attempts of Eugene Debs, Big Bill Haywood, Woody Guthrie, and others to present Americans with a socialism they could recognize and embrace? Or perhaps, more to the point, did Gompers not accurately represent a significant constituency—and maybe a majority—within the American working classes? As for the institutional arguments, there is no feature of the American state, of significance, which is unique to the United States and which would explain the exceptionalism phenomenon in its totality. The American rejection of collectivism has been rather thorough. A satisfying explanation of that reality would have to be founded on some broader process or dynamic rather than on the failures of a particular union or party, the foibles of one individual labor leader, or the ramifications of one particular custom or institutional device.

Perhaps one might argue, as Werner Sombart did when he first posed the exceptionalism question, that because the United States appears to be a relatively wealthy society, there has been no strong desire or need for a left.[12] This argument would be more persuasive, however, if it were not so clear that the distribution of resources in the United States is hardly equitable (from a comparative perspective) and if real poverty did not exist to the extent that it does (see Table 7.4). Prosperous or not in the aggregate, average Americans do not have the security

Table 7.4. Poverty Rates in Selected Countries

Country	Population below Income Poverty Line (%), 1989–94	Human Poverty Index (HPI-2), 1995
Australia	12.9	12.5
Belgium	5.5	12.4
Canada	11.7	12
Denmark	7.5	12
Finland	6.2	11.8
France	7.5	11.8
Germany	5.9	10.5
Ireland	11.1	15.2
Italy	6.5	11.6
Japan	11.8	12
Netherlands	6.7	8.2
New Zealand	9.2	12.6
Norway	6.6	11.3
Spain	10.4	13.1
Sweden	6.7	6.8
United Kingdom	13.5	15
United States	19.1	16.5

Source: United Nations Development Programme, *Human Development Report, 1998* (New York: Oxford University Press, 1998), p. 186.
Notes: The figures in the first column are based on a European Union/Organization for Economic Cooperation and Development (EU/OECD) standard pegged at 50% of the median-adjusted disposable personal income. The figures in the second column are based on Human Development Report Office calculations.

in terms of employment, welfare, or health care that citizens of other industrialized nations take for granted. Faced with hardship, the average American does not have the support of the state that individuals elsewhere can claim as a right.

Race or demographic heterogeneity is an important factor to consider in the effort to understand exceptionalism because, in contrast to the other theories offered, every aspect of American life has been affected by the way Americans have chosen to characterize and process their differences. While it is tempting to view the existence of blacks in the United States as a minor issue at most, race is the ghost with a permanent seat at the table of American life, the spirit whose existence gives definition to all others. Thus one would expect race to affect the American left as well. Although the South is commonly dismissed (inaccurately) as an undifferentiated reservoir of reaction, it is in this part of the country that the left came undone consistently, and until the 1960s it is from this region that the most influential and conservative political actors and movements emerged. The power of conservatives in the Senate and the barriers to basic public policy developments in the United States can be traced directly to the role of racial conflict in southern politics (rather than the pervasive influence of Lockean liberalism or individualism). Indeed, despite the changes brought about by the second Reconstruction that was the civil rights movement, the South has continued to be on the cutting edge of American politics and life (with the other parts of the country not far behind).

Last, I want to emphasize that neither the left nor race are static, immutable entities. The history of the left in the United States, as elsewhere, has revealed a certain dynamism. Certainly those Americans who lived before World War II would remember a society in which a domestic Communist Party was a reality, in which the CIO's John Lewis was a powerful and respected political actor. Earlier generations would remember Eugene Debs and his successor Norman Thomas, and they might have voted in elections that sent Socialists to Congress.[13] In other words, in contrast to the present, there were eras when the American labor movement and the left were credible actors and presences. The left has had periods of prominence (often followed by periods of invisibility and weakness). What is significant, though, is that the American left has always been weaker than its counterparts elsewhere that experienced the same cycles of influence and marginality. When Eugene Debs was gaining the support of a million Americans in his presidential bids in the first two decades of this century, leftist leaders were winning elections and forming governments in Europe. When the AFL and CIO were working closely behind the scene with the New Deal Democrats, representatives of leftist parties and workers were at the decision-making table in the various European legislatures. Finally, while the New Deal and Great Society administrations made great strides in the context of American public policy history, from a broader comparative perspective these achievements appear rather limited and belated.

Similarly, to suggest that race is the variable that explains the puzzle of American exceptionalism is not to imply that some unchanging force has had a consistent role in and impact on American life. Whiteness, blackness, and otherness have been made and remade in American history, and these constructions have proved to be rather flexible in certain circumstances. The whiteness that in the mid–nineteenth century had trouble absorbing Irish and German immigrants and rejected Chinese Americans as unassimilable now stands at the beginning of the twenty-first seemingly ready and able to welcome Asians and many Hispanics. At different points, in different areas, and among different groups, the walls of racial difference have proved relatively permeable and on occasion have been toppled: for example, the brief and unexpected moment that was the civil rights movement. Over the course of the twentieth century, literal blackface lost its legitimacy, as the ability of politicians to use explicitly racist language to justify their resistance to progressive policy alternatives decreased. Thus here I use race to refer to an ongoing nuanced and fluid process, particularly observable in the arenas of popular culture, with the recognition that although this dynamic has been a constant presence in American life, its contours have shifted and its significance need not be seen as a given, an inevitable restraining force on the development of new, more inclusive conceptions of American community and citizenship.

Liberty and Confinement inside the House of Labor

Nevertheless, up to this point, the choices to make and remake race have produced the conflicted language of self and community that has characterized American social discourse, shaped even the claims of those movements seeking to challenge the status quo, and consequently made the economic and policy objectives of the conventional left more difficult to achieve. As noted by Edmund Morgan, early American conceptions of freedom and equality were unique not simply because they appeared to ignore or contradict the realities of slavery (and later Jim Crow segregation) but also because they were formed as an apparent acknowledgment of and in conscious contrast to the absence of liberty experienced by blacks.[14] Before and after the Revolutionary War, whites emphasized freedom and individual rights precisely because of the awareness of the presence of unfree or excluded populations inside the nation's borders.

Just as John Locke used the language of slavery to criticize royal absolutism while participating in the profits of slavery through his investments in the Royal African Company and writing constitutions for the Carolinas that gave "every freeman . . . absolute power and authority over his negro slaves," Thomas Jefferson's broad claims about the natural rights and liberties of citizens and the tyranny of the British have to be understood in tandem with his own ownership of slaves and his rather negative assessment of the capacities of free blacks.[15] Despite Louis Hartz's assertions regarding the dominance of northern notions of individualism and liberalism, the South can claim Locke, as well as Jefferson, along with the other defenders of southern practices before and after the Civil War

(from John Calhoun to George Wallace) who have put the same metaphors regarding slavery and liberty into service to buttress their appeals for relief from the
ambitions of abolitionists and integrationists, as well as leftists and supporters of
a progressive social welfare state.

Those seeking to advance the interests of women in the nineteenth century,
although mobilized by their experiences in the abolitionist movement, which
they supported and occasionally led, were quite clear in their assertions that to
deny women basic civil rights—particularly the right to vote—would be to reduce them to the level of chattel slavery. Abolitionist Henry Ward Beecher contrasted the state of "refined and cultivated women on the one side" with "the
rising cloud of emancipated Africans," on the other, concluding that it was "more
important that women should vote than . . . the black man" (Beecher also took
time to suggest that women should be valued above the Irish, "the great emigrant
band of the Emerald Isle").[16] For leading first-wave feminists (and abolitionists)
such as Elizabeth Cady Stanton, it was clear that the rights of white women should
come before those of blacks and that emancipation made the claims of women
only that much more urgent and their situation that much more dire. Her successor among the ranks of suffragettes, Susan B. Anthony, calculating that the cause
needed the support of southern whites (women and men alike) went so far as to
discourage blacks (including Frederick Douglass) from participating in the meetings of the National American Women's Suffrage Association and supported the
organization's decision to sell female suffrage as a means of overcoming the votes
of blacks, Asians, and other immigrants (especially when combined with literacy
tests).[17] The subsequent wave of the feminist movement would not be as explicitly racist in terms of its organizing strategies, despite its frequent appeal to race-
based metaphors (e.g., woman as "nigger"), but it would be almost as divorced
from the concerns and realities of nonwhite women (and men).[18]

Although nativism was an integral part of the worldviews of most actors in
the nineteenth century, newcomers were also quick to recognize that becoming
white and being allowed to move freely within the nonblack community were important achievements. "To enter the white race," suggests Noel Ignatiev in *How
the Irish Became White*, "was a strategy to secure an advantage in a competitive
society."[19] From the ranks of first- and second-generation Americans—for example, the Socialist Party's Victor Berger and the American Federation of Labor's
Samuel Gompers—would emerge some of the most ardent patriots and nativists
and some of the most willing contributors to the cause of American racialism.[20]
As slave traders and owners, nationalists, nativists, and feminists would use the
status of blacks as a metaphor to dramatize their own circumstances, the first-

Table 7.5. Black Residents in Neighborhoods Where
Average Black Resides (%), 1930 and 1970

City	1930	1970
Boston	19.2	66.1
Chicago	70.4	89.2
Los Angeles	25.6	73.9
New York	41.8	60.2
Philadelphia	27.3	75.6

Source: Douglas S. Massey and Nancy A. Denton, *American Apartheid: Segregation and the Making of the Underclass* (Cambridge: Harvard University Press, 1994), p. 48.

generation American leaders of the labor movement were no less willing to put racial understandings into play that would strengthen, in their minds, their own claims to citizenship and social status.

Beyond the efforts to clarify the distinction between their own citizenship status and that of the descendants of slaves, white workers were motivated to seek a separation between their occasionally integrated work spaces and their home lives. Ira Katznelson contends: "What is distinctive about the American experience is that the linguistic, cultural, and institutional meaning given to the differentiation of work and community . . . has taken a sharply divided form."[21] The disjunction between these two realms—in Katznelson's words, the division "between the language and practice of a politics of work and those of a politics of community"—has reinforced the fragmented and conflicted character of American working-class aspirations.[22] The willingness of UAW-affiliated workers in Detroit to organize around a white conservative populism in the 1940s to delay or prevent the erection of housing for blacks, just as their counterparts among the steelworkers in Chicago resisted similar developments in their own neighborhoods with violence in the 1950s (after raising no objections to like arrangements for whites two decades earlier), raises an obvious question: how can solidarity be achieved on the shop floor when it is being strenuously avoided and undermined elsewhere?

This tension between life at work and life at home has become more observable in the North (see Table 7.5) over the course of the last fifty years, whereas the South has actually become more integrated in its neighborhoods and public schools. Perhaps one of the best examples of this work-home dichotomy are the Levittowns that were established in New York (in Nassau County), New Jersey, and Pennsylvania. These communities, built in the post–World War II period, either explicitly refused admission to blacks through restrictive covenants (stipu-

Table 7.6. Population in Levittown, New York, by Race, 1960–1990

Category	1960	1970	1980	1990
Total population	65,276	65,440	57,045	53,286
White	65,056	65,128	56,354	51,883
Black	57	44	45	137
Other	163	268	646	1,266

Source: New York Times, Sunday, December 23, 1997, p. 23.
Note: The 1990 figure for other includes 950 Asians and Pacific Islanders and 31 American Indians and Aleuts.

lating that the houses not "be used or occupied by any persons other than members of the Caucasian race") or were not shown to black home buyers.[23] In the 1948 *Shelley v. Kraemer* decision, the Supreme Court ruled that racially restrictive covenants were not legally enforceable, but simple mob violence often sufficed to achieve the same end, as was the case in the Pennsylvania Levittown in 1957. Integration, of even the slightest degree, did not begin in the New Jersey community until 1960. Although William J. Levitt, the owner of Levitt and Sons, the company behind the projects, was Jewish, he was not convinced that his housing developments could affect what he believed to be the immutable racial mores of the time, one way or the other: "The Negroes in America are trying to do in 400 years what the Jews in the world have not wholly accomplished in 600 years. As a Jew, I have no room in my mind or heart for racial prejudice. But I have come to know that if we sell one house to a Negro family, then 90 or 95 percent of our white customers will not buy into the community. That is their attitude, not ours. As a company, our position is simply this: We can solve a housing problem, or we can try to solve a racial problem, but we cannot combine the two."[24] Levitt, the grandson of a rabbi, built housing in Long Island that refused Jewish applicants admission, but what is more remarkable about the Levittown phenomenon and the associated legacy of segregation — the Long Island community is the most segregated suburb in the United States (see Table 7.6) — is that like Henry Ford, a notorious anti-Semite, Levitt insisted on building his projects with nonunion labor that worked, consistent with Taylorism, in specialized teams to perform specialized tasks (e.g., one crew devoted to painting one color in the different divisions). With a workforce that included up to fifteen thousand workers completing, at its peak, thirty-six houses a day, the Levittown process in some ways typifies the American reconciliation of class and race: an under- or unorganized workforce mass-building racialized segmented communities.

Last, the role of the federal government is significant in the Levittown saga.

Before the civil rights era, the state was not only slow or reluctant to challenge segregation but at times actually reinforced or increased the distance between racial groups. The individuals who moved into the Levittowns often depended on loans subsidized by the Federal Housing Administration (FHA), the Home Owners' Loan Corporation, and the Veterans Administration, which consciously and actively helped millions of Americans buy homes in segregated neighborhoods, because the federal government's public-housing policies generally conformed to and expanded on local practices with respect to residential segregation.[25] As Desmond King notes, "Federal housing programmes were designed and implemented in a way which favoured White home-buyers and ensured that Black Americans continued to be restricted in their choice of area in which to live."[26] The federal government, before and after the New Deal, played a significant role in racializing public spaces in the United States, restricting the opportunities available to African Americans and reinforcing the conflicts between (white) homeowners' rights and (black) civil rights.

The metaphorical contrasting of liberty with slavery and the definition of freedom as the distance one can place between oneself and the situation of blacks have also been evident in the actions of some "blacks" themselves. One can certainly read Homer Plessy's plea in front of the Supreme Court for relief from Louisiana's Jim Crow laws as a request for release from the iron cages of "blackness." His contention that he was "seven-eighths Caucasian and one-eighth African . . . that the mixture of colored blood was not discernible in him, and that he was entitled to every right, privilege, and immunity secured to citizens of the United States of the white race" was consistent with the efforts of Louisiana Creoles to distinguish themselves as much as possible from the local Negro population.[27] Whereas such strategies hinged more explicitly on color and complexion in Plessy's day, the post-1968 physical and spiritual flight of the black middle classes can be interpreted as being part of the same process, as part of the drive to achieve freedom, a racialized freedom that entails being as far as possible from the stereotyped confines of "black life."[28] It is not surprising, then, that many blacks have interpreted the call for multiracial categories in the census as an attempt on the part of some individuals to jump the fence and abandon the ship—or prison—of black community.[29]

For the most, though, playing off the reality of being "black" has not been a strategy available to African Americans: their calls for liberty and freedom have rarely been tinged with the same combination of irony and desperation that has characterized the pleas of some of these other groups. The black struggle for equality and freedom has been relatively unconflicted in this sense (although there have been problematic assumptions about class, gender, and sexuality), and it is for this reason that the speeches, marches, and cultural expressions of the civil rights movement have resonated so widely throughout the world. The focus in this discussion has been on the factors and forces related to race and heterogeneity that have weakened the American left; nevertheless, I want to emphasize that the conflicted development of community in the United States has been accompanied by a thorough exclusion of blacks from unions, from a wide range of employment possibilities, and from quality housing of their own choice. This marginalization, supported and abetted by the state, has sacrificed generations and severely circumscribed black life chances. Too often debates about race and politics, reparations, and affirmative action are detached from any real understanding of the depth of the historical (and contemporary) violence that has been visited on blacks and the ritualized, almost fetishistic, dismissal of the humanity of African Americans.

The point of this discussion, though, is to identify the implications of the aggregate decisions over time to stigmatize black labor, black skin, and black life, beyond the damage done to African Americans. These decisions, along with the racialization of the freedom struggles of white labor, have also affected non-black Americans to the extent that one must really question Sean Wilentz's assertion that the exceptionalism phenomenon is a "colossal non-problem." If white Americans had benefited from the exclusion of blacks—and Asians and other groups at other times—from the privileges associated with membership in the "white republic," to use Alexander Saxton's term, perhaps one might justify, on the basis of some bare-bones, instrumentalist, and amoral calculus, the choices that have been made. What is clear, though, is that the limited, complicated, and conflicted liberties that Jacksonian Americans have achieved do not equal those achieved by their counterparts in other societies. The universal acceptance of race as a meaningful index of social status and the commonly used racialized metaphors and language of freedom have restricted the benefits accruing to all American citizens. That workers and leftists shared these racial understandings with employers, slaveowners, and others is not surprising. Indeed, given the widespread agreement that the republican community could not include nonwhites, with the consequence that maintaining functioning communities would prove to be impossible, what is remarkable is that any individuals and movements were able to transcend these restrictions (e.g., to varying degrees, some of the branches of the Populist Party, the IWW, the post-1928 Communist Party, the CIO before World War II, and the administration of Lyndon Baines Johnson in the mid-1960s).

Sitting by the Gateway

The conventional left is clearly in decline throughout the West. In the United Kingdom, France, Italy, Germany, Austria, and even Sweden, leftist parties are not faring as well with their respective electorates as they did even ten years ago. Over the same period, movements have emerged in some of these countries—for example, in France, Germany, Austria, and Italy—demanding that government limit the influx of "others" from non-European nations and increasingly from other parts of Europe. Indeed, one of the first major upsurges in support for Margaret Thatcher came in 1978 after she referred to Britons feeling "rather swamped" by immigrants from the Commonwealth, a comment that brought her party, the Conservatives, much of the backing that the more explicitly xenophobic British National Front had at the time. As these sentiments have become popular and have mobilized electorates, the conventional left has lost its appeal in the eyes of a growing segment of its potential constituency.

Although the electoral fortunes of the conventional left appear to be in decline, many of its public policy objectives have been realized. The right to vote and constitutional support for that right have been institutionalized in every Western European state. Similarly, in all these countries, the state has acted so as to extend health care coverage to all its citizens. While the formulas and underlying principles vary, the societies have chosen to socialize the benefits of health care technology (and to control the cost of providing health care benefits). And unionized labor in these societies has realized many of its basic goals: official recognition as the representative of the working classes, unemployment benefits, sick-pay compensation, occupational safety regulations, mandated vacation periods, and so on. Families have the benefit of developed parental leave legislation and extensive public-housing schemes where it has been determined that the free market will not suffice. Owing to the efforts of the various Green movements, some headway has been made in regulating the effects of industrial production on the environment (although elements of the conventional left have resisted these advancements).[30] Finally, as a consequence of more informal cultural processes, citizens now enjoy generally safer environments.

Overall, the arguments and institutions of the economic right have succeeded in remaking these various societies and have brought about a thorough fragmentation of their different cultures, yet a certain public policy equilibrium has been established, an equilibrium that survived even the effects of a decade of Thatcherism in England; the 1990 poll tax fiasco was probably an indication of the outer limits of her mandate. Thus regardless of the party in power, it appears that these societies will not go "backward" in their willingness to support the provision of certain public goods (besides immigration policy, one issue that might engender much debate is the degree to which the state should be involved in the economy). While the battles between the left's "economists" and the various prefascist and fascist movements have given the economic right the opportunity to achieve many of its own goals, these societies have still chosen to maintain a certain collective sensibility.

In Canada, a similar equilibrium has been reached in terms of the public goods provisions available to the country's citizens. The primary difference between Canada and Western Europe is that linguistic conflict in Canada has hampered the New Democratic Party's efforts to achieve national support. Similarly, the drive to establish a national culture has been frustrated by the diverse traditions brought to the country by different peoples, with the result that a certain cultural pluralism has been accepted and institutionalized. Despite these linguistic and cultural tensions, the Canadian federal structure has allowed the provinces to create a public goods delivery apparatus that might not have been possible in a more centralized or evenly heterogeneous society, by varying the scale of political interaction. In other words, if French Canada and the province of Quebec did not overlap to the degree that they do, the federal structure would not have been an adequate means of mitigating the effects of the country's demographic and linguistic heterogeneity. Yet tensions between European and non-European communities have arisen, and the antagonisms generated by the linguistic divide continue to threaten the long-term viability of the Canadian federation itself.[31]

Throughout the world, there has been an accelerated fragmentation of the frequently romanticized understandings and customs that previously bound different communities. The effort to resist this fragmentation has been hampered by the confusions generated by an increasingly interactive world community and the tensions created by antagonistic conceptions of gender identity and difference. The various conscious and unconscious attempts to prevent the institutionalization of alienation in its different aspects have also been complicated by the tendency of some movements and peoples to process their alienation by attempting to universalize it, as well as by the general inclination to "make things big." The end result has been the fracturing of the often idealized harmonies and mediums that provided their adherents with a means of understanding and responding to their circumstances collectively.

The left's inability to recognize the meaning and implications of these false dichotomies and its acceptance of the notion that big is always better have confounded its efforts to recognize and interpret its role and function in the maintenance and realization of a collective sensibility and human civilization. The particular and exceptional extent to which the American left has been removed from the main stage of American life has been a direct function of its inability or unwillingness to transcend these hurdles in an especially demographically diverse context, and a result of the popular attachment to a realm — race — that can generate few larger meanings, resilient identities, or practical moralities.

NOTES

Chapter One

1. Wilentz, "Against Exceptionalism," p. 18.
2. Ibid., p. 3.
3. Fredrickson, "From Exceptionalism to Variability," pp. 588–89.
4. Or in Wilentz's terms, "events and movements." See Wilentz, "Against Exceptionalism," p. 5. Examples of analysts who have approached the question in the same manner are, as already mentioned, Wilentz, *Chants Democratic;* Voss, *Making of American Exceptionalism;* Salvatore, *Eugene V. Debs;* Shannon, *Decline of American Communism;* and Diggins, *American Left.*
5. Wilentz, "Against Exceptionalism," p. 3. For a comparative analysis of some of the public goods listed in this paragraph, see Leichter, *Comparative Approach to Policy Analysis;* Heidenheimer, Heclo, and Teich, *Comparative Public Policy;* Headey, *Housing Policy;* Kimball, *Disconnected;* Piven and Cloward, *Why Americans Don't Vote;* and Kennett and Anderson, *Gun in America.*
6. For some interesting examples of organic leftist politics emerging out of mainstream popular culture, see Denselow, *When the Music's Over.*
7. Neither the United States nor the South are static entities. The United States continues to change in terms of its demographic composition, and external conditions and developments (for example, globalization, cultural convergence, the image consciousness that maintaining foreign policy credibility can involve) present ongoing opportunities for a "different" America.
8. Berelson, Lazarsfeld, and McPhee, *Voting,* p. 209.
9. The three major parties of the left currently operating in the United States—the Greens (which has had some impact on political life in the state of New Mexico), the New Party, and the Labor Party—have yet to attract significant support from voters. For a more detailed discussion of the French exception, see Chapter 2.
10. Rose, "How Exceptional is the American Political Economy?," p. 101.
11. On the other hand, the tax burden the American government places on its citizens is also the lowest among its Western counterparts. For 1994, government tax revenues represented 58.6 percent of Denmark's gross domestic product (GDP), 56.2 percent of Sweden's GDP, 55.2 percent of Norway's GDP, and 54 percent of Finland's, with the Netherlands falling at 51.2 percent; Belgium, 50.0 percent; France, 49.5 percent; Austria, 48 percent; Italy, 46.3 percent; Germany, 46.1 percent; Canada, 42 percent; Spain, 39.5 percent; Britain, 36.4 percent; and the United States, 31.6 percent. See Nathaniel C. Nash, "Europeans Brace Themselves for Higher Taxes," *New York Times,* February 24, 1995.
12. Turner suggested that "the most important effect of the frontier [on societal values and inclinations] has been in the promotion of democracy.... [T]he frontier is productive of individualism ... [and] frontier individualism has from the beginning promoted democ-

racy." From "The Significance of the Frontier in American History," in *Early Writings of Frederick Jackson Turner*, p. 219. In this spirit Anthony King suggests that "the state plays a more limited role in America than elsewhere because Americans, more than other people, want it to play a limited role." See "Ideas, Institutions, and the Policies of Governments," p. 418.

13. Potter, *People of Plenty.* One argument that flows from the Turner and Potter theses, to some extent, is that the struggle for universal manhood franchise rights gave rise to many of the socialist and social democratic campaigns in Europe; in the United States manhood suffrage rights were granted during the Jacksonian era. Both Switzerland (1848) and Australia (in the 1850s) extended such rights during the same period, and (as will be discussed in Chapter 5) obvious limitations have been placed on voting rights in the American instance.

14. Eric Foner, "Why Is There No Socialism in the United States?," p. 61.

15. See, for example, James C. Davies, "Toward a Theory of Revolution," pp. 5–19, and Gurr, *Why Men Rebel.*

16. More recent figures (1994) indicate that the relative poverty rates have not changed, with the United States having the highest poverty rate (19.1 percent) after government transfers are factored in (on the basis of market incomes alone, poverty rates are roughly similar among Western nations, with Britain and Belgium on the high end and Germany on the low end). See Bruce Little, "Examining the Poverty of Nations," *Globe and Mail,* August 27, 1995 (and Table 7.4 in this volume).

17. World War I, for example, provoked the splintering of many of the individual socialist parties that made up the Second International. In *American Labor Unions,* Karson suggests that the Catholic Church, along with the influence of Catholicism, might explain American labor exceptionalism. The Catholic Church sought to orient the American labor movement toward a more reformist and moderate path in the first half of the century. The United States, though, was hardly the only country in this period which had a significant number of Catholics in its working classes.

18. One manner in which this reform/revolution tension was particularly relevant will be discussed in the Chapter 3. See Cantor, *Divided Left;* Shannon, *Decline of American Communism;* and Weinstein, *Decline of Socialism.* A related argument is that the craft (as opposed to industrial) orientation of American labor unions, as well as the skilled/unskilled divisions within the working class, reduced the effectiveness of the American union movement. See Gordon, Reich, and Edwards, *Labor Market Segmentation,* and Gordon, Reich, and Edwards, *Segmented Work, Divided Workers.* Again, these splits were not unique to the American case. For an interesting discussion of the effects and possible ramifications of these divisions in the European labor movements, see Kumar, *Rise of Modern Society,* especially chapter 6, pp. 131–68.

19. Weinstein, *Corporate Ideal.* See also Galambos, *Public Image of Big Business;* Galambos, *Rise of the Corporate Commonwealth;* Lustig, *Corporate Liberalism;* and, one of the earlier expositions of the corporate liberal thesis, Kolko, *Triumph of Conservatism.* In a related vein, in *Hammer and Hoe,* Kelley writes, "When we ponder Werner Sombart's question, 'Why is there no socialism in the United States?' in light of the South, violence and lawlessness loom large" (p. xii).

20. McGerr, *Decline of Popular Politics.* For one example of the "two-party resilience" thesis, see Norman Thomas, *Socialism Re-examined.*

21. This counterargument is made by McCormick: "The most visible result [of the institutionalization of the Democratic and Republican Parties] was the appearance of new third parties with bold and specific governmental programs. Under Eugene V. Debs's leader-

ship, the Socialist Party of America reached a peak of strength between 1910 and 1912 when dozens of towns and cities elected Socialist mayors and Debs won nearly a million votes as a presidential candidate." See McCormick, *Party Period,* p. 177.

22. Key, *Southern Politics,* p. 16.

23. Hartz, *Founding of New Societies,* p. 75. In *Continental Divide,* Lipset advances the same argument in the context of a comparison of the American and Canadian political cultures.

24. Hartz, *Founding of New Societies,* p. 106.

25. As Pocock states, "We have found that a 'bourgeois ideology,' a paradigm for capitalist man as *Zoon politikon,* was immensely hampered in its development by the omnipresence of Aristotelian and civic humanist values which virtually defined rentier and entrepreneur as corrupt, and that if indeed capitalist thought ended by privatizing the individual, this may have been because it was unable to find an appropriate way of presenting him as citizen. 'Bourgeois ideology,' which old-fashioned Marxism depicted as appearing with historic inevitability, had, it seems, to wage a struggle for existence and may never finally have won it." See Pocock, "Virtue and Commerce," p. 127 (quotation in text), and Pocock, "Machiavellian Moment Revisited," pp. 460–61.

26. Wilentz, "Artisanal Republican Festivals and the Rise of Class Conflict in New York City, 1788–1837," in *Working Class America,* ed. Frisch and Walkowitz, p. 38.

27. This same theme is developed in Salvatore, *Eugene V. Debs.*

28. Wilentz, "Artisanal Republican Festivals," p. 63. In *Myth of American Individualism,* Barry Alan Shain argues that the predominance of liberal individualist ideals in the eighteenth century has been exaggerated and that the republicanism which thrived then was closer to what he terms "reformed-Protestant communalism" than the secular republicanism suggested by analysts such as Wilentz.

29. Kloppenberg, "Virtues of Liberalism," p. 28.

30. Isaac, "Republican vs. Liberalism?," p. 351. Kloppenberg notes in specific reference to the interaction of these philosophies and the rise of American socialism that "the principles of autonomy and popular sovereignty had been enshrined, and they exerted a powerful hold on the American imagination. When the challenge of socialism emerged in the nineteenth century, it was not so much co-opted by a liberal consensus as it was preempted by the nation's own prior commitment to liberty and equality" ("Virtues of Liberalism," p. 32).

31. Kraditor, "American Radical Historians," p. 140.

32. Saxton, *Indispensable Enemy,* p. 1. A similar understanding lies at the heart of Edmund Morgan's *American Slavery, American Freedom.* Suggesting that America can be seen as "colonial Virginia writ large," Morgan contends that colonial conceptions of equality were not only racially circumscribed but also imaginable only because all white Virginians were automatically and effectively "equal in not being slaves" (pp. 387, 381). Sean Wilentz and Nick Salvatore, among others, have both been criticized for failing to give proper consideration to the implications of "whiteness" with regard to American labor. See Ignatiev, *How the Irish Became White,* p. 183; Goldfield, *Color of Politics,* p. 149; and, for a broader comment on the phenomenon, Painter, "French Theories in American Settings," pp. 92–95.

33. See Rogers M. Smith, *Civic Ideals,* p. 8.

34. Fields, "Slavery, Race, and Ideology," p. 118.

35. Tensions relating to immigration are beginning to influence political developments in Western Europe and Canada, and it is conceivable that in the near future immigration-related issues will have greater public policy and public good–related implications. These developments are discussed in greater detail in Chapters 3, 6, and 7.

36. For one perspective on the way federal arrangements have reduced the impact of linguistic tensions in Canadian politics, see Richard Iton, " 'Race' and Language in American and Canadian Politics," in *Identity, Rights, and Constitutional Transformation,* ed. Hanafin and Williams, pp. 111–31.

37. Although slavery did exist in Canada, it was on a much smaller scale and for a shorter time period.

38. See Linne, *A General System of Nature,* and Buffon, *Oeuvres Complètes de Buffon.*

39. As to Linne's and Buffon's motivations, Montagu writes, "In an age of nationalist and imperialist expansion, national pride played no small part in the naming and classification of fossil as well as living forms of men." See Montagu, "Introduction," in *Concept of Race,* ed. Montagu, p. xv.

40. Ibid., pp. xvi, 9. In the same spirit, Johann Herder, the eighteenth-century proponent of the particularist conception of *Volksgeist,* wrote: "I could wish the distinctions between the human species, that have been made from a laudable zeal for discriminatory science, not be carried beyond the due bounds. Some for instance have thought fit, to employ the term *races* for four or five divisions, originally made in consequence of country or complexion: but I see no reason for this appellation. Race refers to a difference of origin, which in this case does not exist. . . . In short, there are neither four or five races, nor exclusive varieties, on this Earth. Complexions run into each other: forms follow the genetic character: and upon the whole, all are at last but shades of the same great picture, extending through all ages, and over all parts of the Earth." See *Philosophy of the History of Man,* p. 298.

41. For a relatively early discussion of the Americanization of race, see Handlin, "The Linnaean Web," in *Race and Nationality in America,* pp. 71–92.

42. See Spencer Rich, "Caribbean Hispanics Seen Divided by Race in U.S.," *Washington Post,* October 26, 1989, p. A18. Significantly, Canadian census figures were, until recently, broken down on the basis of mother tongue and country of origin. As a result it was not known exactly how many "whites," "blacks," "Asians," or others lived in the country. Not surprisingly, because of a push to collect census data from those alarmed by non-European immigration and by ethnic and immigrant groups wishing to ascertain the size of their own communities, questions about race are now included.

43. That New York's Puerto Ricans and Florida's Cubans, the first predominantly Democrats and the latter Republicans, are both lumped in the Hispanic category, is one indication of the limited utility of the grouping.

44. Any attempt to talk about difference is fraught with risk given the history of the usage of terms such as "race" and "culture." Even the terms "ethnicity" and "demographic heterogeneity" can be read (and, in this case, misread) as an endorsement of the notion that there are empirical differences on the basis of which one can distinguish human populations. That is not the sense in which the terms are being used in this discussion. On the other hand, it should not be necessary to forgo all consideration of culture and ethnicity, difference and particularistic attachments, as long as it is recognized that these categories are always constructed, flexible, and mutable, although often quite real to their adherents. It is in this spirit that Henry Louis Gates Jr. writes in *Colored People,* p. xv, "Part of me admires those people who can say with a straight face that they have transcended any attachment to a particular community or group . . . but I always want to run around behind them to see what holds them up." The term "demographic heterogeneity" is being used to acknowledge, in a neutral manner, that peoples are prone to attributing significance to a number of issues including ethnicity, religion, and aspects of physical appearance, among

others, and to recognize that the potential exists for social conflict and certain dynamics to occur. At the minimum, the term is used to recognize that "diverse societies," however defined, always face a different—and perhaps more difficult—kind of struggle in trying to mobilize toward collective goals, although the rewards arguably are greater than those achievable in more homogeneous societies.

45. For a discussion of the incorporation of the Irish, see Ignatiev, *How the Irish Became White*.

46. Quoted in Steven A. Holmes, "Figuring Out Hispanic Influence," *New York Times*, August 16, 1998.

47. Michael Lind, "The Beige and the Black," *New York Times Magazine*, August 16, 1998, p. 38.

48. Richard Rodriguez, quoted in "A Dialogue on Race with President Clinton," p. 2. The Hispanic category overlaps with the traditional racial categories. In other words, a number of Hispanics are "black." It is not clear whether the predictions about the relative size of the two groups incorporate this understanding. Regarding the future of race in American life, the push to create biracial categories might only give more life to the existing language of race rather than contribute to its obsolescence. Some blacks have also noted that current methods of calibrating difference are necessary for the purposes of counting with regard to the implementation of affirmative action programs and have consequently expressed concerns about the push to modify or abandon these classifications. See Lawrence Wright, "One Drop of Blood."

49. Among those who have pursued this line of argument are Du Bois, *Black Reconstruction in America*; Saxton, *Indispensable Enemy*, and *Rise and Fall of the White Republic*; Mink, *Old Labor and New Immigrants*; Roediger, *Wages of Whiteness*; Ignatiev, *How the Irish Became White*; Quadagno, *Color of Welfare*; Lewis, "Promise and Peril of Class"; and Goldfield, *Color of Politics*.

50. Roediger, *Wages of Whiteness*, p. 5.

51. Denning, *Cultural Front*.

Chapter Two

1. Quoted in Brody, "Barriers of Individualism," *Dissent*, Winter 1989, p. 73.

2. Ibid.

3. Saxton, *Indispensable Enemy*, p. 12.

4. See Commons et al., *History of Labor*, 1:412–17.

5. The union also sought monetary reform, and specifically banking reform, to satisfy its significant agrarian constituency.

6. Commons et al., *History of Labor*, 2:90.

7. From Stephens's address to the Knights' assembly of January 12, 1871, "History of the Knights of Labor," in *Labor Movement*, ed. McNeill, pp. 402–3.

8. Quoted in Dulles and Dubofsky, *Labor in America*, p. 126.

9. Quoted in McNeill, *Labor Movement*, p. 425.

10. Quoted in ibid., pp. 426–27.

11. Dulles and Dubofsky, *Labor in America*, pp. 127–34, and Commons et al., *History of Labor*, 2:339, 396, 413.

12. Selig Perlman, "End of Secrecy in the Knights and Deviation from First Principles," in Commons et al., *History of Labor*, 2:349.

13. Dulles and Dubofsky, *Labor in America*, p. 141.

14. The actual numbers given are 510,351 members in 1887 and 75,000 in 1893 in Commons et al., *History of Labor*, 2:413, and Dulles and Dubofsky, *Labor in America*, p. 134, respectively.

15. Commons et al., *History of Labor*, 2:390. Craft unions organized workers within their specific trades. Industrial unions organized workers by industry. The industrial unions, consequently, included skilled and unskilled workers. Craft unions were, naturally, less inclined to consider the interests of the unskilled and often pursued their interests over and against those of unskilled labor. The willingness of craft unions to maintain or create a hierarchy within the working class was reflected in their support for reform, often initiated from above, rather than "radical" change.

16. The AFL was established officially on December 8, 1886.

17. Dulles and Dubofsky, *Labor in America*, p. 142.

18. Gompers quoted in Brody, "Barriers of Individualism," p. 74.

19. Selig Perlman, "The Great Upheaval, 1884–1886," in Commons et al., *History of Labor*, 2:357.

20. From Reid, *Negro Membership in American Labor Unions*, p. 24. Barriers to the recruitment of unskilled labor included high dues and initiation fees.

21. It is probably no coincidence that industrial unions really succeeded only after large-scale immigration ceased. As Dulles and Dubofsky suggest, "As the workers' ranks were constantly swelled by new arrivals, a tremendous reservoir of potential strikebreakers was always at hand to furnish cheap replacements for those who dared to take part in any union activity" (*Labor in America*, pp. 121–22).

22. Mink, *Old Labor and New Immigrants*, p. 68.

23. Dulles and Dubofsky, *Labor in America*, p. 147.

24. Brody, "Barriers of Individualism," pp. 74–75.

25. Ibid., p. 75.

26. Quoted in Takaki, *Different Mirror*, p. 195.

27. Saxton, *Indispensable Enemy*, p. 19.

28. Ibid., p. 18.

29. Quoted in McNeill, *Labor Movement*, p. 429.

30. Ibid., p. 430.

31. Ibid., p. 433. It is interesting to note that many of the individuals who put forward these arguments were of Irish descent. Nativist distrust of Irish verticalist loyalties was a factor, as already noted, in the Know-Nothing assaults on Catholic immigrants.

32. Ibid., p. 435.

33. Saxton, *Indispensable Enemy*, p. 261. The term "coolie" was used to suggest (incorrectly) that the Chinese immigrants represented unfree or indentured labor.

34. Ibid., p. 265.

35. Quoted in ibid., p. 122.

36. Quoted in ibid., p. 62.

37. Quoted in Tsai, *Chinese Experience in America*, p. 16.

38. See Ira B. Cross, *Labor Movement in California*, pp. 84–85.

39. Kingston, *China Men*, p. 144. The immigrants themselves were understandably displeased with the treatment they received from their fellow Americans. "When I first came, Chinese [were] treated worse than dog," remembered one. "Oh, it was terrible, terrible." Another resident of San Francisco's Chinatown in the 1870s recollects: "We were simply terrified; we kept indoors after dark for fear of being shot in the back. Children spit upon us as we passed by and called us rats." See Takaki, *Different Mirror*, p. 208. At the same

time, most of these immigrants characterized their fellow Americans as quite foreign as well (consequently the frequent references by Chinese immigrants to "demons," "devils," and "barbarians") and occasionally in equally derogatory terms. Suggested one of these immigrants, Lee Chew: "It was the jealousy of other nationalities—especially the Irish—that raised all the outcry against the Chinese. . . . The Chinese were persecuted, not for their vices, but for their virtues. . . . Irish fill the almshouses and prisons and orphan asylums, Italians are among the most dangerous of men, Jews were unclean and ignorant. Yet they are all let in, while Chinese . . . are shut out." See Holt, *Life Stories of Undistinguished Americans*, pp. 184–85.

40. Saxton, *Indispensable Enemy*, p. 1.

41. The AFL's state secretary in California, Paul Scharrenberg, suggested that the law was necessary to "maintain California for us and our kind of people." See Kwong, *Forbidden Workers*, p. 150.

42. In "The Anti-Chinese Agitation in California," in Commons et al., *History of Labor*, Selig Perlman makes the following (striking and ironic) observation: "The anti-Chinese agitation in California, culminating as it did in the Exclusion Act of 1882, was doubtless the most important single factor in the history of American labor, for without it the entire country might have been overrun by Mongolian labor, and the labor movement might have become a conflict of races instead of one of classes" (2:252–53).

43. Versions of this argument can be found in Saxton's *Indispensable Enemy;* Kung, *Chinese in American Life*, pp. 75–76; Chen, *Chinese of America*, p. 150; and Gyory, *Closing the Gate*.

44. See Marshall, *The Negro and Organized Labor*, p. 6.

45. Spero and Harris, *Black Worker*, p. 3.

46. Quoted in Thomas Wagstaff, "Call Your Old Master—'Master': Southern Political Leaders and Negro Labor during Presidential Reconstruction," in *Black Labor in America*, ed. Cantor, p. 15. For a vivid description of the similarities between slavery and the black work experience after emancipation, see "The Life Story of a Negro Peon," in *Life Stories of Undistinguished Americans*, ed. Holt, pp. 114–23.

47. Emancipation caused some southerners to consider replacing black labor with Asian labor, an arrangement some perceived as being probably cheaper than any scheme to hand out "forty acres and a mule" to each freedman. One gloating Kentucky farmer warned the new citizens, "Work nigger or starve," in the apparent belief that Chinese workers would soon force the blacks to compete, unsuccessfully, for employment. Despite a temporary excitement about the possibilities, as well as attempts to contact the appropriate labor contractors, few Chinese laborers actually went to the Southeast. The failure of this plan appears to have been related to a basic Chinese unwillingness to participate. See Barth, *Bitter Struggle*, pp. 188–97. Regarding black responses to Chinese immigration, see Philip S. Foner and Rosenberg, *Racism, Dissent, and Asian Americans*, pp. 212–42.

48. Spero and Harris, *Black Worker*, p. 3.

49. Wilentz, *Chants Democratic*, p. 264.

50. Ibid.

51. See Bernstein, *New York City Draft Riots*.

52. See Staudenraus, *African Colonization Movement;* Read, *Negro Problem Solved;* and Redkey, *Black Exodus*.

53. Reid, *Negro Membership in American Labor Unions*, p. 23.

54. See Commons et al., *History of Labor*, 2:146–51.

55. See Marshall, *The Negro and Organized Labor*, p. 12.

56. See Philip S. Foner, *Organized Labor and the Black Worker,* p. 28.

57. See ibid., pp. 23-26, and Sylvis, *Life, Speeches, and Essays of William H. Sylvis,* pp. 339-46.

58. For the white leaders of the NLU, the Republicans were the representatives of capital. For blacks, the Grand Old Party (GOP) was the party of Lincoln. At that point, in 1869, Ulysees S. Grant was president, and Isaac Myers, speaking for the black delegates in attendance from Maryland and Pennsylvania, stated that "the colored men of the country thoroughly indorse him [Grant]." See Philip S. Foner, *Organized Labor and the Black Worker,* p. 26.

59. Philip S. Foner and Lewis, *Black Worker,* p. 52, preface.

60. See ibid., p. 273.

61. Ibid., p. 283.

62. From August Meier and Elliot Rudwick's "Attitudes of Negro Leaders toward the American Labor Movement from the Civil War to World War I," in *The Negro and the American Labor Movement,* ed. Jacobsen, p. 33.

63. Ibid., p. 37.

64. See Philip S. Foner and Lewis, *Black Worker,* p. 13.

65. See ibid., p. 43.

66. Quoted in Saxton, *Indispensable Enemy,* p. 271.

67. Quoted in ibid., p. 273. At the AFL's 1900 convention, with regard to the impending expiry of the Chinese Restriction Act, it was stated that "surely our recent experience with the Chinese is no inducement for the relaxation of the laws for their rigid exclusion from our country." Two years later, at the federation's twenty-second convention, it was asserted that "to permit [the Chinese] to come to this country, under any circumstances, is treason to our civilization and to our race." See American Federation of Labor, *Report of Proceedings,* 20th convention (1900), p. 27, and ibid., 22d convention (1902), p. 145. For a more detailed explanation of Gompers's views with regard to nonwhite immigration, see Gompers, *Seventy Years of Life and Labor,* pp. 160-67.

68. Marshall, *The Negro and Organized Labor,* p. 19.

69. See Herbert Hill, "Anti-Oriental Agitation and the Rise of Working-Class Racism," *Society,* January/February 1973, pp. 43-48, and Gwendolyn Mink, *Old Labor and New Immigrants,* p. 79.

70. Marc Karson and Ronald Radosh, "The American Federation of Labor and the Negro Worker, 1894-1949," in *The Negro and the American Labor Movement,* ed. Jacobsen, pp. 158-59.

71. Marshall, *The Negro and Organized Labor,* p. 15.

72. Paul B. Worthman, "Black Workers and Labor Unions in Birmingham, Alabama, 1897-1904," in *Black Labor in America,* ed. Cantor, p. 62.

73. Marshall, *The Negro and Organized Labor,* pp. 16-17.

74. Ibid., p. 17.

75. Reid, *Negro Membership in American Labor Unions,* p. 47.

76. Ibid., p. 50.

77. See Livesay, *Samuel Gompers and Organized Labor,* p. 158.

78. Reid, *Negro Membership in American Labor Unions,* p. 40.

79. Ibid., p. 139.

80. Spero and Harris, *Black Worker,* pp. 85-86.

81. Marshall, *The Negro and Organized Labor,* p. 11.

82. Ibid., p. 10.

83. See Philip S. Foner, *American Socialism and Black Americans,* pp. 89-90.

84. Meier and Rudwick, "Attitudes of Negro Leaders," p. 37.

85. Philip S. Foner, *American Socialism and Black Americans,* p. 90.

86. From the introduction to Washington, *Up from Slavery,* p. v.

87. Bracey, Meier, and Rudwick, *Black Nationalism in America,* p. xl.

88. Cruse, *Rebellion or Revolution?,* p. 83.

89. Ibid., p. 211. For two divergent perspectives on Booker T. Washington, see Baker, *Modernism,* and Reed, *W. E. B. Du Bois and American Political Thought.*

90. "Nonintegrationism" is used in this discussion to refer to the broad category of philosophies connected primarily by their common rejection of integrationism (for whatever reason). "Nationalist approaches" are a subset of this category, and the term is used to refer to those philosophies that *actively* seek to increase or celebrate differences between their adherents and other groups. Booker T. Washington was a nonintegrationist in that he rejected integration (although his reasons for that choice are not absolutely clear). One cannot safely, on the basis of his public record, categorize Washington as a nationalist.

91. Philip S. Foner, *American Socialism and Black Americans,* p. 92.

92. This quotation is from the same passage in which Washington proposes, "In all things that are purely social we can be as separate as the fingers, yet one as the hand in all things essential to mutual progress." See his *Up from Slavery,* pp. 161–62.

93. See Matthews, *Quest for an American Sociology,* p. 66, and Washington, *Man Farthest Down.*

94. "Verticalism" refers to the tendency of an ethnic or cultural group to be organized hierarchically and therefore to be resistant to the class appeals of labor and leftist movements.

95. Meier and Rudwick, "Attitudes of Negro Leaders," p. 41.

96. Booker T. Washington, "The Negro and the Labor Unions," *Atlantic Monthly,* June 1913, p. 756. It should be noted that the article in question is, on the whole, a rather balanced assessment of the problems blacks faced in their dealings with unions and that Washington urges unions and all workers to eliminate discrimination. Significantly, it was written after the election of a Democratic president (Woodrow Wilson) and in a period when Washington was much more willing to challenge Jim Crow given that his patronage connections had been severed and his "machine" was no longer as omnipotent as it previously had been. For an indication of his inclinations before this relative transformation, see the January 1898 edition of the *Southern Estates Farm Magazine* for an article entitled "The Best Free Labor in the World."

97. Norrell, "Caste in Steel," p. 671.

98. Herbert G. Gutman, "The Negro and the United Mine Workers of America: The Career and Letters of Richard L. Davis and Something of Their Meaning, 1890–1900," in *The Negro and the American Labor Movement,* ed. Jacobsen, pp. 74–75. See also Joe W. Trotter, "Class and Racial Inequality: The Southern West Virginia Black Coal Miners' Response, 1915–1932," in *Organized Labor in the Twentieth-Century South,* ed. Zieger, pp. 60–83.

99. Gutman, "The Negro and the United Mine Workers," p. 51.

100. Ibid., p. 50.

101. Ibid., p. 51. Gutman's reading of the UMW has been criticized for romanticizing the union's racial record and downplaying the extent to which black mine workers experienced discrimination. See Spero and Harris, *Black Worker,* pp. 352–75; Herbert Hill, "Myth-Making as Labor History: Herbert Gutman and the United Mine Workers of America," *International Journal of Politics, Culture, and Society* 2 (Winter 1988): 132–200; and Ignatiev, *How the Irish Became White,* pp. 180–82. In *Challenge of Interracial Unionism,* Daniel Letwin suggests that on occasion "the Alabama UMW challenged the hardening norms of

segregation" (p. 6), and he argues for a more nuanced and fluid reading of the class and racial dynamics operating among workers and their unions in the South.

102. Perlman, "Great Upheaval," 2:360.

103. Dubofsky, *We Shall Be All,* p. 21.

104. Ibid., p. 22.

105. Fred Thompson, editor of the IWW's *Industrial Worker,* quoted in ibid., p. 25.

106. *Proceedings of the Founding Convention of the IWW,* preface.

107. Ibid.

108. Ibid., p. 1. Two other differences between the two unions were the higher dues charged by the AFL and the greater centralization of the IWW.

109. Pelling, *American Labor,* p. 114.

110. Tensions within the organization led to the formation of a dissident IWW at one point, DeLeon's effective expulsion, and Debs's distancing.

111. Dubofsky, *We Shall Be All,* p. ix.

112. It is ironic, perhaps, that a UMW official was presiding over the AFL when the racially exclusive International Association of Machinists (IAM) was finally admitted, given that the UMW was supposedly relatively progressive in this area. Also, at the same time that Gompers was facing off against the socialists within the AFL, Terence Powderly was himself dethroned by socialists in the Knights of Labor, which resulted, a year later, in the 1895 expulsion of the members of Daniel DeLeon's Socialist Labor Party from the order. For Gompers's own account of his defeat and his activities afterward, see *Seventy Years of Life and Labor,* pp. 106–12.

113. From Pelling, *American Labor,* p. 115. For V. I. Lenin's assessment of Gompers's class politics, see Stearn, *Gompers,* pp. 118–19.

114. Following tradition, one of the demands was further exclusion of Chinese immigrants.

115. James Weinstein, in *Corporate Ideal,* suggests that a liberal corporatist ethic defined the era and characterized the activities of the NCF. Some members of the AFL did question Gompers's participation in the NCF. See American Federation of Labor, *Report of Proceedings,* 25th convention (1905), pp. 145, 159, 181–82. For Gompers's response, see Stearn, *Gompers,* pp. 40–43, and American Federation of Labor, *Report of Proceedings,* 31st convention (1911).

116. See American Federation of Labor, *Report of Proceedings,* 26th convention (1906), p. 100.

117. See ibid., pp. 101–2.

118. Gompers, *Should a Political Labor Party Be Formed?,* p. 10. Gompers also contended that "an independent political labor party becomes either radical, so-called, or else reactionary, but it is primarily devoted to one thing and that is vote-getting. Every sail is trimmed to the getting of votes. The question of the conditions of Labor, the question of the standards of Labor, the question of the struggles and the sacrifices of Labor, to bring into the lives and the work of the toilers—all that is subordinated into the consideration of votes for the party" (ibid., pp. 10–11). Clearly, Gompers was also afraid that any labor party in the United States would be dominated by the Socialist Party, for which he had little affection. In contrast, Socialist (and AFL supporter) Victor Berger argued that "there is only one way left for the working class and for the common people in general. That is to send socialists to Congress, in order that the voice of labor may be heard in the national legislature of our country" (*American Socialist,* October 17, 1914, p. 1).

119. The American labor movement also had to compete with the individualist values propagated in some quarters suggesting that "the strikebreaker was the real American

hero." This suggestion was made by Charles Eliot, a Harvard University professor, who also urged that "no sacrifice [be made] of the independent American worker to the labor union." Quoted in Walter Galenson, "The Historical Role of American Trade Unionism," in *Unions in Transition,* ed. Lipset, p. 45.

120. American Federation of Labor, *Report of Proceedings,* 40th convention (1920), p. 276.

121. Ibid., 41st convention (1921), pp. 129–30. At the AFL's 45th convention, it was plainly stated that "the position of the American Federation of Labor on the Asiatic Exclusion question has been affirmed and reaffirmed so often that it should be known to all within and out of the labor movement" (ibid. [1925], p. 170). Three years later a resolution was adopted calling for Secretary of Labor James J. Davis to "repudiate" a statement made by his assistant secretary at a Chinese-American Citizens Alliance dinner in New York (October 7, 1928) suggesting that immigration laws might be amended so as to allow American-born Chinese individuals to sponsor wives from China. See ibid., 48th convention (1928).

122. At its 36th convention in 1916 a delegate from the Laborers' Friendly Society of Japan, B. Suzuki, urged the AFL to approach the immigration and labor question from a broader perspective: "When the labor movement is restricted only to a single country, and does not extend outside its national boundary, it is evident that a country, where laborers have no power and their wages are cheap, will finally control the destiny of the world's industry, and cheap labor will monopolize the labor market of the world." Suzuki also encouraged the AFL to send delegates to the conventions of Japanese unionists. See ibid., 36th convention (1916), p. 190.

123. Ibid., 47th convention (1927), p. 338.

124. Ibid., 51st convention (1931), p. 73.

125. See Gillian Creese, "Class, Ethnicity, and Conflict: The Case of Chinese and Japanese Immigrants," in *Workers, Capital, and the State in British Columbia,* ed. Warburton and Coburn, p. 69.

126. See ibid., p. 73.

127. Trades and Labor Congress of Canada, *Report of Proceedings,* 36th convention (1920), p. 191.

128. Ibid., p. 26.

129. Ibid., 37th convention (1921), pp. 213–14.

130. Ibid., 36th convention (1920), p. 24.

131. J. N. Bell, one of the TUC's delegates to the 1906 AFL convention, sympathized with his American brothers about their concerns regarding Chinese labor, noting that the TUC was against further Chinese immigration to South Africa, which was, in his view, undercutting the wages and job security of "Englishmen." See American Federation of Labor, *Report of Proceedings,* 26th convention (1906), pp. 121–23.

132. Just as the new immigrants of the mid–nineteenth century, the Irish and Germans, quickly learned the doctrines of nativism and resisted the Chinese, even the newest arrival in this country in the early decades of this century soon assumed the popular attitude toward blacks. In her essay "Immigrants in the New South: Italians in Louisiana's Sugar Parishes, 1880–1910" (in *American Working Class Culture,* ed. Cantor), Jean Ann Scarpaci describes how Italian workers eventually came to interpret the place of blacks in American society and shape their own expectations and sense of status. As one observer recounts: "One Italian informant . . . said he and his family had been badly mistreated by a French plantation owner near New Roads. When asked how he had been mistreated, he stated that he and his family were made to live among the negroes and were treated in the same manner. At first he did not mind because he did not know any difference, but when he learned

the position that Negroes occupied in this country, he demanded that his family be moved to a different house and be given better treatment" (p. 389). Concludes Scarpaci, "Thus, the exposure of the Italian immigrant to white prejudices ultimately influenced his attitude toward Southern blacks. He realized that treatment equal to that accorded the black was inferior treatment" (p. 390). Echoes Dubofsky in *We Shall Be All*, "Only the Negro's presence kept the Italians, the Pole, and the Slav above society's mudsill" (p. 8.). Despite the marked heterogeneity of the American working class, when faced with the issue of the black worker as American citizen, a striking attitudinal homogeneity developed.

133. In the 1900–1910 period, 170,000 blacks moved north, 454,000 in the next decade, and 749,000 between 1920 and 1930. See Marable, *Race, Reform, and Rebellion,* p. 8, and Marshall, *The Negro and Organized Labor,* p. 21.

134. See American Federation of Labor, *Report of Proceedings,* 36th convention (1916), pp. 223, 255.

135. Meier and Rudwick, "Attitudes of Negro Leaders," p. 46.

136. See Tuttle, *Race Riot.*

137. Frazier, *Negro Family,* p. 447.

138. See Marshall, *The Negro and Organized Labor,* pp. 23–25.

139. American Federation of Labor, *Report of Proceedings,* 38th convention (1918), p. 199.

140. At the 1920 convention, a representative of the interests of black workers even stated, "We are not trying for, nor do we want what is called 'social equality,' as some are trying to insinuate." See ibid., 40th convention (1920), p. 263.

141. Ibid., 45th convention (1925), p. 134. In the NAACP's *Annual Report* for 1924, the following question was asked: "Is it not time . . . that black and white labor get together? Is it not time for white unions to stop bluffing and for black laborers to stop cutting off their noses [i.e., gaining employment through strikebreaking] to spite their faces?" See National Association for the Advancement of Colored People, *Annual Report* (1924), p. 49.

142. See Marshall, *The Negro and Organized Labor,* pp. 23–25, 39.

143. American Federation of Labor, *Report of Proceedings,* 42d convention (1922), pp. 118–19.

144. Marshall, *The Negro and Organized Labor,* p. 25.

145. The porters also played a major role in distributing the different black newspapers from city to city. North of the border, the BSCP was a significant organization in African Canadian communities and in politics, because in Canada, as in the United States, the railway porters were in many ways perceived to be among the elite of black workers and the railroads tended to fill porters' positions with black candidates exclusively.

146. Pelling, *American Labor,* pp. 105–6, and Rayback, *History of American Labor,* p. 295.

147. The actual estimate is 5,110,000. See Rayback, *History of American Labor,* pp. 295–96.

148. Ibid., p. 291.

149. Lochnerism generally refers to conservative readings of the Fourteenth Amendment regarding state regulatory rights and of the Fifth Amendment and the commerce clause regarding the ability of the federal government to regulate the economy and undertake redistributive measures.

150. These new approaches included the creation of company unions, stock distribution plans, profit sharing, and the application of the ideas developed in Frederick Taylor's time and motion studies to the organization of workers and the workplace.

151. Grubbs, *Struggle for Labor Loyalty,* p. 131.

152. Rayback, *History of American Labor,* pp. 296, 315.

153. Ibid.

154. From Raymond Wolters, "Closed Shop and White Shop: The Negro Response to Collective Bargaining, 1933–1935," in *Black Labor in America*, ed. Cantor, pp. 137–38.

155. See ibid., pp. 138, 143.

156. American Federation of Labor, *Report of Proceedings*, 54th convention (1934), p. 334.

157. Ibid., 55th convention (1935), pp. 812, 814. At this convention, Green and A. Philip Randolph debated the number of AFL internationals that excluded blacks (with Green claiming that only five did and Randolph citing twenty cases). Randolph's estimation was certainly closer to the truth.

158. The AFL and NAACP found themselves on opposite sides of the issue—with the association making it clear that its opposition was not to "the *closed* shop but against the *white* shop"—and the NAACP's San Francisco branch picketed the AFL's 1934 convention in the city with loudspeakers and billboards reading "Best of luck—A.F. of L., White Labor Must Smash the Color Line in its own Interest." See National Association for the Advancement of Colored People, *Annual Report* (1934), pp. 12–14.

159. There were also concerns expressed by black leadership about the effective racial imbalances and exclusions built into the National Recovery Administration because those fields in which black workers were concentrated (e.g., within the textiles industry) were characteristically not targeted by the new programs. In the NAACP's *Annual Report* for 1933, it was noted that "the cotton textile code deliberately excluded about 12,000 colored workers by its specific provision that the clause relating to minimum wages and maximum hours should not apply to 'outside crews and cleaners.' Most of the colored employees in the cotton textile industry are in these categories." See National Association for the Advancement of Colored People, *Annual Report* (1933), p. 6. A. Philip Randolph introduced a resolution at the AFL's 1933 convention seeking the federation's support for a complaint against these exclusions. See American Federation of Labor, *Report of Proceedings*, 53d convention (1933). The failure of the New Deal–era programs to tackle Jim Crow will be discussed in more depth in Chapters 4 and 5.

160. See Wolters, "Closed Shop," pp. 142–44.

161. Clear evidence of the NAACP's support for the principle of labor organization—at a point when organized labor still discriminated against black workers—can be found in the resolution passed at the association's 1939 convention calling for the organization "to accord preference to employers of union labor in all purchases of supplies and in all letting of contracts involving the employment of labor." See National Association for the Advancement of Colored People, *Annual Report* (1939), p. 17.

162. Wolters, "Closed Shop," p. 152.

163. See Morris, *Conflict within the AFL*, p. 108.

164. For an extended discussion of the birth of the CIO, see Galenson, *CIO Challenge*.

165. See the American Federation of Labor, *Report of Proceedings*, 52d convention (1932). Lewis introduced a successful resolution calling for the federation's affiliates to contribute funds toward the BSCP's dispute with the Pullman Company. After the split, Randolph urged the AFL to pursue a conciliatory approach to the CIO and criticized efforts to Red-bait the breakaway unions: "Communism is not an issue in this controversy. As a matter of fact, the members of the C.I.O., the United Mine Workers of America, the International Garment Workers of America, the Amalgamated Clothing Workers of America were not accused of Communistic tendencies before this split. Why would they then be suddenly accused of being Communistic? Everybody knows John L. Lewis is not a Communist." See American Federation of Labor, *Report of Proceedings*, 57th convention (1937), p. 396.

166. See Philip S. Foner, *Paul Robeson Speaks*, p. 135.

167. Marshall, *The Negro and Organized Labor*, p. 39.

168. National Association for the Advancement of Colored People, *Annual Report* (1940), p. 9.

169. Horne, *Black and Red*, p. 49.

170. In *If He Hollers Let Him Go*, Chester Himes offers a description of the interplay of wartime developments and black and female labor in the context of West Coast industry.

171. Marshall, *The Negro and Organized Labor*, p. 41. In "Union Conservatism: A Barrier to Racial Equality," Julius Jacobsen supports this contention: "The alliance of Negro and labor organizations, particularly the CIO, continued in the post war period. A tribute to its effectiveness was Truman's surprise victory in the 1948 presidential election." From *The Negro and the American Labor Movement*, ed. Jacobsen, p. 8.

172. Marshall, *The Negro and Organized Labor*, p. 49.

173. Ford was also a vicious anti-Semite.

174. Blacks made up 12.2 percent of Ford's employees in 1930 but only 4 percent of the industry's total workforce. See Marshall, *The Negro and Organized Labor*, p. 35.

175. See James S. Olson, "Race, Class, and Progress: Black Leadership and Industrial Unionism, 1936–1945," in *Black Labor in America*, ed. Cantor, pp. 159–61.

176. Mine Workers and CIO chief John L. Lewis had addressed the NAACP's 1940 convention, and other CIO executives (such as Philip Murray and Walter Reuther) would serve on the NAACP's board.

177. Marshall, *The Negro and Organized Labor*, p. 29.

178. See American Federation of Labor, *Report of Proceedings*, 61st convention (1941), p. 476.

179. See ibid., pp. 483–84, 487.

180. Marshall, *The Negro and Organized Labor*, p. 44. The first constitution of the Brotherhood of Railway Clerks of America (written in 1900) limited membership to "any white person of good moral character who is 18 years of age or over, and who has had at least six months actual experience in Railroad Clerical Work, and who shall at the time of making application for membership be in the employ of some railroad Company." While the age limit was dropped to seventeen in the 1905 constitution (and pushed back to eighteen in 1906) and gender inclusivity was recognized in the 1910 version, the racial exclusion would remain until 1947. See Brotherhood of Railway Clerks of America, *Constitution and By-Laws*, 1900–1947.

181. Marshall, *The Negro and Organized Labor*, p. 215.

182. Ibid., p. 42.

183. The first FEPC was established in August 1941 and lasted until January 1943. A second committee was launched in May 1943 and terminated its activities in June 1946.

184. The NAACP, for its part, protested Roosevelt's decision in 1942 to change the status of the FEPC from an independent agency that reported directly to the president to an organization that was subsumed under the umbrella of the War Manpower Commission. The commission already included two agencies—the United States Employment Service and the United States Office of Education—that "permitted and encouraged" discrimination. See National Association for the Advancement of Colored People, *Annual Report* (1942), pp. 4–6.

185. A number of states outside the South established counterparts to the FEPC in this period: New York and New Jersey in 1945; Massachusetts in 1946; Connecticut in 1947; and New Mexico, Oregon, Rhode Island, and Washington in 1949. Other states followed in the 1950s and early 1960s: Alaska in 1953; Michigan, Minnesota, and Pennsylvania in 1955; Wisconsin and Colorado in 1957; California and Ohio in 1959; Delaware in 1960; Illinois, Kansas, and Missouri in 1961; and Indiana, Hawaii, Iowa, and Vermont in 1963. The 1944 *Steele*

v. Louisville and Nashville Railroad Company Supreme Court decision also played a role in forcing unions to reexamine their membership policies.

186. Under "criteria . . . useful in spotting a Communist front," a 1956 Senate subcommittee report lists, "Is the organization repudiated as Communist-controlled by such outstanding organizations as the American Federation of Labor, the American Legion, or its own former constituents?" See U.S. Senate, Subcommittee to Investigate the Administration of the Internal Security Act and Other Internal Security Laws of the Committee on the Judiciary, *The Communist Party of the United States of America; What It Is, How It Works: A Handbook for Americans,* 84th Cong., 2d sess. (Washington, D.C.: Government Printing Office, 1956), pp. 93–96.

187. Marshall, *The Negro and Organized Labor,* p. 44.

188. Norrell, "Caste in Steel," pp. 673, 680, 684. See also Judith Stein, "Southern Workers in National Unions: Birmingham Steelworkers, 1936–1951," in *Organized Labor in the Twentieth-Century South,* ed. Zieger, pp. 183–222. Hudson's own understanding is that both race and political affiliation contributed to his expulsion. See Painter, *Narrative of Hosea Hudson,* pp. 352–62, and for a detailed discussion of the situation of black Communists in Alabama in this period, Kelley, *Hammer and Hoe.*

189. Norrell, "Caste in Steel," pp. 677, 679, 680, 688. In Ellison's *Invisible Man,* one of the more unforgettable characters is the old, black paint mixer who fears the helpers sent to him by the union are seeking to learn and then take away his job.

190. Ibid., p. 676.

191. See Marshall, *The Negro and Organized Labor,* pp. 192–95.

192. *Crisis,* January 1956, p. 35.

193. See *AFL-CIO Constitution* (Washington, D.C.: American Federation of Labor–Congress of Industrial Organizations, 1955), art. 2, sec. 4.

194. At the NAACP's 1961 convention it was resolved that the organization "call upon all branches and state and area conferences to try to prevent the use of Negroes and other racial minorities for strike-breaking purposes during labor disputes." See National Association for the Advancement of Colored People, *Annual Convention Resolutions,* 52d convention (1961), pp. 18–20. The same year, the NAACP's Herbert Hill issued a critical assessment of the trade unions' record on racial discrimination, noting in particular the interpenetration of white supremacist movements (including the Ku Klux Klan) and labor unions in the South, and the rigid exclusion of black workers from the construction trades throughout the country. See Herbert Hill, *Racism within Organized Labor.*

195. Randolph was, at the time, the only black member of the AFL-CIO's executive council (and an NAACP vice-president).

196. Marshall, *The Negro and Organized Labor,* p. 72.

197. Ibid., p. 68.

198. The early 1960s also saw the beginning of tensions between blacks and Jews within the labor movement—focusing on allegations of racism within the New York–based garment workers union (ILGWU)—and eventually outside the labor movement as well. The late 1960s produced the more aggressive and more explicitly political League of Revolutionary Black Workers. Like the TULC, the league was based in Detroit among the autoworkers. Among other goals, the organization sought UAW support for a campaign to end the Vietnam War, the diversion of military and defense spending to meet the needs of lower-income constituencies, a decrease in income taxes, and an increase in profit and industrial taxes. Consequently, the league stated that "millions of dollars which black Detroit-area workers pour into the union coffers every year could be used to build new homes, schools, universities, libraries, recreation and social centers, rifle ranges, food co-

ops, small industries, etc. . . . . We have already spent too much in supporting the needs of white America, and we want the white ruling class, also Reuther [UAW president Walter Reuther] and the auto barons, to keep out of the business of the black community." See Marshall, *The Negro and Organized Labor,* pp. 69, 72–79, 258.

199. Ibid., p. 80.

200. Ibid., p. 14.

201. Title VII originally included companies with one hundred employees or more, but eventually coverage was extended to those firms employing twenty-five or more workers. Although the courts were initially active with regard to interpreting the legislation, by the mid-1970s more conservative views had begun to prevail (e.g., *Washington v. Davis,* 426 U.S. 229 [1975], in which the Supreme Court argued that intent to discriminate must be proven before Title VII can be invoked, and *Teamsters v. United States,* 431 U.S. 324 [1977], which stated that seniority systems that reinforce discrimination were not necessarily forbidden by the Civil Rights Act).

202. See Philip S. Foner, Lewis, and Cvornyek, *Black Worker since the AFL-CIO Merger,* pp. 36–38.

203. See Vernon F. Jordan Jr., "Black People and the Unions," in *Historic Speeches,* ed. Haliburton, p. 157.

204. It has been suggested that Richard Nixon lent his support to these programs partly because they would aggravate tensions between white labor and blacks with the result that the Democratic Party coalition would be that much weaker. With regard to the Philadelphia Plan, Meany also stated: "I can say to you that we don't like this Plan. We feel it is political in nature. . . . We won't get in its way. We know it will fall of its own dead weight." See Archie Robinson, *George Meany and His Times,* p. 291.

205. See Ronald B. Taylor, *Chavez and the Farm Workers,* and Levy, *Cesar Chavez.*

206. The restriction and exclusion policies of the federal government with regard to Chinese immigrants, which labor supported, reinforced by the unions' own exclusion of those Chinese citizens that remained, meant that most Chinese workers were employed in businesses inside the various Chinese communities and were often as exploited and unorganized as their white counterparts elsewhere. See Kwong, *Forbidden Workers,* pp. 139–59.

207. For more detailed discussions of these developments, see ibid. and Gómez-Quiñones, *Mexican American Labor.*

208. Dubofsky, *We Shall Be All,* p. 377.

209. Herbert Hill, "The AFL-CIO and the Black Worker," *Journal of Intergroup Relations* 10 (Spring 1982): 78.

210. See Mancur Olson, *Logic of Collective Action.*

211. The Teamsters were ejected from the AFL-CIO in the late 1950s but have since been readmitted. In fall 1991 they underwent an NLRB-supervised election as a result of allegations of voting irregularities and mob links within the union's structure. Even after the election of a reform slate, headed by Ron Carey, the union continues to be plagued by allegations of corruption.

212. David S. Broder, "Mainstream Democratic Group Stakes Claim on Party's Future," *Washington Post,* May 3, 1991, p. A15. In the foreword to Zieger's *American Workers, American Unions,* Stanley Kutler writes: "Two decades earlier, organized labor was both courted and feared as a political force. By 1985, political candidates began to question whether such support was a liability. The question, in short, was whether unions had become irrelevant" (p. vii).

213. Broder, "Mainstream Democratic Group Stakes Claim," p. A15. Obviously, after the election of DLC product Bill Clinton in 1992 and his failure to bring about comprehen-

sive health care reform, as well as his support of welfare reform and free trade (e.g., North American Free Trade Agreement [NAFTA]), labor's distrust was justified.

214. In fact, in three of the four elections before 1992, the Teamsters executive endorsed the Republican candidate.

215. Esther Fuchs, quoted in Michael Specter, "N.Y. News Strike: Unions Still Bark, but Some Doubt They Can Bite," *Washington Post,* November 3, 1990, p. A10.

216. Dubofsky also suggests that "the AFL-CIO (and Meany in particular) remained the nation's most steadfast anti-Communist institution in the 1960s." See *We Shall Be All,* pp. 378, 382.

217. In fact, in the 1980s the government's role in labor relations was to encourage and support union busting. "It marked a complete shift in public opinion," suggests Jo-Ann Mart, a spokeswoman for the Amalgamated Clothing and Textile Workers Union, with regard to the PATCO incident. "It was never considered a real option to just ignore the employees and hire new ones. Now it is done all the time." See Specter, "N.Y. News Strike," p. A10. Ironically, Reagan himself had been president of the AFL-affiliated Screen Actors Guild in the late 1940s. A similar process in the field of professional football turned out to the benefit of the employees. But, clearly, football players are highly skilled and specialized workers.

218. See Evelyn Richards, "U.S. Firms Stage Competitive Revival," *Washington Post,* May 20, 1991, p. A8. In Zieger's *American Workers, American Unions,* economic writer Bob Kuttner suggests that the decline in the traditional manufacturing sector brings into question the middle-class aspirations and standing of labor: "A service economy . . . needs engineers and executives at one extreme—and millions of secretaries, fast-food workers, sales clerks, computer operators, and janitors at the other. . . . [I]t becomes increasingly difficult to maintain the United States as a middle-class society" (p. 195).

219. In 1985, 16 percent of the world's workforce was unionized; by 1995, that number had dropped to 8.5 percent. See International Labour Organization, *World Labour Report,* p. 6.

220. In 1968, 44 percent of all potential union members (including registered unemployed) and 45 percent of all employed workers in the United Kingdom were unionized. The corresponding numbers for 1979, just before Thatcher, are 54.4 percent and 57.5 percent, and for 1983, 46.3 and 53.9 percent. See Edwards, Garonna, and Todtling, *Unions in Crisis and Beyond,* p. 81, and International Labour Organization, *World Labour Report,* pp. 237–38.

221. One explanation given for the French case is the traditionally "weak link between membership and benefits," as individual potential members have had less incentive to join unions when they can get the benefits anyway (Edwards, Garonna, and Todtling, *Unions in Crisis and Beyond,* pp. 176–77). Other reasons offered are the high level of infighting between communist unions such as the Confédération Générale du Travail (CGT) and the socialist unions such as the Force Ouvrière (FO), French "individualism," and the greater predominance of small industries and businesses in the French economy. Val R. Lorwin suggests that the syndicalist legacy has discouraged French labor unions from establishing stable organizations and structures: "Unfortunately, French labor has continued the habits of the 'heroic period' of the youthful CGT and stressed solidarity rather than solidity of organization. Thus it has turned a source of occasional strength into a permanent weakness." See "Reflections on the History of the French and American Labor Movements," *Journal of Economic History* 17, no. 1 (1957): 36. Jelle Visser notes that "students of French unions have questioned the comparability of unionization rates across countries," and he posits that "while taking a membership card in French unions is held to be a commitment

to militancy, across its borders (for instance, in Britain or Belgium) membership is believed to be propped up with administrative measures (social insurance checkoff, closed shop). French unions *are* incomparable," contends Visser, concluding that "perhaps union members in France [are] better compared to unpaid union organizers and shop stewards in Britain." See Visser, "The Strength of Union Movements in Advanced Capitalist Democracies: Social and Organizational Variations," in *Future of Labour Movements*, ed. Regini, pp. 22–23. The ability of French unions to bring many parts of the country to a virtual standstill in late 1995 and the strike by Air France workers before the 1998 World Cup are indications that French unions are stronger than their numbers might suggest. As one participant (and transportation worker) in the 1995 strikes stated, "I don't even belong to the union, but I think it's great that so many guys are willing to go out on the picket lines to fight against unfair treatment." See Craig R. Whitney, "French Labor Feud Is Still Bubbling in Marseilles," *New York Times*, December 31, 1995, sec. 1, p. 14. On this general point, see also International Labour Organization, *World Labour Report*, p. 7.

222. "Roughly" is the key word here. For a more detailed consideration of the differences and similarities between the two situations, see Richard Iton, " 'Race' and Language in American and Canadian Politics," in *Identity, Rights, and Constitutional Transformation*, ed. Hanafin and Williams, pp. 111–31.

223. See David Brody, "The Breakdown of Labor's Social Contract," in *Legacy of Dissent*, ed. Mills, p. 376.

224. Again, from a comparative perspective, the change in labor costs — that is, the cost of labor per item produced — in the 1982 to 1989 period increased 50 percent in Sweden (in local currency, 45 percent in U.S. currency) and 12 percent in Britain (in local currency, 7 percent in U.S. currency), and it decreased 5 percent in the United States. Evelyn Richards writes: "At the same time that U.S. workers were turning out more goods per hour, labor costs were being held down through the introduction of new labor-saving technology, layoffs and wage restraint by industry and labor unions. This sweeping undertaking has caused pain. Since 1980, 2 million workers have been cut from the U.S. manufacturing payroll. Millions more have accepted — or been forced to accept — reductions in earnings. Yet because of productivity gains, manufacturing today accounts for a slightly larger share of total U.S. economic output than it did a decade ago." These same costs decreased 11 percent in Japan in local currency but increased 62 percent in U.S. currency. The differences between local and U.S. currency figures, in the period cited, are related to the decline of the American dollar versus the yen. The statistics are from Richards, "U.S. Firms Stage Competitive Revival," p. A8.

225. The most recent evidence of labor's powerlessness was the bipartisan endorsement of fast-track negotiations of a free-trade pact with Mexico and the almost total dismissal of labor's arguments and interests. The United States is also one of the few industrialized countries that has not ratified either of the two basic International Labour Office (ILO) conventions: no. 87 recognizing the right to organize, and no. 98 recognizing collective bargaining. Canada, Japan, Austria, Belgium, Denmark, Finland, France, Germany, Ireland, Italy, Luxembourg, the Netherlands, Norway, Sweden, the United Kingdom, and Australia have all ratified the first. Except for Canada and Switzerland, these countries have all ratified the second convention as well. See International Labour Organization, *World Labour Report*, pp. 256–57.

226. Geoghegan, *Which Side Are You On?*, p. 4.

227. There were rumors that some labor activists were seeking to establish a labor-based independent political movement. See William Greider, "Labor's Brand New Day," *Rolling*

Stone, October 17, 1991, pp. 39, 40, 106, and Jonathan Tasini, "Giants in the Land of Cotton," *Village Voice,* October 22, 1991, pp. 31–42. These rumors were proven to be true in June 1996 with the launching of the Labor Party. The new party, though, has yet to run any candidates.

228. Refuting Booker T. Washington's "fingers of the hand" argument for the feasibility of Jim Crow, Randolph contended at the same convention that "as a matter of fact, the white and black workers cannot be organized separately as the fingers on my hand." See American Federation of Labor, *Report of Proceedings,* 56th convention (1936), p. 660.

Chapter Three

1. For discussions of the resilience of the two-party system, see Mazmanian, *Third Parties,* and Smallwood, *Other Candidates.*

2. In *Sectionalism and American Political Development,* Richard Franklin Bensel makes the argument "that sectional competition . . . has been and remains the dominant influence on the American political system" (p. xix). In his development of his central thesis, Bensel suggests that geography is the most important factor explaining sectional divisions and gives less weight to racial factors than, for example, does V. O. Key in *Southern Politics;* see pp. 253–54.

3. New Orleans was, after New York, the main port of immigration and, along with other centers along the Mississippi River, developed strong nativist movements. See Overdyke, *Know-Nothing Party in the South.*

4. As I will discuss in Chapter 6, the specific concerns raised by the Know-Nothings were further delegitimized by the push in this era to define "whiteness."

5. As prevailing customs came to penetrate the Republican Party as well, separate black-and-tan and lily-white factions developed to compete for the right to represent the southern GOP and claim the spoils of patronage. These conditions and arrangements were one means by which Booker T. Washington and his disciples were able to accumulate power, although they could deliver no votes. (Perhaps it would be more accurate to suggest that their power lay precisely in their promises not to deliver votes to anyone.) See Walton, *Black Republicans.* Referring to the attitude of some of the black Republican bodies in the South, Walton observes: "In some localities, indeed, the Black and Tan organizations became merely self-seeking groups with no concern for the welfare of the Black community" (p. 46). Although the election of Woodrow Wilson in 1912 temporarily disempowered Washington and his associates, it was not until the election of Herbert Hoover in 1928 that black Republicans were totally locked out of the patronage market — a situation that lasted until the 1980s.

6. Key, *Southern Politics,* pp. 5, 44.

7. The turn-of-the-century franchise restrictions also removed many whites from the voting rosters, as I will discuss in Chapter 5.

8. An early example would be the Lodge Force Bill, which proposed to use federal power to enforce and maintain the Reconstruction effort.

9. See Walton, *Black Republicans,* pp. 36–37.

10. See McMath, *Populist Vanguard.*

11. See Goodwyn, *Populist Moment,* pp. 118–23, and Hicks, *Populist Revolt,* p. 115. The actual number, Goodwyn suggests, is closer to 250,000.

12. From Norman Pollack, *Populist Response to Industrial America,* p. 68.

13. The strongest Populist states in the 1892 elections were North Dakota, Idaho, Nevada,

Colorado, and Kansas. Slightly weaker in support were South Dakota, Wyoming, Nebraska, and Alabama and then Texas, Montana, Washington, Oregon, Georgia, North Carolina, Florida, and Mississippi. See Hicks, *Populist Revolt,* p. 263.

14. See Shaw, *Wool-Hat Boys,* p. 169.

15. Palmer, *Man over Money,* p. 202.

16. Shaw, *Wool-Hat Boys,* p. 176.

17. From the *Greensboro Daily Record,* September 29, 30, 1892. See also Hicks, *Populist Revolt,* p. 244. Like most of the labor movements emerging from the ashes of Jeffersonian rhetoric and labor republican ideology, the Populists were antistrike. In the South, this antistrike position was involved, to an extent, with the question of race. As Shaw writes, "Like the mill owners, white farmers desired an ample supply of servile workers. The land-lord needed tenants at planting time, and the yeoman required pickers at harvest. Their position became clear in September, 1891, when the Colored Farmers' Alliance began a cotton-pickers strike in Texas. The white Farmers' Alliance denounced the uprising, and fifteen Texas strikers were killed in shootouts. Georgia farmers ominously warned their pickers not to follow the Texans' lead" (*Wool-Hat Boys,* p. 169).

18. Argersinger, *Populism and Politics,* p. 112.

19. Ibid.

20. From the summer of 1891, quoted in ibid., p. 95. As to the allegations about his place of birth, Peffer was actually born in Pennsylvania.

21. From Hicks, *Populist Revolt,* p. 239.

22. Klan violence also was used to retard black education by burning schools, and black economic development, by threatening or killing rural commune organizers. See Newton and Newton, *Racial and Religious Violence in America,* and Anderson and Moss, *Facts of Reconstruction.* These general conditions provoked a French observer to comment in 1867 that "any Democrat who did not manage to hint that the Negro is a degenerate gorilla would be considered lacking in enthusiasm" (Walton, *Black Republicans,* p. 24).

23. Shaw, *Wool-Hat Boys,* pp. 80-81.

24. Hicks, *Populist Revolt,* p. 243.

25. Palmer, *Man over Money,* p. 59.

26. Ibid. The instances in which the southern Populists encouraged and supported black suffrage were linked to the likelihood that those votes would be for the People's Party. According to Shaw, the attitude of the white Populists toward blacks was purely instrumental: "Some of the men who disenfranchised . . . blacks in the 1870s and 1880s became Populists in the 1890s. It was unlikely that these public officials suddenly became more tolerant of black voters. Instead, they were faced with the classic Populist dilemma: because the third party would split the white vote, they were forced to appeal to blacks" (*Wool-Hat Boys,* p. 84).

27. See Woodward, *Strange Career of Jim Crow,* p. 61.

28. Shaw, *Wool-Hat Boys,* p. 86.

29. The Populists also consistently called for the popular election of senators to Congress, a change that did not come about until 1913.

30. The widespread adoption of the primary system is one result of the Populist movement. The primary system made possible "reform" administrations such as James Vardaman's in Mississippi. See Kirwan, *Revolt of the Rednecks.*

31. Quoted in Walton, *Black Republicans,* p. 32.

32. Kirwan, *Revolt of the Rednecks,* p. 101.

33. Hicks, *Populist Revolt,* p. 251.

34. John Rayner, quoted in Goodwyn, *Populist Moment,* p. 329.

35. Peter Argersinger argues that the attention paid to "sham issues" allowed the two major parties to survive without responding to the more serious issues that needed to be addressed: "The tariff, the bloody shirt, the lost Cause, and white supremacy dominated political discussion before Populism: issues essentially irrelevant to the massive problems the nation confronted in industrialization, urbanization, expansion, and immigration; but issues which would, because of their emotional content, mobilize electorates in state, section, and nation to maintain the dominance of self-seeking groups and parties. More than that, such sham issues often intensified national problems which continued to fester, unsolved, and diverted attention from real problems. Dependent upon traditional loyalties or ethnic-cultural cleavages for electoral support, old parties could not or would not formulate relevant policies for pressing economic, social, racial, and political difficulties. The two-party system did not meet the need to articulate constituent demands directly into the political framework" (*Populism and Politics*, p. 305).

36. Pollack, *Populist Response to Industrial America*, p. 85.

37. As I already mentioned, these orientations fed the fears of nativists and set off Know-Nothing movements across the country.

38. See Seretan, *Daniel DeLeon*, p. 47.

39. Ibid., p. 219.

40. See Reeve, *Life and Times of Daniel DeLeon*, p. 135.

41. From Philip S. Foner, *American Socialism and Black Americans*, p. 77. It should also be noted that DeLeon probably lived for awhile on his uncle's slave plantation in Curaçao as a child. See Seretan, *Daniel DeLeon*, p. 5.

42. Reeve, *Life and Times of Daniel DeLeon*, pp. 165–66.

43. Ibid., pp. 166–67. In DeLeon's defense, the suffragettes of this period were overwhelmingly middle- and upper-class and often racist as well.

44. See Reeve, *Life and Times of Daniel DeLeon*, pp. 159–64.

45. See Kipnis, *American Socialist Movement*, p. 19.

46. Ibid., p. 28.

47. Salvatore, *Eugene V. Debs*, p. 286.

48. Weinstein, *Decline of Socialism*, p. 9.

49. Kipnis, *American Socialist Movement*, pp. 46–47.

50. Berger brought Debs a copy of Karl Marx's *Das Kapital* while Debs was incarcerated. It is not clear whether Debs became a socialist at that point or had already moved toward a socialist orientation before his imprisonment. See Salvatore, *Eugene V. Debs*, p. 150.

51. Ibid., pp. 12–18.

52. Ibid., p. 46.

53. Weinstein, *Decline of Socialism*, p. 11.

54. See Salvatore, *Eugene V. Debs*, p. 73.

55. See ibid., pp. 264–67, 325.

56. The actual numbers were 4,119,538 for Roosevelt in 1912 and 4,822,856 for La Follette in 1924. See Smallwood, *Other Candidates*, p. x.

57. Hanagan, "Response to Sean Wilentz," p. 33.

58. See ibid.

59. Ibid.

60. Salvatore, *Eugene V. Debs*, p. 271.

61. Ibid.

62. Section 3 of the Espionage Act declared guilty of a felony "whoever, when the United States is at war, shall willfully cause or attempt to cause insubordination, disloyalty, mutiny, or refusal of duty in the military or naval forces . . . or shall willfully obstruct the recruiting

or enlistment service." See Cox, *The Court and the Constitution*, p. 218. Debs was arrested in June 1918 under this act. The American Socialists were the only Western socialist party, for whatever reasons, to uphold the principle of internationalism and officially oppose the war (in contrast to the AFL's unqualified support). The party's major publication, the *American Socialist*, carried such headlines as "Capitalism Gone Mad!," "U.S. Socialists Must Halt World Murder," "Shall We Go to War for Morgan and Rockefeller?," and "Murderous War Is the Inevitable Result of Murderous European Capitalism." As a result, some members left the party. See the *American Socialist*, August 15, 1914, August 29, 1914, September 5, 1914, and September 12, 1914.

63. See Weinstein, *Corporate Ideal.*

64. Kipnis, *American Socialist Movement*, p. 429.

65. Weinstein, *Decline of Socialism*, pp. viii, 2.

66. Weinstein writes that "Haywood's constituents existed on the edges of society [and that] . . . Haywood did not share with Berger, Hillquit, or Debs the view that capitalism might survive for a considerable time. His was an apocalyptic vision of the revolution. Believing that it would occur at any time, he did not see the need to develop long-term strategy" (ibid., p. 14).

67. For the details of this particular academic debate—over the significance of Haywood's dismissal from the National Executive Committee—see ibid., pp. 40-50.

68. One could also add the tensions arising from the issue of centralization and the disproportionate representation of the New York, Chicago, and other northeastern factions, in a period when the party's votes were coming from the West.

69. Weinstein, *Decline of Socialism*, p. 54.

70. Of Debs, Salvatore suggests, "In certain contexts, Debs's position on the role of women was quite progressive. . . . But another aspect of Debs's thought concerning women also influenced his public attitudes and dominated his private images: [Debs speaking] . . . 'If man, the titan, makes the world big, woman, the enchantress, makes it beautiful'" (*Eugene V. Debs*, pp. 215-16).

71. See *American Socialist*, February 27, 1915, p. 3, and July 24, 1915, p. 1.

72. Quoted in Pollack, *Populist Response to Industrial America*, p. 84.

73. Salvatore, *Eugene V. Debs*, p. 104. Salvatore also notes that Debs had similarly negative attitudes toward Jewish immigrants.

74. From Durden, *Climax of Populism*, p. 142.

75. From Kipnis, *American Socialist Movement*, p. 281.

76. Ibid., p. 286.

77. *Proceedings of the National Convention of the American Socialist Party* (Chicago, May 1908), p. 117.

78. Ibid., p. 108.

79. Ibid., p. 105.

80. Ibid., p. 113.

81. Ibid., p. 260.

82. Ibid., p. 259.

83. Ibid., p. 114.

84. From Kipnis, *American Socialist Movement*, p. 284.

85. See Philip S. Foner, *American Socialism and Black Americans*, p. 87, and Salvatore, *Eugene V. Debs*, p. 227. Debs fought against the establishment of the American Railway Union's color bar with no success.

86. Philip S. Foner, *American Socialism and Black Americans*, p. 111.

87. Salvatore, *Eugene V. Debs*, p. 226.

88. Ibid., p. 227.

89. From Philip S. Foner, *American Socialism and Black Americans,* p. 106.

90. *Proceedings of the National Convention of the American Socialist Party* (Chicago, May 1908), pp. 110–11.

91. From Philip S. Foner, *American Socialism and Black Americans,* pp. 105–6.

92. Ibid., p. 125.

93. As Kipnis writes, for the center and right wings of the party, "socialism would solve the race question in the only possible manner — complete segregation" (*American Socialist Movement,* p. 132).

94. Ibid., pp. 133, 134. The suggestion that the SP gave little attention to the situation of blacks is supported by the absence of articles or editorials addressing the issue in the pages of the *American Socialist.*

95. Ibid., p. 423.

96. Weinstein, *Decline of Socialism,* p. 73.

97. From Philip S. Foner, *American Socialism and Black Americans,* p. 106.

98. Another argument that can be invoked to explain the SP's "failure" is that the presence of unassimilated language federations within the party prevented it from establishing an effective centralized internal communications network. As Richard F. Hamilton writes, "A problem that faced the old Socialist party at the time of its first appearance was the division of the working class into many foreign language subcommunities. In contrast to the experience of linguistically homogeneous countries, the educational and organizational tasks of the American party were extremely complicated" (*Class and Politics,* p. 541). Ethnic tensions also played a role in the party's post–World War I splintering, revealing a pattern of events and developments consistent with the heterogeneity thesis.

99. The expulsions cost the SP in membership. In January 1919 the party had 109,589 members; by July of that year the number had dropped to 39,750. See Draper, *Roots of American Communism,* p. 158.

100. As Irving Howe and Lewis Coser write, "Yet nothing that was happening in American domestic life could mean so much as the sudden outbreak, first in February, 1917, and then in October, of the two Russian Revolutions. . . . All the talk, the dreams, the theories — everything that to even the least doubting or least contemplative of socialist minds must sometimes have seemed dim and elusive now took on the force of reality. That a working-class state could be proclaimed in the most backward country of Europe, that the Lenin who yesterday had been a mere *émigré* lost in the fogs of factional dispute should today command the palace of the Czars — this seemed visible triumphant proof that the final victory of socialism was at hand (*American Communist Party,* p. 25).

101. Draper, *Roots of American Communism,* p. 110.

102. The disproportionate presence of immigrants in the Communist Party meant that anti-Communist movements were reinforced by anti-immigrant sentiment, and vice versa.

103. A reading of the *Communist* newspaper (established in 1919 as the official paper of the Communist Party of America) makes the degree of this factionalism apparent. More energy was expended identifying and criticizing the Party's enemies on the left than on almost any other subject.

104. Ruthenberg, Party secretary, was succeeded by Lovestone upon the former's death in 1927.

105. Some critics of the IWW argued that pursuing labor organization outside the established American Federation of Labor — that is, dual unionism — would weaken the labor movement as a whole. Accordingly, Foster said at the time: "The AFL and big independent unions are not hopeless. . . . It would be a basic error . . . to reject the existing trade

unions altogether. . . . Under present conditions there is no room for a genuine dual labor movement in the United States." From Howe and Coser, *American Communist Party*, p. 238.

106. Members of TUEL were branded as dual unionists in 1923 by the AFL's leadership, and many members were expelled. Foster, however, hung on.

107. See Ottanelli, *Communist Party of the United States*, p. 20.

108. See Lewy, *Cause That Failed*, pp. 7, 307. The Party's membership did not exceed fifteen thousand until 1933.

109. Ibid., p. 307. The CPUSA ceased to exist officially in 1991.

110. See, among others, ibid.; Howe and Coser, *American Communist Party*; Draper, *Roots of American Communism*; Shannon, *Decline of American Communism*; and Klehr, *Heyday of American Communism*. For an overview of the academic debate about the extent to which the CPUSA was controlled by the Comintern, see Isserman, "Three Generations," pp. 517–45.

111. The Voorhis legislation led the CPUSA to disassociate itself from the Comintern formally and temporarily, though not spiritually.

112. The Popular Front became the Democratic Front in 1938.

113. See Ottanelli, *Communist Party of the United States*, p. 209.

114. Howe and Coser, *American Communist Party*, p. 340.

115. Ibid.

116. Shannon, *Decline of American Communism*, p. 6.

117. In the spring of 1945, Jacques Duclos, a member of the French Communist Party, wrote an article in *Cahiers du Communisme* suggesting that Browder's actions constituted a "notorious revision" of the movement's tenets. Duclos's article was seen as having been authorized by the Comintern and led to Browder's dismissal and Foster's elevation the same spring. Ottanelli argues that Foster's return to pre–Popular Front policies "irreparably isolated the CPUSA during the red scare of the postwar years" (*Communist Party of the United States*, p. 215).

118. See Lewy, *Cause That Failed*, pp. 216–21.

119. Wallace's 1948 campaign managed to persuade 1,157,326 voters. Strom Thurmond's Dixiecrat campaign the same year garnered 1,176,125 voters. See Smallwood, *Other Candidates*, p. x.

120. Du Bois would later write that the idea "of letting a few of our capitalists share with whites in the exploitation of our masses, would never be a solution to our problem" (*Autobiography*, p. 290).

121. From Philip S. Foner, *American Socialism and Black Americans*, p. 357.

122. Du Bois, *Writings in Periodical Literature*, p. 40.

123. See Du Bois, *Autobiography*, p. 264. Not coincidentally, while Du Bois was supporting Wilson, his archnemesis during this period, Booker T. Washington was supporting the GOP candidate. Wilson's victory cost Washington significantly in terms of status in Washington, D.C., and access to power and patronage.

124. Du Bois quotes Wilson, the future president, stating, "I want to assure them [blacks] that should I become President of the United States they may count upon me for absolute fair dealing, for everything by which I could assist in advancing the interests of their race in the United States" (*Autobiography*, p. 264). It was the same Woodrow Wilson who would invite Thomas Dixon, his former student at the Johns Hopkins University, to screen David Wark Griffith's celebration of the first wave of the Ku Klux Klan, *Birth of a Nation* (largely based on Dixon's novel and play *The Clansman*), at the White House. Wilson was cited as a source in the film's credits and after the screening said, "It is like writing history with lightning." See Silva, *Focus on "Birth of a Nation"*, p. 108. The book, play, and movie (per

capita, one of the most popular films ever) are credited with mobilizing a second wave of Klan activity.

125. For a discussion of these developments, Wilson's actions at Versailles, and Du Bois's disillusionment, see Lauren, *Power and Prejudice,* and W. E. B. Du Bois, "Close Ranks," in *W. E. B. Du Bois,* ed. Lewis, p. 697.

126. From Philip S. Foner, *American Socialism and Black Americans,* p. 300.

127. The Red scare following the war sharply reduced the Socialist influence in Harlem and elsewhere, resulting in the collapse of the Harlem Socialist club and relegation of explicit socialist politics to the background in the pages of the *Messenger.* See Naison, *Communists in Harlem,* p. 9.

128. Manning Marable writes in *From the Grassroots* that "if the Socialist Party was, as Randolph believed, the highest expression of working class consciousness, and if blacks were overwhelmingly working class, then no other political formation could address blacks' interests as well as the party. Race and ethnicity played no role in the 'scientific evolution' of class contradictions; class was an economic category without cultural or social limits. Randolph increasingly viewed any form of black nationalism as a major obstacle between white and black workers in the struggle toward socialist democracy" (p. 66).

129. Marshall, *The Negro and Organized Labor,* p. 72.

130. From *Philosophy and Opinions of Marcus Garvey,* p. xvii.

131. See Martin, *Race First,* p. 234.

132. From Vincent, *Black Power and the Garvey Movement,* p. 194. Garvey met with white supremacist groups (such as the Ku Klux Klan) and defended those encounters on the grounds that racist whites were simply more honest about their intentions than were liberals.

133. To a lesser extent, Washington was also active in Pan-Africanist circles.

134. Martin, *Race First,* p. 13. The Black Star Liner was modeled on similar transportation efforts launched by Irish American (the Green Star Liner) and Polish American immigrant communities.

135. From Weinstein, *Decline of Socialism,* p. 73.

136. From Martin, *Race First,* p. 273.

137. Ibid.

138. See Huggins, *Harlem Renaissance.*

139. From Philip S. Foner, *American Socialism and Black Americans,* p. 301.

140. Reid, *Negro Membership in American Labor Unions,* p. 128.

141. From Philip S. Foner, *American Socialism and Black Americans,* p. 302.

142. From Lewy, *Cause That Failed,* p. 36.

143. As noted in the previous chapter, Randolph refused to support the Red-baiting of the CIO that took place after the CIO's expulsion from the AFL in 1937.

144. Du Bois, *Autobiography,* pp. 290–91.

145. From Martin, *Race First,* p. 222.

146. The membership of the ABB and the UNIA reflected the influence of West Indian immigrants on the politics and general culture of the Harlem Renaissance years.

147. From Herb Boyd, "Blacks and the American Left," *Crisis,* February 1988, p. 24.

148. Like most blacks of the period, Garvey consistently criticized the restrictive policies of the AFL.

149. Martin, *Race First,* pp. 235–36.

150. For all it is worth, the Federal Bureau of Investigation's J. Edgar Hoover was convinced that Garvey was a Bolshevist. See ibid., pp. 221, 253.

151. In this same context, Garvey suggested that "the greatest enemies of the Negroes are

among those who hypocritically profess love and fellowship for him, when, in truth and deep down in their heart, they despise and hate him." See Garvey, *Philosophy and Opinions of Marcus Garvey*, pp. 69–70, and Martin, *Race First*, p. 240.

152. Martin, *Race First*, p. 240.

153. From ibid., p. 221.

154. The emergence of the UNIA brought to the surface simmering tensions between Caribbean immigrants and African Americans as well. For the details of this development, see Cruse, *Crisis of the Negro Intellectual;* Clarence Walker, *Deromanticizing Black History;* and W. A. Domingo, "Gift of the Black Tropics," in *Harlem Renaissance Reader,* ed. Lewis.

155. In *Race First,* Martin questions the validity of the charges, conviction, and deportation.

156. The UNIA's foreign branches in the West Indies, Canada, England, and elsewhere lasted much longer, even beyond Garvey's death in 1941. Some branches still exist in the United States and Canada and certainly elsewhere.

157. See Martin, *Race First*, p. 225.

158. From ibid., p. 224.

159. Ibid., p. 229. In 1939, from his exile in Mexico, Leon Trotsky restated this principle: "It is very possible the Negroes also through self-determination will proceed to the proletarian dictatorship in a couple of gigantic strides, ahead of the great bloc of white workers. They will then furnish the vanguard. I am absolutely sure that they will in any case fight better than the white workers. That, however, can happen only provided the Communist party carries on an uncompromising merciless struggle not against the supposed national prepossessions of the Negroes but against the colossal prejudices of the white workers and gives it no concession whatever" (ibid., p. 231).

160. See Ottanelli, *Communist Party of the United States,* p. 38. The charge against Yokinen was that he failed to protest the expulsion of a Negro from a meeting of the Finnish Labor Club where he, Yokinen, was employed as a janitor. Stated Israel Amter, a CPUSA leader, in announcing the trial, "White chauvinism is not confined to drawing the color line in Jim Crow fashion. There are subtler forms of white chauvinism, such as the attitude of people who say they have no objections to the Negro as long as he stays in his place. Then there is the crass white chauvinism of the American Federation of Labor which, in many places, will not allow a Negro to join a union." The trial was held at the Harlem Casino, located at the intersection of 116th Street and Lenox Avenue, and was "conducted as nearly as possible in accordance with legal procedure in Soviet Russia." See "Reds Here to Stage 'Chauvinism' Trial," *New York Times,* February 28, 1931, p. 22.

161. Lewy, *Cause That Failed,* p. 301.

162. Ottanelli, *Communist Party of the United States,* pp. 42–43. For a more detailed discussion of the role of blacks in the CPUSA in the South, see Painter, *Narrative of Hosea Hudson.*

163. Naison, *Communists in Harlem,* p. xvii.

164. That there might be tension between these two positions was not, at least immediately, perceived to be a problem.

165. I call Wright's Pan-Africanism "peculiar" because it seemed more the result of frustration than conviction. See R. Wright, *White Man, Listen!*

166. Richard Wright, "I Tried to Be a Communist," September 1944, p. 56.

167. From Margaret Walker, *Richard Wright, Daemonic Genius,* p. 282.

168. One famous example of the clash between blacks and whites on the left over the function of black art is the debate that followed the publication of Irving Howe's "Black Boys and Native Sons" in *Dissent.* See Howe, *Selected Writings,* pp. 119–39, and Ralph Elli-

son's response, "The World and the Jug," in *Shadow and Act,* pp. 107–43. Harold Cruse, in *The Crisis of the Negro Intellectual,* discusses these tensions and the problems arising from the application of Marxism to the American situation: "Marxist conceptions become mechanically rooted in the thinking patterns much as do religious dogmas—so much so that if the Negro Marxist does not free his mind from these dogmatic categories, he remains forever unable to deal with new American realities. He will oppose every set of political, economic or cultural conceptions that do not square with his ingrained dogmas. The influence of European Marxism on the thinking of the American Negro has been disastrous" (p. 419). Cruse also commented on the cultural inadequacies of the Marxist model: "In our consideration of Marxism-Leninism (as a European intellectual product) we must keep in mind that European Marxism-Leninism did not produce a politico-cultural model, but a politico-economic-class model. That this was so is crucial for our understanding as to why European 'Marxist-Leninist' models have been so inapplicable to many features of the Black experience, especially the cultural" ("The Amilcar Cabral Politico-Cultural Model," *Black World* 24 [December 1974]: 24).

169. Cruse, *Crisis of the Negro Intellectual,* p. 174.

170. Perhaps, more to the point, Randolph recognized that if he was explicit about his atheism he would never garner much support from black laborers. See Pfeffer, *A. Philip Randolph.* The history recounted by Kelley in *Hammer and Hoe* suggests that many blacks in the South were able to sustain and reconcile their faiths in Christianity and communism.

171. From Boyd, "Blacks and the American Left," p. 27. A similar reconciliation of "tribalism" and "communism" was attempted by the African socialists who tried to find in the values of their own heritage a natural foundation for socialism. See Ottaway and Ottaway, *Afrocommunism,* and Cedric J. Robinson, *Black Marxism.*

172. See Padmore, *Pan-Africanism or Communism,* p. 268.

173. Lewy, *Cause That Failed,* p. 295.

174. For one account of the effect of the revelations concerning the Soviet persecution of Jews and an insight into some of the interactions between Jewish and black Communists, see Fast, *Being Red.* For other accounts of these relations, see Ossie Davis and Dee, *With Ossie and Ruby,* and Cruse, *Crisis of the Negro Intellectual.* Gerald Horne suggests that the Suez crisis also aggravated tensions between the two groups. See "The Red and the Black: The Communist Party and African-Americans in Historical Perspective," in *New Studies,* ed. Brown et al., p. 227. In *Blackface, White Noise,* Michael Rogin provides an interesting analysis of the changing nature of black-Jewish relations in the first half of the twentieth century.

175. In the article "Paul Robeson: Wrong," Walter White argued that "minorities like the Negro would be insane to cast their lot with the Communists" (*Negro Digest,* March 1950). While White and Wilkins struggled to distinguish the NAACP's operations from any affiliation with suspected communists, blacks were among the strongest public critics of the HUAC investigations, especially given the committee's tendency to read support for integration as a symptom of communism. In the pages of the *Pittsburgh Courier,* J. A. Rogers noted the willingness of Red-baiters to overlook and/or uphold segregation, asking, "What has this committee [HUAC] done against an un-American activity older than Communism and far more galling to Negroes, namely Jim Crow?" (January 8, 1954). See also Horne, *Black and Red,* pp. 201–21.

176. As Du Bois explained his move to nonintegrationism, "It was clear to me that agitation against race prejudice and a planned economy for bettering the economic condition of the American Negro were not antagonistic ideals but part of one ideal; that it did not increase segregation; the segregation was there and would remain for many years. But

now I proposed that in economic lines, just as in lines of literature and religion, segregation should be planned and organized and carefully thought through. This plan did not establish a new segregation; it did not advocate segregation as the final solution of the race problem; exactly the contrary; but it did face the facts and faced them with thoughtfully mapped effort" (*Dusk of Dawn*, p. 305).

177. Robeson's role in the McCarthy drama will be discussed in more detail in Chapter 6.

178. See the *New York Times*, June 20, 1949, p. 7, and Duberman, *Paul Robeson*, p. 346.

179. Du Bois, *Autobiography*, p. 370.

180. It appears that Thurgood Marshall gave reports to the Federal Bureau of Investigation in the late 1950s and early 1960s regarding perceived efforts of the "communists" to infiltrate the NAACP. These allegations have not yet been proven. See Randall Kennedy, "Thurgood Marshall and the FBI," *IntellectualCapital*, December 5, 1996.

181. Arthur Miller's *The Crucible* is an interesting depiction of the era.

182. It was partly his belief that Versailles was an attempt to maintain the racial status quo on a global basis that led Du Bois to convene the first Pan-African Congress in 1919.

183. See Egerton, *Speak Now against the Day*, p. 454.

184. See Lee and Solomon, *Unreliable Sources*, p. 94.

185. See Desmond King, *Separate and Unequal*, pp. 33–34.

186. Arguments that a new moral conscience had developed or that American blacks were more aggressive in this period do not have much logical appeal. There was no evidence of any greater sincere sensitivity to the issue on the part of Americans, and African Americans were as aggressive in other periods as they were in the 1950s and early 1960s.

187. See *Common Sense*, no. 8 (1944): 421. In Randolph's view, such a party would support the following objectives: minority rights; a restored Fair Employment Practices Committee; antilynching legislation; increases in the minimum wage; a thirty-hour workweek; federal aid to education; the "socialization of key industries," including banking, transportation, and energy; the defeat of imperialism; and the alliance of labor, farmers, and white-collar workers.

Chapter Four

1. Some credit for what would become the New Deal alliance should go to Al Smith, the Democratic Party's Catholic candidate for president in 1928.

2. See Lowi, *Personal President*, pp. 48–49.

3. The exact point at which the New Deal era ended is a subject of debate. For instance, in "The Rise of the 'Silent Majority'" in *Rise and Fall of the New Deal Order*, ed. Fraser and Gerstle, Jonathan Rieder suggests, "The New Deal collapsed in the 1960s" (p. 243). In another essay in the same collection, Gerstle and Fraser state, "When Ronald Reagan assumed office in January of 1981, an epoch in the nation's political history came to an end" (p. ix).

4. Scammon and Wattenberg, *Real Majority*, p. 39.

5. Ibid., p. 58.

6. On the basis of his own experiences and data, Republican activist Kevin Phillips made similar arguments in *The Emerging Republican Majority*, a book that reportedly influenced Richard Nixon's decision to coopt the racial wedge issues identified with George Wallace in 1964 and 1968 and develop a "southern strategy" for the 1972 campaign.

7. Edsall and Edsall, *Chain Reaction*, p. 4. For a discussion of the alienation of northern, white Catholics from the Democratic Party, see Freedman, *Inheritance*.

8. See Stanley Greenberg, *Middle Class Dreams*, p. 34; emphasis added.

9. Ibid., p. 39.

10. A similar thesis is advanced in Sleeper, *Closest of Strangers*.

11. From Stanley Greenberg, *Middle Class Dreams*, p. 39.

12. Kristi Andersen has offered cogent arguments about the effects of newly enfranchised voters on the politics of the late 1920s and early 1930s and the role of conversion (vote changing) as opposed to mobilization (new voters) in the forging of new alignments. See *Creation of a Democratic Majority*.

13. Quoted in Egerton, *Speak Now against the Day*, p. 93. Al Smith's 1928 campaign, especially his ability to garner support from black voters in New York, was the first sign that the northern black vote might be available to the Democratic Party.

14. See ibid., p. 110.

15. See Patterson, *Congressional Conservatism and the New Deal*, p. 13.

16. Edwin Witte, quoted in Skocpol, *Social Policy in the United States*, p. 159. The administration of Social Security would become fundamentally a federal responsibility after the 1974 collapsing of a number of welfare programs into the Supplementary Security Insurance (or SSI) program. In "Race and Social Welfare Policy," Gareth Davies and Martha Derthick argue that such other factors as the difficulty of including in the social security plan seasonal and agricultural workers (who were similarly excluded initially in the plans of other countries such as the United Kingdom and Canada) and the apparent support of members of the Roosevelt administration for the exclusion on fiscal and administrative grounds should be considered when assessing the motives underlying the decision to exclude these groups. Indeed, they suggest that "the temporary omission of such workers was less significant than was the creation of a new, wholly national program of retirement insurance" (p. 233). Similar claims are offered with regard to the decision to leave the administration of the Aid to Dependent Children program to the states, as Davies and Derthick cite the concerns of some states, primarily southern, that a national program involving mandated state contributions might bankrupt those states with minimal or nonexistent programs and expenditure histories in this area (pp. 226–32).

17. See House Committee on Ways and Means Hearings on the Economic Security Act, 74th Cong., 1st sess., 1935, pp. 125, 127.

18. Houston also testified in front of the House Ways and Means Committee, suggesting that "from the point of view of the Negro, it would be much easier to get fair enforcement of a Federal law than to get a really effective old-age assistance law passed by southern legislatures." See Senate Finance Committee Hearings on the Economic Security Act, 74th Cong., 1st sess., 1935, p. 641, and House Committee on Ways and Means Hearings on the Economic Security Act, 74th Cong., 1st sess., 1935, pp. 641–43.

19. See National Association for the Advancement of Colored People, *Annual Report* (1934, 1935, 1936, 1937, and pp. 13–14 in 1938).

20. Roberts's "change of heart" was first apparent in the Court's 5–4 decision in the *West Coast Hotel v. Parrish* case (1937) — dealing with minimum wages for women — which was settled before the court-packing plan was announced but after Roosevelt's landslide victory in 1936, which might have influenced Roberts's calculations. The NLRB decision, which gave support to the rights of workers to organize unions, came after the proposal. Roosevelt's efforts to push the court-packing proposal through long after it was clear it would not succeed — indeed, after it was no longer necessary given retirements from the Supreme Court — only further aggravated his growing number of opponents. See Patterson, *Congressional Conservatism and the New Deal*, p. 125.

21. Roosevelt's most consistent opponents in the Senate during this era, from within his own party, included Virginia's Glass, North Carolina's Bailey, Oklahoma's Thomas P. Gore,

Maryland's Millard E. Tydings, Virginia's Harry Flood Byrd, South Carolina's Ellison D. Smith, Georgia's Walter George, New York's Royal Copeland (a former Republican), and Nebraska's Edward R. Burke (a consistent voice against labor interests, who, after being denied the party's nomination in 1940, supported the Republican presidential candidate Wendell Wilkie).

22. Quoted in Patterson, "Failure of Party Realignment in the South," pp. 602–3.

23. Quoted in Patterson, *Congressional Conservatism and the New Deal*, p. 257.

24. Wilson made the comments in a 1913 letter to NAACP secretary Oswald Garrison Villard. Traditional arguments concerning the risk to white women that desegregated workplaces might incur were also offered. Thomas Dixon, author of the play on which *The Birth of a Nation* was based and a former student of Wilson's, included the following comments in a letter he sent to his former professor after the appointment of a black to a post in the Treasury Department: "I am heartsick over the announcement that you have appointed a Negro to boss white girls as Register of the Treasury. The establishment of Negro men over white employees . . . has in the minds of many thoughtful men and women long been a serious offense against the cleanliness of our social life." For a more detailed discussion of these practices and the extent to which government actions reinforced segregation, see Desmond King, *Separate and Unequal*. The quotations cited are from pages 5 and 12 respectively.

25. The requirement that government job seekers submit a photograph was justified as a means of preventing fraudulent applications and assisting "appointing officers to form some opinion in regard to eligibles certified." In response the NAACP contended that "the policy of the civil service commission in requiring photographs of applicants permits of color discrimination in an easy way. . . . A number of cases could be cited where persons who had successfully passed civil service examinations had been directed, often by telegraph, to report for duty, only to be informed, when they did appear, that an error had been made and that there were no vacancies." This requirement was dropped (after a long protest campaign from the NAACP and others) and replaced with fingerprinting in 1940. See the National Association for the Advancement of Colored People, *Annual Report* (1917–1918), p. 44; (1939), p. 15; (1940), p. 11; and Desmond King, *Separate and Unequal*, p. 48.

26. Roosevelt's popularity was indeed higher in the South than it was elsewhere in the country throughout this period. See Gallup, *Gallup Opinion Poll*, pp. 51–187.

27. The United States Employment Service (USES), which was created in 1933, was turned over to the states in 1946. Before and after the transfer the agency had a reputation for discriminating against black job seekers in the job opportunities made available to them, the location of USES relative to black neighborhoods, and the resources devoted to black clients. See Desmond King, *Separate and Unequal*, pp. 173–89.

28. The record with regard to regulatory policy is different.

29. See Egerton, *Speak Now against the Day*, p. 500, and Key, *Southern Politics*, p. 333.

30. See the *Birmingham News*, May 9, 1948, and Key, *Southern Politics*, p. 334.

31. Sundquist, *Politics and Policy*, p. 386.

32. Richard F. Hamilton, *Class and Politics*, p. 536. Similarly in *Dynamics of the Party System*, James Sundquist argues that the "Reagan revolution" did not constitute or signal the establishment of a new alignment, as the new right and old right issues "do not cluster well." Suggesting that economic issues were too powerful to be crowded out by social concerns, he questioned the realigning capacity of the various items that constituted the "Social Issue" and concluded, "For most people, moral causes are something to indulge in when times are prosperous and inflation is held within bounds of tolerance. But when the

economy is sick, those issues must be put aside" (p. 441). In *Sectionalism and American Political Development,* Richard Franklin Bensel contends that "the civil rights legislation passed in the 1960s has effectively and permanently removed the 'race question' as the primary basis of sectional conflict. The lower classes have been enfranchised, and regional urbanization and industrialization have proceeded apace" (p. 253). Bensel suggests that sectional differences remain but that they are not rooted in racial conflict. Lastly, V. O. Key was optimistic, on the basis of his reading of the late 1940s South, that race would become less of a factor in depressing class politics as urbanization and industrialization proceeded and as a result of the activities of the labor movement in the South. See "Is There a Way Out?" in *Southern Politics.*

33. See Sundquist, *Dynamics of the Party System,* p. 359.

34. Quoted in Leuchtenburg, "Old Cowhand from Dixie," p. 96. After the defeat of Nelson Rockefeller and his supporters at the GOP's 1964 convention, no serious Republican candidates for national office would promote any significant degree of racial liberalism (with the possible exceptions of Jack Kemp and Colin Powell).

35. Quoted in ibid., pp. 96–97.

36. Regarding George Wallace, see Dan Carter, *Politics of Rage.*

37. This development—the reestablishment of a significant black voting constituency in the South—resulted in 1972 in the election to Congress of the first blacks from the South since Reconstruction: Andrew Young (Georgia) and Barbara Jordan (Texas).

38. Before the 1978 decision to lift the tax-exempt status of segregated and religious private schools, the evangelical movement was largely unorganized. The challenges to the gender status quo and the changes in the tax regulations mobilized a constituency (most notably in the form of the Moral Majority led by Robert Billings and Jerry Falwell) that had been split between the two major parties and was largely apolitical (and satisfied with the pre–civil rights era racial and gender status quos).

39. The eleven states are Alabama, Arkansas, Florida, Georgia, Louisiana, Mississippi, North Carolina, South Carolina, Tennessee, Texas, and Virginia.

40. Tower's victory in a special election to replace Lyndon Baines Johnson (who had been selected to join John Kennedy's ticket) occurred in a contest in which several Democratic candidates ran for the open seat. Consequently, the Democratic vote was split, which allowed Tower, the Republican, to win.

41. See the *New York Times,* November 5, 1998.

42. Gingrich would be shortly replaced, however, briefly by Louisiana's Robert Livingston and in the long term by Illinois representative Dennis Hastert (the acknowledged leader of the GOP contingent during Hastert's reign, though, has been Texan Tom DeLay).

43. See the *New York Times,* November 5, 1998.

44. Georgia congressman Sanford D. Bishop Jr. is both black and a "blue dog," conservative Democrat. Tennessee House member, Democrat Harold Ford Jr. is also both black and conservative. Conservative J. C. (Julius Caesar) Watts of Oklahoma is the sole black Republican member of Congress.

45. Hartz, *Liberal Tradition in America,* p. 8.

46. While Harry Truman was not from the South but from Kansas, it is clear that his views on race evolved significantly over time from being clearly pro–Jim Crow toward a more liberal disposition.

47. See Orfield, *Public School Desegregation.*

48. The unemployment rate is cited in Peter Brown, *Minority Party,* pp. 25–26.

49. See Thomas Edsall, "Race," p. 61, and Edsall and Edsall, *Chain Reaction,* pp. 258–59.

50. Stanley Greenberg, *Middle Class Dreams*, p. 11.

51. David Roediger, "White Workers, New Democrats, and Affirmative Action," in *House That Race Built*, ed. Lubiano, p. 50.

52. See Charles S. Bullock III, "The Nomination Process and Super Tuesday," in *The 1988 Presidential Election in the South*, ed. Moreland, Steed, and Baker, pp. 3–19. The perhaps amusing result of the Super Tuesday innovation in 1988 was to energize further the campaigns of Michael Dukakis (a northern liberal), Jesse Jackson, and, to a lesser degree, Tennessee's Al Gore. Since then, the other states have moved up their primaries as well, reducing the intended impact of the combined southern primaries.

53. See David S. Broder, "Mainstream Democratic Group Stakes Claim on Party's Future," *Washington Post*, May 3, 1991, p. A15.

54. George Bush visited the county twice during the 1992 campaign. The GOP won 39 percent of the vote, and the Democrats won 38 percent. See Stanley Greenberg, *Middle Class Dreams*, pp. 52–53. Clinton did win the state of Michigan.

55. Yet the Clinton administration did defend affirmative action, making a record number of appointments of blacks, Hispanics, and women to the various departments of the executive branch, and during the crises that marked his second term, African Americans were particularly supportive of the president.

56. Organized labor's financial support for the Democratic Party in the 1996 elections indicated both its potential strength (as Republicans clearly were affected by the advertising campaigns conducted by the AFL-CIO between March and November) and its weakness: the Democratic Party has been barely responsive to organized labor's concerns.

57. As late as 1995, Theda Skocpol expressed optimism with regard to the Clinton administration's promise in the area of social policy: "Perhaps an effort is under way to build a new broad coalition—cross-class and cross-racial—in support of public sector initiatives to help all children and families in America [including] . . . relevant programs [such as] . . . wage supplements for low-wage workers; improved job training and retraining for all American workers; child support for all single custodial parents; access to health care for all American families; and assistance to working families in obtaining health care." See Skocpol, "African Americans in U.S. Social Policy," in *Classifying by Race*, ed. Peterson, pp. 150–51.

58. Suggests John Kenneth Galbraith, "The new Congress that came to office in the United States in early 1995 representing the conservative will expressed its intention to dismantle much of the welfare state, much of the modern regulatory apparatus of government, and to limit drastically the role of government in general. This was the broad promise broadly enunciated. Then came the specific legislation, the assault on particular functions and regulations. . . . [T]hese are proving far from popular. . . . Some dramatic and well-publicized exceptions possibly apart, the welfare state and its basic programs will survive" (*Good Society*, pp. 12–13).

59. For example, Scammon and Wattenberg refer to a video that would include clips of first "a young, clean-cut black man seated at a lunch counter," then "a jagged plate-glass window [through which] . . . comes a grinning young black . . . carrying a television set," and finally "a group of black students [emerging] from a campus building they have recently 'taken over' . . . carrying rifles" as an accurate description of the evolving image of blacks (i.e., Sidney Poitier to Huey Newton) in the minds of whites over the course of the 1960s (*Real Majority*, pp. 41–42).

60. Most of the race riots up to that point had involved white attacks on blacks. The 1935 riot in Harlem was one of the first in which white people were not directly involved as participants. See Cheryl Lynn Greenberg, *"Or Does It Explode?"*

61. Commenting on the "dam . . . that has for over twenty years blocked prospects for a constructive engagement of the political parties on the issues of race, poverty, bifurcating incomes, employment policy, and educational reform," the Edsalls seem not to realize that these same circumstances have prevailed throughout this century in American policymaking. In *Politics and Policy*, Sundquist discusses a similar deadlock in the policymaking process in the two decades leading up to the Kennedy assassination and the activism of the Johnson administration. The Edsalls' further suggestions — "Throughout the past decade, the South has been on the cutting edge of national politics," and "race has increasingly become the defining characteristic of partisanship" in the South — are remarkable, especially given that Key's *Southern Politics* is cited in the same chapter. See Edsall and Edsall, *Chain Reaction*, pp. 257 and 259.

62. Edsall, "Race," p. 86.

Chapter Five

1. To some extent, all conventional public goods — for example, health care, public transportation, and environmental policies — are intermediate in that they are means to a certain way of life.

2. *Lemon v. Kurtzman*, 403 U.S. 602 (1971).

3. Durkheim, *De la Division du Travail Social*.

4. As Theodore Lowi argues in reference to the nature of the demands placed on the executive branch in the United States: "The costs of [placing too much responsibility on the executive] . . . outweigh the benefits because deceit is inherent in the present structure. Since more is demanded than can ever be delivered, and since the payoff is pinpointed personally on the president — that's where the buck stops — deceit will always be used to save the president as well as to defend the fundamental interests of the state" (*Personal President*, p. 175).

5. Peter J. Coleman, "The World of Intervention, 1880–1940," in *New Deal and Its Legacy*, ed. Eden, p. 54.

6. Anne O'Hare McCormick, "As He Sees Himself," *New York Times Magazine*, October 16, 1938, p. 2. For an interesting consideration of the degree of interaction that took place between American and European policymakers and advisers in the decades before World War II, see Rodgers, *Atlantic Crossings*.

7. As Arnold Heidenheimer, Hugh Heclo, and Carolyn Teich Adams state, the "United States is not the most active nation in the welfare field." See *Comparative Public Policy*, p. 187. For an analysis of the politics of the 1996 welfare rollback, see Mink, *Welfare's End*.

8. One reason the 1995 figure for Greece is so low is the large percentage of government expenditure devoted to interest payments (37.7 percent). If interest payments are subtracted, 31.5 percent of the remaining expenditure was devoted to social welfare in Greece; the corresponding figure for the United States is 37.5 percent.

9. See Heidenheimer, Heclo, and Adams, *Comparative Public Policy*, p. 189.

10. In *Three Worlds of Welfare Capitalism*, Esping-Andersen identifies three different categories of welfare state: liberal welfare states such as the United States, Australia, and Canada; corporatist welfare states such as France, Germany, Austria, and Italy; and social democratic welfare states such as Sweden, Norway, and Denmark. In liberal welfare states, universal public programs are few and modest; in corporatist systems, the programs are more often inclusive but are not structured so as to redistribute resources significantly; and social democratic welfare state programs tend to be both inclusive and redistributive.

11. Roughly similar dynamics meant that after their 1965 creation, Medicaid (means-

tested medical care for the poor) would be administered by the states, and Medicare (health care for the aged) would be administered by the federal government.

12. Quadagno, *Color of Welfare,* p. 21. Blacks did, however, benefit from the New Deal jobs programs established in the North. Although similarly situated groups were initially excluded from these types of programs in Canada and the United Kingdom, racial considerations clearly had a significant influence in the American decision-making process.

13. Quadagno, *Color of Welfare,* p. 10.

14. Other possible policy areas might include public education, child care provisions, gun control, and progressive industrial relations regulations.

15. Quoted in Barbara Vobejda, "Baby Boomers Could Trigger Huge Health Care Crisis," *Washington Post,* January 4, 1992, p. A3. On this point, see also Bruce C. Vladeck and James P. Firman, "The Aging of the Population and Health Services," in *Health Care Policy in America,* ed. Berki; and Judith R. Lave and Herbert A. Silverman, "Financing the Health Care of the Aged," in *Health Care Policy in America,* ed. Berki.

16. Sixteen percent of the population is completely uninsured; 8 percent are covered by Medicare and Medicaid, 68 percent have employer-based coverage, and 8 percent have other arrangements (i.e., individual policies). See the *New York Times,* October 10, 1999, sec. 4, pp. 1, 16; the *Washington Post,* Health section, May 7, 1991, p. 5; *Washington Post,* Health section, January 21, 1992, pp. 10–11; and "Policy Changes Fail to Fill Gaps in Health Coverage," *New York Times,* August 9, 1998, sec. 1, pp. 1, 18.

17. See the *New York Times,* May 16, 1993, p. E3; the *Washington Post,* September 15, 1998, p. A1; and Glied, *Chronic Condition,* p. 6.

18. This continues to be a problem despite federal legislation passed in 1996 requiring insurance companies to make policies available — at whatever price — to individuals with preexisting conditions. See "Policy Changes Fail to Fill Gaps," pp. 1, 18.

19. Patients with private insurance and their insurers are charged roughly 128 percent of the actual cost of the services they receive.

20. As a result of increasing costs there has been a push to "ration" Medicaid services in some states. Oregon has recently proposed such a reorganization. See Spencer Rich, "As Medicaid Outlays Soar, Millions Lack Coverage," *Washington Post,* November 15, 1991, p. A21; Spencer Rich, "Task Force Says Medicaid Costs May Reach 200 Billion Dollars in 1996," *Washington Post,* July 11, 1991, p. A16; Michael Specter, "Medicaid's Malady," *Washington Post,* July 8, 1991, pp. A1 and A8; Michael Specter, "Plan Covers All Needy but Not All Ailments," *Washington Post,* July 1, 1991, pp. A1 and A12; and Drew Altman, "Health Care for the Poor," in *Health Care Policy in America,* ed. Berki.

21. See Spencer Rich, "Medicare Trust Funds' Outlook Bleak," *Washington Post,* April 2, 1991, p. A19, and Robert Pear, "Medicare Prognosis: Unwieldy Growth Fueled by More Fees and Beneficiaries," *New York Times,* March 10, 1991, p. 4E.

22. Moore, *Social Origins of Dictatorship and Democracy.*

23. See Maynard, *Health Care in the European Community,* pp. 5–45.

24. See ibid., pp. 78–106, and Roemer and Roemer, *Health Care Systems,* pp. 129–72.

25. Klein, *Politics of the NHS,* p. 1, and Maynard, *Health Care in the European Community,* pp. 186–213.

26. See Klein, *Politics of the NHS,* p. 1.

27. Ibid., p. 195.

28. See John Mohan, "Health Care Policy and the State in 'Austerity Capitalism,'" in *State in Action,* ed. Simmie and King, p. 77.

29. See ibid.

30. One reason health care costs in the United States are higher may be the tendency to

perform more expensive and possibly unnecessary procedures. For instance, 205 tonsillectomies per 100,000 population are performed in the United States as compared with 89 in Canada, 61 in Japan, 65 in Sweden, and 26 in the United Kingdom. The corresponding numbers for coronary bypasses are 61 for the United States, 26 for Canada, 1 in Japan, and 6 in the United Kingdom. For hysterectomies, the figures are 90 for Japan, 145 for Sweden, 250 for the United Kingdom, 479 for Canada, and 557 for the United States. Appendectomies are less likely to be performed on a per capita basis in the United States (130 per 100,000 population) than in the United Kingdom (131), Canada (143), Sweden (168), and Japan (244). These figures are from 1980. See OECD, *Health Care Systems in Transition: The Search for Efficiency* (Paris: OECD, 1990), p. 22, and William Claiborne, "No Quick Fix," *Washington Post,* Health section, July 23, 1991, p. 12.

31. American physicians also make, on average, much more than their counterparts elsewhere. In 1990 the average physician's salary (in American dollars) in Sweden was $39,991, $45,021 in Japan, $51,118 in the United Kingdom, $53,405 in France, and $84,819 for Canadian doctors. The average salary in the United States for doctors in 1989 was $155,800. See OECD, *U.S. Health Care at the Cross-Roads, 1992,* Health Policy Studies no. 1 (Paris: OECD, 1992), p. 89. The figure for West German doctors in 1986 was $88,394.

32. See Claiborne, "No Quick Fix," p. 12.

33. See Spencer Rich, "Health Care Paperwork Called Waste," *Washington Post,* May 2, 1991, p. A1; Spencer Rich, "Study Finds Rx for U.S. in Canada Health Plan," *Washington Post,* October 18, 1991, p. A19; and Spencer Rich, "GAO: Canadian-Style Health Insurance Would Save 67 Billion Dollars," *Washington Post,* June 4, 1991, p. A21.

34. See Spencer Rich, "Two Studies Differ Sharply on Health Care Overhaul," *Washington Post,* January 11, 1992, p. A11.

35. Ibid.

36. Spencer Rich, "National Health Insurance No Panacea, Sullivan Says," *Washington Post,* February 20, 1991, p. A4.

37. From Michael Specter, "Health Care in Canada: A Model with Limits," *Washington Post,* December 18, 1989, p. A4. One factor that has clearly contributed to the absence of widespread popular support for comprehensive health care reform among Americans is their lack of understanding of arrangements elsewhere. Consequently, when German, British, and Canadian health care arrangements have been demonized throughout this century by opponents of reform in the United States and when the claim has been made (e.g., James Todd's statement) that the United States has the "best health care system in the world," American citizens have not had the ability (the resources or data) to evaluate these assertions accurately.

38. From Rich, "Health Care Paperwork Called Waste," p. A1.

39. From Constance Matthiessen, "Should the U.S. Copy Canada?," *Washington Post,* Health section, November 27, 1990, p. 13. Theodore Marmor and Jerry Mashaw describe what they call "an all too typical example" of one of the consequences of the American health care system: "A California real estate agent . . . lost her savings, her house and eventually her life to breast cancer. A change of job meant the loss of her health insurance, and she was unable to afford a 1,000 dollar-a-month temporary policy. The diagnosed breast cancer — now a pre-existing condition — left her uninsurable." See Victor Cohn, "Moving on Health Care Reform," *Washington Post,* Health section, January 21, 1992, p. 11.

40. From Matthiessen, "Should the U.S. Copy Canada?," p. 13.

41. From Specter, "Health Care in Canada," p. A4.

42. From ibid. Another aspect of the health care reform debate is the desirable mix between general practitioners (oriented toward cheaper preventive care) and specialists

(typically more expensive and necessary when preventive measures have failed or have not been taken). The United States has a particularly high specialist to general practitioner ratio, a ratio that other countries have lowered through policies and subsidies. For a discussion of these issues and others related to the applicability of the Canadian model to the United States, see Rachlis and Kushner, *Strong Medicine,* pp. 188–218.

43. From ibid., p. A4. At times, at the most superficial level, "socialized" health care has been presented as un-American. During a debate over health care reform in California at the end of the Progressive Era, the AMA distributed an anti–health care reform pamphlet reading "Made in Germany: Do You Want It in California?" with a picture of the unpopular kaiser. Attacks on the British National Health Service some forty years later led the editors of the *British Medical Journal* to criticize "the vulgarity and cheapness of the AMA's past and present attacks upon the National Health Service." See Heidenheimer, Heclo, and Adams, *Comparative Public Policy,* pp. 18–25.

44. From Vicki Kemper and Viveca Novak, "The Great American Health-Care Sellout," *Washington Post,* October 13, 1991, p. C4. One New Deal official predicted in 1936, "As long as the medical profession is opposed we will not have health insurance." See Heidenheimer, Heclo, and Adams, *Comparative Public Policy,* p. 25.

45. See Kemper and Novak, "Great American Health-Care Sellout," pp. C1, C4.

46. The 1989 repeal of the catastrophic health care program was a further reflection of the divisions within the AARP. The more vocal wealthy seniors were able to eliminate a program that would have been of great assistance to the unmobilized poorer senior constituency.

47. See American Federation of Labor, *Report of Proceedings,* 36th convention (1916), p. 145.

48. See Gompers, *Labor and the Common Welfare,* p. 119.

49. Poen, *Harry S. Truman versus the Medical Lobby,* p. 12.

50. See National Health Conference, *Proceedings of the United States Interdepartmental Committee,* pp. 29–32.

51. The destruction brought about by the Second World War in England and the experience of providing emergency health care services in a time of crisis undoubtedly made the move toward health care rationalization appear more conceivable to the English in contrast to their American counterparts, who were barely affected by World War II inside their own borders.

52. Rodgers, *Atlantic Crossings,* p. 4.

53. Ibid., p. 3.

54. See Poen, *Harry S. Truman versus the Medical Lobby,* p. 107. For a list of those groups suspected to be affiliated with the CPUSA, see U.S. Senate, Subcommittee to Investigate the Administration of the Internal Security Act and Other Internal Security Laws of the Committee on the Judiciary, *The Communist Party of the United States of America; What It Is, How It Works: A Handbook for Americans,* 84th Cong., 2d sess. (Washington, D.C.: Government Printing Office, 1956).

55. See Poen, *Harry S. Truman versus the Medical Lobby,* p. 88.

56. At this point, organized labor began to see collective bargaining as a possibly more feasible means of securing health care benefits.

57. See "AMA Statement on Truman Health Plan," *New York Times,* April 25, 1949, p. 8, and Skidmore, *Medicare and the American Rhetoric of Reconciliation,* p. 71.

58. See James Sundquist, "For the Old, Health Care," in *Politics and Policy,* pp. 287–321; Skidmore, *Medicare and the American Rhetoric of Reconciliation;* and Poen, *Harry S. Truman versus the Medical Lobby.*

59. The National Medical Association (NMA), a black medical group, supported Truman's 1945 health care proposals, to the displeasure of the AMA. As a result, pressure was placed on the AMA and its affiliates to drop their color bars. The Baltimore County Medical Society did so in 1948. One year later, the Missouri State Medical Association dropped "white" from its membership requirements, as did the Florida State Medical Association in 1950. In 1949 the AMA accepted its first black delegate and passed a resolution in 1950 encouraging its local affiliates to review their own practices. In 1949, for the first time, the NMA decided not to take a position on health care reform, despite a warning from one member that "if you support [through inaction] the stand against Truman, you will receive a pat on the back from the AMA, but condemnation from ten million Negroes and the NAACP." See McCoy and Ruetten, *Quest and Response,* pp. 162, 187.

60. Roughly 59 percent of all blacks under sixty-five had private health insurance in 1989, and 17 percent were covered by Medicaid. In the same year, among whites under sixty-five, 80 percent had private health insurance, and 6 percent relied on Medicaid. Of the completely uninsured, 71 percent are members of families with a full-time worker, 14 percent are members of a family with a part-time worker, and 15 percent are members of families without any employment-derived income. See Don Colburn, "The Black-White Health Gap," *Washington Post,* Health section, April 5, 1988, pp. 12–15; "Black Health Crisis," *Baltimore Sun,* Health section, February 14, 1989; Amy Goldstein, "Conference Looks at Inequities in U.S. Health Care," *Washington Post,* November 2, 1991, p. A13; and Cohn, "Moving on Health Care Reform," pp. 10–11. For another discussion of how race can affect the distribution of health care, see David Mariniss, "Prescription Written in Black and White," *Washington Post,* April 3, 1991, pp. A1, A4.

61. Continuing, the editorial states, "Medicaid coverage by poverty-line demarcations and physician payments are the lowest in many states that have the largest population of blacks; mainstream private medicine, particularly in large cities such as our nation's capital, has turned its back on the poor; most physicians refuse even to see such patients." See Lundberg, "National Health Care Reform," p. 2566.

62. Quoted in the *Washington Post,* Health section, January 21, 1992, p. 11.

63. Skocpol, *Boomerang,* p. 113.

64. These proposals still proved to be susceptible to attack from the right (and, to a lesser degree, the left). The Clinton administration proposed to reform the American health care system by (1) encouraging the growth of HMOs; (2) creating a government body that would evaluate the plans offered by different HMOs and making these evaluations available to the public; (3) establishing a basic minimum plan and using the tax code to discourage individuals from purchasing more expensive plans (i.e., by making higher individual health care expenditures nondeductible); (4) requiring employers either to cover their employees or to pay into a public fund that would; and (5) expanding Medicaid to cover the uninsured. Perhaps the most significant long-term proposal was to allow states to opt out and adopt a single-payer system as exists in Canada. Possible weaknesses included the lack of a cost-control mechanism and the persistence of unnecessary administrative costs and institutions (i.e., the insurance companies). Actually, the plan would have added only one layer of administration. It was also not clear if the proposals would in reality have covered the uninsured and underinsured or lessened the burden on American businesses.

65. Near the end of Clinton's first term, in the summer of 1996, minor legislation was passed that would increase portability—the ability of individuals to carry health insurance from job to job—and restrict the ability of insurance companies to refuse policies to those with preexisting conditions. Subsequent legislation was passed to set up the Children's Health Insurance Program. Nevertheless, the number of children without insurance

seems to have increased because of cuts in welfare programs that have led recipients to forgo the Medicaid benefits for which their children might still be eligible and because a number of employers are cutting back on coverage to the dependents of their workers. See "Policy Changes Fail to Fill Gaps," pp. 1, 18, and "Many States Slow to Use Children's Insurance Fund," *New York Times,* May 9, 1999, pp. 1, 16. Since the failure of the Clinton Health Care Plan in 1994, most of the attention regarding health care policy has been devoted to HMO reform and instituting a patient's bill of rights (thus far unsuccessful) and to saving money in public health care programs such as Medicare and Medicaid to achieve deficit reduction. See the *Washington Post,* September 27, 1994, p. A1; August 11, 1998, p. A1; and October 10, 1998, p. A1; and the *New York Times,* October 10, 1999, sec. 4, pp. 1, 16.

66. These references are drawn from an interadministration memo ("Talking about Health Care") circulated in the 1993-94 period and cited in Skocpol, *Boomerang,* pp. 114, 117; emphasis added.

67. Ibid., p. 118. Observed Drew Altman of the Henry J. Kaiser Family Foundation in 1998, four years after the collapse of the Clinton health care proposals, the situation of the uninsured "is the biggest problem we face in American health care, and it's not on the political agenda." See "Policy Changes Fail to Fill Gaps," p. 18.

68. Skocpol, *Boomerang,* p. 117. At another point Skocpol remarks on "the anxiety many crafters of the Health Security [the Clinton plan] message felt to make the new proposal appealing to already-insured middle-class Americans, in a nation where electoral politics and public discussions are profoundly biased upward in the class scale" (p. 118). It is interesting, given the history of the linkage between class and racial understandings, that she does not consider race as a factor in contributing to the failure of the Clinton health care proposals.

69. This is much easier to argue in hindsight. The first draft of this manuscript was written before Clinton's election in expectation that health care reform was indeed coming.

70. Piven and Cloward, *Why Americans Don't Vote,* p. 4.

71. Working from a different perspective, Seymour Martin Lipset suggests in *Political Man* that nonvoters are more likely to be antidemocratic and authoritarian: "Various American studies indicate that those lower-class individuals who are nonvoters, and who have little political interest, tend to reject the democratic norms of tolerance" (p. 116 n).

72. Piven and Cloward, *Why Americans Don't Vote,* p. 9.

73. One example of the significance of nonvoting is offered by John Petrocik, who suggests that the "margin for Ronald Reagan in 1980 was made possible by a failure of prospective Carter voters to turn out on election day." See Petrocik, "Voter Turnout and Electoral Preference: The Anomalous Reagan Elections," in *Elections in America,* ed. Scholzman, p. 253. Similarly, John Kenneth Galbraith contends that "had there been a full turnout at the election [the 1994 midterm elections, which gave the Republicans control of both houses of Congress], both the result and the reaction would have been decidedly different. The sense of social responsibility for the poor would have been greatly enhanced" (*Good Society,* p. 139).

74. For a discussion of the relevant issues and data, see Rosenstone and Hansen, *Mobilization, Participation, and Democracy in America.*

75. Lipset, *Political Man,* p. 185.

76. George F. Will, "In Defense of Nonvoting," *Newsweek,* October 10, 1983, p. 96.

77. Piven and Cloward, *Why Americans Don't Vote,* p. 12.

78. Francis G. Wilson, "Inactive Electorate and Social Revolution," p. 76. This article was written in 1936 at a point when significant barriers to voting existed.

79. Lipset, *Political Man,* p. 229.

80. Teixeira, *Why Americans Don't Vote,* p. 8.

81. Piven and Cloward, *Why Americans Don't Vote,* p. 17.

82. Burnham, "System of 1896," p. 167. In *Critical Elections and the Mainsprings of American Politics,* Burnham suggests that "the American peculiarity of personal registration ought not to be received by analysts as a given" (p. 83).

83. As a consequence of a 1972 Supreme Court decision, most states' residence requirements have been eliminated or reduced to thirty days. For a discussion of barriers to voting in the United States, as opposed to in the United Kingdom, see Reeve and Ware, *Electoral Systems,* pp. 52–55. Some states have eliminated most of these barriers and allow same-day registration and voting (and Oregon is experimenting with mail-in voting).

84. As a publication of the British Information Service, "Parliamentary Elections in Britain," states: "The register of electors is compiled by electoral registration officers. . . . To ascertain the names of the people in his area who are qualified to be registered, the registration officer either sends a standard form to every separate residence in his area for completion by the occupant, or conducts a door-to-door canvass, as may be thought best suited to the area concerned. Provisional electors' lists are then published and displayed . . . to enable claims and objections to be lodged. . . . The registry must be published not later than 15th February each year and comes in force 16th February." Cited in Kimball, *Disconnected,* pp. 303–4. Canada has recently moved toward establishing a permanent voters' list with inclusive procedures to register those who move between elections.

85. See Chambers and Burnham, *American Party Systems.* Australia and Switzerland, however, did establish universal manhood suffrage in the 1840s and 1850s respectively.

86. The republican argument that the rights and dignity of citizens (i.e., white males) ought to be respected, as discussed in Chapter 2, would require easy access to the vote for all and offer little support for property qualifications.

87. As noted, Booker T. Washington did not, at least publicly, offer much opposition to these restrictions.

88. Woodward, *Strange Career of Jim Crow,* pp. 68–69.

89. "In the off-year congressional election of 1926," Burnham notes, "only 8.5 percent of the South's potential voters actually went to the polls." See Burnham, *Current Crisis in American Politics,* p. 139.

90. McCormick, "Party Period and Public Policy," p. 295.

91. Quoted in McGerr, *Decline of Popular Politics,* p. 46.

92. For a discussion of the effects of literacy tests in the North, see Riker, *Democracy in the United States,* pp. 59–60.

93. Piven and Cloward, *Why Americans Don't Vote,* p. 93.

94. From Giddings, *When and Where I Enter,* p. 124.

95. Ibid.

96. This willingness on the part of white feminists to endorse restrictions on the black vote led W. E. B. Du Bois to suggest that "the Negro race has suffered more from the antipathy and narrowness of women both North and South than from any other single source" (ibid., p. 125). Similar tensions between blacks and feminists developed over the issues of the Fifteenth Amendment and how the Nineteenth Amendment, which lifted gender restrictions on the franchise, would be enforced in the South.

97. As Richard McCormick suggests, "Changes in politics and governance at the beginning of the twentieth century marked the start of a new political era, distinct in its patterns of participation from the party period before it. Early in the 1900s, electoral turnout fell and party loyalties became weaker, while new avenues of political participation opened up. In the same years, distributive policies came under sustained assault, while the gov-

ernment's regulatory and administrative functions were strengthened" ("Party Period and Public Policy," p. 295).

98. For one analysis of the weakening of the patronage system, see Skowronek, *Building a New American State.*

99. It might be tempting to argue that the 1919 passage of the Nineteenth Amendment was the cause of these low figures, but the decline in turnout preceded this development. As Piven and Cloward note, "The downward trend began before 1920, and it persisted afterwards, even when the lower rates of voting by women are taken into account." Nevertheless, some have argued that a greater reluctance of women in the immigrant communities to vote might have at least temporarily effectively increased the voting power of "native" Americans. See *Why Americans Don't Vote,* pp. 55–56.

100. Thirty-six percent of eligible voters turned out for the 1998 midterm elections (the lowest midterm turnout since 1942). See ibid., p. 161, and *Keesing's Record of World Events, 1992,* vol. 38, no. 11, 1992.

101. The term "Hispanics" is placed in quotation marks because of the constructed nature of the category as discussed in the Chapter 1. Income and education continue to correlate with nonvoting. Those with college degrees are almost twice as likely to register to vote as those with elementary school education, and the employed are 15 to 20 percent more likely to register and vote than the unemployed. See Piven and Cloward, *Why Americans Don't Vote,* pp. 204–5.

102. Burnham, *Current Crisis in American Politics,* pp. 157–58.

103. The importance of money to the prevalence of antileftist political movements is perhaps one of the most significant legacies of the 1896 election. McKinley and the Republican National Committee, under the guidance of future National Civic Federation leader Marcus Hanna, spent $3.5 million in comparison with the $300,000 spent by the Bryan-led Democratic-Populist fusion ticket. See McGerr, *Decline of Popular Politics,* pp. 140–41.

104. See Piven and Cloward, "Northern Bourbons," pp. 39–42, and *New York Times,* May 21, 1995, June 10, 1995, September 3, 1995, and December 3, 1995. Admit Piven and Cloward, "Voter registration reform is no magic bullet. The period ahead will show whether it makes a difference" ("Northern Bourbons," p. 42).

105. See Heidenheimer, Heclo, and Adams, *Comparative Public Policy,* pp. 189, 257–81; Meyer and Oster, *Deregulation and the Future of Intercity Passenger Travel;* Paul Taylor, "New Push on for Parental Leave," *Washington Post,* March 21, 1991, p. A19; and Mary Jordan, "Nationwide Tests Urged for Schools," *Washington Post,* January 25, 1992, p. A1. As public spaces and institutions, such as public schools, are abandoned, the fight to maintain bus service in many southern towns and cities is becoming a civil rights issue of sorts. See Rick Bragg, "Buses Again Concern Civil Rights Veterans," *New York Times,* June 16, 1996. Similarly, it is obvious that progressive changes in gender policies, issues, and relations will not result in the United States until the cultural and racial (as well as class) insensitivities of feminism are overcome, the misogyny and homophobia evident in the various "racial" groups are transcended, and ultimately until gender is "deracialized." From the battles over the Fifteenth and Nineteenth Amendments to the undercutting effects of race on the understanding of gender issues in the Clarence Thomas and O. J. Simpson cases, the two realms clearly are intimately related.

106. Gilens, " 'Race Coding' and White Opposition to Welfare," p. 601; emphasis added.

107. See Mink, *Welfare's End,* p. 23.

108. Theda Skocpol, "African Americans in U.S. Social Policy," in *Classifying by Race,* ed. Peterson, p. 129.

109. See Tocqueville, *Democracy in America,* 1:373; emphasis added.

Chapter Six

1. "Culture" in the narrow sense refers to music, arts, language, and aesthetics in general. "Culture" in the broad sense refers to "a whole way of life" and would include economic and political practices and institutions as well as the standard anthropological realms of human existence.

2. See Esping-Andersen, *Three Worlds of Welfare Capitalism.*

3. One way in which cultural institutions might differ from modern health care institutions in the West is that the former are more likely to have been created by society (like the left itself) than to have been "provided" by the state (such as health care).

4. Receiving greater recognition are gender implications associated with the arrangement of health care systems (e.g., related to the interpretation of symptoms). Similarly, education policies and policing strategies have been challenged on the basis of their potential gender, ethnic, and class biases. The conventional left and labor unions—that is, intermediate public goods—are, as has been suggested, also susceptible to these claims and challenges. Some of the problems faced by these movements of the left were caused by their inability to satisfy particularistic claims successfully.

5. One of the most striking examples of this process can be found in the social sciences where each discipline—for example, economics, sociology, political science, history, anthropology, and theology—seems to operate according to its own normative values and in terms of its own preferred concepts and methodologies to the point that communication across disciplines is nearly impossible.

6. In much the same manner, Antonio Gramsci suggested that cultural forces constructed as a *hegemony* could prevent popular understanding of the nature of the relations of production in the economic realm. See Walter Benjamin, "The Work of Art in the Age of Mechanical Reproduction," in *Illuminations,* pp. 217–51, and Gramsci, *Letters from Prison.*

7. Quoted in Denning, *Cultural Front,* p. 381.

8. See Adorno, *Prisms,* pp. 130–32.

9. Excerpted from an interview with Cornel West by James Ledbetter, "Cornel U.," *Vibe,* September 1993, p. 66.

10. The manner in which Taylorism was incorporated in the 1920s is an example. The principles of scientific management could have been used to increase efficiency without necessarily increasing the hierarchical nature of the workplace as they did.

11. The use of video cameras for surveillance purposes and as a means of drawing citizens further into the television process as "collaborators" (e.g., *America's Funniest Home Videos*) illustrates how new technology can be used to reinforce market operations and penetration. Yet video cameras have also enabled individuals to make films for their own consumption and the market that challenge "the industry's" hegemony and, in the case of the Rodney King beating, give citizens a better understanding of how the police (as agents of the state) behave in certain circumstances.

12. The questioning of the merits of national bilingualism coincided with an assault on the linguistic rights of French-speaking Canadians in Manitoba, Ontario, and New Brunswick and, later, on English-speaking Canadians in the province of Quebec. The claims of the First Nations, Inuit, or aboriginal population have characteristically been overlooked, although this group has often acted to ensure that its interests are recognized and respected. For consideration of these developments, see Carens, *Is Quebec Nationalism Just?*

13. Note Brian McKenna and Susan Purcell: "Rosemount [a francophone neighborhood in Montreal] had sent more than its fair share of young men to be murdered in the muck of Flanders. Many people were baffled that French-Canadian boys would volunteer to risk

life and limb for an English king in a foreign land, but if a fellow wanted to chance being buried under the Union Jack that was his business. As long as it was done voluntarily. But now the government in Ottawa was talking of dragooning young men. To promote conscription in Quebec was to invite sedition, if not worse. 'Let them talk of conscription,' said the [francophone] nationalists among the crowd after Sunday mass, 'and we'll talk of secession' " (*Drapeau*, p. 4).

14. John Herd Thompson and Seager, *Canada*, p. 172.

15. For a more detailed discussion of these developments, see Yorke, *Axes, Chops, and Hot Licks.*

16. Lawrence Levine refers to these unifying beliefs and symbols—for instance, the mythological attributes of the Constitution, the George Washington cherry tree story, the Liberty Bell, and the significance of the Fourth of July—as "invented tradition" (a term he borrows from Eric Hobsbawm). See *Highbrow/Lowbrow*, p. 229.

17. George F. Will, "The Cult of Ethnicity," *Washington Post*, July 14, 1991, p. C7.

18. See, for example, Hoffmann, *Gulliver's Troubles.*

19. Quoted in Edmund Morris, "Just Americans," *Washington Post*, Sunday, February 12, 1989, p. C7.

20. Dobbert, *Disintegration of an Immigrant Community*, p. 431.

21. At the time the Czechs were apparently considered to constitute a distinct race. See Kenneth D. Miller, *Czecho-Slovaks in America*, pp. 105-6. The term "race" was used at this time to distinguish francophones and anglophones in Canada as well. Suggests André Siegfried in 1907, "An immemorial struggle persists between French and English. . . . In the first place, and above all, it is a racial problem" (*Race Question in Canada*, p. 1).

22. Chada, *Czechs in the United States*, p. 231.

23. Ibid., p. 233.

24. Ibid., p. 234. Suggest Nathan Glazer and Daniel Patrick Moynihan, "The American descendents of immigrants diverge markedly from the people of the old country. . . . The powerful assimilatory influences of American society operate on all who come into it, making the children of immigrants and even immigrants themselves a very different people from those they left behind." See *Beyond the Melting Pot*, p. 12.

25. Asks Michael Novak, "What do people have to lose before they can qualify as true Americans?" See *Rise of the Unmeltable Ethnics*, p. xxi.

26. Levine, *Highbrow/Lowbrow*, pp. 192, 195.

27. Quoted in ibid., p. 221.

28. Quoted in ibid., p. 177.

29. Ibid. The terms "highbrow" and "lowbrow" were drawn from the field of craniology and the argument that the superior races (i.e., northern Europeans) had literally higher brows (foreheads) than did those whose cranial capacity was smaller and whose brows were supposedly lower. Even these physiobiological arguments were reasoned in a dubious manner. See Montagu, *Concept of Race*, pp. 93-94, 234-38.

30. Rogin, *Blackface, White Noise*, p. 78.

31. Levine, *Highbrow/Lowbrow*, p. 9. For a discussion of how the disintegrative effects of the industrialization process influenced the relevance of American Protestantism, see Susan Curtis, "Work and Salvation in Corporate America," in *Consuming Faith*, pp. 16-35.

32. Austro-Marxist Bauer suggested that "the national character of each nation [would] stamp itself on its socialism [and that] the nearer the working class of a country comes to taking power, the more must it adapt its practices and methods of struggle to the national peculiarities of its battlefield. Similarly, the socialist ideology of the working class becomes more closely linked with the national cultural heritage, as it absorbs more culture. . . . Our

task must not be to stamp out national peculiarities but to bring about national unity in national diversity." See Otto Bauer, "National Character and the Idea of a Nation," in *Essential Works of Socialism,* ed. Howe, p. 132.

33. The producer in question was Gary David Goldberg. See Bill Carter, "CBS Is Taking a Risk with New Series Set in Brooklyn in the 50's," *New York Times,* September 19, 1991, pp. C15, C18.

34. Continuing, Mason lamented, in his characteristic manner: "They worry too much about which age group might be left out: 'If they're 12, they won't understand it, so all this is out. If they're over 60, it's too young; if they're over 12, it's too old. This is not for the Midwest, this is not for the South.' Before you know it, you've got a show about two kids: 'Did you eat lunch yet? You didn't eat?' This is the conversation. My God!" See Tom Shales, "Jackie Mason's 'Soup,' a Post-Mortem," *Washington Post,* November 17, 1989, p. D8.

35. Robertson, *Dispossessed Majority,* p. 233.

36. See Morris, "Just Americans," p. C7, and David Von Drehle, "In N.H. Town, Voters Find Democrats Are No Field of Dreams," *Washington Post,* February 15, 1992, p. A21.

37. Traveling between the United States and Canada, I find one difference that is immediately discernible is the degree to which the "ethnic" communities have been maintained, physically and culturally, in Canada. Comparing, for instance, German, Italian, Irish, Jewish, Greek (white), Chinese, Filipino, Korean, Vietnamese and Japanese (Asian), and Afro-Caribbean and African (black) immigrant cohorts, it appears that in the context of American racialism there has been less support for the preservation of particularistic traditions and ways of life (at least outside of New York City). Lastly, the presence of aboriginal populations in both the United States and Canada contributed to the promotion of a white/nonwhite dichotomy, the difference being that the push to define whiteness in the United States was even stronger because of the presence of a significant black population.

38. Roediger, *Wages of Whiteness,* p. 3.

39. Ignatiev, *How the Irish Became White,* p. 1.

40. In *Playing in the Dark,* Toni Morrison argues that perceptions of "blackness" and of Africans in America have influenced significantly the development of conceptions of "whiteness" and have had a pervasive influence on American literature.

41. Toll, *Blacking Up,* p. 5.

42. Ibid.

43. Continuing, Twain recollects, "I remember the first Negro musical show I ever saw. It must have been in the early forties. It was a new institution. In our village of Hannibal . . . it burst upon us as a glad and stunning surprise" (*Autobiography of Mark Twain,* p. 64).

44. See Alexander Saxton, "Blackface Minstrelsy," in *Rise and Fall of the White Republic.*

45. Lott, *Love and Theft,* p. 163.

46. Toll, *Blacking Up,* p. 65.

47. Toll suggests that the songs of Stephen Foster helped in that regard, in their creation of "an idealized world that had all the virtues that Northern society seemed to lack" (ibid., p. 37).

48. Rogin, *Blackface, White Noise,* pp. 11–12. At another point Rogin contends, "American politics was organized around antiblack racism rather than anti-Semitism. . . . Jewish immigrants and their children inherited and often struggled against the racial representations that signified American belonging" (p. 165).

49. See Ely, *Adventures of Amos 'n' Andy;* Joe Wood, "Do the White Thing: Young Black Teenagers," *Village Voice,* March 1991, pp. 10–11; David Mills, "It's a White Thing," *Washington Post,* July 14, 1991, pp. G1 and G4; and Frith, *Sound Effects,* p. 15.

50. Quoted in Frith, *Sound Effects,* p. 15. Similarly, Toll notes that in the 1930s roughly 40

million individuals, or one-third of all Americans, listened to *Amos 'n' Andy* and that "to avoid losing customers, movie theaters played *Amos 'n' Andy* in their lobbies, and Atlantic City merchants piped it onto the boardwalk; utility companies reported a drop in water pressure as the program ended and people flushed their toilets." See *Entertainment Machine*, pp. 54–55.

51. See Norman Mailer, "The White Negro," in *Legacy of Dissent*, ed. Nicolaus Mills, p. 157, and Jack Kerouac, "On the Road Again," *The New Yorker*, June 22 and 29, 1998, p. 56.

52. Lott, *Love and Theft*, p. 234.

53. In his article in the *Atlantic Monthly* explaining his departure from the CPUSA, Richard Wright cites as one source of his disaffection the party's abandonment of the John Reed Clubs, which provided a number of young writers their first opportunities to develop their skills, as part of its Popular Front policy reorientation. See "I Tried to Be a Communist," *Atlantic Monthly*, August 1944, p. 69. Wright is one of the individuals Denning mentions who continued to produce work consistent with the Popular Front after his decision to leave the CPUSA. See Denning, *Cultural Front*, p. 26.

54. Rogin, *Blackface, White Noise*, p. 162, and Denning, *Cultural Front*, p. 8.

55. For example, the jazz producer Norman Granz organized concerts in support of the defendants. The convictions were subsequently overturned.

56. In the "zoot suit" riots of 1943, white servicemen attacked Mexican American, Filipino, and black youths wearing the flamboyant, cloth-consuming outfits during a period in which fabric was being rationed and young men who were not serving in the military were suspected of being unpatriotic draft dodgers. These riots were followed by similar disturbances throughout the country (e.g., Detroit, Philadelphia, Chicago, and New York City). See Robin D. G. Kelley, "The Riddle of the Zoot: Malcolm Little and Black Cultural Politics during World War II," in *Malcolm X*, ed. Joe Wood, pp. 155–82.

57. Suggests Michael Rogin with regard to *Body and Soul*, "If any film gives credence to the hallucinatory charge that a Communist conspiracy was seizing control of Hollywood . . . this is the one" (*Blackface, White Noise*, pp. 211–12).

58. The Count Basie Orchestra, "It's the Same Old South," *Four to a Bar* (Parade 2030, 1994).

59. Naison, "Paul Robeson and the American Labor Movement," in *Paul Robeson*, ed. Stewart, p. 179.

60. Carby, *Race Men*, p. 101.

61. Michael Denning suggests that the character of Charles Foster Kane might have been a combination of William Randolph Hearst and Henry Luce, publisher of *Time*, *Life*, and *Fortune* magazines. Hearst also was one of the subjects of John Dos Passos's *U.S.A.* (1938). See Denning, *Cultural Front*, pp. 384–94.

62. Hernton, *The Sexual Mountain and Black Women Writers*. For discussions of the interconnections between racial and gender politics in American politics, see Angela Y. Davis, *Women, Race, and Class;* Evans, *Personal Politics;* and Giddings, *When and Where I Enter*.

63. For one discussion of Friedan's experiences in this period, see Horowitz, *Betty Friedan*.

64. Holiday, with Dufty, *Lady Sings the Blues*, p. 94.

65. "We identified with the Rosenbergs," suggests Dee's husband, Ossie Davis, "because they were of the Left, they were obvious targets for the FBI, and they were Jews." See Ossie Davis and Dee, *With Ossie and Ruby*, pp. 232, 238.

66. Denning, *Cultural Front*, p. 338. Although the kind of explicit racism characteristic of the left, labor, and the CPUSA pre-1928 was not a significant issue during the Popular Front

period, Billie Holiday suggests that Barney Josephson was reluctant to give Hazel Scott, at that point an aspiring jazz singer, an opportunity to audition to play at Café Society because "she was too dark." Scott did eventually get the audition and the job. See Holiday, with Dufty, *Lady Sings the Blues,* p. 91.

67. For the details of this particular debate, see Angela Y. Davis, *Blues Legacies and Black Feminism,* pp. 181–97, and Denning, *Cultural Front,* pp. 338–48. Although Lewis Allan wrote the words for "Strange Fruit," to the extent that a vocalist writes by singing (e.g., Frank Sinatra, Betty Carter, Cassandra Wilson) by adding layers of meaning in the process of performance and interpretation, Holiday certainly can justifiably claim — as she apparently did on occasion — that she cowrote the song.

68. McKay, *Harlem,* pp. 248–49.

69. See Naison, *Communists in Harlem,* p. 212.

70. Quoted in Duberman, *Paul Robeson,* pp. 176–77.

71. Naison, *Communists in Harlem,* p. 204.

72. Quoted in Duberman, *Paul Robeson,* p. 177. In Robeson's defense, jazz changed substantially over the course of the period in question.

73. The durability of the conflicts of the McCarthy era was still evident more than forty years later. The decision to give Elia Kazan an honorary Oscar at the 1999 Academy Awards show (on March 21, 1999) generated a lot of debate. Arthur Laurents, one of the individuals blacklisted as a result of the McCarthy era, stated on the eve of the show, "I think Kazan's motive is what is so awful. He couldn't have worked in movies unless he testified. . . . [Giving him the Oscar] says it was O.K., we can forget about it now. . . . I do not want him honored as a person for something he did that was despicable." Quoted in "Decades Later, Naming Names Still Matters," *New York Times,* March 14, 1999, sec. 2, p. 4. From the stage at the Oscars, the comedian Chris Rock would call Kazan a "rat." Kazan has asserted that "if you want an apology now because I . . . name[d] names to the House committee, you've misjudged my character. The 'horrible, immoral thing' I would do, I did out of my true self. Everything before was . . . posturing. The people who owe . . . an explanation . . . are those who, year after year, held the Soviets blameless for all their crimes" (*Life,* p. 460).

74. See American Business Consultants, *Red Channels.*

75. Fast would eventually publish the novel, the story of a slave revolt, himself (which would subsequently, of course, be turned into a successful movie). See Fast, *Being Red.*

76. According to Ossie Davis, "Whereas in Hollywood actors, stars, and celebrities seemed to be stumbling over each other, rushing to clear their own names by pointing the accusing finger at their friends and associates, on Broadway, it was different. Though we, too, were a community besieged, we held ourselves above such perfidious behavior. We knew how to defend ourselves and how to fight back. No. Broadway was not Hollywood. We had organization, we had a philosophy based on what we considered to be our First Amendment rights, we had a galaxy of heroes, including Paul [Robeson], and we had an objective, which was to fight the witch-hunt" (Ossie Davis and Dee, *With Ossie and Ruby,* p. 226). Arthur Laurents has observed, "There was absolutely no blacklist in the theater. . . . Broadway producers were individuals, not corporate producers" ("Decades Later," p. 24).

77. Ossie Davis and Dee, *With Ossie and Ruby,* p. 200.

78. Stated Eleanor Roosevelt after Robinson's appearance, "Mr. Robeson does his people great harm in trying to line them up on the Communist side of the political picture. Jackie Robinson helped them greatly by his forthright statements" (Duberman, *Paul Robeson,* pp. 360–61).

79. See Walter White, "The Strange Case of Paul Robeson," *Ebony,* February 1951.

80. See Testimony of Hazel Scott, *Hearing before the House Committee for Un-American*

Activities, 81st Cong., 2d sess., September 22, 1950; Charles V. Hamilton, *Adam Clayton Powell,* p. 196; and Haygood, *King of the Cats,* p. 162.

81. Quoted in Duberman, *Paul Robeson,* p. 391.

82. Quoted in Denning, *Cultural Front,* pp. 317–18.

83. Ossie Davis and Dee, *With Ossie and Ruby,* p. 234.

84. *Red Channels,* pp. 79–84, 129–30, and 157–58. Actors Harry Belafonte and Sidney Poitier were able to escape a similar fate possibly because they, along with Dizzy Gillespie, were warned by Paul Robeson to keep their distance lest they be targeted as well (they were also just beginning their careers during this period). Recalled Dizzy Gillespie, "One time I was playing at the Apollo Theatre at the height of the McCarthy era and I received a telegram from him [Paul Robeson] saying that he had come by to see me but that he didn't come backstage because he didn't want to put pressure on me." Perhaps ironically, Gillespie was, at least at one point, a "card-carrying Communist." As he notes in his autobiography, "At those communist dances, they were always trying to convert you. As a matter of fact, I signed one of those cards; I never went to a meeting, but I was a card-carrying communist because it was directly associated with my work." See Duberman, *Paul Robeson,* p. 391; Bruce Cook, "Singer/Activist Paul Robeson Dies: A Tragic Hero," *Rolling Stone,* March 11, 1976, p. 15; and Gillespie, with Fraser, *To Be, or Not . . . to Bop,* p. 80.

85. Denning, *Cultural Front,* p. 14.

86. Quoted in ibid., p. 309.

87. Duke Ellington, quoted in John Pittman, "The Duke Will Stay on Top!," in *Duke Ellington Reader,* ed. Mark Tucker, p. 149.

88. See Angela Davis, *Blues Legacies and Black Feminism,* p. 184. Continuing, Davis contends that the song "put the elements of protest and resistance back at the center of contemporary black musical culture" and reduced the distance "between fame and commercial success on the one hand and social consciousness in music on the other" (ibid.).

89. Holiday and Dufty, *Lady Sings the Blues,* p. 84.

90. Holiday's recording of "Strange Fruit" was released by special arrangement by Milt Gabler's Commodore Records. See Holiday and Dufty, *Lady Sings the Blues,* p. 85, and Angela Davis, *Blues Legacies and Black Feminism,* p. 195.

91. Bogle, *Toms, Coons, Mulattoes, Mammies, and Bucks,* p. 127.

92. Robert Gordon, *It Came from Memphis,* p. 49.

93. Binford, quoted in Guralnick, *Last Train to Memphis,* p. 46.

94. This campaign was aided by the advance warning civil rights groups had: the film was based on a popular novel, Thomas Dixon's *The Clansman* (1905), that subsequently generated a touring play and pageants before the film was made and released.

95. Koppes and Black, "Blacks, Loyalty, and the Motion-Picture Propaganda in World War II," p. 405.

96. Quoted in Roeder, *Censored War,* p. 44. An interesting parallel case is the resistance of francophones during World War I to being drafted to serve in the Canadian armed forces under the direction of the British. "To preach Holy War for the liberties of the peoples overseas, and to oppress the national minorities in Canada [i.e., the francophone populations]," argued francophone leader Henri Bourassa, "is, in our opinion, nothing but odious hypocrisy." See Bourassa, "Mr. Bourassa's Reply to Capt. Talbot Papineau," in *Readings in Canadian History,* ed. Francis and Smith, p. 362.

97. This, according to OWI survey data, was a process that had already started. A dialogue between African Americans and Japanese authorities had been initiated at the 1919 Paris Peace Conference when Japan introduced a motion calling for the acceptance of a principle of racial equality, as a challenge to the implicit white supremacist assumptions in

play at the meetings, which the chairman of the League of Nations Commission, Woodrow Wilson, successfully blocked (even though a majority of the delegates voted in favor of the plank). See Lauren, *Power and Prejudice,* pp. 88–107, and Koppes and Black, "Blacks, Loyalty, and Motion-Picture Propaganda," pp. 385–86.

98. Roeder, *Censored War,* p. 44.

99. Ibid., p. 46.

100. Ibid., p. 57. Initially, photos of *all* wounded soldiers were censored because of a concern about public reaction and support back home for the war. This prohibition against images of injured and dead white soldiers was eventually relaxed. See ibid., pp. 7–25.

101. Quoted in Koppes and Black, "Blacks, Loyalty, and Motion-Picture Propaganda," p. 390.

102. Quoted in ibid., p. 388; emphasis added.

103. A. Philip Randolph, "Why Should We March?," *Survey Graphic,* November 1942, p. 488.

104. Quoted in Koppes and Black, "Blacks, Loyalty, and Motion-Picture Propaganda," p. 394.

105. Ira Katznelson, "Was the Great Society a Lost Opportunity?," in *Rise and Fall of the New Deal Order,* ed. Fraser and Gerstle, p. 188, and Denning, *Cultural Front,* pp. 35–37, 466–70.

106. Denning, *Cultural Front,* p. 467.

107. Ibid., pp. 469–70.

108. Continuing, Sinatra suggested, "By means of its almost imbecilic reiteration, and sly, lewd, in plain fact, dirty lyrics . . . it [rock and roll] manages to be the martial music of every sideburned delinquent on the face of the earth. . . . It is the most brutal, ugly, desperate, vicious form of expression it has been my misfortune to hear." Offered Elvis Presley, in a rather gracious response, "I admire the man. He has a right to say what he wants to say. He is a great success and a fine actor, but . . . he's mistaken about this. This is a trend, just the same as he faced when he started years ago." Quoted in Guralnick, *Last Train to Memphis,* p. 437.

109. Jonathan Rieder, "The Rise of the 'Silent Majority,' " in *Rise and Fall of the New Deal Order,* ed. Fraser and Gerstle, p. 247.

110. Denning, *Cultural Front,* p. 32.

111. Rogin, *Blackface, White Noise,* p. 199.

112. "I saw—I don't remember when, but I saw as a child—I thought to myself: suppose that I would have been born *black,*" Phillips has remarked. See Guralnick, *Last Train to Memphis,* pp. 60, 134, and 500.

113. Marcus, *Mystery Train,* p. 208.

114. Quoted in Wexler and Ritz, *Rhythm and the Blues,* p. 134.

115. Ward, *Just My Soul Responding,* pp. 5 and 38.

116. Ibid., p. 3.

117. Ibid., p. 120.

118. Depending on the source, Phillips's payoff is either a million or a billion dollars. For the lower estimate, see David Nicholson, "Please Mr. Postman . . . If Elvis Deserves a Stamp, So Do America's Black Rockers," *Washington Post,* January 26, 1992, p. C5, and for the higher calculation, see Guralnick, *Last Train to Memphis,* p. 500. Regarding the "white Negro" concept, see Mailer, "White Negro."

119. Quoted in Ward, *Just My Soul Responding,* p. 137.

120. This statement in an article in *Tan* magazine is quoted in ibid., p. 136.

121. Ibid.

122. Public Enemy, "Fight the Power," *Music from Do the Right Thing,* Motown, 1989.

123. Although it occurred at the same time that significant class movements in American politics were marginalized, the civil rights movement unleashed class tensions among African Americans. As a result, the (limited) black engagement with blackface forms (e.g., Bert Williams) led—after the delegitimizing of literal blackface and the lessened pressure to "Tom"—to a new form of masking in which some blacks would engage stereotypes of lower-income black life in what Nelson George has called "ghettocentricity" as a way of establishing credibility and authenticity with white and black audiences. According to George, "Ghettocentricity means making the values and lifestyles of America's poverty-stricken urban homelands central to one's being." See Nelson George, "Ghettocentricity," in *Buppies, B-boys, Baps, and Bohos,* pp. 95–97. One example of this phenomenon might be the work of Long Island's Eddie Murphy on the animated sitcom *The PJs.* In contemporary hip hop (e.g., Public Enemy's Chuck D and GangStarr's Guru) this masking has allowed black artists to cross the line as had white peers (Vanilla Ice and Eminem) and in common to continue the blackface tradition of transgression combined with the containment or exclusion of truly progressive class, gender, and cultural politics. The roots of this development can be traced, perhaps, to the work of Leroi Jones (later, Amiri Baraka) and the example set by an earlier scion of the black middle class, the conflicted and complicated Miles Davis. For interpretations of Miles Davis, see Miles Davis and Troupe, *Miles;* Cleage, *Deals with the Devil;* and Hazel Carby, "Playin' the Changes," in *Race Men,* pp. 135–65.

124. The gap between the norms prevailing in popular culture and formal politics explains the mixed reaction to the emergence of the former wrestler Jesse Ventura as governor of Minnesota. This same tension would undoubtedly affect the presidential campaign of the actor and director Warren Beatty if he were to seek the nomination of Ross Perot's Reform Party for 2000. Business tycoon Donald Trump's attempts to persuade talk show host Oprah Winfrey to serve as his running mate (again, on the Reform ticket for 2000) indicates that the line between the two realms—formal politics and popular culture—has blurred, at least in the eyes of some Americans. Ronald Reagan's political successes, naturally, represent one example of this phenomenon.

125. Springsteen's onstage relationship with Clemons during the heyday of the E Street Band is consistent with a tradition in American literature, vaudeville, radio, and film that includes Huckleberry Finn and Jim, Jack Benny and "Rochester," Humphrey Bogart and "Sam," John Garfield and Canada Lee, Sidney Poitier and Tony Curtis, Richard Pryor and Gene Wilder, Sylvester Stallone and Carl Weathers, Eddie Murphy and Nick Nolte, Mel Gibson and Danny Glover, Wesley Snipes and Woody Harrelson, and, more recently, as a possible reflection of the changing place of Asian Americans in the context of the racial polarization characteristic of American life, Chris Tucker and Jackie Chan. The E Street Band's name is a reference to the street on which keyboardist Sancious's mother lived.

126. Bruce Springsteen, "My Hometown," *Born in the U.S.A.,* Columbia, 1984.

127. Bruce Springsteen, "Born in the U.S.A.," *Born in the U.S.A.*

128. Cullen, *Born in the U.S.A.,* pp. 64–65. It is interesting to note that Hootie and the Blowfish, a rock band which became popular in the mid-1990s with white audiences (including Bill Clinton) while featuring a black lead singer, chose, intentionally, to obscure the racial identities of the band's members on the cover of their first release, *Cracked Rear View* (Atlantic, 1994). Some of the album's lyrics, though, did address racial issues.

129. Quoted in Marsh, *Glory Days,* p. 234.

130. Quoted in ibid., pp. 237–38.

131. Quoted in ibid., p. 238.

132. Quoted in ibid., p. 26.

133. Quoted in Werner, *Change Is Gonna Come*, p. 247.

134. Quoted in Marsh, *Glory Days*, p. 229.

135. Quoted in Cullen, *Born in the U.S.A.*, p. 13.

136. See Randall Robinson, *Defending the Spirit*, p. 273. In 1999 Jordan did offer public support and contribute funds to the presidential campaign of the former basketball player and senator Democrat Bill Bradley. See the *New York Times,* October 3, 1999, p. 1.

137. When Bob Dole's campaign tried to do the same thing in 1996, Springsteen immediately spoke out against it. Dole's campaign also used Sam and Dave's 1960s rhythm and blues hit "Soul Man."

138. Bobby McFerrin, "Don't Worry, Be Happy," *Simple Pleasures,* EMI, 1988. The Clinton campaign would choose Fleetwood Mac's less ambiguous "Don't Stop (Thinking about Tomorrow)" in 1992 to frame its promise of better days to come. When former Klansman David Duke borrowed pop singer Bryan Adams's "Everything I Do (I Do It for You)" for his Louisiana gubernatorial campaign, Adams threatened to sue.

139. It is for this reason that the specifically political arguments raised by the advocates of the American Negro school (e.g., Ralph Ellison, Albert Murray, Stanley Crouch, and Wynton Marsalis) are so unconvincing: the obvious influence of African Americans on mainstream American culture and the possibility that all Americans are cultural mulattoes do not mean that blacks have been similarly accepted into the formal political structures of the (white) republic. For the clearest statement of the views of this particular school, see Ellison, *Shadow and Act.*

140. See Denselow, *When the Music's Over,* pp. 138–42.

141. See Nager, *Memphis Beat,* p. xiv. For other considerations of the significance of Memphis as a major musical center and crossroads, see Guralnick, *Sweet Soul Music;* Guralnick, *Last Train to Memphis;* and Robert Gordon, *It Came from Memphis.*

142. Indeed, given Clinton's need for the support of both black voters and the Reagan Democrat constituencies, it was conceivably all good, if rather bewildering, politics.

143. The various African American cultural traditions have been similarly shaped and warped by the effects of racialism in the United States. Particularly in the last thirty years, it has become evident that these cultural practices and the mediums that shape them are unlikely to sustain or nurture perspectives that might enable the various black communities to understand and process effectively the changes occurring in their circumstances.

144. See Karl Marx, "Contribution to the Critique of Hegel's *Philosophy of Right:* Introduction," in *Marx-Engels Reader,* ed. Robert C. Tucker, p. 21. The statement is made in the following context: "But in Germany every class lacks the logic, insight, courage and clarity which would make it a negative representative of society. Moreover, there is also lacking in every class the generosity of spirit which identifies itself, if only for a moment, with the popular mind; that genius which pushes material force to political power, that revolutionary daring which throws at its adversary the defiant phrase: *I am nothing and I should be everything*" (ibid.).

Chapter Seven

1. See, for instance, Hartz, *Liberal Tradition in America;* Wilentz, *Chants Democratic;* Eric Foner, "Why Is There No Socialism in the United States?"; and Laslett and Lipset, *Failure of a Dream?*

2. See Theda Skocpol, "African Americans in U.S. Social Policy," in *Classifying by Race,* ed. Peterson, p. 129.

3. See the *New York Times,* March 30, 1997, p. A8.

4. See the *Globe and Mail,* June 2, 1997, p. B1.

5. The overlapping of "left" and "far right" also indicates the difficulty involved in balancing economic and cultural concerns without lapsing into fascism or sterile economism.

6. See, for instance, Scammon and Wattenberg, *Real Majority;* Edsall, *Chain Reaction;* Peter Brown, *Minority Party;* Sleeper, *Closest of Strangers;* and Stanley Greenberg, *Middle Class Dreams.* One notable exception to this pattern is Goldfield, *Color of Politics.*

7. With regard to the convergence thesis, see Eric Foner, "Why Is There No Socialism in the United States?," pp. 57–80, and Rose, "How Exceptional Is the American Political Economy?," pp. 91–115.

8. Burt, "Women's Issues," pp. 111–12.

9. Notes Pippa Norris, "Although changes have been implemented by all administrations, a large share of the credit has been claimed by Socialist governments. It was [François] Mitterand who initiated the Ministry for Women's Rights in France, [Andreas] Papandreaou, leader of PASOK [the Panhellenic or Greek Socialist Movement], who created the Greek Council for Equal Rights, and the Labour Party which set up the Equal Opportunities Commission to monitor equal pay in Britain. Feminists who work within left-wing parliamentary parties, in a broad coalition with other disadvantaged groups, claim that this strategy can be an effective way to improve the position of women. Yet many other feminists are skeptical about how far political parties, as part of the patriarchal power structure, can have any fundamental impact on the position of women." See *Politics and Sexual Equality,* p. 4.

10. The conventional left, identified with the interests of white, male workers, has been resistant to other new social movements such as the environmental cause and identity politics that are not rooted in whiteness, as well as feminist mobilization.

11. See Lenin, *Imperialism,* and Cardoso, *Dependency and Development in Latin America.* David Cameron argues that one factor analysts have often overlooked when explaining the growth of public economies is the exposure (i.e., vulnerability) of the state in question to the global economy. "Governments in small open economies," he posits, "have tended to provide a variety of income supplements in the form of social security schemes, health insurance, unemployment benefits, job training, employment subsidies to firms, and even investment capital." See "Expansion of the Public Economy," p. 1260.

12. Sombart, *Why Is There No Socialism in the United States?*

13. There is currently one socialist in the House of Representatives, Vermont's Bernie Saunders.

14. See Edmund Morgan, *American Slavery, American Freedom.* Eric Foner makes a similar argument in *Slavery and Freedom.*

15. See Locke, "Fundamental Constitutions of Carolina," p. 196. For one analysis of Locke's "racial politics," see Farr, " 'So Vile and Miserable an Estate,' " pp. 263–89. On the tensions between Thomas Jefferson's words and actions, see O'Brien, "Thomas Jefferson," pp. 53–74. Jefferson's legacy is further complicated by his apparent personal involvement with his slave Sally Hemings despite his public condemnation of miscegenation.

16. See Angela Y. Davis, *Women, Race and Class,* pp. 71–72.

17. For an intriguing contemporary consideration of the ways in which racial and ethnic considerations can affect the creation of policies targeting violence against women, see Crenshaw, "Mapping the Margins," pp. 1241–99.

18. In a somewhat similar fashion, although with different implications, modern campaigns for gay and lesbian liberation have (correctly) compared homophobic impulses with racist sentiment and on that basis have questioned the legitimacy of the exclusion of uncloseted lesbians and gays from the military. The gay rights movement, certainly

post-Stonewall, has drawn many of its strategies and rituals from the civil rights movement. Black-inspired music and icons have also provided the soundtrack and look, respectively, for some of the more publicized aspects of gay nightlife (e.g., disco and black female singers, or "divas"). Consequently, the near-riot that took place on June 12, 1979, at a Chicago White Sox game involving the smashing of disco records—admission was ninety-eight cents if one brought a disco record to be destroyed—has to be understood as both a homophobic and racist "celebration." At the same time, despite its brief history, the mainstream gay rights movement does have a reputation for marginalizing the concerns of people of color, as some subcultures are known for promoting exotic and fundamentally stereotypical images of black men and women. See Boykin, *One More River to Cross*, pp. 212–35.

19. Ignatiev, *How the Irish Became White*, p. 2.

20. Regarding Gompers's own status as an immigrant and his nativism, Nick Salvatore makes the following interesting argument: "Gompers's repeated insistence that he is not an immigrant and his frequent, almost bizarre, pointing of his finger at 'them,' the foreign-born, as he asserts his native roots would, if taken literally, seem ridiculous. But Gompers is not denying the very immigrant background that, in another context, he proudly proclaims. Rather, his denial is a more complicated statement whose ultimate audience is the native-born worker and especially the native-born executive and politician. In distancing himself and those he represents from the new immigrants, Gompers both praises the success of an earlier process of Americanization and offers his services as a member of the indigenous culture in this new context." See Salvatore's introduction to *Seventy Years of Life and Labor*, by Gompers, pp. xxxiii–xxxiv.

21. Katznelson, *City Trenches*, p. 19.

22. Ibid., p. 194.

23. Vose, *Caucasians Only*, p. 125.

24. *New York Times*, December 23, 1997, p. 23.

25. Indeed the FHA's underwriting manuals encouraged private developers to institute racially exclusive housing arrangements so as to enhance market values, create neighborhood stability, and protect the "character" of the community. See Vose, *Caucasians Only*, pp. 125–27, 225–27, and Sugrue, *Origins of the Urban Crisis*, p. 182.

26. Desmond King, *Separate and Unequal*, p. 202.

27. See *Plessy v. Ferguson* 163 U.S. 537; 41 L. Ed. 256; 16 S. Ct. 1138 (1896).

28. This sentiment provides the foundation for much of the work of the essayist Shelby Steele. See *Content of Our Character*. Similarly, the comedian Chris Rock has suggested that "there's like, a civil war going on with black people, and there's two sides: there's black people . . . and there's niggas. And niggas have got to go! Every time black people want to have a good time, ign'ant-ass niggas [expletive] it up! . . . I *love* black people, but I *hate* niggas, brother. Oh, I hate niggas! Boy, I wish they'd let me join the Ku Klux Klan!" (quoted in David Kamp, "The Color of Truth," *Vanity Fair*, August 1998, p. 167).

29. For a discussion of the relevant issues, see Lawrence Wright, "One Drop of Blood," *The New Yorker*, July 25, 1994, and Njeri, *Last Plantation*.

30. As regards environmental policy, the United States, it is generally agreed, has been more aggressive in terms of passing legislation. Yet actual enforcement has often been lacking, and the environmental problems facing Americans are significantly greater than those facing other Western industrialized nations on a per capita basis. The relatively developed legal apparatus that exists to deal with environmental concerns (and, to some degree, gender issues) can be partly understood as the result of the absence of a strong conventional left, the force that has resisted environmental and gender advancements in other industri-

alized societies (e.g., the labor/socialist/Green dynamics evident in Swedish politics over the last twenty-five years). The resistance of labor to some environmental campaigns derives from the threat to labor's short-term interests (i.e., protecting existing jobs) by the call for industry to make the long-term state of the environment a higher priority. See Vogel, *National Styles of Regulation;* Brickman, Jasanoff, and Ilgen, "The Comparison of National Policies," in *Controlling Chemicals;* and George Hoberg, "Comparing Canadian Performance in Environmental Policy," in *Canadian Environmental Policy,* ed. Boardman.

31. In a similar manner, Scottish nationalism and Irish nationalism presently constitute a threat to the long-term viability of Great Britain. Regarding Canada's future, the combination of economic conservatism, linguistic antagonisms, nativist sentiments, and a frustration with the federalist status quo have given rise to the Reform Party (based primarily in the Canadian West), a movement that may also signal a significant reorientation of Canadian politics. A similar set of concerns led to the election of the Progressive Conservatives in the province of Ontario in 1995 on a platform (welfare cuts, tax cuts, antiemployment equity) that drew more inspiration from the American Republican Party than it did from any previous incarnation of the Progressive Conservatives in Canada.

BIBLIOGRAPHY

Abella, Irving, and David Millar, eds. *The Canadian Worker in the Twentieth Century.* Toronto: Oxford University Press, 1978.

Abrams, Douglas Carl. *Conservative Constraints: North Carolina and the New Deal.* Jackson: University of Mississippi Press, 1992.

Adorno, Theodor W. *Prisms.* London: Spearman, 1967.

Alba, Richard D. *Ethnic Identity: The Transformation of White America.* New Haven: Yale University Press, 1990.

Allsop, Judith. *Health Policy and the NHS: Towards 2000.* 2d ed. London: Longman, 1995.

American Business Consultants. *Red Channels: The Report of Communist Influence in Radio and Television.* New York: American Business Consultants, 1950.

American Federation of Labor. *Report of Proceedings.* 1894–1955. Washington, D.C.: American Federation of Labor. Microfilm.

Anbinder, Tyler Gregory. *Nativism and Slavery: The Northern Know-Nothings and the Politics of the 1850s.* New York: Oxford University Press, 1992.

Anderson, Benedict. *Imagined Communities: Reflections on the Origin and Spread of Nationalism.* London: Verso, 1983.

Anderson, Eric, and Alfred A. Moss Jr., eds. *The Facts of Reconstruction: Essays in Honor of John Hope Franklin.* Baton Rouge: Louisiana State University Press, 1991.

Anderson, Jervis. *A. Philip Randolph: A Biographical Portrait.* New York: Harcourt Brace Jovanovich, 1986.

Andersen, Kristi. *The Creation of a Democratic Majority, 1928–1936.* Chicago: University of Chicago Press, 1979.

Argersinger, Peter H. *Populism and Politics: William Alfred Peffer and the People's Party.* Lexington: University Press of Kentucky, 1974.

Aronowitz, Stanley. *False Promises: The Shaping of American Working Class Consciousness.* New York: McGraw-Hill, 1973.

———. *From the Ashes of the Old: American Labor and America's Future.* Boston: Houghton Mifflin, 1998.

———. *Roll over Beethoven: The Return of Cultural Strife.* Middletown: Wesleyan University Press, 1993.

Avakumovic, Ivan. *Socialism in Canada: A Study of the CCF-NDP in Federal and Provincial Politics.* Toronto: McClelland and Stewart, 1978.

Baggott, Rob. *Health and Health Care in Britain.* 2d ed. London: Macmillan, 1998.

Baker, Houston A., Jr. *Blues, Ideology, and Afro-American Literature: A Vernacular Theory.* Chicago: University of Chicago Press, 1984.

———. *Modernism and the Harlem Renaissance.* Chicago: University of Chicago Press, 1987.

Baraka, Imamu Amiri (formerly Leroi Jones). *The Autobiography of Leroi Jones.* Chicago: Lawrence Hill, 1997.

Barker, Lucius J., and Ronald Walters, eds. *Jesse Jackson's 1984 Presidential Campaign: Challenge and Change in American Politics.* Urbana: University of Illinois Press, 1989.

Barr, Nicholas. *The Economics of the Welfare State.* 3d ed. New York: Oxford University Press, 1998.

Barth, Gunther. *Bitter Struggle: A History of the Chinese in the United States, 1850–1870.* Cambridge: Harvard University Press, 1964.

Baum, Dale. *The Civil War Party System: The Case of Massachusetts, 1848–1876.* Chapel Hill: University of North Carolina Press, 1984.

Bell, Bernard W., Emily Grosholz, and James B. Stewart, eds. *W. E. B. Du Bois: On Race and Culture.* New York: Routledge, 1996.

Bell, Daniel. "Reflections on the Negro and Labor." *New Leader,* January 21, 1963, 18–20.

Benjamin, Walter. *Illuminations.* Edited by Hannah Arendt, translated by Harry Zohn. New York: Schocken, 1969.

Bensel, Richard Franklin. *Sectionalism and American Political Development, 1880–1980.* Madison: University of Wisconsin Press, 1984.

Berelson, Bernard, Paul Lazarsfeld, and William McPhee. *Voting: A Study of Opinion Formation in a Presidential Campaign.* Chicago: University of Chicago Press, 1954.

Berghe, Pierre van den. *Race and Racism: A Comparative Perspective.* New York: Wiley, 1967.

Berki, S. E., ed. *Health Care Policy in America.* Beverly Hills: Sage, 1983.

Berlin, Isaiah. *Four Essays on Liberty.* New York: Oxford University Press, 1970.

Bernstein, Iver. *The New York City Draft Riots.* New York: Oxford University Press, 1990.

Best, Geoffrey, ed. *The Permanent Revolution: The French Revolution and Its Legacy, 1789–1989.* Chicago: University of Chicago Press, 1988.

Biles, Roger. *The South and the New Deal.* Lexington: University Press of Kentucky, 1994.

Black, Earl. *Southern Governors and Civil Rights: Racial Segregation as a Campaign Issue in the Second Reconstruction.* Cambridge: Harvard University Press, 1976.

———. *The Vital South: How Presidents Are Elected.* New York: Columbia University Press, 1992.

Blakely, Edward J., and Mary Gail Snyder. *Fortress America: Gated Communities in the United States.* Washington, D.C.: Brookings Institution Press/Lincoln Institute of Land Policy, 1997.

Blaskey, George T. *Hard Times and the New Deal in Kentucky, 1929–1939.* Lexington: University Press of Kentucky, 1986.

Blendon, Robert J., and Jennifer Edwards. "Caring for the Uninsured: Choices for Reform." *Journal of the American Medical Association* 265, no. 19 (May 15, 1991): 2563–65.

Boardman, Robert, ed. *Canadian Environmental Policy: Ecosystems, Politics, and Process.* Toronto: Oxford University Press, 1992.

Bogle, Donald. *Toms, Coons, Mulattoes, Mammies, and Bucks: An Interpretive History of Blacks in American Films.* New York: Continuum, 1989.

Bok, Derek. *The State of the Nation: Government and the Quest for a Better Society.* Cambridge: Harvard University Press, 1996.

Book of Vital World Statistics, The. New York: Economist Books, 1990.

Boykin, Keith. *One More River to Cross: Black and Gay in America.* New York: Anchor, 1996.

Bracey, John, August Meier, and Elliot Rudwick, eds. *Black Nationalism in America.* New York: Bobb-Merrill, 1970.

Brickman, Ronald, Sheila Jasanoff, and Thomas Ilgen. *Controlling Chemicals: The Politics of Regulation in Europe and the United States*. Ithaca: Cornell University Press, 1985.

Brinkley, Alan. *Liberalism and Its Discontents*. Cambridge: Harvard University Press, 1998.

Brody, David. "Barriers of Individualism." *Dissent,* Winter 1989, pp. 71–77.

Brotherhood of Railway Clerks of America. *Constitution and By-Laws*. 1900, 1905, 1906, 1910, and 1947. Cincinnati: Brotherhood of Railway Clerks of America. Microfilm.

Brown, Michael E., Randy Martin, Frank Rosengarten, and George Snedeker, eds. *New Studies in the Politics and Culture of U.S. Communism*. New York: Monthly Review Press, 1993.

Brown, Peter. *Minority Party: Why Democrats Face Defeat in 1992 and Beyond*. Washington, D.C.: Regnery Gateway, 1991.

Brown, Wendy. *States of Injury: Power and Freedom in Late Modernity*. Princeton: Princeton University Press, 1995.

Browning, Rufus P., Dale Rogers Marshall, and David H. Tabb, eds. *Racial Politics in American Cities*. 2d ed. New York: Longman Publishers, 1997.

Buffon, Georges Louis Leclerc. *Oeuvres Complètes de Buffon*. Brussels: Lejeune, 1828.

Bullard, Robert. *Confronting Environmental Racism: Voices from the Grassroots*. Boston: South End, 1993.

Burleigh, Michael, and Wolfgang Wippermann. *The Racial State: Germany, 1933–1945*. Cambridge: Cambridge University Press, 1991.

Burnham, Walter Dean. *Critical Elections and the Mainsprings of American Politics*. New York: W. W. Norton, 1970.

———. *The Current Crisis in American Politics*. New York: Oxford University Press, 1982.

———. "The System of 1896: An Analysis." In *The Evolution of American Electoral Systems,* edited by Paul Kleppner et al., pp. 147–202. Westport: Greenwood, 1981.

Burt, Sandra. "Women's Issues and the Women's Movement in Canada since 1970." In *The Politics of Gender, Ethnicity, and Language in Canada,* edited by Alan Cairns and Cynthia Williams, pp. 111–69. Toronto: University of Toronto Press, 1986.

Cameron, David. "The Expansion of the Political Economy: A Comparative Analysis." *American Political Science Review* 72 (December 1978): 1243–61.

Campbell, Colin, and William Christian. *Political Parties and Ideologies in Canada: Liberals, Conservatives, Socialists, Nationalists*. Toronto: McGraw-Hill Ryerson, 1990.

Cantor, Milton. *The Divided Left: American Radicalism, 1900–1975*. New York: Hill and Wang, 1978.

———, ed. *American Workingclass Culture: Explorations in American Labor and Social History*. Westport: Greenwood, 1979.

———, ed. *Black Labor in America*. Westport: Negro Universities Press, 1969.

Capeci, Dominic J., Jr. *Race Relations in Wartime Detroit: The Sojourner Truth Housing Controversy*. Philadelphia: Temple University Press, 1984.

Caraway, Nancie. *Segregated Sisterhood: Racism and the Politics of American Feminism*. Knoxville: University of Tennessee Press, 1991.

Carby, Hazel. *Race Men*. Cambridge: Harvard University Press, 1998.

Cardoso, Fernando Henrique. *Dependency and Development in Latin America*. Berkeley: University of California Press, 1979.

Carens, Joseph H., ed. *Is Quebec Nationalism Just?: Perspectives from Anglophone Canada*. Montreal: McGill-Queen's University Press, 1995.

Carnoy, Martin. *Faded Dreams: The Politics and Economics of Race in America*. New York: Cambridge University Press, 1994.

Carter, Dan. *The Politics of Rage: George Wallace, the Origins of the New Conservatism, and the Transformation of American Politics.* New York: Simon and Schuster, 1996.

Carter, Stephen L. *Reflections of an Affirmative Action Baby.* New York: Basic, 1991.

Chada, Joseph. *The Czechs in the United States.* Chicago: SVU Press, 1981.

Chambers, William Nisbet, and Walter Dean Burnham. *The American Party Systems: Stages of Political Development.* New York: Oxford University Press, 1975.

Chapman, Audrey, ed. *Health Care Reform: A Human Rights Approach.* Washington, D.C.: Georgetown University Press, 1994.

Chen, Jack. *The Chinese of America.* San Francisco: Harper and Row, 1980.

Cheng, Lucie, and Edna Bonacich, eds. *Labor Immigration under Capitalism.* Berkeley: University of California Press, 1984.

Clarke, John Henrik, ed. *Marcus Garvey and the Vision of Africa.* New York: Vintage, 1974.

Cleage, Pearl. *Deals with the Devil and Other Reasons to Riot.* New York: Ballantine, 1993.

Cohen, Lizabeth. *Making a New Deal: Industrial Workers in Chicago, 1919–1939.* New York: Cambridge University Press, 1990.

Collier, Ken. *After the Welfare State.* Vancouver: New Star Books, 1997.

Commons, John R., David J. Saposs, Helen L. Sumner, E. B. Mittelman, H. E. Hoagland, John B. Andrews, and Selig Perlman. *History of Labor in the United States.* Vols. 1–2. New York: Augustus M. Kelley, 1966.

Cooper, Wayne F. *Claude McKay: Rebel Sojourner in the Harlem Renaissance.* New York: Schocken Books, 1987.

Copland, Aaron, and Vivian Perlis. *Copland: 1900 through 1942.* New York: St. Martin's/Marek, 1984.

———. *Copland: Since 1943.* New York: St. Martin's, 1989.

Cornell, Stephen. *The Return of the Native: American Indian Political Resurgence.* New York: Oxford University Press, 1988.

Cox, Archibald. *The Court and the Constitution.* Boston: Houghton Mifflin, 1987.

Crenshaw, Kimberle. "Mapping the Margins: Intersectionality, Identity Politics, and Violence against Women of Color." *Stanford Law Review* 43 (July 1991): 1241–99.

Cronon, Edmund David. *Black Moses: The Story of Marcus Garvey and the Universal Negro Improvement Association.* Madison: University of Wisconsin Press, 1955.

Cross, Ira B. *A History of the Labor Movement in California.* Berkeley: University of California Press, 1935.

Cruse, Harold. *The Crisis of the Negro Intellectual: From Its Origins to the Present.* New York: William Morrow, 1967.

———. *Plural but Equal: A Critical Study of Blacks and Minorities and America's Plural Society.* New York: Quill/William Morrow, 1987.

———. *Rebellion or Revolution?* New York: William Morrow, 1968.

Cullen, Jim. *Born in the U.S.A.: Bruce Springsteen and the American Tradition.* New York: HarperCollins, 1997.

Curtis, Susan. *A Consuming Faith: The Social Gospel and Modern American Culture.* Baltimore: Johns Hopkins University Press, 1991.

Daniel, Clete. *Chicano Workers and the Politics of Fairness: The FEPC in the Southwest, 1941–1945.* Austin: University of Texas Press, 1991.

Danziger, Sheldon H., and Daniel H. Weinberg, eds. *Fighting Poverty: What Works and What Doesn't.* Cambridge: Harvard University Press, 1986.

Davidson, Chandler. *Race and Class in Texas Politics.* Princeton: Princeton University Press, 1990.

————, ed. *The Quiet Revolution in the South*. Princeton: Princeton University Press, 1994.

Davies, Gareth, and Martha Derthick. "Race and Social Welfare Policy: The Social Security Act of 1935." *Political Science Quarterly* 112, no. 2 (1997): 217–35.

Davies, James C. "Toward a Theory of Revolution." *American Sociological Review* 27 (February 1962): 5–19.

Davis, Angela Y. *An Autobiography*. New York: Random House, 1974.

————. *Blues Legacies and Black Feminism*. New York: Vintage, 1998.

————. *Women, Race, and Class*. New York: Vintage, 1983.

Davis, Benjamin J. *Communist Councilman from Harlem: Autobiographical Notes Written in a Federal Penetentiary*. New York: International Publishers, 1969.

Davis, F. James. *Who Is Black? One Nation's Definition*. University Park: Pennsylvania State University Press, 1991.

Davis, Miles, and Quincy Troupe. *Miles: The Autobiography*. New York: Simon and Schuster, 1990.

Davis, Ossie, and Ruby Dee. *With Ossie and Ruby: In This Life Together*. New York: William Morrow, 1998.

Dawson, Michael. *Behind the Mule: Race and Class in African-American Politics*. Princeton: Princeton University Press, 1994.

Denning, Michael. *The Cultural Front: The Laboring of American Culture in the Twentieth Century*. New York: Verso, 1997.

Denselow, Robin. *When the Music's Over: The Story of Political Pop*. London: Faber and Faber, 1989.

Desan, Phillippe, ed. *Humanism in Crisis: The Decline of the French Renaissance*. Ann Arbor: University of Michigan Press, 1991.

DeVeaux, Scott. *The Birth of Bebop: A Social and Musical History*. Berkeley: University of California Press, 1997.

"Dialogue on Race with President Clinton, A." Special edition of *The NewsHour*, moderated by Jim Lehrer, July 9, 1998. Transcript online at <http://www.pbs.org>.

Diggins, John. *The American Left in the Twentieth Century*. New York: Harcourt Brace Jovanovich, 1973.

————. "The Misuses of Gramsci." *Journal of American History* 75, no. 1 (1988): 141–45.

Dionne, E. J. *Why Americans Hate Politics*. New York: Simon and Schuster, 1991.

Diop, Cheikh Anta. *The African Origin of Civilization, Myth or Reality*. New York: Lawrence Hill, 1974.

Dobbert, Guido. *The Disintegration of an Immigrant Community: The Cincinnati Germans, 1870–1920*. New York: Arno, 1980.

Donald, David. *Charles Sumner and the Rights of Man*. New York: Alfred A. Knopf, 1970.

Douglas, Clifford Hugh. *Credit-Power and Democracy*. London: Cecil Palmer, 1920.

Draper, Theodore. *The Roots of American Communism*. New York: Viking, 1957.

Drinnon, Richard. *Facing West: The Metaphysics of Indian Hating and Empire Building*. Minneapolis: University of Minnesota Press, 1985.

Duberman, Martin. *Paul Robeson*. New York: Knopf, 1988.

Dubofsky, Melvin. *The State and Labor in Modern America*. Chapel Hill: University of North Carolina Press, 1994.

————. *We Shall Be All: A History of the Industrial Workers of the World*. Chicago: Quadrangle, 1969.

Du Bois, W. E. B. *The Autobiography of W. E. B. Du Bois*. New York: International Publishers, 1968.

———. *Black Reconstruction in America.* Cleveland: Old Meridian, 1935.

———. *Dusk of Dawn: An Essay toward an Autobiography of a Race Concept.* New York: Harcourt, Brace and Company, 1936.

———. *The Selected Writings of W. E. B. Du Bois.* Edited by Walter Wilson. New York: New American Library, 1970.

———. *The Souls of Black Folk.* New York: New American Library, 1969.

———. *Writings in Periodical Literature, 1891–1909.* Millwood: Kraus-Thomson Organization, 1982.

———. *Writings in Periodical Literature, 1910–1934.* Millwood: Kraus-Thomson Organization, 1982.

Dulles, Foster Rhea, and Melvin Dubofsky. *Labor in America.* Arlington Heights: Harlan Davidson, 1984.

Dumas, Evelyn. *The Bitter Thirties in Quebec.* Montreal: Black Rose, 1975.

Durden, Robert F. *The Climax of Populism: The Election of 1896.* Lexington: University Press of Kentucky, 1966.

Durkheim, Émile. *De la Division du Travail Social.* Paris: Presses Universitaires de France, 1960.

Eden, Robert, ed. *The New Deal and Its Legacy: Critique and Reappraisal.* Westport: Greenwood, 1989.

Edsall, Thomas. "Race." *Atlantic Monthly,* May 1991, pp. 53–86.

Edsall, Thomas, and Mary Edsall. *Chain Reaction: The Impact of Race, Rights, and Taxes in American Politics.* New York: Norton, 1991.

Edwards, Richard, Paulo Garonna, and Franz Todtling, eds. *Unions in Crisis and Beyond: Perspectives from Six Countries.* Dover: Auburn House Publishing, 1986.

Egerton, John. *Speak Now against the Day: The Generation before the Civil Rights Movement in the South.* Chapel Hill: University of North Carolina Press, 1994.

Elections since 1945: A Worldwide Reference Compendium. Chicago: St. James, 1989.

Ellison, Ralph. *The Invisible Man.* New York: Random House, 1952.

———. *Shadow and Act.* New York: Vintage, 1964.

Ely, Melvin Patrick. *The Adventures of Amos 'n' Andy: A Social History of an American Phenomenon.* New York: Free Press, 1991.

Emerson, Ken. *Doo-Dah! Stephen Foster and the Rise of American Popular Culture.* New York: Simon and Schuster, 1997.

Ergang, Robert. *Herder and the Foundations of German Nationalism.* New York: Columbia University Press, 1931.

Esping-Andersen, Gøsta. *The Three Worlds of Welfare Capitalism.* Cambridge: Polity, 1990.

Espiritu, Yen Le. *Asian American Panethnicity.* Philadelphia: Temple University Press, 1992.

Evans, Sara. *Personal Politics: The Roots of Women's Liberation in the Civil Rights Movement and the New Left.* New York: Knopf, 1979.

Farias, Victor. *Heidegger and Nazism.* Philadephia: Temple University Press, 1989.

Farr, James. " 'So Vile and Miserable an Estate': The Problem of Slavery in Locke's Political Thought." *Political Theory* 14 (May 1986): 263–89.

Fast, Howard. *Being Red.* New York: Houghton Mifflin, 1990.

Feigert, Frank. *Canada Votes.* Durham: Duke University Press, 1989.

Ferry, Luc, and Alain Renault. *Heidegger and Modernity.* Chicago: University of Chicago Press, 1990.

Fields, Barbara Jeanne. *Slavery and Freedom on the Middle Ground: Maryland during the Nineteenth Century.* New Haven: Yale University Press, 1985.

———. "Slavery, Race, and Ideology in the United States of America." *New Left Review* 181 (May/June 1990): 95–118.

Finlay, John. *Social Credit: The English Origins.* Montreal: McGill-Queens University Press, 1972.

Fitzmaurice, John. *Québec and Canada: Past, Present, and Future.* New York: St. Martin's, 1985.

Foner, Eric. *Slavery and Freedom in Nineteenth-Century America.* Oxford: Clarendon, 1994.

———. "Why Is There No Socialism in the United States?" *History Workshop* 17 (Spring 1984): 57–80.

Foner, Philip S. *American Socialism and Black Americans.* Westport: Greenwood, 1977.

———. *Organized Labor and the Black Worker, 1619–1973.* New York: Praeger, 1974.

———, ed. *Paul Robeson Speaks: Writings, Speeches, Interviews, 1918–1974.* New York: Brunner/Mazel Publishers, 1978.

Foner, Philip S., and Daniel Rosenberg, eds. *Racism, Dissent, and Asian Americans from 1850 to the Present: A Documentary History.* Westport: Greenwood, 1993.

Foner, Philip S., and Ronald L. Lewis, eds. *The Black Worker during the Era of the Knights of Labor.* Philadelphia: Temple University Press, 1978.

Foner, Philip S., Ronald Lewis, and Robert Cvornyek, eds. *The Black Worker since the AFL-CIO Merger, 1955–1980.* Philadelphia: Temple University Press, 1984.

Francis, R. Douglas, and Donald B. Smith, eds. *Readings in Canadian History: Post-Confederation.* 2d ed. Toronto: Holt, Rinehart, and Winston, 1986.

Fraser, Steve, and Gary Gerstle, eds. *The Rise and Fall of the New Deal Order, 1930–1980.* Princeton: Princeton University Press, 1989.

Frazier, E. Franklin. *Black Bourgeoisie.* Glencoe: Free Press, 1957.

———. *The Negro Family in the United States.* Chicago: University of Chicago Press, 1939.

Fredrickson, George M. "America's Diversity in Comparative Perspective." *Journal of American History* 85, no. 3 (December 1998): 859–75.

———. *The Black Image in the White Mind: The Debate on Afro-American Character and Destiny.* New York: Harper and Row, 1971.

———. "From Exceptionalism to Variability: Recent Developments in Cross-National Comparative History." *Journal of American History* 82, no. 2 (September 1995): 587–604.

———. *White Supremacy: A Comparative Study in American and South African History.* New York: Oxford University Press, 1981.

Freedman, Samuel G. *The Inheritance: How Three Families and America Moved from Roosevelt to Reagan and Beyond.* New York: Simon and Schuster, 1996.

Frisch, Michael, and Daniel Walkowitz, eds. *Working-Class America: Essays on Labor, Community, and American Society.* Urbana: University of Illinois Press, 1982.

Frith, Simon. *Sound Effects: Youth, Leisure, and the Politics of Rock 'n' Roll.* New York: Pantheon, 1981.

Galambos, Louis. *The Public Image of Big Business, 1880–1940.* Baltimore: Johns Hopkins University Press, 1975.

———. *The Rise of the Corporate Commonwealth: U.S. Business and Public Policy in the Twentieth Century.* New York: Basic, 1988.

Galbraith, John Kenneth. *The Affluent Society.* Boston: Houghton Mifflin, 1969.

————. *The Culture of Contentment.* Boston: Houghton Mifflin, 1992.

————. *The Good Society: The Humane Agenda.* Boston: Houghton Mifflin, 1996.

Galenson, Walter. *The American Labor Movement, 1955–1995.* Westport: Greenwood, 1996.

————. *The CIO Challenge to the AFL.* Cambridge: Harvard University Press, 1960.

————. *Comparative Labor Movements.* New York: Prentice-Hall, 1952.

Gallup, George. *The Gallup Opinion Poll: Public Opinion, 1935–1971.* Vol. 1. New York: Random House, 1972.

Gans, Herbert J. *The Levittowners: Ways of Life and Politics in a New Suburban Community.* New York: Pantheon, 1967.

Garvey, Marcus. *Philosophy and Opinions of Marcus Garvey.* Edited by Amy Garvey. London: Frank Cass, 1967.

Gates, Henry Louis, Jr. *Colored People.* New York: Vintage, 1994.

Geertz, Clifford. *The Interpretation of Cultures: Selected Essays.* New York: Basic, 1973.

Geoghegan, Thomas. *Which Side Are You On? Trying to Be for Labor When It's Flat on Its Back.* New York: Farrar, Straus, and Giroux, 1991.

George, Nelson. *Buppies, B-boys, Baps, and Bohos: Notes on Post-Soul Black Culture.* New York: HarperCollins, 1992.

————. *The Death of Rhythm and Blues.* New York: Pantheon, 1988.

————. *Where Did Our Love Go? The Rise and Fall of the Motown Sound.* New York: St. Martin's, 1985.

Gerstle, Gary. "Race and the Myth of the Liberal Consensus." *Journal of American History* 82, no. 2 (September 1995): 579–86.

Giddings, Paula. *When and Where I Enter: The Impact of Black Women on Race and Sex in America.* New York: Bantam, 1985.

Gilens, Martin. " 'Race Coding' and White Opposition to Welfare." *American Political Science Review* 90, no. 3 (September 1996): 593–604.

Gillespie, Dizzy, with Al Fraser. *To Be, or Not . . . to Bop: Memoirs.* Garden City: Doubleday, 1979.

Gioia, Ted. *The History of Jazz.* New York: Oxford University Press, 1997.

Glazer, Nathan, and Daniel Patrick Moynihan. *Beyond the Melting Pot: The Negroes, Puerto Ricans, Jews, Italians, and Irish of New York City.* Cambridge: MIT Press, 1963.

Glied, Sherry. *Chronic Condition: Why Health Care Reform Fails.* Cambridge: Harvard University Press, 1997.

Goldfield, Michael. *The Color of Politics: Race and the Mainsprings of American Politics.* New York: New Press, 1997.

Goldman, Albert. *Elvis.* New York: Avon, 1981.

Gomez, Michael A. *Exchanging Our Country Marks: The Transformation of African Identities in the Colonial and Antebellum South.* Chapel Hill: University of North Carolina Press, 1998.

Gómez-Quiñones, Juan. *Mexican American Labor, 1790–1990.* Albuquerque: University of New Mexico Press, 1994.

Gompers, Samuel. *Labor and the Common Welfare.* New York: E. P. Dutton, 1919.

————. *Seventy Years of Life and Labor: An Autobiography.* Edited by Nick Salvatore. Ithaca: ILR Press, 1984.

————. *Should a Political Labor Party Be Formed?* Washington, D.C.: Executive Council of the American Federation of Labor, 1918.

Goodwyn, Lawrence. *The Populist Moment: A Short History of the Agrarian Revolt in America.* New York: Oxford University Press, 1978.

Gordon, David, Michael Reich, and Richard Edwards, eds. *Labor Market Segmentation.* Lexington: D. C. Heath, 1975.

————, eds. *Segmented Work, Divided Workers: The Historical Transformation of Labor in the United States.* New York: Cambridge University Press, 1982.

Gordon, Robert. *It Came from Memphis.* Boston: Faber and Faber, 1995.

Government Finance Statistics Yearbook, 1991. Washington, D.C.: International Monetary Fund, 1991.

Gozzi, Raymond, Jr. *New Words and a Changing American Culture.* Columbia: University of South Carolina Press, 1990.

Gramsci, Antonio. *Letters from Prison.* New York: Harper and Row, 1973.

Grantham, Dewey W. *The South in Modern America: A Region at Odds.* New York: HarperCollins, 1994.

Greenberg, Cheryl Lynn. *"Or Does It Explode?": Black Harlem in the Great Depression.* New York: Oxford University Press, 1991.

Greenberg, Stanley. *Middle Class Dreams: The Politics and Power of the New American Majority.* New York: Times Books, 1995.

Greenberg, Stanley, and Theda Skocpol, eds. *The New Majority: Toward a Popular Progressive Politics.* New Haven: Yale University Press, 1997.

Greene, Jack P. *Pursuits of Happiness: The Social Development of Early Modern British Colonies and the Formation of American Culture.* Chapel Hill: University of North Carolina Press, 1988.

Gregor, A. James. *Young Mussolini and the Intellectual Origins of Fascism.* Berkeley: University of California Press, 1979.

Grubbs, Frank L, Jr. *The Struggle for Labor Loyalty: Gompers, the A.F. of L., and the Pacifists, 1917–1920.* Durham: Duke University Press, 1968.

Guinier, Lani. *The Tyranny of the Majority: Fundamental Fairness in Representative Democracy.* New York: Free Press, 1994.

Guralnick, Peter. *Last Train to Memphis: The Rise of Elvis Presley.* Boston: Little, Brown, 1994.

————. *Sweet Soul Music: Rhythm and Blues and the Southern Dream of Freedom.* New York: HarperPerennial, 1986.

Gurr, Ted. *Why Men Rebel.* Princeton: Princeton University Press, 1970.

————, ed. *Violence in America.* Vol. 2. London: Sage, 1989.

Gyory, Andrew. *Closing the Gate: Race, Politics and the Chinese Exclusion Act.* Chapel Hill: University of North Carolina Press, 1998.

Haar, Charles M. *Suburbs under Seige: Race, Space, and Audacious Judges.* Princeton: Princeton University Press, 1996.

Haliburton, Warren J., ed. *Historic Speeches of African Americans.* New York: Franklin Watts, 1993.

Hall, Stuart. *The Hard Road to Renewal: Thatcherism and the Crisis of the Left.* London: Verso, 1988.

Hamilton, Charles V. *Adam Clayton Powell, Jr.: The Political Biography of an American Dilemma.* New York: Collier Books, 1991.

Hamilton, Richard F. *Class and Politics in the United States.* New York: John Wiley and Sons, 1972.

Hanafin, Patrick J., and Melissa S. Williams, eds. *Identity, Rights, and Constitutional Transformation.* Aldershot: Ashgate, 1999.

Hanagan, Michael. "Response to Sean Wilentz." *International Labor and Working Class History* 26 (Fall 1984): 31–36.

Handlin, Oscar. *Race and Nationality in America.* Boston: Little, Brown, 1948.

Hanson, Russell. *The Democratic Imagination in America: Conversations with Our Past.* Princeton: Princeton University Press, 1985.

Hartz, Louis. *The Founding of New Societies: Studies in the History of the United States, Latin America, South Africa, Canada, and Australia.* New York: Harcourt, Brace, and World, 1964.

―――. *The Liberal Tradition in America: An Interpretation of American Political Thought since the Revolution.* New York: Harcourt, Brace, and World, 1955.

Haygood, Wil. *King of the Cats: The Life and Times of Adam Clayton Powell, Jr.* Boston: Houghton Mifflin, 1993.

Headey, Bruce. *Housing Policy in the Developed Economy.* London: Croom Helm, 1978.

Heidenheimer, Arnold, Hugh Heclo, and Carolyn Teich Adams, eds. *Comparative Public Policy: The Politics of Social Choice in Europe and America.* New York: St. Martin's, 1975.

Henry, Charles P. *Culture and African-American Politics.* Bloomington: Indiana University Press, 1990.

Herder, Johann. *Outlines of a Philosophy of the History of Man.* Translated by Thomas Churchill. London: J. Johnson, 1803.

Hernton, Calvin C. *The Sexual Mountain and Black Women Writers: Adventures in Sex, Literature, and Real Life.* Garden City: Doubleday, 1987.

Hicks, John D. *The Populist Revolt: A History of the Farmers' Alliance and the People's Party.* Minneapolis: University of Minnesota Press, 1931.

Hill, Herbert. "The AFL-CIO and the Black Worker." *Journal of Intergroup Relations* 10 (Spring 1982).

―――. "Myth-Making as Labor History: Herbert Gutman and the United Mine Workers of America." *International Journal of Politics, Culture, and Society* 2 (Winter 1988): 132–200.

―――. *Racism within Organized Labor: A Report of Five Years of the AFL-CIO, 1955–1960.* New York: Labor Department, National Association for the Advancement of Colored People, 1961.

Hill, Robert A., and Barbara Bair, eds. *Marcus Garvey: Life and Lessons.* Berkeley: University of California Press, 1987.

Himes, Chester. *If He Hollers Let Him Go.* Garden City: Doubleday, Doran, 1946.

―――. *Lonely Crusade.* New York: Thunder's Mouth Press, 1997.

Hirsch, Arnold. *Making the Second Ghetto in Chicago, 1940–1960.* New York: Cambridge University Press, 1983.

Hirsch, Arthur. *The French Left.* Montreal: Black Rose, 1982.

Hirshey, Gerri. *Nowhere to Run: The Story of Soul Music.* New York: Viking, 1984.

Hitler, Adolf. *Mein Kampf.* Los Angeles: Angriff, 1981.

Hoberman, J. *The Red Atlantis: Communist Culture in the Absence of Communism.* Philadelphia: Temple University Press, 1998.

Hochschild, Jennifer. *The New American Dilemma: Liberal Democracy and School Desegregation.* New Haven: Yale University Press, 1984.

Hodges, James. *New Deal Labor Policy and the Southern Cotton Textile Industry, 1933–1941.* Knoxville: University of Tennessee Press, 1986.

Hoffmann, Stanley. *Gulliver's Troubles: Or the Setting of American Foreign Policy.* New York: McGraw-Hill, 1968.

Holiday, Billie, with William Dufty. *Lady Sings the Blues.* New York: Avon, 1956.

Holt, Hamilton, ed. *The Life Stories of Undistinguished Americans: As Told by Themselves.* New York: Routledge, 1990.

Horne, Gerald. *Black and Red: W. E. B. Du Bois and the Afro-American Response to the Cold War, 1944–1963.* Albany: State University of New York Press, 1986.

———. *Black Liberation/Red Scare: Ben Davis and the Communist Party.* Newark: University of Delaware Press, 1994.

———. *Communist Front? The Civil Rights Congress, 1946–1956.* Rutherford: Fairleigh Dickinson University Press, 1988.

Horowitz, Daniel. *Betty Friedan and the Making of "The Feminine Mystique": The American Left, the Cold War, and Modern Feminism.* Amherst: University of Massachusetts Press, 1998.

Hoston, Germaine A. *Marxism and the Crisis of Development in Prewar Japan.* Princeton: Princeton University Press, 1986.

———. *The State, Identity, and the National Question in China and Japan.* Princeton: Princeton University Press, 1994.

Howe, Irving. *Selected Writings, 1950–1990.* New York: Harcourt Brace Jovanovich, 1990.

———, ed. *Essential Works of Socialism.* New York: Holt, Rinehart, and Winston, 1970.

Howe, Irving, and Lewis Coser, eds. *The American Communist Party: A Critical History.* New York: DeCapo, 1974.

Huggins, Nathan. *Harlem Renaissance.* New York: Oxford University Press, 1971.

Hyde, Samuel, Jr. *Pistols and Politics: The Dilemmas of Democracy in Louisiana's Florida Parishes, 1810–1899.* Baton Rouge: Louisiana State University Press, 1996.

Ignatiev, Noel. *How the Irish Became White.* New York: Routledge, 1995.

International Labour Organization, *World Labour Report: Industrial Relations, Democracy, and Social Stability.* Geneva: International Labour Office, 1997.

Isaac, Jeffrey C. "Republicanism vs. Liberalism?: A Reconsideration." *History of Political Thought* 9, no. 2 (Summer 1988): 349–77.

Isserman, Maurice. "Three Generations: Historians View American Communism." *Labor History* 26, no. 4 (1985): 517–45.

Jacobsen, Julius, ed. *The Negro and the American Labor Movement.* Garden City: Anchor, 1968.

Jacoway, Elizabeth, Dan T. Carter, Lester C. Lamon, and Robert C. McMath Jr., eds. *The Adaptable South: Essays in Honor of George Brown Tindall.* Baton Rouge: Louisiana State University Press, 1991.

Janoski, Thomas, and Alexander M. Hicks, eds. *The Comparative Political Economy of the Welfare State.* New York: Cambridge University Press, 1994.

Jones, Jacqueline. *American Work: Four Centuries of Black and White Labor.* New York: W. W. Norton, 1998.

Jones, Leroi. *Blues People: The Negro Experience in White America and the Music That Developed from It.* New York: William Morrow, 1963.

Jordan, Winthrop. *White over Black: American Attitudes toward the Negro, 1550–1812.* Chapel Hill: University of North Carolina Press, 1968.

Karson, Marc. *American Labor Unions and Politics, 1900–1918.* Carbondale: Southern Illinois University Press, 1958.

Kater, Michael. *Different Drummers: Jazz in the Culture of Nazi Germany.* New York: Oxford University Press, 1992.

———. *The Twisted Muse: Musicians and Their Music in the Third Reich.* New York: Oxford University Press, 1997.

Katznelson, Ira. *Black Men, White Cities: Race, Politics, and Migration in the United States, 1900-30, and Britain, 1948-68.* Chicago: University of Chicago Press, 1976.

———. *City Trenches: Urban Politics and the Patterning of Class in the United States.* Chicago: University of Chicago Press, 1981.

Kaufmann, Walter, ed. *Existentialism from Dostoevsky to Sartre.* New York: Meridian, 1956.

Kazan, Elia. *A Life.* New York: Alfred A. Knopf, 1988.

Keil, Charles. *Urban Blues.* Chicago: University of Chicago Press, 1966.

Kelley, Robin D. G. *Hammer and Hoe: Alabama Communists during the Great Depression.* Chapel Hill: University of North Carolina Press, 1990.

———. *Race Rebels: Culture, Politics, and the Black Working Class.* New York: Free Press, 1994.

Kennett, Lee, and James L. Anderson. *The Gun in America: The Origins of a National Dilemma.* Westport: Greenwood, 1975.

Key, V. O., Jr. "A Theory of Critical Elections." *Journal of Politics* 17 (1955): 3-18.

———. *Southern Politics in State and Nation.* New York: Alfred A. Knopf, 1949.

Kimball, Penn. *The Disconnected.* New York: Columbia University Press, 1972.

King, Anthony. "Ideas, Institutions, and the Policies of Governments: A Comparative Analysis, Part III." *British Journal of Political Science* 3 (October 1973): 409-23.

King, Desmond S. "Political Centralization and State Interests in Britain." *Comparative Political Studies* 21, no. 4 (January 1989): 467-94.

———. *Separate and Unequal: Black Americans and the US Federal Government.* New York: Oxford University Press, 1995.

King, Martin Luther, Jr. *Where Do We Go from Here: Chaos or Community?* New York: Harper and Row, 1967.

———. *Why We Can't Wait.* New York: Harper and Row, 1963.

Kingston, Maxine Hong. *China Men.* New York: Vintage International, 1989.

Kingston, Paul. *Anti-Semitism in France during the 1930s.* Hull: University of Hull Press, 1983.

Kipnis, Ira. *The American Socialist Movement, 1897-1912.* New York: Columbia University Press, 1952.

Kirp, David L., John P. Dwyer, and Larry A. Rosenthal. *Our Town: Race, Housing, and the Soul of Suburbia.* New Brunswick: Rutgers University Press, 1995.

Kirwan, Albert D. *Revolt of the Rednecks: Mississippi Politics, 1876-1925.* Lexington: University Press of Kentucky, 1951.

Klehr, Harvey. *The Heyday of American Communism: The Depression Decade.* New York: Basic, 1984.

Klein, Rudolph. *The Politics of the NHS.* 2d ed. New York: Longman, 1995.

Kleppner, Paul, Walter Dean Burnham, Ronald P. Formisano, Samuel P. Hays, Richard Jensen, and William G. Shade, eds. *The Evolution of American Electoral Systems.* Westport: Greenwood, 1981.

Kloppenberg, James. "The Virtues of Liberalism: Christianity, Republicanism, and Ethics in Early American Discourse." *Journal of American History* 74, no. 1 (1987): 9-33.

Kolko, Gabriel. *The Triumph of Conservatism: A Re-interpretation of American History, 1900-1916.* Glencoe: Free Press, 1963.

Koppes, Clayton R., and Gregory D. Black. "Blacks, Loyalty, and the Motion-Picture Propaganda in World War II." *Journal of American History* 73, no. 2 (June 1986): 383-406.

Kraditor, Aileen. "American Radical Historians in Their Heritage." *Past and Present* 56 (August 1972): 136–53.

———, ed. *Up from the Pedestal: Selected Writings in the History of American Feminism.* Chicago: Quadrangle, 1968.

Kumar, Krishan. *The Rise of Modern Society: Aspects of the Social and Political Development of the West.* New York: Basil Blackwell, 1988.

Kung, Shien-Woo. *Chinese in American Life: Some Aspects of Their History, Status, Problems, and Contributions.* Seattle: University of Washington Press, 1962.

Kurien, George Thomas. *The New Book of World Rankings.* 3d ed. New York: Facts on File, 1991.

Kwong, Peter. *Forbidden Workers: Illegal Chinese Workers and American Labor.* New York: New Press, 1997.

Kymlicka, Will. *Finding Our Way: Rethinking Ethnocultural Relations in Canada.* Toronto: Oxford University Press, 1998.

———. *Multicultural Citizenship: A Liberal Theory of Minority Rights.* New York: Clarendon, 1995.

Kymlicka, Will, and Ian Shapiro, eds. *Ethnicity and Group Rights.* New York: New York University Press, 1997.

Lacqueur, Walter, ed. *Fascism: A Reader's Guide.* Berkeley: University of California Press, 1976.

Laslett, John H. M., and Seymour Martin Lipset, eds. *Failure of a Dream? Essays in the History of American Socialism.* New York: Anchor, 1974.

Lauren, Paul Gordon. *Power and Prejudice: The Politics and Diplomacy of Racial Discrimination.* Boulder: Westview, 1996.

Lee, Martin A., and Norman Solomon. *Unreliable Sources.* New York: Carol Publishing, 1990.

Leichter, Howard M. *A Comparative Approach to Policy Analysis: Health Care Policy in Four Nations.* Cambridge: Cambridge University Press, 1979.

Lenin, Vladimir I. *Imperialism.* London: M. Lawrence, 1933.

Letwin, Daniel. *The Challenge of Interracial Unionism: Alabama Coal Miners, 1878–1921.* Chapel Hill: University of North Carolina Press, 1998.

Leuchtenburg, William. *Franklin D. Roosevelt and the New Deal, 1932–1940.* New York: Harper and Row, 1963.

———. "The Old Cowhand from Dixie." *Atlantic Monthly,* December 1992, pp. 92–100.

Levine, Lawrence. *Black Culture and Black Consciousness: Afro-American Folk Thought from Slavery to Freedom.* New York: Oxford University Press, 1977.

———. *Highbrow/Lowbrow: The Emergence of Cultural Hierarchy in America.* Cambridge: Harvard University Press, 1988.

Levy, Jacques E. *Cesar Chavez: Autobiography of La Causa.* New York: W. W. Norton, 1975.

Lewis, David Levering. "The Promise and Peril of Class in the Problem of the Twentieth Century," *Good Society* 7, no. 3 (Fall 1997): 1–7.

———. *W. E. B. Du Bois: Biography of a Race, 1868–1919.* New York: Henry Holt, 1993.

———. *When Harlem Was in Vogue.* New York: Alfred A. Knopf, 1981.

———, ed. *The Portable Harlem Renaissance Reader.* New York: Penguin, 1994.

———. *W. E. B. Du Bois: A Reader.* New York: Henry Holt, 1995.

Lewis, Rupert, and Patrick Bryan, eds. *Garvey: His Work and Impact.* Kingston: Institute of Social and Economic Research and the Department of Extra-Mural Studies, University of the West Indies, 1988.

Lewy, Guenter. *The Cause That Failed: Communism in American Political Life.* New York: Oxford University Press, 1990.

Lincoln, C. Eric. *The Black Muslims in America.* 3d ed. Trenton, N.J.: Africa World Press, 1994.

——, ed. *Martin Luther King, Jr.: A Profile.* New York: Hill and Wang, 1968.

Linne, Carl von. *A General System of Nature.* London: Lackington, Allen, 1806.

Lipset, Seymour Martin. *Agrarian Socialism.* Berkeley: University of California Press, 1950.

——. *Continental Divide: The Values and Institutions of the United States and Canada.* Toronto: Canadian-American Committee, 1989.

——. *Political Man: The Social Bases of Politics.* Garden City: Doubleday and Company, 1963.

——, ed. *Unions in Transition: Entering the Second Century.* San Francisco: Institute for Contemporary Studies, 1986.

Livesay, Harold. *Samuel Gompers and Organized Labor in America.* Boston: Little, Brown, 1978.

Locke, John. "The Fundamental Constitutions of Carolina." In *The Works of John Locke,* 10:175–99. London: Thomas Tegg, 1823.

López, Antoinette Sedillo, ed. *Latino Employment, Labor Organizations, and Immigration.* New York: Garland Publishing, 1995.

Lorwin, Lewis. *The American Federation of Labor: History, Policies, and Prospects.* Washington, D.C.: Brookings Institution, 1933.

——. *Labor and Internationalism.* New York: Macmillan, 1929.

Lorwin, Val R. "Reflections on the History of the French and American Labor Movements." *Journal of Economic History* 17, no. 1 (1957): 25–44.

Lott, Eric. *Love and Theft: Blackface Minstrelsy and the American Working Class.* New York: Oxford University Press, 1993.

Lowi, Theodore. *The Personal President: Power Invested, Promise Unfulfilled.* Ithaca: Cornell University Press, 1985.

Lowith, Karl. *From Hegel to Nietzsche: The Revolution in Nineteenth-Century Thought.* Translated by David E. Green. New York: Columbia University Press, 1991.

Lubiano, Wahneema, ed. *The House That Race Built.* New York: Vintage, 1997.

Lundberg, George D. "American Health Care System Management Objectives: The Aura of Inevitability Becomes Incarnate." *Journal of the American Medical Association* 269, no. 19 (May 19, 1993): 2554–55.

——. "National Health Care Reform: An Aura of Inevitability Is upon Us." *Journal of the American Medical Association* 265, no. 19 (May 15, 1991): 2566–67.

Lustig, Jeffrey. *Corporate Liberalism: The Origins of Modern American Political Theory, 1890–1920.* Berkeley: University of California Press, 1982.

Luxemburg, Rosa. *Selected Writings.* Edited by Horace B. Davis. New York: Monthly Review, 1976.

Lynch, Matthew, and Stanley Raphael. *Medicine and the State.* Springfield: Charles C. Thomas, 1963.

McCormick, Joseph P., and Charles E. Jones. "Deracialization Revisited: Thinking through the Dilemma." In *Dilemmas of Black Politics: Leadership, Strategy, and Issues,* edited by Georgia Persons, pp. 66–84. New York: HarperCollins, 1993.

McCormick, Richard. *The Party Period and Public Policy: American Politics from the Age of Jackson to the Progressive Era.* New York: Oxford University Press, 1986.

————. "The Party Period and Public Policy: An Exploratory Hypothesis." *Journal of American History* 66 (September 1979): 279–98.

McCoy, Donald R., and Richard T. Ruetten. *Quest and Response: Minority Rights and the Truman Administration.* Lawrence: University Press of Kansas, 1973.

McGerr, Michael. *The Decline of Popular Politics: The American North, 1865–1928.* New York: Oxford University Press, 1986.

McHenry, Dean E. *The Third Force in Canada: The Co-operative Commonwealth Federation, 1932–1948.* Toronto: Oxford University Press, 1950.

McInniss, Grace. *J. W. Woodsworth: A Man to Remember.* Toronto: Macmillan, 1953.

McKay, Claude. *Harlem: Negro Metropolis.* New York: E. P. Dutton, 1940.

————. *Home to Harlem.* Boston: Northeastern University Press, 1987.

McKenna, Brian, and Susan Purcell. *Drapeau.* Markham: Penguin, 1980.

Mackie, Thomas, and Richard Rose. *The International Almanac of Electoral History.* 3d ed. Washington, D.C.: Congressional Quarterly, 1991.

MacLean, Nancy. *Behind the Mask of Chivalry: The Making of the Second Ku Klux Klan.* New York: Oxford University Press, 1994.

McMath, Robert C. *Populist Vanguard: A History of the Southern Farmers' Alliance.* Chapel Hill: University of North Carolina Press, 1975.

McNeill, George, ed. *The Labor Movement: The Problem of Today.* Boston: A. M. Bridgeman, 1886.

Mailer, Norman. *The White Negro.* San Francisco: City Lights, 1957.

Mandle, W. F. *Anti-Semitism and the British Union of Fascists.* New York: Barnes and Noble, 1968.

Marable, Manning. *Beyond Black and White: Rethinking Race in American Politics and Society.* New York: Verso, 1995.

————. *From the Grassroots.* Boston: South End, 1980.

————. *Race, Reform, and Rebellion: The Second Reconstruction in America, 1945–1982.* Jackson: University Press of Mississippi, 1984.

Marcus, Greil. *Mystery Train: Images of America in Rock 'n' Roll Music.* New York: E. P. Dutton, 1982.

Marmor, Theodore. *Understanding Health Care Reform.* New Haven: Yale University Press, 1994.

Marsh, Dave. *Born to Run: The Bruce Springsteen Story.* Vol. 1. New York: Thunder's Mouth Press, 1996.

————. *Glory Days: The Bruce Springsteen Story.* Vol. 2. New York: Thunder's Mouth Press, 1996.

Marshall, Ray. *The Negro and Organized Labor.* New York: John Wiley and Sons, 1965.

Martin, Tony. *Race First: The Ideological and Organizational Struggles of Marcus Garvey and the Universal Negro Improvement Association.* Westport: Greenwood, 1976.

Marx, Karl. *Capital.* Edited by Frederick Engels. New York: International Publishers, 1967.

————. *The Manifesto of the Communist Party.* Peking: Foreign Languages Press, 1965.

Matthews, Fred H. *Quest for an American Sociology: Robert E. Park and the Chicago School.* Montreal: McGill-Queen's University Press, 1977.

Maynard, Alan. *Health Care in the European Community.* Pittsburgh: University of Pittsburgh Press, 1975.

Mazmanian, Daniel. *Third Parties in Presidential Elections.* Washington, D.C.: Brookings Institution, 1974.

Meisel, James H. *The Genesis of Georges Sorel: An Account of His Formative Period Followed by a Study of His Influence.* Westport: Greenwood, 1982.

Melendez, Edwin, Clara Rodriguez, and Janis Barry Figueroa, eds. *Hispanics in the Labor Force: Issues and Policies.* New York: Plenum, 1991.

Mertz, Paul E. *New Deal Policy and Southern Rural Poverty.* Baton Rouge: Louisiana State University Press, 1978.

Meyer, John R., and Clinton V. Oster Jr. *Deregulation and the Future of Intercity Passenger Travel.* Cambridge: MIT Press, 1987.

Miller, Arthur. *The Crucible: A Play in Four Acts.* New York: Viking, 1953.

Miller, Kenneth D. *The Czecho-Slovaks in America.* New York: George H. Doran, 1922.

Mills, Charles W. *Blackness Visible: Essays on Philosophy and Race.* Ithaca: Cornell University Press, 1998.

———. *The Racial Contract.* Ithaca: Cornell University Press, 1997.

Mills, Nicolaus, ed. *Legacy of Dissent: Forty Years of Writing from "Dissent" Magazine.* New York: Touchstone, 1994.

Mink, Gwendolyn. *Old Labor and New Immigrants in American Political Development: Union, Party, and State, 1875–1920.* Ithaca: Cornell University Press, 1986.

———. *Welfare's End.* Ithaca: Cornell University Press, 1998.

Misgeld, Klaus, Karl Molin, and Klas Amark, eds. *Creating Social Democracy.* University Park: Pennsylvania State University Press, 1992.

Modibo, Coulibaly, Rodney D. Green, and David M. James. *Segregation in Federally Subsidized Low-Income Housing in the United States.* Westport: Praeger, 1998.

Moe, Richard, and Carter Wilkie. *Changing Places: Rebuilding Community in the Age of Sprawl.* New York: Henry Holt, 1997.

Montagu, Ashley, ed. *The Concept of Race.* New York: Free Press of Glencoe, 1964.

Montgomery, David. *Beyond Equality: Labor and the Radical Republicans, 1862–1872.* Urbana: University of Illinois Press, 1981.

Moore, Barrington. *Social Origins of Dictatorship and Democracy: Lord and Peasant in the Making of the Modern World.* Boston: Beacon, 1966.

Moore, Jesse Thomas, Jr. *A Search for Equality: The National Urban League, 1910–1961.* University Park: Pennsylvania State University Press, 1981.

Moreland, Laurence W., Robert P. Steed, and Tod A. Baker, eds. *The 1988 Presidential Election in the South: Continuity amidst Change in Southern Party Politics.* New York: Praeger, 1991.

Morgan, Edmund. *American Slavery, American Freedom: The Ordeal of Colonial Virginia.* New York: W. W. Norton, 1975.

Morgan, Ted. *A Covert Life: Jay Lovestone, Communist, Anti-Communist, and Spymaster.* New York: Random House, 1998.

Morin, Claude. *Quebec versus Ottawa: The Struggle for Self-Government, 1960–1972.* Toronto: University of Toronto Press, 1976.

Morris, James O. *Conflict within the AFL: A Study of Craft versus Industrial Unionism, 1901–1938.* Ithaca: Cornell University Press, 1958.

Morrison, Toni. *Playing in the Dark: Whiteness and the Literary Imagination.* Cambridge: Harvard University Press, 1992.

Mouffe, Chantal, and Ernesto Laclau. *Hegemony and Socialist Strategy: Towards a Radical Democratic Politics.* London: Verso, 1985.

Murray, Albert. *Hero and the Blues.* St. Louis: University of Missouri Press, 1973.

———. *The Omni-Americans: New Perspectives on Black Experience and American Culture.* New York: Outerbridge and Dienstfrey, 1970.

———. *Stomping the Blues.* New York: McGraw-Hill, 1976.

Murray, Charles. *Losing Ground: American Social Policy, 1950–1980.* New York: Basic, 1984.

Mussolini, Benito. *The Corporate State.* New York: Howard Fertig, 1975.

Myrdal, Gunnar. *An American Dilemma.* New York: McGraw-Hill, 1944.

Nager, Larry. *Memphis Beat: The Lives and Times of America's Musical Crossroads.* New York: St. Martin's, 1998.

Naison, Mark. *Communists in Harlem during the Depression.* Urbana: University of Illinois Press, 1983.

National Association for the Advancement of Colored People. *Annual Convention Resolutions.* 1933–1965. New York: National Association for the Advancement of Colored People.

———. *Annual Report.* 1910–1970. New York: National Association for the Advancement of Colored People.

National Health Conference. *Proceedings of the United States Interdepartmental Committee to Coordinate Health and Welfare Activities.* Washington, D.C.: Government Printing Office, 1938.

Newton, Michael, and Judy Ann Newton. *Racial and Religious Violence in America: A Chronology.* New York: Garland, 1991.

Nisenson, Eric. *Blue: The Murder of Jazz.* New York: St. Martin's, 1997.

Njeri, Itabari. *The Last Plantation: Color, Conflict, and Identity; Reflections of a New World Black.* Boston: Houghton-Mifflin, 1997.

Nolte, Ernst. *Three Faces of Fascism: Action Française, Italian Fascism, National Socialism.* Translated by Leila Vannewitz. New York: Holt, Rinehart, and Winston, 1966.

Norrell, Robert J. "Caste in Steel: Jim Crow Careers in Birmingham, Alabama." *Journal of American History* 73, no. 3 (1986): 669–94.

Norris, Pippa. *Politics and Sexual Equality: The Comparative Position of Women in Western Democracies.* Boulder: Lynne Rienner Publishers, 1987.

Novak, Michael. *The Rise of the Unmeltable Ethnics: Politics and Culture in the Seventies.* New York: Macmillan, 1972.

O'Brien, Conor Cruise. "Thomas Jefferson: Radical and Racist." *Atlantic Monthly,* October 1996, pp. 53–74.

Oestreicher, Richard. "Urban Working-Class Political Behavior and Theories of American Electoral Politics, 1870–1940." *Journal of American History* 74, no. 4 (1987): 1257–86.

Okihiro, Gary. *Margins and Mainstreams: Asians in American History and Culture.* Seattle: University of Washington Press, 1994.

Olson, Mancur. *The Logic of Collective Action: Public Goods and the Theory of Groups.* Cambridge: Harvard University Press, 1965.

Olssen, Andrée Levesque. *The Canadian Left in Quebec during the Great Depression.* Durham: Duke University Press, 1973.

Omi, Michael, and Howard Winant. *Racial Formation in the United States: From the 1960s to the 1990s.* New York: Routledge, 1994.

O'Reilly, Kenneth. *Nixon's Piano: Presidents and Racial Politics from Washington to Clinton.* New York: Free Press, 1995.

Orfield, Gary. *Public School Desegregation in the United States, 1968–1980.* Washington, D.C.: Joint Center for Political Studies, 1983.

Ottanelli, Fraser M. *The Communist Party of the United States.* New Brunswick: Rutgers University Press, 1991.

Ottaway, Marina, and David Ottaway. *Afrocommunism.* New York: Africana Publishing, 1986.

Overdyke, W. Darrell. *The Know-Nothing Party in the South.* Binghamton: Vail-Ballou, 1950.

Padmore, George. *Pan-Africanism or Communism.* Garden City: Doubleday, 1971.

Painter, Nell Irvin. "French Theories in American Settings: Some Thoughts on Transferability." *Journal of Women's History* 1 (Spring 1989): 92–95.

———. *The Narrative of Hosea Hudson: His Life as a Negro Communist in the South.* Cambridge: Harvard University Press, 1979.

Palmer, Bruce. *Man over Money: The Southern Populist Critique of American Capitalism.* Chapel Hill: University of North Carolina Press, 1980.

Pangle, Tom L. *The Spirit of Modern Republicanism: The Moral Vision of the American Founders and the Philosophy of Locke.* Chicago: University of Chicago Press, 1988.

Panitch, Leo, and Donald Swartz. *The Assault on Trade Union Freedoms.* Toronto: Garamond, 1988.

Patterson, James T. *Congressional Conservatism and the New Deal: The Growth of the Conservative Coalition in Congress, 1933–1939.* Lexington: University Press of Kentucky, 1967.

———. "The Failure of Party Realignment in the South." *Journal of Politics* 27 (August 1965): 602–17.

———. *The New Deal and the States: Federalism in Transition.* Princeton: Princeton University Press, 1969.

Pelling, Henry. *American Labor.* Chicago: University of Chicago Press, 1960.

———. *Origins of the Labour Party.* 2d ed. London: Oxford University Press, 1965.

Persons, Georgia, ed. *Dilemmas of Black Politics: Issues of Leadership and Strategy.* New York: HarperCollins College Publishers, 1993.

Peterson, Paul E., ed. *Classifying by Race.* Princeton: Princeton University Press, 1995.

Pfeffer, Paula F. *A. Philip Randolph: Pioneer of the Civil Rights Movement.* Baton Rouge: Louisiana State University Press, 1990.

Phillips, Kevin. *The Emerging Republican Majority.* New Rochelle: Arlington House, 1969.

———. *Post-Conservative America: People, Politics, and Ideology in a Time of Crisis.* New York: Randon House, 1982.

Piazza, Tom. *Blues Up and Down: Jazz in Our Time.* New York: St. Martin's, 1997.

Pierson, Christopher. *Beyond the Welfare State: The New Political Economy of Welfare.* Cambridge: Polity, 1991.

Piven, Frances Fox, and Richard A. Cloward. "Northern Bourbons: A Preliminary Report on the National Voter Registration Act." *PS,* March 1996, pp. 39–42.

———. *Poor People's Movements: Why They Succeed, How They Fail.* New York: Vintage, 1979.

———. *Why Americans Don't Vote.* New York: Pantheon, 1988.

Pocock, J. G. A. "The Machiavellian Moment Revisited: A Study in History and Ideology." *Journal of Modern History* 53 (March 1981).

———. "Virtue and Commerce in the Eighteenth Century." *Journal of Interdisciplinary History* 3, no. 1 (1972).

Poen, Monte M. *Harry S. Truman versus the Medical Lobby: The Genesis of Medicare.* Columbia: University of Missouri Press, 1979.

Pollack, Howard. *Aaron Copland: The Life and Work of an Uncommon Man.* New York: Henry Holt, 1999.

Pollack, Norman. *The Populist Response to Industrial America: Midwestern Populist Thought.* Cambridge: Harvard University Press, 1962.

Pontusson, Jonas. *The Limits of Social Democracy: Investment Politics in Sweden.* Ithaca: Cornell University Press, 1992.

Potter, David. *People of Plenty: Economic Abundance and the American Character.* Chicago: University of Chicago Press, 1954.

Proceedings of the Founding Convention of the IWW. New York: Merit Publishers, 1969.

Quadagno, Jill. *The Color of Welfare: How Racism Undermined the War on Poverty.* New York: Oxford University Press, 1994.

Quain, Kevin, ed. *The Elvis Reader.* New York: St. Martin's, 1992.

Quinn, Herbert F. *The Union Nationale: Quebec Nationalism from Duplessis to Levesque.* Toronto: University of Toronto Press, 1983.

Rachlis, Michael, and Carol Kushner. *Strong Medicine: How to Save Canada's Health Care System.* Toronto: HarperCollins Publishers, 1994.

Rayback, Joseph. *A History of American Labor.* New York: Free Press, 1966.

Read, Hollis. *The Negro Problem Solved; or, Africa as She Was, as She Is, and She Shall Be. Her Curse and Her Cure.* New York: A. A. Constantine, 1864.

Redkey, Edwin S. *Black Exodus: Black Nationalist and Back-to-Africa Movements, 1890–1910.* New Haven: Yale University Press, 1969.

Reed, Adolph, Jr. *The Jesse Jackson Phenomenon: The Crisis of Purpose in Afro-American Politics.* New Haven: Yale University Press, 1986.

———. *W. E. B. Du Bois and American Political Thought: Fabianism and the Color Line.* New York: Oxford University Press, 1997.

———. "W. E. B. Du Bois and the Bases of His Political Thought." *Political Theory* 13 (August 1985): 431–56.

———, ed. *Race, Politics, and Culture: Critical Essays on the Radicalism of the 1960s.* Westport: Greenwood, 1986.

———. *Without Justice for All: The New Liberalism and Our Retreat from Racial Equality.* Boulder: Westview, 1999.

Reeve, Andrew, and Alan Ware. *Electoral Systems: A Comparative and Theoretical Introduction.* London: Routledge, 1992.

Reeve, Carl. *The Life and Times of Daniel DeLeon.* New York: Humanities, 1972.

Regini, Marino, ed. *The Future of Labour Movements.* London: Sage, 1992.

Reid, Ira De A. *Negro Membership in American Labor Unions.* New York: Alexander, 1930.

Resnick, Phillip. *The Masks of Proteus: Canadian Reflections on the State.* Montreal: McGill-Queens University Press, 1990.

Reynolds, Barbara. *Jesse Jackson: The Man, the Movement, the Myth.* Chicago: Nelson-Hall, 1975.

Rifkin, Jeremy. *The End of Work: The Decline of the Global Work Force and the Dawn of the Post-Market Era.* New York: G. P. Putnam's Sons, 1995.

Riker, William H. *Democracy in the United States.* New York: Macmillan, 1965.

Robertson, Wilmot. *The Dispossessed Majority.* Cape Canaveral: Howard Allen, 1973.

Robeson, Paul. *Here I Stand.* New York: Othello Associates, 1958.

Robin, Martin, ed. *Radical Politics and Canadian Labour, 1880–1930.* Kingston: Industrial Relations Centre, Queens University, 1968.

Robinson, Archie. *George Meany and His Times.* New York: Simon and Schuster, 1981.

Robinson, Cedric J. *Black Marxism: The Making of the Black Radical Tradition.* London: Zed, 1983.

Robinson, Randall. *Defending the Spirit.* New York: Dutton, 1998.

Rodgers, Daniel T. *Atlantic Crossings: Social Politics in a Progressive Age.* Cambridge: Harvard University Press, Belknap Press, 1998.

Roeder, George H., Jr. *The Censored War: American Visual Experience during World War Two.* New Haven: Yale University Press, 1993.

Roediger, David R. *Towards the Abolition of Whiteness: Essays on Race, Politics, and Working Class History.* New York: Verso, 1994.

———. *The Wages of Whiteness: Race and the Making of the American Working Class.* New York: Verso, 1991.

Roemer, Milton I. *National Health Care Systems of the World.* New York: Oxford University Press, 1991.

Roemer, Milton I., and Ruth J. Roemer. *Health Care Systems and Comparative Manpower Policies.* New York: Marcel Dekker, 1981.

Rogin, Michael. *Blackface, White Noise: Jewish Immigrants in the Hollywood Melting Pot.* Berkeley: University of California Press, 1996.

Rose, Richard. "How Exceptional Is the American Political Economy?" *Political Science Quarterly* 104, no. 1 (Spring 1989): 91–115.

Rosenstone, Steven, and John Mark Hansen. *Mobilization, Participation, and Democracy in America.* New York: Macmillan, 1993.

Salvatore, Nick. *Eugene V. Debs: Citizen and Socialist.* Urbana: University of Illinois Press, 1982.

Sartre, Jean Paul. *Anti-Semite and Jew.* New York: Schocken, 1948.

Saxton, Alexander. *The Indispensable Enemy: Labor and the Anti-Chinese Movement in California.* Berkeley: University of California Press, 1971.

———. *The Rise and Fall of the White Republic: Class, Politics, and Mass Culture in Nineteenth-Century America.* London: Verso, 1990.

Scales-Trent, Judy. *Notes of a White Black Woman: Race, Color, Community.* University Park: Pennsylvania State University Press, 1995.

Scammon, Richard, and Ben Wattenberg. *The Real Majority.* New York: Coward-McCann, 1970.

Schain, Martin. "Immigration and Changes in the French Party System." *European Journal of Political Research* 16, no. 6 (November 1988).

Schlesinger, Arthur, Jr. *The Disuniting of America: Reflections on a Multicultural Society.* New York: Norton, 1991.

Scholzman, Kay, ed. *Elections in America.* London: Allen and Unwin, 1987.

Schorske, Carl. *German Social-Democracy, 1905–1917: The Development of the Great Schism.* Cambridge: Harvard University Press, 1955.

Schrecker, Ellen. *Many Are the Crimes: McCarthyism in America.* Boston: Little, Brown, 1998.

Schulman, Bruce J. *From Cotton Belt to Sunbelt: Federal Policy, Economic Development, and the Transformation of the South, 1930–1980.* New York: Oxford University Press, 1991.

Schwab, Larry M. *The Illusion of a Conservative Reagan Revolution.* New Brunswick: Transaction Publishers, 1991.

Seretan, L. Glen. *Daniel DeLeon: The Odyssey of an American Marxist.* Cambridge: Harvard University Press, 1979.

Shafer, Byron. *Is America Different? A New Look at American Exceptionalism.* New York: Oxford University Press, 1991.

Shain, Barry Alan. *The Myth of American Individualism: The Protestant Origins of American Political Thought.* Princeton: Princeton University Press, 1994.

Shannon, David. *The Decline of American Communism: A History of the Communist Party of the United States since 1945.* New York: Harcourt, Brace, 1959.

Shaw, Barton C. *The Wool-Hat Boys: Georgia's Populist Party.* Baton Rouge: Louisiana State University Press, 1984.

Siegfried, André. *The Race Question in Canada.* London: Everleigh Nash, 1907.

Silva, Fred, ed. *Focus on "Birth of a Nation."* Englewood Cliffs, N.J.: Prentice-Hall, 1971.

Simmie, James, and Roger King, eds. *The State in Action: Public Policy and Politics.* New York: Pinter, 1990.

Sitkoff, Harvard. *A New Deal for Blacks: The Emergence of Civil Rights as a National Issue.* New York: Oxford University Press, 1978.

Skidelsky, Robert. *Oswald Mosely.* New York: Holt, Rinehart, and Winston, 1975.

Skidmore, Max J. *Medicare and the American Rhetoric of Reconciliation.* [University]: University of Alabama Press, 1970.

Skocpol, Theda. *Boomerang: Clinton's Health Care Security Effort and the Turn against Government in U.S. Politics.* New York: W. W. Norton, 1996.

———. *Protecting Soldiers and Mothers: The Political Origins of Social Policy in the United States.* Cambridge: Harvard University Press, 1992.

———. *Social Policy in the United States: Future Possibilities in Historical Perspective.* Princeton: Princeton University Press, 1995.

Skowronek, Stephen. *Building a New American State: The Expansion of National Administrative Capacities, 1877–1920.* New York: Cambridge University Press, 1982.

Sleeper, Jim. *The Closest of Strangers: Liberalism and the Politics of Race in New York.* New York: W. W. Norton, 1990.

Smallwood, Frank. *The Other Candidates: Third Parties in Presidential Elections.* Hanover: University Press of New England, 1983.

Smith, Douglas L. *The New Deal in the Urban South.* Baton Rouge: Louisiana State University Press, 1988.

Smith, Lillian. *Strange Fruit.* New York: Reynal and Hitchcock, 1944.

Smith, Rogers M. *Civic Ideals: Conflicting Ideals of Citizenship in U.S. History.* New Haven: Yale University Press, 1997.

Sombart, Werner. *Why Is There No Socialism in the United States?* White Plains: M. E. Sharpe, 1976.

Sorel, Georges. *Reflections on Violence.* Glencoe: Free Press, 1950.

Spero, Sterling B., and Abram L. Harris. *The Black Worker.* New York: Columbia University Press, 1931.

Stanley, Harold W. *Voter Mobilization and the Politics of Race: The South and Universal Suffrage, 1952–1984.* London: Praeger, 1987.

State of Black America, 1970–1996. Edited by Janet Dewart. New York: Urban League, 1996.

Staudenraus, P. J. *The African Colonization Movement, 1816–1865.* New York: Columbia University Press, 1961.

Stearn, Gerald Emanuel, ed. *Gompers.* Englewood Cliffs: Prentice-Hall, 1971.

Steele, Shelby. *The Content of Our Character: A New Vision of Race in America.* New York: St. Martin's, 1990.

Sternhell, Zeev. *Maurice Barrès et le Nationalisme Français.* Paris: A. Colin, 1972.

———. *Neither Right nor Left: Fascist Ideology in France.* Berkeley: University of California Press, 1986.

Stewart, Jeffrey C., ed. *Paul Robeson: Artist and Citizen.* New Brunswick, N.J.: Rutgers University Press, 1998.

Strauss, George, Daniel G. Gallagher, and Jack Fiorito, eds. *The State of the Unions.* Madison: Industrial Relations Research Association, 1991.

Sugrue, Thomas. *The Origins of the Urban Crisis: Race, Industrial Decline, and Housing in Detroit, 1940–1960.* Princeton: Princeton University Press, 1996.

Sundquist, James. *Dynamics of the Party System: Alignment and Realignment of Political Parties in the United States.* Washington, D.C.: Brookings Institution, 1983.

———. *Politics and Policy: The Eisenhower, Kennedy, and Johnson Years.* Washington, D.C.: Brookings Institution, 1968.

Sylvis, James C., ed. *The Life, Speeches, and Essays of William H. Sylvis* (Philadelphia, 1872).

Takagi, Dana Y. *The Retreat from Race: Asian Admissions and Racial Politics.* New Brunswick: Rutgers University Press, 1993.

Takaki, Ronald. *A Different Mirror: A History of Multicultural America.* Boston: Little, Brown, 1993.

———. *Iron Cages: Race and Culture in Nineteenth-Century America.* New York: Oxford University Press, 1979.

———. *Strangers from a Distant Shore: A History of Asian Americans.* New York: Penguin, 1990.

Taylor, Arthur. *Notes and Tones.* New York: Da Capo, 1993.

Taylor, Ronald B. *Chavez and the Farm Workers.* Boston: Beacon, 1975.

Teixeira, Ruy A. *Why Americans Don't Vote: Turnout Decline in the United States, 1960–1984.* Westport: Greenwood, 1987.

Thomas, J. C. *Chasin' the Trane.* New York: Da Capo, 1975.

Thomas, Norman. *Socialism Re-examined.* New York: Norton, 1963.

Thompson, E. P. *The Makings of the English Working Class: Customs in Common.* New York: Vintage, 1963.

Thompson, John Herd, and Allen Seager. *Canada, 1922–1939: Decades of Discord.* Toronto: McClelland and Stewart, 1985.

Tiersky, Ronald. "Declining Fortunes of the French Communist Party." *Problems of Communism* 37 (September 1988): 1–22.

———. *France in the New Europe.* Belmont: Wadsworth, 1994.

Tindall, George B. *The Emergence of the New South, 1913–1945.* Baton Rouge: Louisiana State University Press, 1967.

Tocqueville, Alexis de. *Democracy in America.* 2 vols. New York: Vintage, 1945.

Toll, Robert C. *Blacking Up: The Minstrel Show in Nineteenth-Century America.* New York: Oxford University Press, 1974.

———. *The Entertainment Machine: American Show Business in the Twentieth Century.* New York: Oxford University Press, 1982.

Trades and Labour Congress of Canada. *Report of Proceedings.* 1920 and 1921. Ottawa: Trades and Labour Congress of Canada, 1920, 1921.

Trudeau, Pierre Elliot. *Federalism and the French-Canadians.* New York: St. Martin's, 1968.

Tsai, Shih-Shau Henry. *The Chinese Experience in America.* Bloomington: Indiana University Press, 1986.

Tucker, Mark, ed. *The Duke Ellington Reader.* New York: Oxford University Press, 1993.

Tucker, Robert, ed. *The Marx-Engels Reader.* New York: W. W. Norton, 1972.

Turner, Frederick Jackson. *The Early Writings of Frederick Jackson Turner.* Madison: University of Wisconsin Press, 1938.

Tuttle, William. *Race Riot: Chicago in the Red Summer of 1919.* New York: Atheneum, 1970.

Twain, Mark. *The Autobiography of Mark Twain.* New York: Harper and Row, 1959.

United Nations Development Programme. *Human Development Report, 1998.* New York: Oxford University Press, 1998.

Urwin, Derek W., ed. *Politics in Western Europe Today.* London: Longman, 1990.

Valdez, R. Burciaga, Hal Morgenstern, E. Richard Brown, Roberta Wyn, Chao Wang, and William Cumberland. "Insuring Latinos against the Costs of Illness." *Journal of the American Medical Association* 269 (February 17, 1993): 889–94.

Vallières, Pierre. *L'Urgence de Choisir.* Montreal: Éditions Parti Pris, 1971.

———. *White Niggers of America.* Toronto: McClelland and Stewart, 1971.

Vargas, Zaragosa. *Proletarians of the North: A History of Mexican Industrial Workers in Detroit and the Midwest, 1917–1933.* Berkeley: University of California Press, 1993.

Vincent, Theodore. *Black Power and the Garvey Movement.* Berkeley: Ramparts, 1973.

Vogel, David. *National Styles of Regulation: Environmental Policy in Great Britain and the United States.* Ithaca: Cornell University Press, 1986.

Vose, Clement. *Caucasians Only: The Supreme Court, the NAACP, and Restrictive Covenant Cases.* Berkeley: University of California Press, 1959.

Voss, Kim. *The Making of American Exceptionalism: The Knights of Labor and Class Formation in the Nineteenth Century.* Ithaca: Cornell University Press, 1993.

Walker, Clarence. *Deromanticizing Black History: Critical Essays and Reappraisals.* Knoxville: University of Tennessee Press, 1991.

Walker, Margaret. *Richard Wright, Daemonic Genius: A Portrait of the Man, a Critical Look at His Work.* New York: Warner, 1988.

Walton, Hanes, Jr. *Black Republicans: The Politics of the Black and Tans.* Metuchen: Scarecrow Press, 1975.

Warburton, Rennie, and David Coburn, eds. *Workers, Capital, and the State in British Columbia.* Vancouver: University of British Columbia Press, 1988.

Ward, Brian. *Just My Soul Responding: Rhythm and Blues, Black Consciousness, and Race Relations.* Berkeley: University of California Press, 1998.

Washburn, Patrick S. *A Question of Sedition: The Federal Government's Investigation of the Black Press during World War II.* New York: Oxford University Press, 1986.

Washington, Booker T. *The Man Farthest Down: A Record of Observation and Study in Europe.* Garden City: Doubleday, Page, 1912.

———. *Up from Slavery: An Autobiography.* New York: Dodd, Mead, 1965.

Wasserman, Earl, ed. *Aspects of the Eighteenth Century.* Baltimore: Johns Hopkins University Press, 1965.

Wattenberg, Ben. *Values Matter Most: How Republicans or Democrats or a Third Party Can Win and Renew the American Way of Life.* New York: Free Press, 1995.

Watts, Jerry Gafio. *Heroism and the Black Intellectual: Ralph Ellison, Politics, and Afro-American Intellectual Life.* Chapel Hill: University of North Carolina Press, 1994.

Weinstein, James. *The Corporate Ideal in the Liberal State, 1900–1918.* Boston: Beacon, 1968.

———. *The Decline of Socialism in America, 1912–1925.* New York: Monthly Review, 1967.

Weiss, Nancy J. *Farewell to the Party of Lincoln: Black Politics in the Age of FDR.* Princeton: Princeton University Press, 1983.

Werner, Craig. *A Change Is Gonna Come: Music, Race, and the Soul of America.* New York: Plume, 1998.

Wexler, Jerry, and David Ritz. *Rhythm and the Blues: A Life in American Music.* New York: St. Martin's, 1993.

Whayne, Jeannie M. *A New Plantation South: Land, Labor, and Federal Favor in Twentieth-Century Arkansas.* Charlottesville: University Press of Virginia, 1996.

Wiesenthal, Helmut. *Realism in Green Politics: Social Movements and Ecological Reform in Germany.* Manchester: Manchester University Press, 1993.

Wilentz, Sean. "Against Exceptionalism: Class Consciousness and the American Labor Movement, 1790–1920." *International Labor and Working Class History,* no. 26 (Fall 1984): 1–24.

————. *Chants Democratic: New York City and the Rise of the American Working Class, 1788–1850.* New York: Oxford University Press, 1984.

Wilkins, Roy, with Tom Mathews. *Standing Fast: The Autobiography of Roy Wilkins.* New York: Viking, 1982.

Williams, Melissa. *Voice, Trust, and Memory: Marginalized Groups and the Failings of Liberal Representation.* Princeton: Princeton University Press, 1998.

Wilson, Francis G. "The Inactive Electorate and Social Revolution." *Southwestern Social Science Quarterly* 16 (March 1936): 73–84.

Wilson, William Julius. *The Declining Significance of Race: Blacks and Changing American Institutions.* Chicago: University of Chicago Press, 1978.

————. *The Truly Disadvantaged: The Inner City, the Underclass, and Public Policy.* Chicago: University of Chicago Press, 1987.

————. *When Work Disappears: The World of the New Urban Poor.* New York: Knopf, 1996.

Wish, Harvey. *Society and Thought in Modern America.* New York: David McKay, 1962.

Wood, Joe, ed. *Malcolm X: In Our Own Image.* New York: St. Martin's, 1992.

Wood, Gordon S. *The Creation of the American Republic, 1776–1787.* Chapel Hill: University of North Carolina Press, 1969.

————. *The Radicalism of the American Revolution.* New York: Vintage, 1991.

Woodsworth, J. S. *Strangers within Our Gates.* Toronto: Missionary Society of the Methodist Church, 1909.

Woodward, C. Vann. *The Strange Career of Jim Crow.* New York: Oxford University Press, 1957.

Wright, James D. *Under the Gun: Weapons, Crime, and Violence in America.* New York: Aldine, 1983.

Wright, Lawrence. "One Drop of Blood." *The New Yorker,* July 25, 1994, pp. 46–55.

Wright, Richard. "I Tried to Be a Communist." Parts 1 and 2. *Atlantic Monthly,* August 1944, pp. 61–70; September 1944, pp. 48–56.

————. *The Outsider.* New York: Harper, 1953.

————. *White Man, Listen!* Garden City: Anchor, 1964.

Wrobel, David. *The End of American Exceptionalism: Frontier Anxiety from the Old West to the New Deal.* Lawrence: University Press of Kansas, 1993.

Yorke, Ritchie. *Axes, Chops, and Hot Licks.* Edmonton: Hurtig, 1971.

Young, Walter D. *The Anatomy of a Party: The National CCF, 1932–1961.* Toronto: University of Toronto Press, 1969.

Zieger, Robert H. *American Workers, American Unions, 1920–1985.* Baltimore: Johns Hopkins University Press, 1986.

————, ed. *Organized Labor in the Twentieth-Century South.* Knoxville: University of Tennessee Press, 1991.

INDEX